Perspectives in Law, Business and Innovation

Over the last three decades, interconnected processes of globalization and rapid technological change—particularly, the emergence of networked technologies—have profoundly disrupted traditional models of business organization. This economic transformation has created multiple new opportunities for the emergence of alternate business forms, and disruptive innovation has become one of the major driving forces in the contemporary economy. Moreover, in the context of globalization, the innovation space increasingly takes on a global character. The main stakeholders—innovators, entrepreneurs and investors—now have an unprecedented degree of mobility in pursuing economic opportunities wherever they arise. As such, frictionless movement of goods, workers, services, and capital is becoming the "new normal".

This new economic and social reality has created multiple regulatory challenges for policymakers as they struggle to come to terms with the rapid pace of these social and economic changes. Moreover, these challenges impact across multiple fields of both public and private law. Nevertheless, existing approaches within legal science often struggle to deal with innovation and its effects.

Paralleling this shift in the economy, we can, therefore, see a similar process of disruption occurring within contemporary academia, as traditional approaches and disciplinary boundaries—both within and between disciplines—are being re-configured. Conventional notions of legal science are becoming increasingly obsolete or, at least, there is a need to develop alternative perspectives on the various regulatory challenges that are currently being created by the new innovation-driven global economy.

The aim of this series is to provide a forum for the publication of cutting-edge research in the fields of innovation and the law from a Japanese and Asian perspective. The series will cut across the traditional sub-disciplines of legal studies but will be tied together by a focus on contemporary developments in an innovation-driven economy and will deepen our understanding of the various regulatory responses to these economic and social changes.

The series editor and editorial board carefully assess each book proposal and sample chapters in terms of their relevance to law, business, and innovative technological change. Each proposal is evaluated on the basis of its academic value and distinctive contribution to the fast-moving debate in these fields.

All books and chapters in the Perspectives in Law, Business and Innovation book series are indexed in Scopus.

Mateo Aboy
Marcelo Corrales Compagnucci • Timo Minssen
Editors

Quantum Technology Governance I

Law and Regulation

Springer

Editors
Mateo Aboy
Faculty of Law
University of Cambridge
Cambridge, UK

Marcelo Corrales Compagnucci
CeBIL, Faculty of Law
University of Copenhagen
Copenhagen, Denmark

Timo Minssen
CeBIL, Faculty of Law
University of Copenhagen
Copenhagen, Denmark

ISSN 2520-1875 ISSN 2520-1883 (electronic)
Perspectives in Law, Business and Innovation
ISBN 978-981-95-8370-6 ISBN 978-981-95-8371-3 (eBook)
https://doi.org/10.1007/978-981-95-8371-3

This Springer imprint is published by the registered company Springer Nature Singapore Pte Ltd.
The registered company address is: 152 Beach Road, #21-01/04 Gateway East, Singapore 189721, Singapore

Preface

Quantum technologies have progressed from early-stage foundational research to a core strategic priority, reshaping agendas in research policy and security strategy. As capabilities in quantum computing, cryptography, and sensing advance, they highlight important intersections with existing legal and regulatory frameworks, prompting governments, firms, and other stakeholders alike to engage with governance considerations earlier in the technology life cycle than in prior waves of innovation.

This two-volume series offers a systematic and interdisciplinary examination of the legal, regulatory, and ethical dimensions of quantum technologies, advancing original and timely contributions to the emerging discourse on quantum technology governance. As the first comprehensive anthology to integrate these domains, it provides a scholarly collection that captures the global scope of recent developments in quantum governance, law, and policy.

Quantum Technology Governance I: Law and Regulation—the present volume—offers a systematic and interdisciplinary examination of the legal and regulatory architecture shaping quantum technologies. It addresses how emerging capabilities in quantum computing, cryptography, and sensing intersect with intellectual property law, cybersecurity frameworks, export control regimes, and public international law. These technologies introduce non-classical features that stress-test existing governance systems, requiring interpretive flexibility, anticipatory policymaking, and evidence-based strategies rather than wholesale doctrinal reform. The chapters in this volume explore:

- *Foundational intersections between quantum information technologies and law*, including the governance-stack model that aligns regulatory tools with technical layers.
- *Intellectual property strategies*—patents, trade secrets, and open innovation—and their coexistence in a "superposition" across the quantum stack.
- *Empirical patent trends and policy implications*, mapping global filings and their impact on innovation and disclosure.
- *Cybersecurity regulation in the quantum age*, addressing vulnerabilities such as "harvest now, decrypt later" attacks and the transition to post-quantum cryptography.

- *Export control* challenges and opportunities, analyzing plurilateral coordination and modular enforcement strategies.
- *Public international law and geopolitical dimensions*, examining effects-based norms, attribution, and strategic governance frameworks.

Collectively, these contributions provide policymakers, scholars, and technologists with a roadmap for navigating the legal and regulatory landscapes of quantum technologies as they transition from theoretical constructs to practical deployment.

Volume II: *Frameworks, Standards and Ethics* complements this legal focus by addressing governance frameworks for particular applications, international standards as governance tools, and ethical considerations.

Designed to serve both as an accessible entry point and a rigorous resource, this two-volume series equips stakeholders to leverage quantum technologies responsibly while safeguarding societal interests. With contributions from leading experts across disciplines and jurisdictions, it advances a nuanced understanding of how governance can meet the technical, legal, and ethical demands of the quantum era.

This publication was made possible by the generous support of a Novo Nordisk Foundation (NNF) grant for a scientifically independent Collaborative Research Program in Bioscience Innovation Law (Inter-CeBIL Program—grant no. NNF23SA0087056).

Cambridge, UK Mateo Aboy
Copenhagen, Denmark Marcelo Corrales Compagnucci
Copenhagen, Denmark Timo Minssen

Contents

Editors and Contributors

About the Editors

Mateo Aboy is Director of Research in Technology & Law (Biomedical Innovation, AI, QT, and Law) at the Faculty of Law, University of Cambridge. He is a member of the Centre for Law, Medicine & Life Sciences (LML) and the Centre for IP & Information Law (CIPIL) at the University of Cambridge. His multidisciplinary background includes a combination of law, engineering, regulatory science, and management experience. He holds degrees in electrical and computer engineering (BS, BSEE, MSECE, MPhil/DEA, PhD ECE), law (LLB, SJD/PhD/LLD), and international management (MBA), as well as professional registrations as Professional Chartered Engineer (CEng, EU/ES COIT), Certified Licensing Professional (CLP), Patent Practitioner with a Bar Admission/licensed to practice in patent cases before the US Patent Office (USPTO), Fellow of Information Privacy (FIP, IAPP), Certified Privacy Information Professional (CIPP/E), Certified Privacy Manager (CIPM), Lead Implementer of Information Security Management Systems—ISMS (ISO 27001), Lead Auditor of Medical Device Quality Management Systems (ISO 13485), Lead Implementer of Privacy Information Management Systems—PIMS (ISO 27701), and Certified Data Protection Officer (C-DPO). Mateo's research seeks to understand the drivers of technology-based innovation, IP incentives, and the determinants of how emergent technologies are protected, regulated, funded, developed, adopted, and used in practice. He is the author of more than 200 scholarly articles published in leading scientific, engineering, and legal journals. His professional experience includes work in various senior roles both in private sector and in academia. He holds over 20 patents as an inventor.

Marcelo Corrales Compagnucci is Associate Professor and Associate Director at the Center for Advanced Studies in Bioscience Innovation Law (CeBIL), Faculty of Law, University of Copenhagen, Denmark. He is also Inter-CeBIL Research Affiliate at the Petrie-Flom Center for Health Law Policy, Biotechnology, and Bioethics at Harvard Law School. He specializes in information technology, AI governance, privacy, data protection, and data security law. His research interests are the legal issues involved in disruptive innovation technologies and biomedicine. He is the founder of CORCOM IT Law Consulting. His past activities have included working as a consultant and lawyer for law firms and IT companies. He was also a research associate with the Institute for Legal Informatics (IRI) at Leibniz Universität Hannover in Germany, and a visiting research fellow in various research centers around the world, including Harvard Law School, Cambridge University, the Max Planck Institute, University of Edinburgh, Turin University, and the Academia Sinica in Taiwan. He has a Doctor of Laws (LL.D.) degree from Kyushu University in Japan. He also holds a Master of Laws (LL.M.) in international economics and business law from Kyushu University, and an LL.M. in law and information technology and an LL.M. in European intellectual property law, both from the University of Stockholm in Sweden. He has several publications in the field of IT Law. His most recent book collections co-edited with various authors include *Generative AI, Contracts, Law and Design* (Springer, 2025), *International Transfers of Health Data: A Global Perspective* (Springer, 2024), *AI in eHealth: Human Autonomy, Data Governance and Privacy in Healthcare* (Cambridge University Press, 2022), *Smart Contracts: Technological, Business and Legal Perspectives* (Hart Publishing, 2021), and *Legal Design: Integrating Business, Design and Legal Thinking with Technology* (Edward Elgar Publishing, 2021).

Timo Minssen is Professor of Law at the University of Copenhagen (UCPH), specializing in Health & Life Science Innovation. He is the Director of UCPH's Center for Advanced Studies in Bioscience Innovation Law (CeBIL) and holds the UNESCO Co-Chair in the Right to Science. Timo is also an Inter-CeBIL Research Affiliate at Harvard Law School and at the University of Cambridge, as well as Associate Member of the Centre of Genomics and Policy at McGill University. His research and practice concentrate on IP, Competition, and Regulatory Law in health and life science technologies, including AI, quantum technologies, advanced medical technologies, and biotechnologies.Timo holds a German law degree from the University of Göttingen, and biotech and IP-related LL.M. M.I.C.L., LL.Lic., and LL.D. degrees from Lund and Uppsala University. Previously, he was an Epigenetics fellow at the Pufendorf Institute for Advanced Studies and Visiting Professor at the Technical University of Munich, the Universities of Cambridge and Oxford, Waseda Law School, Harvard Law School, and the Max Planck Institute for Innovation and Competition. In 2007, he also held the position of Associate Professor at the Chicago-Kent College of Law, teaching a course in comparative European and US patent law. Moreover, he was trained in the German Court system, the European Patent Office, law firms, and start-ups.Timo is Scientific Advisory Board Member of the Munich Intellectual Property Law Centre (MIPLC). He also serves as an advisor to the WHO, WIPO, the EU Commission, companies, national governments, and law firms. At UCPH, he leads several interdisciplinary research projects on legal issues in emerging biotechnologies, precision medicine, AI-assisted surgery, medical device technologies, ATMPs, antimicrobial resistance, pandemic preparedness, advanced medical computing, and sustainable innovation. He is the PI and grant holder of a large research program in bioscience innovation law, funded by the Novo Nordisk Foundation and involving international core partners, such as Harvard, DTU, and the Universities of Cambridge and Michigan.His research comprises 8 books and 240+ publications in leading law and science journals. It is frequently featured in international media, such as *The Economist*, *Financial Times*, *El Mundo*, *Politico*, *Times of India*, *WHO Bulletin*, and *Times Higher Education*.

Contributors

Mateo Aboy Centre for Law, Medicine and Life Sciences (LML) and Centre for Intellectual Property and Information Law (CIPIL), University of Cambridge, Cambridge, UK

Lee Andrew Bygrave Norwegian Research Center for Computers and Law (NRCCL), University of Oslo, Oslo, Norway

Marcelo Corrales Compagnucci Center for Advanced Studies in Bioscience Innovation Law (CeBIL), University of Copenhagen, Copenhagen, Denmark; Inter-CeBIL Research Affiliate at the Petrie-Flom Center for Health Law Policy, Biotechnology, and Bioethics, Havard Law School, Cambridge MA, US

Cristina Crespo Centre for Law, Medicine and Life Sciences (LML) and Centre for Intellectual Property and Information Law (CIPIL), University of Cambridge, Cambridge, UK

Peter Alexander Earls Davis Center for Advanced Studies in Bioscience Innovation Law (CeBIL), University of Copenhagen, Copenhagen, Denmark

Urs Gasser Technical University of Munich (TUM), Munich, Germany

Gabriela Lenarczyk Center for Advanced Studies in Bioscience Innovation Law (CeBIL), University of Copenhagen, Copenhagen, Denmark

Timo Minssen Center for Advanced Studies in Bioscience Innovation Law (CeBIL), University of Copenhagen, Copenhagen, Denmark; LML Research Affiliate at the University of Cambridge, Cambridge, UK; Inter-CeBIL Research Affiliate at the Petrie-Flom Center for Health Law Policy, Biotechnology, and Bioethics, Havard Law School, Cambridge MA, US; Associate Member of the Centre of Genomics and Policy at McGill University, Montreal, Canada

Elija Perrier Centre for Quantum Software and Information, University of Technology, Sydney, NSW, Australia; Centre for Law, Medicine and Life Sciences (LML), University of Cambridge, Cambridge, United Kingdom

Quantum Technology Governance: Legal and Regulatory Perspectives

Mateo Aboy, Marcelo Corrales Compagnucci, and Timo Minssen

Abstract This chapter offers an overview of *Quantum Technology Governance: Law & Regulation*, highlighting the foundational role of quantum information technology (QIT) and the legal, regulatory, and geopolitical considerations arising from its recent advancements. It maps how quantum computing, communication, and sensing intersect with established legal and governance frameworks across intellectual property, cybersecurity, export controls, and international law.

The chapter introduces a progressive analytical structure that begins with QIT's ontological and governance foundations before turning to domain-specific regulatory considerations and global strategic implications. It synthesizes key themes developed throughout the volume, including adaptive legal interpretation; layered governance mechanisms such as the governance-stack model; mixed intellectual property strategies combining patents, trade secrets, and open innovation; empirical patent trends; EU and US approaches to quantum-enabled cybersecurity risks; the evolution of export control architectures; and the application of effects-based norms in public international law.

Across these domains, the chapter identifies a recurring theme of regulatory adaptability. Although QIT introduces non-classical features that stress-test existing legal and policy systems, we argue that many challenges can be met through inter-

M. Aboy (✉)
Centre for Law, Medicine and Life Sciences (LML) and Centre for Intellectual Property and Information Law (CIPIL), University of Cambridge, Cambridge, UK
e-mail: ma608@cam.ac.uk

M. C. Compagnucci · T. Minssen
Center for Advanced Studies in Bioscience Innovation Law (CeBIL), University of Copenhagen, Copenhagen, Denmark

LML Research Affiliate at the University of Cambridge, Cambridge, UK

Inter-CeBIL Research Affiliate at the Petrie-Flom Center for Health Law Policy, Biotechnology, and Bioethics, Havard Law School, Cambridge MA, US

Associate Member of the Centre of Genomics and Policy at McGill University, Montreal, Canada

M. Aboy et al. (eds.), *Quantum Technology Governance I*, Perspectives in Law, Business and Innovation, https://doi.org/10.1007/978-981-95-8371-3_1

pretive flexibility, evidence-based policymaking, and technology governance rather than wholesale doctrinal reform. By integrating legal analysis, empirical insights, and international governance perspectives, the chapter provides policymakers, technologists, scholars, and practitioners with a roadmap for responsible quantum governance as technologies transition from theoretical potential to practical deployment.

Keywords Quantum technology governance · Quantum law · Quantum regulation · Quantum innovation

1 Introduction

Quantum technologies represent a paradigm shift in computing, communication, and sensing, promising unprecedented advancements in fields ranging from cryptography and drug discovery to materials science and quantum simulation. At the heart of this revolution lies quantum information technology (QIT), which harnesses principles of quantum mechanics such as superposition and entanglement to process information beyond the capabilities of classical systems for certain tasks. This second-generation quantum revolution builds on the first, which gave rise to foundational technologies like transistors, lasers, and MRI technologies, by explicitly leveraging quantum mechanical phenomena. For instance, superposition allows quantum bits (qubits) to exist in multiple states simultaneously, enabling exponential computational speedups for certain tasks, while entanglement enables correlations that defy classical locality, opening doors to secure communication protocols.[1]

This transformative potential introduces key implications for technology governance, law, regulation, and international standards.[2] As quantum systems evolve from theoretical constructs to practical applications—evident in milestones like demonstrations of quantum advantage with programmable processors— they raise questions about intellectual property (IP) protection, cybersecurity vulnerabilities, international export controls, and geopolitical strategies. For instance, the dual-use nature of QIT—spanning civilian innovations like pharmaceutical simulations and military applications such as advanced decryption—amplifies risks of proliferation and strategic imbalances, necessitating frameworks that balance open innovation with security imperatives.[3]

These implications are compounded by the nature and pace of innovation, which can stress-test existing legal frameworks and can create governance vacuums that could exacerbate risks like data breaches and even threats to global security. For example, quantum threats to cybersecurity, such as "harvest now, decrypt later" attacks exploiting Shor's algorithm to undermine asymmetric encryption, may require anticipatory technology governance initiatives. Similarly, the surge in patent filings—reflecting a 14.5% compound annual growth rate from 2001 to 2025—highlights the need for policies that continue to encourage disclosure to

---

[1] Aboy et al. (2022).

[2] Aboy et al. (2025).

[3] Kop et al. (2024a).

enrich the public domain, countering tendencies toward trade secrecy in capital-intensive fields.[4]

This book, *Quantum Technology Governance*: *Law & Regulation*, addresses these imperatives by bringing together interdisciplinary perspectives from law, policy, technology, and international relations. It aims to provide scholars, policymakers, practitioners, and technologists with a comprehensive roadmap for navigating the legal and regulatory landscapes of quantum technologies.

Drawing on concepts like the SEA (safeguarding, engaging, advancing)[5] and governance-stack model which aligns regulatory instruments with QIT's technical layers from hardware to algorithms, the volume explores how existing laws can be applied or adapted, where new guidance or regulations may be needed, and the broader implications for society in an era of quantum advantage. By examining both domestic and international dimensions, including the application of effects-based norms from public international law and export controls, the book underscores the need for sensible technology governance (*engagement*) to ensure that quantum technologies continue to advance and benefit humanity (*advancement*) while mitigating potential downside risks and harms (*safeguarding*).[6]

The structure of the book is designed to build progressively from foundational concepts to specialized regulatory considerations and global considerations. Following this introduction, the subsequent chapters delve into key aspects of quantum technology governance. Below is an overview of the book's structure and contents.

2 Quantum Information Technologies and the Law

This area establishes the foundational intersection between quantum information technologies (QIT) and legal principles, emphasizing quantum's unique ontological features and their governance implications. It distinguishes between first- and second-generation quantum technologies, where second-generation innovations like quantum computing leverage superposition and entanglement in ways that challenge classical legal assumptions about certainty and reproducibility, and examine to what extent it may be possible to accommodate QIT governance through interpretive legal and regulatory adaptations rather than doctrinal overhauls. The governance-stack model aligns regulatory tools with QIT layers—from hardware to algorithms—enabling targeted risk management and clarifying that much of QIT falls under existing computational laws, potentially reducing the need for entirely new frameworks. Quantum's probabilistic nature raises novel issues in areas like liability and contracts, such as attributing errors in quantum-induced outcomes, but these may be possible to be addressed via information-theoretic lenses that treat QIT as an extension of classical systems.[7]

[4] Aboy et al. (2022).

[5] Kop et al. (2024a).

[6] Kop et al. (2024a, b).

[7] Perrier and Aboy (2026a, b).

The analysis reveals potential impacts on privacy and evidence standards, where the no-cloning theorem complicates data duplication, yet indirect verification methods help preserve legal enforceability. By framing QIT's affordances (e.g., ultra-precise sensing, decryption) the discussion highlights opportunities for ethical governance, advocating multidisciplinary approaches to balance innovation with societal risks without prematurely restricting development.[8]

This foundational chapter sets the stage for subsequent chapters on law and regulation, illustrating how quantum's core principles necessitate a cohesive thread of interpretive flexibility across legal domains to foster responsible advancement.[9]

3 IP Law: Patents, Trade Secrets, and Open Innovation

This area explores IP strategies in quantum information technology, portraying a "superposition" where patents, trade secrets, and open innovation coexist strategically across the quantum stack. Firms blend these tools contextually (e.g., using trade secrets for tacit know-how in hardware layers like cryogenic systems, while patents protect reproducible inventions) allowing balanced protection, as evidenced by the surge in filings since 2014. Openness via frameworks like IBM's Qiskit fosters ecosystems and network effects, providing competitive advantages for incumbents and access for researchers and startups, countering fears of exclusionary IP. Quantum's probabilistic features test patent doctrines like enablement. The chapter analyzes to what extent the patent system is capable of accommodating QIS inventions.[10]

Trade secrecy's role endures due to export controls and R&D complexities, yet patents encourage disclosure, enriching the public domain and mitigating thicket risks in a diverse owner landscape. The layered approach—calibrating IP at specific stack levels—optimizes private incentives and public goals, reframing debates from proprietary versus open to integrated models that support equitable innovation amid geopolitical tensions. Building on the foundational governance-stack model, this chapter weaves in the theme of adaptive legal tools, showing how IP strategies not only protect quantum innovations but also inform broader policy trends analyzed in subsequent empirical mappings.[11]

[8] Perrier and Aboy (2026a, b).

[9] Perrier and Aboy (2026a, b).

[10] Lenarczyk et al. (2026).

[11] Lenarczyk et al. (2026).

4 Patenting Trends and Policy Implications

This chapter provides an updated empirical mapping of quantum technology patents from 2001 to October 2025, revealing trends that inform innovation policy and counter overprotection concerns. The USPTO and EPO now grant approximately 2500 patents annually under quantum classifications, reflecting a 14.5% CAGR and acceleration driven by breakthroughs like error-corrected qubits, underscoring sustained R&D investment without slowdown.[12]

It reports that the patent system is promoting early disclosure of quantum inventions that otherwise could be kept secret. In fact, about 54% of quantum-related disclosures are already in the public domain, including over 6500 expired patent grants, progressively enriching a quantum information commons that raises novelty thresholds and narrows future claims, benefiting open innovation. Analysis of these patents reveals patent claim structures mirroring semiconductor patents, highlighting continuity with classical tech and cautioning against unharmonized reforms that could distort global filings.[13]

Diversity among top owners (e.g., spanning IBM, Google, startups such as IonQ and Rigetti, universities, and governments) indicates lower concentration than in IT markets, supporting competition and IP leverage for SMEs in capital-intensive fields. Geopolitical shifts, such as China's lead in filings, amplify security implications, urging evidence-based policies that balance disclosure incentives with technology monitoring, while affirming patents' role in countering trade secrecy in strategic areas. This data-driven perspective extends the adaptive IP narrative, providing empirical grounding for the regulatory challenges in cybersecurity and export controls that follow, ensuring governance remains evidence-informed across quantum's evolving landscape.[14]

5 Quantum and Cybersecurity Law

This area examines EU cybersecurity regulations' adequacy against quantum threats, advocating proactive reforms for resilience. It identifies two core challenges: (1) "harvest now, decrypt later" attacks and (2) quantum potentially outpacing classical cryptography measures through algorithms like Shor's algorithm, exposing vulnerabilities in asymmetric encryption that demand urgent post-quantum cryptography (PQC) transitions.[15]

EU concepts like "state of the art" and "appropriate measures" under NIS2 and GDPR may fail to address future threats materializing today, necessitating

[12] Aboy et al. (2026).

[13] Aboy et al. (2026).

[14] Aboy et al. (2026).

[15] Davis et al. (2026b).

enhancements such as quantum-risk assessments to protect critical infrastructure and quantum-specific information security standards. PQC offers practical solutions without specialized hardware, with NIST's standards providing an emerging blueprint, yet integration complexities in legacy systems highlight the need for policy focus on interoperability and implementation.[16]

Anticipatory governance through multi-layered strategies (e.g., combining law, regulation, regulatory guidance, international standards, and judicial decisions) may enable the EU to leverage its regulatory capacity amid global efforts like the Commission's PQC Roadmap. While quantum key distribution emerges as a potential defense, the analysis stresses balanced approaches that account for uncertainties, urging shifts to future-oriented controls to safeguard information security in an evolving threat landscape. Linking back to the patent trends' emphasis on disclosure and innovation, this section highlights how cybersecurity adaptations must align with broader governance threads, paving the way for export controls as another layer of protective strategy in quantum's international context.[17]

6 Quantum and Export Control Law

This area analyzes export controls on quantum technologies, mapping US and EU measures while identifying enforcement opportunities and challenges. It notes the shift to plurilateral coordination outside multilateral frameworks like Wassenaar, enabling targeted restrictions on quantum stacks from hardware to software amid US-China-EU rivalries, as seen in 2022–2025 iterations.[18]

Quantum's layered nature allows granular controls, such as on cryogenic systems or cloud-access models, offering dynamic enforcement tied to physical footprints and modularity, enhancing efficacy over intangible assets. Challenges include regulating know-how and avoiding fragmentation, with US "deemed exports" and EU variations risking compliance burdens, yet opportunities arise from centralized infrastructure for verifiable restrictions.[19]

The dual-use potential heightens national security rationales, but empirical gaps in multilateral regimes underscore the need for adaptive strategies that balance collaboration with prevention of proliferation. Forward-looking frameworks should leverage quantum-specific affordances (e.g., component-level targeting) to inform coordinated policies, ensuring controls adapt to diffusion without unduly hindering global R&D in this nascent field. This regulatory focus complements the cybersecurity emphasis on anticipatory measures, reinforcing a unified thread of proactive

[16] Davis et al. (2026b).

[17] Davis et al. (2026b).

[18] Davis et al. (2026a).

[19] Davis et al. (2026a).

governance that extends into international law, where export controls serve as a bridge between domestic protections and global norms.[20]

7 Quantum and International Law: Strategic and Geopolitical Dimensions

This area investigates quantum information technologies' implications for public international law, integrating strategic and geopolitical dimensions. QIT's embedding within classical infrastructures allows existing doctrines (like those in the Tallinn Manual) to apply effects-based norms to quantum operations without fundamental changes, maintaining continuity in sovereignty and due diligence.[21]

Quantum ontology could complicate attribution and jurisdiction, yet functional definitions focused on outcomes enable interpretive refinements, as in probabilistic causation during cyber operations. Game theory models reveal patterns of cooperation and competition, with quantum decryption altering informational asymmetries and urging new norms to manage arms races and equitable access.[22]

Dual-use export controls provide an immediate governance interface, constraining transfers while shaping capability distribution, with calls for multilateral reforms to address entangled systems. The analysis proposes strategic frameworks for geopolitical governance, emphasizing law's likely flexibility to accommodate QIT's non-classical features through incremental evolution, fostering transparency and accountability in peacetime and conflict scenarios. Culminating the first volume's progressive exploration, this section ties together the adaptive themes from foundational law, IP strategies, patent trends, cybersecurity, and export controls, advocating for interconnected global approaches to harness quantum's potential responsibly.[23]

8 Discussion

The analyses presented across this volume reveal that QIS challenge existing governance structures not by rendering them obsolete, but by exposing areas where interpretive flexibility, empirical grounding, and anticipatory foresight are most needed. A central insight emerging from the contributions is that QIT's disruptive potential lies not only in its technical characteristics (e.g., probabilistic computation, entanglement-enabled communication, and ultra-sensitive sensing) but also in the

[20] Davis et al. (2026a).

[21] Perrier and Aboy (2026a, b).

[22] Perrier and Aboy (2026a, b).

[23] Perrier and Aboy (2026a, b).

nature, pace and asymmetry of its development across companies, industries, and jurisdictions. These dynamics create governance pressures that test the adaptability of legal and regulatory systems while simultaneously revealing opportunities to strengthen them.

First, the volume shows that *quantum technologies are inherently layered*, spanning hardware, control systems, algorithms, and applications. This layered architecture reinforces the importance of governance-stack approaches that align regulatory tools with specific technical strata. Such alignment helps avoid both overbroad regulatory interventions and excessively narrow measures that fail to address systemic risks.

Second, the contributions collectively show that existing legal doctrines and regulatory frameworks possess significant latent adaptability. Whether in IP law, cybersecurity regulation, export controls, or public international law, many longstanding principles—such as enablement, proportionality, and effects-based norms—likely already provide conceptual room to address quantum-specific complexities. Rather than demanding wholesale legal reinvention, quantum technologies more often call for recalibration, updated interpretation, clear guidance, standards, and targeted supplementation.

Third, the volume highlights the importance of *empirical evidence*—including patent analytics, cybersecurity threat modeling, and export control enforcement data—in informing quantum governance. These empirical perspectives illuminate technological trajectories, reveal the dispersion or concentration of capabilities, and help identify where regulatory asymmetries or vulnerabilities may emerge.

Finally, we emphasize the need for *governance that jointly optimizes advancing and safeguarding*. QIT's dual-use nature, global research ecosystem, and strategic implications require approaches that preserve openness for scientific progress while managing proliferation risks, competitive distortions, and geopolitical tension. As the volume shows, multilateral coordination (e.g., across standard-setting bodies, export control regimes, cybersecurity frameworks, and interpretive guidance in international law) will be essential to preventing fragmented or inconsistent regulatory landscapes that could impede innovation or exacerbate systemic risks.

Taken together, the contributions in this volume illustrate that effective quantum governance must be empirically informed, adaptive, and internationally engaged. As QIT transitions from theoretical work to practical deployment, governance systems must evolve in tandem, ensuring that innovation proceeds responsibly while upholding security, transparency, and public trust.

9 Conclusion

Collectively, the first volume's scholarly contributions reveal a recurring theme of adaptability in quantum governance, where existing legal frameworks (i.e., bolstered by interpretive flexibility and evidence-based insights) may be able accommodate quantum's unique challenges without necessitating wholesale reforms.

From the foundational governance-stack model that layers regulatory tools across QIT components to the "superposition" of IP strategies blending patents, secrets, and openness, the narrative underscores how quantum innovations more likely extend rather than completely rupture classical paradigms. Empirical patent trends further affirm this, showing robust growth and a burgeoning public domain that counters overprotection fears while highlighting geopolitical dynamics, such as China's rising dominance, which amplify the need for balanced incentives in capital-intensive fields.

This adaptive thread extends into specialized domains, where cybersecurity reforms advocate multi-layered strategies to mitigate threats like quantum decryption, aligning with global standards for resilient infrastructure. Export controls, in turn, leverage quantum's modular nature for targeted enforcement, bridging domestic security with international collaboration amid plurilateral shifts. Culminating in public international law, the analysis integrates these elements through effects-based norms and game-theoretic modeling, proposing frameworks that foster equitable access and transparency. Together, these insights equip stakeholders to navigate quantum's transition from theory to application, emphasizing multidisciplinary cooperation to harness its transformative power equitably and ethically.

By synthesizing these contributions, the book not only maps the current quantum governance landscape in terms of existing laws and regulations but also charts pathways for future resilience, calling for proactive policies that balance innovation and security. As quantum technologies mature, this interconnected approach ensures they advance societal progress (*advancement*) while mitigating risks (*safeguarding*), positioning governance as a dynamic enabler rather than a constraint.

Acknowledgments This work was made possible through the generous support of the Novo Nordisk Foundation (NNF) via a grant for the scientifically independent Collaborative Research Program in Bioscience Innovation Law (Inter-CeBIL Program—Grant No. NNF23SA0087056).

References

Aboy M, Minssen T, Kop M (2022) Mapping the patent landscape of quantum technologies: patenting trends, innovation and policy implications. IIC 53:853–882

Aboy M et al (2025) Quantum technology governance: a standards-first approach. Science 380(6760):575–578

Aboy M, Crespo C, Minssen T (2026) Mapping the patent landscape of quantum technologies: evolving patenting trends and policy implications. In: Aboy M, Corrales Compagnucci M, Minssen T (eds) *Quantum technology governance I: law & Regulation*, perspectives in law, business and innovation. Springer Nature, Singapore. (forthcoming)

Davis P, Aboy M, Minssen T (2026a) Regulatory challenges and opportunities of export controls on quantum computing. In: Aboy M, Corrales Compagnucci M, Minssen T (eds) *Quantum technology governance I: law & Regulation*, perspectives in law, business and innovation. Springer Nature, Singapore. (forthcoming)

Davis P et al (2026b) EU Cybersecurity regulation in the quantum age. In: Aboy M, Corrales Compagnucci M, Minssen T (eds) *Quantum technology governance I: law & Regulation*, perspectives in law, business and innovation. Springer Nature, Singapore. forthcoming

Kop M et al (2024a) Towards responsible quantum technology: safeguarding, engaging and advancing quantum R&D. UC Law Sci Technol J 15(1):63–94

Kop M et al (2024b) Ten principles for responsible quantum innovation. Quantum Sci Technol 9(3):035013

Lenarczyk G, Minssen T, Aboy M (2026) IP in superposition: patents, trade secrets, and open innovation in quantum information technology. In: Aboy M, Corrales Compagnucci M, Minssen T (eds) *Quantum technology governance I: law & Regulation*, perspectives in law, business and innovation. Springer Nature, Singapore. (forthcoming)

Perrier E, Aboy M (2026a) Quantum information technology & the law. In: Aboy M, Corrales Compagnucci M, Minssen T (eds) *Quantum technology governance I: law & Regulation*, perspectives in law, business and innovation. Springer Nature, Singapore. (forthcoming)

Perrier E, Aboy M (2026b) Quantum information technologies and public international: strategic, legal, and geopolitical dimensions. In: Aboy M, Corrales Compagnucci M, Minssen T (eds) *Quantum technology governance I: law & Regulation*, perspectives in law, business and innovation. Springer Nature, Singapore. (forthcoming)

Quantum Information Technology and the Law

Elija Perrier and **Mateo Aboy**

Abstract Quantum information technology (QIT) encompasses a collection of emerging innovations—quantum computing, quantum communication, and quantum sensing—that leverage unique properties of quantum systems, such as entanglement, superposition, and quantization, in order to process information in ways that are either classically impossible or infeasible. While QIT remains in relative infancy, its potential for unprecedented computational speedups, security of communication, and ultra-precise measurement foreshadows its impacts and risks across economic, strategic, and societal domains. We situate QIT within both its historical and technological context, focusing on the question of what is *sui generis* or unique about QIT with respect to both technical detail and governance imperatives. We identify how the unique ontological properties of quantum systems may raise novel legal conceptual dilemmas and propose a governance-stack model that aligns potential regulatory instruments with specific layers of the QIT technical stack, enabling precise risk assessment and stakeholder-focused regulation. By adopting an information-theoretic lens, we analyze how QIT's novel affordances—ranging from decryption of classical encryption to ultra-precise sensing—may potentially impact legal domains. Our contribution aims to lay a foundation for understanding QIT's legal implications, offering a framework to navigate its opportunities and risks.

Keywords Governance stack · Information · Ontology · Quantum · Uncertainty

E. Perrier (✉)
Centre for Quantum Software and Information, University of Technology, Sydney, NSW, Australia

Centre for Law, Medicine and Life Sciences (LML), University of Cambridge, Cambridge, United Kingdom
e-mail: eper2139@uni.sydney.edu.au

M. Aboy
Centre for Law, Medicine and Life Sciences (LML) and Centre for Intellectual Property and Information Law (CIPIL), University of Cambridge, Cambridge, UK
e-mail: ma608@cam.ac.uk

M. Aboy et al. (eds.), *Quantum Technology Governance I*, Perspectives in Law, Business and Innovation, https://doi.org/10.1007/978-981-95-8371-3_2

1 Introduction

Quantum information technologies (QIT), a set of technologies that leverage the unique properties of quantum mechanics to acquire, store and process information,[1] represent one of the twenty-first century's major technological innovations with potentially far-reaching consequences for economic, strategic and even social systems globally. QIT comprises an expansive set of theoretical and applied disciplines, primarily quantum computing, quantum communication and quantum sensing. By leveraging the unique properties of quantum mechanics, each division of QIT offers the promise of unparalleled information processing capabilities. Quantum computing has the potential, in-principle, to decrypt[2] certain types of classically encrypted data and communications,[3] which could affect aspects of nation States' modern cybersecurity and defense postures. Quantum sensing could potentially contribute to efforts to detect strategic assets like nuclear capable submarines, which might influence nuclear powers' second-strike capabilities.[4] Quantum communication may enable competitive advantage in communication in both peacetime and during conflicts.

The potential scope and impact of QIT is widely considered to be significant. QIT is already a major focus of nation State investment and strategic planning,[5] featuring prominently in global power policy postures.[6] Economically, the potential affordances of quantum simulation[7] and quantum computing open up new means of rapidly accelerating processing power beyond computational limitations of classical computing, enabling both a turbo-charging of the scale of conventional computation, while also unlocking a raft of possible solutions[8] hitherto intractable owing to computational complexity considerations.[9] Quantum communication,[10] especially protocols[11] regarding quantum networks[12] and the quantum internet[13] promise to revolutionize the transfer of information across vast distances. Quantum simulation offers promise in terms of the synthesis of chemical and protein structures in ways that are expected to open new doors to pharmaceutical innovation.[14] Quantum

---

[1] Nielsen Chuang (2011) and Watrous (2018).

[2] Shor (1994, 1997).

[3] Hoofnagle Garfinkel (2021).

[4] Rand (2023).

[5] Monroe et al. (2019).

[6] Bureau of Security (2022).

[7] Daley et al. (2022) and Georgescu et al. (2014).

[8] Bremner et al. (2011).

[9] Papadimitriou (1994).

[10] Cariolaro (2015).

[11] Bassoli et al. (2021).

[12] Kimble (2008).

[13] Rohde (2021).

[14] Flöther et al. (2022).

dot devices offer potentially new levels of measurement enabling medical interventions, diagnosis and treatment at finer-grained scales across health and allied sciences.[15] Post-quantum cryptography[16] is already being promoted by standards' organizations and institutions globally as an anticipatory response to potential decryption risks posed by scalable fault-tolerate quantum devices.

1.1 Novel Technology and Existing Governance

As with all newly emergent technology, details of how such technology ought to be governed remain an open question. This is primarily because QIT remains nascent and not yet developed or deployed at scale. Most QIT remains at the prototype stage. We are yet to see a truly scalable fault-tolerant[17] quantum computer, for example. Quantum sensing is largely limited to specific industry applications (such as in the life sciences). Quantum communication via quantum networks and teleportation[18] remains at the early research and proof of concept stage. Yet it is clear that should these technologies be realized to their full extent, then QIT may have significant potential to impact the rights, obligations and interests of stakeholders from States to individuals.

1.1.1 QIT Has Wide Application

The implications of QIT are wide-ranging due to the unique affordances of quantum information processing such as enabling decryption of classically encrypted data, rapid scaling of the size and velocity of computation and simulation of highly complex systems. Decryption carries consequences for the geopolitical balance of power and strategic State behavior, along with the privacy and security of data and information upon which modern society is built. Quantum simulation opens potential doors to discovering new drugs in ways that could offer profound benefits, but also facilitate malfeasance if misapplied. Quantum sensing enables finer-grained measurement but may also give rise to geopolitical implications from decloaking of strategic submarine assets. Quantum communication and post-quantum cryptography may facilitate a new era in communications infrastructure, yet also render the ability to intercept or decode adversarial activities (including criminal activities) difficult. And the strategic implications of synthesizing artificial intelligence technologies with quantum computing are yet to be examined in any comprehensive way.

[15] Bukowski Simmons (2002).

[16] Bernstein Lange (2017).

[17] Gottesman (1998).

[18] Bennett et al. (1993) and Bouwmeester et al. (1997).

1.1.2 QIT Implications for the Law Are Understudied

The ways in which governance instruments and institutions, including law, legal principles, regulation and judicial interpretation, might respond to QIT remains relatively understudied. As with most early-stage technology, this is due to the absence of data to base even heuristic judgments upon. Quantum computing remains a relatively distant prospect—at least the fully fault-tolerant error correcting kind. Quantum communication is yet to be developed in a way that has direct application and the infrastructure which would be required to underpin quantum networks remains essentially conceptual. Quantum sensing, among the more developed of the QIT sectors, remains limited in its application. This dearth of data makes it understandable as to why there are limited legal responses to the rise of QIT, both in terms of legislation and in terms of anything resembling formal quantification of QIT-related risk.

Legal regimes dealing with QIT specifically are similarly limited. As we discuss, the question of what is *sui generis* about QIT is only just starting to be discussed. QIT will to a considerable extent fall within classes of technology subject to existing governance instruments, such as computational technologies or communication technologies. But almost all such governance instruments do not deal with QIT specifically. Those that do, such as dual use and export controls, only scratch the surface so to speak, usually limited to classification of such technologies as being strategic and obligations that flow from this. The ways in which QIT and the law interact, what is unique (if anything) about their relationship and what responses may be required remains, for the most part, uncharted territory. We aim to address this gap by laying out a set of foundational principles for how the synthesis of QIT and jurisprudential reasoning, quantum technologies and governance, might proceed.

1.2 Contributions

This chapter contributes to the literature by providing an analysis of legal issues and consequences that may arise from the development, use and deployment of QIT. While other chapters in this volume consider normative and policy issues, the focus of this chapter is on how technical features of QIT fit within existing legal concepts, assumptions and requirements as set out in legislation, case law and secondary literature. It is directed at framing the *sui generis* question of QIT and the law: what changes, what stays the same. To this end our contributions are as follows.

1.2.1 Technical Jurisprudential Analysis

We analyze possible consequences from the use of QIT with respect in several areas of law. Our analysis includes a survey of key existing regimes to which QIT use is subject and how the law may respond to novel legal issues arising from QIT use.

1.2.2 Legal Quantum Ontologies

We provide an examination of the consequences of quantum ontology for the law, moving beyond mere recitals of quantum properties such as superposition, entanglement, quantization etc. to consider how the fundamentally distinct ontological nature of QIT does or does not problematize underlying legal assumptions.

1.2.3 Governance Stack Analysis

We identify examples of how to map the relevant QIT technology stack to governance instruments in order to facilitate regulatory objectives, including meeting stakeholder interests, imposing obligations and achieving policy aims such as realization of QIT within desired risk tolerances. We focus upon how the choice of where in the QIT technical stack to regulate affects the appropriate choice of governance instrument, clarifying precisely the extent to which anything quantum per se is the subject of governance as distinct from technology of which QIT is a part. To approach these questions, it is useful to contextualize the emergence of QIT within the broader historical development of quantum mechanics and information technology.

2 A History of Quantum Revolutions

2.1 Quantum Revolutions

The advent and evolution of quantum technologies is often classified into first and second quantum revolutions with associated first and second generation technologies emerging as a result. The first quantum revolution is defined as the inception and initial development of quantum mechanics as the primary scientific theory of reality itself.[19] This revolution established the mathematical foundations and experimental evidence for quantum phenomena, including wave-particle duality, uncertainty principles, and quantized energy levels.[20] These foundational principles were harnessed to create devices—sometimes denoted first-generation quantum technology—such as the transistor[21] and the laser,[22] which collectively transformed electronics, computing, and communications. The demonstration of fundamental quantum effects—such as electron tunnelling—provided an impetus for innovations

[19] Dowling Milburn (2003).

[20] Townsend (2000).

[21] Riordan et al. (1999).

[22] Maiman (1967).

ranging from atomic clocks to semiconductor-based integrated circuits.[23] Taken together, these achievements represent the culmination of what historians and technologists label as the first wave of quantum-enabled inventions, giving rise to advanced instrumentation and the microelectronics revolution.

2.2 *Second Quantum Revolution*

The current era of QIT is often positioned as the so-called 'second quantum revolution'. Its genesis lies in the idea of harnessing quantum mechanical properties directly as a resource (rather than an incidental effect or source of error to mitigate as is the case of short-channel effects in the transistors used in state-of-the art classical computing chips) to perform computation which emerged throughout the late 1970s and early 1980s, in part due to theoretical interest in advancing beyond computational complexity limitations in theoretical computer science and tractability challenges regarding the simulation of physical systems.[24] Feynman famously noted that simulating quantum systems on classical machines can be exponentially costly, suggesting that a universal quantum simulator could bypass these exponential resource demands by operating under the same physical rules it aims to simulate.[25] In parallel, Benioff[26] and Manin[27] provided early mathematical frameworks hinting that quantum-mechanical logic might yield fundamentally new modes of computation. Shor's algorithm and Grover's algorithm were subsequent milestones that catalyzed global research efforts into quantum computing, demonstrating polynomial or exponential speedups over classical methods for certain high-value problems.[28]

This modern era is characterized by the development of theories of quantum information systems—quantum computing, quantum sensing and quantum communication— together with advances in applied computational science have unlocked the potential to exert direct control over quantum mechanical phenomena in order to leverage unique properties of quantum mechanics as a resource itself. This second generation of quantum technologies has been made possible by advances in computational infrastructure, such as highly integrated circuits and control apparatuses enabling extreme fine-grained measurement resolution at submicron scales at which quantum effects become observable. By contrast with the first quantum revolution, the second quantum revolution has involved an intentional harnessing of quantum superposition, entanglement, and non-locality as direct

[23] Dowling Milburn (2003).

[24] Benioff (1980), Feynman (1982) and Manin (1980).

[25] Feynman (1982).

[26] Benioff (1980).

[27] Manin (1980).

[28] Preskill (2021).

technological resources. Rather than incidentally relying on quantum phenomena, second-generation technologies seek to incorporate quantum coherence to surpass classical limits in computing power, sensing precision, and communication security.[29]

Advances in superconducting qubits, ion traps, and photonic integrated circuits, for instance, have enabled practical demonstrations of quantum bits—qubits—along with protocols like quantum key distribution and teleportation (see below for a summary). As a result, modern researchers began to envision fully functional quantum computers for tasks such as factorization, optimisation, and molecular simulation, as well as large-scale quantum networks for ultra-secure communication. Moreover, the second generation of quantum technologies has a specifically information-theoretic focus as devices which leverage quantum mechanics in order to acquire, store and process information. We leverage this informational characterization of quantum technologies as a means of bridging the jurisprudential and technical quantum landscapes, both of which can be cast in information-related terms. These breakthroughs have propelled quantum information science from a domain of theoretical curiosity into a prospective next-generation QIT with, as we set out, non-trivial consequences for regulation, law and governance.

2.3 *Modern State of QIT*

QIT has been under development for over 40 years.[30] The current state of QIT is not homogenous, with different sub-divisions at different levels of maturity. Understanding the current level of technological development is important for legal analysis of QIT impacts. Throughout this work, we consider the current and near-term state of the art of QIT, but also QIT in its anticipated fully-fledged form (despite uncertainties about, for example, which modalities—photonic, trapped ion, superconducting etc—may prevail). In general, as at writing, the state of each of the three primary components of QIT—quantum computing, quantum sensing and quantum communication—is as follows.

2.3.1 Quantum Computing

Fault tolerant quantum computing (FTQC) enabling correction of errors up to arbitrary specificity is yet to be accomplished.[31] In general, the field remains in the noisy intermediate-scale quantum (NISQ)[32] era where quantum computational devices are

---

[29] Nielsen Chuang (2011).

[30] Preskill (2021).

[31] Nielsen Chuang (2011).

[32] Preskill (2018).

limited to a few to up to a thousand qubits, though scalable systems remain in the NISQ era with limited effective logical qubits. Importantly, the types of fidelities and quality assurances on quantum systems—required for reliable and robust results—are often limited to very small systems, with larger qubit networks or systems usually studied from limited perspectives. Moreover, the fundamental barrier to FTQC remains noise and error correction.

2.3.2 Quantum Communication

Quantum communication[33] remains at a prototypical stage. Technological demonstrations of quantum teleportation[34] and quantum networks have been shown to be feasible with small numbers of qubits in controlled settings. However, the sector is regarded as a considerable way off from large-scale networks. The primary challenges remain error correction and noise, together with implementation of the infrastructure required for high-fidelity quantum communication channels at scale.

2.3.3 Quantum Sensing

Quantum sensing[35] is the most mature of the QIT sectors, with quantum dot technology being utilized in prototype medical devices and other industrial applications. However, the type of scaling of quantum sensing devices envisaged for widespread application remains yet to occur. Similarly, while quantum sensing is often discussed in terms of national security infrastructure and adversarial communications, there remain considerable barriers to its use in this context.[36]

In this work, while we remain cognizant of the early-stage of QIT innovation, we consider the legal consequences of likely fully-developed and functional QIT. While uncertainty about QIT remains, especially regarding likely computational substrates upon which scalable fault-tolerant quantum computing or quantum communication will materialize, it is clear that whatever the successful form such QIT assume, there will likely be common legal issues arising from the unique quantum ontologies and characteristics that we address below.

[33] Gisin Thew (2007).

[34] Bouwmeester et al. (1997).

[35] Degen et al. (2017).

[36] Hoofnagle Garfinkel (2021) and Rand (2023).

3 Law and Quantum Technologies

3.1 Law and QIT Innovation

The law is no stranger to novel technology. Nor is it a stranger to technologies leveraging quantum mechanics. And information technology in particular has indeed been central to the development of jurisprudence, from the invention of writing, to the printing press to modern computational systems. How a technology ought to be regulated is the subject matter of both theoretical and applied research into technology governance.[37] The law has shown its capacity to respond to technological advances such as nuclear engineering, biotechnology, the internet and more recently artificial intelligence, in similar ways, albeit with a degree of trial and error that inevitably comes with the arrival of new technological horizons.

3.2 Law and Classical Ontology

Yet as we discuss below, quantum technology arguably falls into distinct class of innovation. This is because although all technology is novel to begin with, almost all technology utilized to any significant degree and which the law governs is what we denote as *classical*, based upon what in the physical sciences are often described as classical assumptions about how objects and subject matter exist, evolve and interact. While the emergence of new technologies may and regularly does challenge legal institutions for a response, rarely does such technology challenge the fundamental underlying classical nature of the law. The law as an institution, social practice, discipline and set of norms is firmly anchored in the classical. This does not mean that the law cannot handle indeterminism. or uncertainty. But it is to recognize that prevailing legal interpretation assumes a classical ontology. The law assumes objects exist in particular ways—that they are persistent, that they are usually in principle observable (even if in practice this is difficult), have a definitive identity and state (again, even if epistemically challenging to access) and subsist or move continuously through time. Similarly, the logic upon which the law is based is by and large classical in its nature: rules, propositions, assertions and declarations upon which the rights, obligations and interests of stakeholders under the law discursively come into being are all based upon an assumption of classical ontology.

For example, propositions of the law—the statements about its subject matter are assumed to be in an underlying sense binary, where uncertainty about the truth of a proposition is similarly demarcated as epistemic. These qualities of jurisprudential reasoning are classical: the things, the objects, the people, the institutions are assumed to behave classically. This ontology informs elementary principles of jurisprudence (often assumed as obvious) such as that the subject matter of a law is

[37] Brownsword (2008) and Brownsword et al. (2017).

ascertainable, that such subject matter may be interacted with or even controlled in a particular manner so as to be governable. The locale of subject matter —persons, places, things—is anchored in a typical Euclidean conceptualization of space. Property is identifiable, locatable, controllable. The list goes on.

3.3 The Challenge of Quantum Ontology

Yet quantum systems, upon which QIT is built, may challenge a number of these foundational assumptions that underpin classical conceptualization within the law. As we set out below, the distinguishing features of quantum are ontologically distinct from classical physics. Certain properties of quantum systems are inherently uncertain, such as the position or momentum of particles. Quantum particles may subsist in coherent superposition states of mutually exclusive measurement outcomes, something fundamentally different from classical states (or classical superposition of waves for example). Quantum particles may be entangled, exhibiting long-range correlations in ways that have been shown to require one of the foundations of classical ontology that objects are locally confined (non-locality being a generally accepted consequence of entanglement and Bell's Theorems). These properties of quantum systems are at the heart of their immense potential in a technological sense, but they are also anchored firmly in an uncanny ontology that is different from how the law usually assumes objects exist. This does not mean that the world of QIT is somehow totally unpredictable, chaotic or ungovernable. Indeed, often we would expect the uncertainty brought about by the quantum nature of technology to be manageable or to not give rise to particular challenges from a jurisprudential perspective. We expand upon these concepts later on in this chapter.

3.4 Existing Law Applicable to QIT

QIT is already subject to existing legal and governance instruments indirectly by virtue of the classification or categories into which it is assigned. Quantum communication technologies would fall within certain definitions and remits of communications laws for example. Quantum computing would fall within governance of computational systems framed in the abstract as applying to for example any form of computational or informational processing. And quantum sensing, as used in life sciences for example, is subject in general to regulations governing the use of devices in medical research and applied contexts. In addition to these sector-specific governance regimes, it is worth noting that quantum technologies, like other emerging technologies, are also indirectly covered by more general instruments. This phenomenon is not unique to QIT but is often observed across nascent technology sectors.

For example, basic principles of contract law, tort law, and trade secret law can apply to the use, development or manufacture of QIT. This may include when, for example, a quantum hardware vendor provides defective components or fails to maintain confidentiality in collaborative research programs. Similarly, environmental laws and guidelines that regulate hazardous substances could indirectly govern aspects of quantum device manufacturing, particularly where specialized materials (e.g., superconducting alloys, cryogenic fluids) are used. While such laws may not explicitly mention quantum as a subject matter or descriptor, they nevertheless impose obligations on stakeholders, including manufacturers, end users, and research institutions arising from QIT use. Reliance on these existing frameworks can create both clarity and confusion: they bring immediate application of the law but are less likely to be tailored to QIT's distinctive attributes where these may be relevant to stakeholder rights or interests, such as entanglement-based communications or probabilistic computing outputs. The history of governance in areas like biotechnology or nanotechnology shows that early reliance on existing regimes has often been supplemented by gradual adaptation once specific quantum-centric concerns emerge. As a result, stakeholders working with QIT—ranging from telecommunication companies implementing quantum key distribution to sensing device manufacturers—face a potentially fragmented governance environment.[38]

4 Classifying Existing Laws

In this section, we set out a high-level summary of some of the key conceptual and structural implications for QIT addressed in a number of subsequent chapters.

4.1 Existing Categories of Law Applicable to QIT

We can identify a few of the key existing legal considerations applicable to QIT as follows:

4.1.1 Verification and Evidence

Legal processes depend on replicable evidence, transparent processes, and definable burdens of proof. Quantum mechanics injects probabilistic verification and no-cloning constraints, potentially problematising legal concepts and processes reliant upon classically deterministic information such as chain-of-custody evidence trail assumptions, patent enablement.

[38] Hoofnagle Garfinkel (2021).

4.1.2 Privacy and Data Security

By enabling decryption of classically encrypted information, QIT escalates privacy and data security risks. As quantum sensors gather new categories of potentially sensitive data, new questions about information security may also emerge. As a result, privacy laws may need to adapt to protect data subject to quantum-based interception or measurement.

4.1.3 Regulatory Alignment

Traditional oversight (e.g., for medical devices, communication standards, or export controls) often presumes classical replicability and locality. In a networked computational setting, QIT's intangible, non-local, nature might in a networked computational setting render it more challenging to define transfers of information across shared resources.

4.1.4 Strategic Asymmetry and Dual Use

As QIT scales, States and major firms could leverage its unique decrypting or simulation powers. The resulting asymmetry raises important geopolitical questions, from cyberwarfare rules to dual-use export restrictions. For example, life sciences R&D may be subject to new forms of dual-use monitoring if quantum simulations facilitate rapid weaponisable biotech.

4.2 Quantum-Specific Laws

There are limited *quantum specific* governance instruments directed principally at technologies classified according to their quantum characteristics or properties. Similarly, there is very limited quantum specific legislation applying to QIT. This is once again understandable given the early prototypical state of the technology and the dearth of data against which to empirically assess QIT risk. As such, the distribution of QIT governance instruments tends to be concentrated into those characteristic of early-stage innovative sectors. This includes a number of proposed frameworks, guidance and emerging standards in quantum governance.[39] In general, across developed economies, the most quantum specific governance legal instruments (legislation, formal regulation) cover three areas—export and dual use controls, cryptographic protocols and ecosystem development. Such legal instruments

---

[39] Aboy et al. (2025).

are in effect legislating or seeking to regulate the trajectory of QIT development, rather than anything approaching the widespread use of QIT per se.

4.2.1 Export Controls and Dual Use

Because QIT is a highly strategic technology, its dissemination and distribution has been the subject of export control and dual use legislation. Export controls applying to integrated circuit components and software to the Commerce Control List, such as those under the recent integrated circuit control laws[40] also cover components relevant to the manufacture of QIT.[41] Rare earth minerals, which are often critical components in QIT production, have also been the subject of policy response in order to secure QIT supply chains.

4.2.2 Cryptographic Protocols

The primary interest in QIT from a national security concerns its impact upon encrypted data and communications. As a result, policy and legislative responses have emerged seeking solutions usually in the form of post-quantum cryptographic protocols (discussed below) in order to mitigate against future QIT-based cyber-attacks. These include the NIST post-quantum cryptography programs to secure communication against QIT adversarial attack.[42]

4.2.3 Quantum Ecosystem Initiatives

There exist a raft of soft-governance policy-oriented frameworks and roadmaps aimed at encouraging the growth of the quantum sector, usually products of the executive rather than legislative wings of governments. Specific legislative examples include the US *National Quantum Initiative* and other similar governmental policies globally.[43]

Although these quantum-specific legal measures are limited, they reflect a common trend in emerging technology governance, where early soft governance instruments[44] are created to pre-empt anticipated strategic risks rather than to holistically shape responsible technology development. Similar to the other early technological initiatives (such as nanotechnology), these quantum-specific instruments have been framed in strategic terms, setting broad goals, timelines, or fund-

[40] CHIPS and Science Act of 2022, Pub. L. No. 117–167, 136 Stat. 1366 (2022).

[41] Allen et al. (2022) and Bureau of Security (2022).

[42] Alagic et al. (2024).

[43] Monroe et al. (2019).

[44] Marchant Gutierrez (2022) and Marchant Wallach (2015).

ing mechanisms for QIT development rather than prescribing detailed regulatory constraints. The dual use characteristics of QIT parallels other domains, such as biotechnology or AI, where technology can be harnessed for civilian or military objectives. This dual use nature prompts heightened international competition and security measures, including trade restrictions and specialized technology transfer controls which have emerged over recent years to apply to QIT and its supply chain elements.

In addition, many governments are also exploring limited, targeted rules addressing specific areas of QIT such as quantum-enabled encryption or quantum-based key exchange.[45] For instance, the U.S. Quantum Computing Cybersecurity Preparedness Act[46] is an example of an early legislative instrument directed towards institutions in adopting post-quantum cryptography. Its aim is to address craft domain-specific regulations as quantum computing evolves. Over time, more comprehensive quantum-specific regulations could emerge, focusing on data privacy, standardization, liability, or sector-specific use cases if the technology matures to the point where existing frameworks become insufficient.

While certain existing laws and regulations take quantum technology as their subject matter, they do not jurisprudentially move much beyond merely applying existing types of regimes, such as dual use, to technologies that meet technical classification as quantum. For example, dual use regimes in the US largely have historically not factored in how the entanglement of quantum networks used for civilian and military purposes may pose challenges (if any) for monitoring, verification and auditing of compliance with dual use rules. Export controls similarly make relatively oblique mention of quantum in the context of well-established control regimes. And quantum ecosystem initiatives largely adopt existing approaches.[47] Intellectual property laws upon which existing patents for quantum technology (such as hardware) are based rely upon generic requirements such as sufficiency of disclosure and existing requirements which QIT must satisfy to be patentable subject matter. This is to be expected as much—if not most—regulation applicable to QIT need not be quantum-specific because the law is not directing outcomes at the quantum mechanical level unlike where, for example, a law that may seek to proscribe or prescribe certain types of quantum computation might (which we argue could be problematic).

[45] Hoofnagle Garfinkel (2021).

[46] Quantum Computing Cybersecurity Preparedness Act, Pub. L. No. 117–260, 136 Stat. 2389 (2022).

[47] Marchant et al. (2024).

5 Related Work

5.1 Technology Governance

Existing literature on quantum technologies and QIT is diverse but often lacks systematic or detailed exposition connecting the underlying technical quantum mechanical properties of QIT to the logic of legal and governance practices. Early work applying technology governance principles to quantum technologies has included a mixture of jurisprudential, ethical and policy-based analysis. Such literature has included frameworks for how to analyze the effects of quantum technology[48] and principles for governance.[49] Other early work situated prospective QIT governance within technology governance debates regarding the extent to which early-stage innovations ought to be lightly regulated so as to not to hamper their development.[50] Policy-oriented studies have examined the institutional procedures by which governance of quantum technologies ought to proceed, arguing for participatory approaches that engender trust in emergent technologies.[51] More broadly, studies into the normative considerations of quantum technologies have sought to consider ethical[52] and design implications.

There have also been a number of non-peer reviewed industry reports and multilateral initiatives examining the implications for quantum governance. Among the more extensive treatments of how governance, law and policy institutions might respond to quantum technologies is Hoofnagle et al.[53] which focuses upon the governance implications of quantum sensing on the basis that it represents the most mature form of QIT. One approach to systematically approaching quantum governance that has sought to synthesize technical and governance instruments is the governance stack model which treats both QIT and its governance in terms of a stack, mapping relationships between them. We adapt such a model below.[54]

5.2 Geopolitical Analysis

Geopolitically, the most detailed study of the implications of quantum sensing for second strike capabilities and decloaking of strategic assets such as nuclear-armed submarines is Rand.[55] This work considers in sober detail the practicalities of claims

[48] Kop (2021a, c).

[49] Kop et al. (2024a).

[50] Johnson (2018).

[51] Ten Holter et al. (2021).

[52] Cortez (2014).

[53] Hoofnagle Garfinkel (2021).

[54] Perrier (2022).

[55] Rand (2023).

that quantum sensing devices may upend geostrategic equilibria based upon nuclear power second-strike capabilities. The work is a timely synthesis of technical exposition and strategic analysis, demonstrating the considerable barriers that would need to be overcome for quantum sensing to pose such a heightened geopolitical risk.[56]

5.3 *Intellectual Property and QIT*

Intellectual property implications of QIT are set out in a number of papers that address key points from an intellectual property perspective, including the patentability of quantum inventions.[57] Beyond theoretical treatments, in an empirical IP study Aboy et al.[58] mapped the landscape of QIT and quantum technology patents, demonstrating an emphasis on hardware patents and that generally the patent system as-is did not provide evidence that patentability challenges were hampering the development of QIT.

A recent systematic review[59] of lessons from emerging technology governance applicable to QIT examines how biotechnology, nanotechnology, and AI might inform effective oversight. The article focuses upon the potential need for early-phase quantum guidance that mirrors those models without imposing undue burdens on innovation. Other literature also considers international instruments in emerging technology, such as treaty or other instruments, for solving cross-border quantum network coordination challenges. While limited, existing legal scholarship underscores the need to consider how general governance frameworks—like those used for nanotech or AI —may be adapted to address quantum's unique affordances.

The governance stack model adopted herein proposes that quantum regulation might be layered, starting from lower-level hardware and culminating in domain-specific, application-level rules. This layered perspective resonates with the emergent idea from AI governance: that regulators need a flexible structure to address risks and responsibilities at each phase of development, including potential synergy with existing multi-lateral initiatives for advanced technology oversight like OECD policy frameworks or ISO/IEC standardization efforts in QIT.[60] Comprehensive quantum governance models remain in formative stages. But, with the literature increasingly merging legal analysis, policy roadmaps, and the lessons gleaned from other frontier technologies to propose more robust responses. However, despite emergent work, there is little research that directly answers precisely what is unique about QIT when it comes to legal frameworks or consequences. This question of the *sui generis* nature of quantum governance: what unique governance requirements

[56] Rohde (2021).

[57] Kop (2021c) and Kop et al. (2024b).

[58] Aboy et al. (2022).

[59] Marchant et al. (2024).

[60] Aboy et al. (2025).

does it generate and give rise to, how is it situated within existing legal frameworks and what ought to be reforms, if any, to domain-specific jurisprudence . This question is the focus of our work. To this end, we frame the question of QIT *sui generis* below.

6 What Is Sui Generis About QIT?

As with any new technological development, the foundation for the study of QIT and the law is to understand the innovative novelty of QIT and the implications, if any, its application. Perhaps the most important and necessary guiding question to answer for quantum governance and jurisprudential perspective regards what is, if anything, *sui generis* about the governance of QIT.[61] The question of *sui generis* compels us to enquire into to whether there is anything *new* from a governance perspective—be it consequential, conceptual, procedural—that arises or ought to arise when technology changes, including information processing technology in general and quantum information processing technologies in particular? We are therefore focused upon the question of whether or not the application of QIT is simply another form of information processing technology already captured by the broad jurisprudence on the use of computational, cyber-technological and information processing technology in general (of which QIT is a subset). These questions are often debated within jurisprudential and technology governance under auspices of the 'technology neutrality' of regulation,[62] whereby governance is technology neutral to the extent it largely is technically agnostic,[63] focused more upon the consequences of any technological use in a specific context. Debates over technology neutrality —the extent to which the law ought to reach into the technical specificities of a particular technology—are common across technology jurisprudence, including emerging scholarship on the governance[64] and ethics[65] of QIT.[66] The answers to these questions depend in part on the operating theory of jurisprudence—its rationale and the justification of governance itself—that one adopts.

---

[61] Perrier (2021, 2022).

[62] Marchant et al. (2024).

[63] Marchant Gutierrez (2022), Marchant Wallach (2015) and Moses (2007, 2017).

[64] Johnson (2018).

[65] Kop (2021a, b) and Kop et al. (2023).

[66] Coenen et al. (2022), Coenen Grunwald (2017), de Wolf (2017), Ten Holter et al. (2021) and Vermaas (2017).

6.1 Quantum Uniqueness

As discussed below and throughout this work, because of its basis in quantum mechanics, QIT may introduce unique differences in how it ought to be construed as a subject matter within the law. Quantum systems exhibit specific properties which are not mere extensions or scalings of classical technology, but are ontologically fundamentally distinct phenomena which have no equivalence in classical physics. These include quantum entanglement and quantum superposition which in a precise way endow quantum technologies which leverage them with different properties from those the law assumes from classical technologies. Quantum systems are also inherently stochastic—not simply in an epistemic way with which the law and governance are already familiar, but physically and ontologically.[67] One of the most significant results of twentieth century physics[68] is that the uncertainty observed in quantum measurement statistics[69]—measurements according to which we infer the existence of objects—is not epistemic, not due to some correctable imperfection in measurement apparatuses. Rather, that uncertainty is physical, real, ontological—and this uncertainty is not merely a peripheral feature of quantum systems, but is instead an uncertainty that affects the primitive ways in which we even define objects by specifying their boundaries, state or evolution over time.

This does not—and this is an important point we emphasize—render quantum phenomena upon which QIT is based somehow 'unknowable' or 'ungovernable' or even unpredictable in ways that mean their control and governance hopeless. Quantum systems and QIT are not unknowable to the law on this basis. Uncertainty is more usefully thought of as a matter of degree and one with which nearly a century of theoretical and applied research has grappled in order to render these inherently uncertain systems controllable. But depending on the type of governance sought (how important specific control over quantum evolution or states is to a particular governance regimes), it does mean that the law may need to adjust or modify in certain circumstances (e.g., instead of focusing on property rights 'in' certain quantum information, the law might instead focus on rights to control such a quantum system given the quantum information technically speaking may lack the precise boundaries usually required of objects capable of being property).

[67] Bartlett et al. (2007) and Harrigan Spekkens (2010).

[68] Bell (1964, 1966, 2004).

[69] Wiseman and Milburn (2010).

6.2 *Coordination of Technology Governance Requires Specificity*

Secondly, the study of QIT and the law, including potentially QIT-specific governance responses can be motivated on the grounds of specificity. While quantum information technologies *qua* information technologies already fall within the abstract ambit of information technology regulation,[70] including instrumental or normative prescriptions and proscriptions applicable thereto, the purpose and function of legal principles, laws and governance instruments is not merely to specify abstract general principles. Rather, details matter, including details as to how, where and under what conditions technology is to be operated, used, monitored, stored and deployed. Specificity is an important feature of the implementation of the law itself and is central to solving the coordination problems in economic and social contexts. Indeed specificity is a hallmark of the logic of all legal systems which rely upon hierarchies of classification in order to determine rights, obligations and interests. And specificity is already a feature of how almost all technology is governed: legislation, regulations, rules, precedents and guidance specifically set out the *how* of technology governance as it applies to a specific technology.

6.3 *Strategic Technologies Require Certainty*

Thirdly, many types of QIT can be considered as strategic technologies, distinct from many others due to their potential unique affordances that may not be available through classical technologies alone. This might be said trivially of all technology that may impact behavior. But QIT is strategic in a different way because of its unique properties and capabilities that are unavailable to stakeholders or adversaries limited to solely classical technology. The strategic implications of QIT mean that its use and deployment can have distinct consequences for economic markets, regulatory behavior and geopolitical positioning. For example, as explored in later chapters, QIT may have particular impact on State strategic behavior given its potential for decryption and simulation (indeed it already affects State behavior strategically as States seek to secure quantum supply-chains on the belief that QIT will genuinely have significant import). Similarly, the possession by market participants of a fully fault-tolerant scalable quantum computer enabling superior optimization strategies to be deployed may have profound implications for information asymmetry in economic activity (as may, for example, the possession of advanced artificial intelligence systems). These potential strategic consequences of QIT may suggest the value of common rules or principles specifically directed at technical features or use of QIT in order to provide certainty to stakeholders. Such rules or principles could

[70] Allenby (2011), Johnson (2018), Johnston (2015) and Moses (2017).

be relevant in geopolitical contexts where regulation and motivation to comply with rules by State actors often relies upon incentives rather than direct legal enforcement.

Technological governance certainty is also important to solving coordination problems, often studied and the subject of game theoretical analyses, of how State actors whose interests do not necessarily align may act cooperatively. The canonical case here from a State sovereignty and national security context is the regulation of nuclear weapons, such as via test-ban, non-proliferation and other international instruments.[71] The monitoring and verification regimes encoded within such instruments play an important role in motivating State behavior to adhere to the terms of such instruments. When it comes to the use of advanced information technologies, such as artificial intelligence of quantum computing, by States for potentially adversarial means, it is therefore reasonable to expect that similar requirements for specificity ought to apply (consider, for example, proposals for regulation of compute levels in respect of artificial intelligence technologies[72]).

6.4 Dual Use of Technology Requires Clarity

A fourth, but related, rationale why technological specificity regarding the governance of QIT in municipal and international law is well-motivated is the *dual use*[73] characteristic of such technologies. Dual use technologies are those which have application both in civilian and adversarial contexts, giving rise to the dilemma of how to regulate the use of and trade in such technologies to afford beneficial utility on the one hand, while limiting their use for adversarial or harmful means by an adversary on the other.[74] Clarity of permitted and proscribed uses is important in the case of dual use regimes in order to provide certainty for stakeholders, actors and users of such technology, especially where the transition from civilian to military use of a technology is relatively frictionless or straight-forward. This is particularly the case where QIT is integrated into other highly sensitive technologies subject to their own dual use or export control regimes, such as AI-related technologies, computational chips and life sciences technologies. QIT already is subject to a degree of dual use regime specificity in a number of jurisdictions, such as the US and Australia, for precisely these reasons.

---

[71] Black-Branch Fleck (2015), Blix (1992) and Niemeyer et al. (2020).

[72] Bengio et al. (2024).

[73] Hoofnagle Garfinkel (2021) and Perrier (2022).

[74] Harris et al. (2016).

6.5 Novel Technologies Require Flexibility

A counterpoint on its face to calls for certainty, clarity and specificity in technological regulation arises from the fact that QIT remains nascent emerging technology. QIT governance faces the classic Collingridge dilemma[75] that early regulation of emergent technology can thwart its development, while leaving regulatory responses too late can embed adverse outcomes applies to QIT. These challenges faced by the application of precautionary principles[76] are important considerations relating to the normative and policy responses of the law and regulatory institutions to QIT. On their face, the risks of undermining novel innovation and the need for adaptivity to (often rapidly) evolving technology leans towards a preference for technology neutrality, where governance specifies outcomes with a purposive goal rather than prescribing or proscribing specific controls on technology (especially at the technical level). These are legitimate concerns, but they are really considerations regarding how the timing and specificity of technology governance are correlated. When (assuming) QIT development occurs as expected—with the onlining of scalable fault-tolerant quantum computers, quantum networks and high-fidelity quantum sensing—there is much that we know now about how such technology must work and would likely be utilized.

There is also much we know about how such systems would materialize (usually in large-scale infrastructure, surrounded by classical computing stacks) and, importantly, where in the technical stack they could be controlled (which in turn informs specifics regarding how they ought to be governed). Moreover, for many domains of the law, such as intellectual property (where degrees of specificity required to meet sufficiency of disclosure standards are relevant) or even the use of QIT within life sciences (quantum dots for example, where the reliability and robustness of information extracted or generated using QIT must satisfy overarching bioinformatics and other rules), QIT is already subject to the specificities and vicissitudes of the law. For these reasons, early-stage uncertainty in innovation may not necessarily argue against technological governance specificity at appropriate times. Instead, it suggests that precaution could involve carefully limiting anticipatory governance given the potential variety in technology development configurations. To facilitate our analysis, we explore in more detail how a governance stack model of technology regulation would apply to QIT.

---

[75] Collingridge (1980).

[76] Aldred (2013), Beyleveld Brownsword (2012), Fisher (2002) and Graham (2004).

7 Governance Stacks, Governance Schemas and Risk

7.1 Overview

To facilitate our analysis, in certain parts throughout this work we adopt and extend a governance stack model of technology regulation. The core idea behind the governance stack approach is that quantum information technologies apply and are deployed at specific locations overall technical processes or procedures used within workflows across economic, social and scientific activity. This may include QIT being a resource for computational simulation or data processing, where quantum devices or quantum effects allow for novel or differentiated outcomes compared with classical computations. Or it may involve QIT used to intercept and decrypt communications during conflict or law enforcement. Decisions about how to govern QIT must be clear about where in the technical stack governance is targeted: is it that the quantum procedures themselves require control or influence? Or just their outcomes or effects upon other parts of the stack? The governance stack model is intended to enable a mapping of the appropriate governance instrument to the appropriate level in the technical stack in a way that is fit for regulatory purpose i.e. that facilitates the regulation of rights, interests and obligations of stakeholders. Our adapted governance stack model has three primary components.

7.1.1 Technical Stack and Process

The technical stack comprises a *vertical* component, thought of as a vertically integrated stack from the basic quantum circuitry that underpins all QIT, through scaffolds and layers of hardware through to the ultimate output of the technology; and a *horizontal* component, which refers to the overall workflow or production process within which QIT forms one integrated component.

7.1.2 Governance Stack

The governance stack comprises an analysis of the hierarchy of governance instruments applicable to the relevant technical stack. This hierarchy can be conceived as extending from State-based formal instruments (such as treaties), through to national and municipal legislation, regulations, executive orders, public instrumentalities, through to civil service organizations and standards organisations. Governance instruments are framed as mediating the rights, interests and obligations among stakeholders (such as between a State and its population, or between individual companies via contracts and so on). Different instruments may be tailored to different objectives (such as certain stakeholder interests) and in application be suited to different layers in the technical stack (often technical standards are more detailed and specific than overarching legislation or treaties).

7.1.3 Information Taxonomies

Into this model we add the idea of information taxonomies as a way of identifying how both QIT and the law relate to information. Information taxonomies are dealt with in more detail below, but in essence they concern inputs (classical input data), processing (computation etc) and outputs (measurement data). QIT as an information technology may be involved in data acquisition via measurement, processing or producing outputs of data. In turn, each of these stages may be the subject directly or indirectly of some governance instrument, which may regulate what or how measurement takes place (in order to ensure veracity of data for example), or types of processing or outputs.

More detail on this approach is set out in the literature.[77] In principle, a heuristic application of this approach would be involve (1) identifying the technical stack elements, (2) identifying the governance stack (including stakeholder objectives) and (3) identifying epistemic QIT impacts on available information and then how any governance instruments ought to regulate that process directly or indirectly given stakeholder interests.

An informational approach is a useful tool for legal analysis of QIT implications. By decomposing QIT into horizontal and vertical components, we can more easily see how a range of intersecting legal regimes coalesce. Rather than, for example, noting that the use of QIT may give rise to data, privacy and intellectual property issues, a detailed stack-based approach can provide a finer-grained analysis. Data considerations, such as complying with data standards requirements, may be an issue arising at the level of quantum memory in the stack. Privacy issues may be not related to the quantum aspect of the technology at all, but rather classical interfaces with the QIT. Intellectual property may give rise to issues only some component or collection of the stack, rather than each part or process.

7.2 Technical Stacks and Governance Stacks

7.2.1 Technical Stack Identification

The first element to ascertain in the governance stack is the technical stack—a hierarchy—of the particular technology in question. We set out a typical QIT stack below. The purpose of the stack is to allow for clear identification of the location and interdependencies of a technology. For example, the quantum aspect of QIT is situated at the very smallest of scales at the lowest layer of any stack using it: within the circuitry. This is one of the reasons second generation quantum technologies are essentially informational. One of the hallmarks of a technology's impact is its capacity to influence or act upon the environment. The capacity for confined and relatively small quantum systems to do so is limited. Their primary use in

[77] Perrier (2022).

technology is for the sensing, encoding, processing and outputting of information. These outputs can then become inputs (not unlike informational outputs of AI) into an actuator or interactive scaffolding. Surrounding the quantum-specific technology elements is a range of technological scaffolding, which may be described in physical or abstract terms. This scaffolding for QIT is classical, including classical circuits, operating systems and signal processing devices. Such classical scaffolding is not itself quantum in that it does not exist and behave in quantum way. This type of distinction is important for understanding how governance may be directed at different layers in the stack (see below). For example highly technical governance, e.g. for how nuclear reactors must function, is usually prescriptive of minutiae, even at atomic levels (control mechanism seek to regulate fission rates for example), while normative social governance, such as regarding how computational platforms may be used or for what purposes are less technically specific.

7.2.2 Governance Stack Identification

Secondly, a governance stack assists in identifying the appropriate instrument e.g. rather than seeking to achieve outcomes at the quantum circuit level, it may be more appropriately done at some other level with purposive goals rather than technical ones. Conversely, should assurance procedures mandate engineering specifications, it may be that these are more appropriately situated at the circuit or technical scaffold level rather than merely in the abstract as a requirement among other stakeholders or levels in the stack. Such an approach recognises that different levels in the technical stack are controllable to different extents and different ways. This affects the extent to which governance can be implemented at that level. As we discuss below, QIT is controllable, but usually in a different way from classical: one cannot for example retain the quantum characteristics of a QIT and somehow control the system's measurement outcomes deterministically if this were a normative aim.

7.3 Integration and Risk

Thirdly, the governance stack model assists in the process of risk assessment central to the development and deployment of any technology. For use cases of QIT, it is important to recognize that QIT will always be integrated within broader classical technology stacks and workflows—QIT will only ever be a component of broader infrastructure. This impacts its risk framing as the context within which QIT is used affects its risk profile, and conversely, the use of QIT within workflows and processes can in principle change total or aggregate measures of risk used to determine the acceptability of an activity. In combination with the stack-based paradigm, we adopt a specifically *risk-centered* approach to QIT and governance. We are interested in how the use of QIT changes risk—both in terms of classification, likelihood of events and so on. Our work does not set out tools and techniques for quantifying such risk per se, but it does recognize that assessment of technology risk is a central element for institutions that rely upon computational technologies—such as artificial intelligence—and which may directly or indirectly utilize QIT.

A risk-centric approach also, we argue, is of particular use for stakeholders considering how the law may (or may not) need to adapt in order to respond to the use of QIT. It may be, for example, that the use of QIT has little or no significant impact upon the types of risks which law and regulation seek to address. Conversely, it may be that the integration of QIT within a workflow or process significantly changes the vectors or properties of risk, potentially opening up new forms of risk to be considered or responded to jurisprudentially (because QIT may enable certain activities that were hitherto physically or computationally infeasible). Or it may be that QIT affects other dimensions of risk, such as scale, scope, breadth or severity of impact. Understanding the variation in risk occasioned by the use of QIT (within the limitations of risk analysis itself) provides a further practical benefit towards understanding the consequences of QIT with which the law and regulation must reckon.

7.4 *Risk and Governance*

A risk-centered and governance-stack model of technology governance thus are complementary. They are focused upon understanding how and where in the technical stack QIT impacts manifest. This in turn allows for finer-grained precision regarding the type, form and extent of governance instruments that ought to be used as controls to manage QIT-related risk. A governance and technical-stack based approach also allows us to cater for important empirical measures of QIT impact. By framing the use of QIT as intervening at some level in the technical stack of an economic, social or scientific workflow, we can then consider how this intervention gives rise to legal consequences. This may include the use of QIT affecting the rights, interests or obligations of stakeholders. A governance stack model helps us to map governance instruments to the appropriate level in a technical stack, thereby allowing us to identify the relevant obligations or rights at stake from such QIT use. The stack model also allows for a finer-grained consideration of exactly what governance seeks to achieve and how it seeks to do so.

For example, this may involve whether the use of QIT or its governance is targeted at the computational level, setting out proscribed computations which ought not be undertaken (e.g. synthesis of proscribed chemical elements for chemical weapons' manufacture), or prescriptions on how, for example, computation unfolds say in pharmaceutical drug design in order to meet bioinformatics requirements on how reliable information from such simulations is. Or it may involve specification of governance instruments relating to the use of QIT in clinical trials which specifies how QIT are measured, utilized or disseminated. Or it may be that the governance instrument in a particular case is not focused on the specific lower-level technical dynamics of a stack, but rather purposively or normatively upon the use of outputs of QIT.

7.5 *Utility of a Risk-Based Stack*

A risk-based approach can help focus our enquiry on the implications of QIT for the law in terms of the following questions:

1. Whether the use of QIT affects, in any way, the application of or objectives of governance instruments?
2. Whether proposed governance regimes covering QIT may affect its use in economic, social or scientific activity?
3. Whether any reform to governance may be necessary or desirable in order to meet the multiple objectives of technology governance in these areas?

Given the relative novelty of both applications of QIT across all sectors, and even more nascent governance regimens for quantum technologies, we adopt a broad focus as to where QIT is likely to apply and be relevant. The sprawling breadth of economic activity as a collocation of interdisciplinary fields together with the complex nuances of quantum information science means that attempts to examine their interrelationship must be handled with care owing to the overt and subtle differences in conceptualization, nomenclature and framing of phenomena. Incorporating (in addition) the thicket of governance frameworks, guidelines, jurisprudence and the like adds more complexity, requiring translation and mappings between concepts, approaches and terms of art which exhibit varying degrees of similarity.

8 Unifying Technology and Law Via Information

8.1 *Information as a Fulcrum Concept*

One of the challenges when approaching the governance of highly technical and highly interdisciplinary sectors lies in finding a common, unifying, set of concepts according to which the conceptual and technical interrelationships among each discipline may be analyzed. Wrangling unified frameworks that allow for translation between concepts in fields, or that show crisply how the governance or laws applicable in one area may directly or indirectly affect the synthesis with technology from other disciplines is a complex task. Much of the study of QIT and the law requires such mediation among distinct technical and jurisprudential disciplines. The complexity and variegated nature of each discipline means it is important to seek a common language, a fulcrum concept or set of concepts, with which to compare and contrast each field. In this work, our choice of fulcrum concept is that of *information* (and information theory). We adopt information as a conceptual means of synthesizing the QIT and the law. Information theory provides a means of organizing and ordering the spectrum of QIT applications along with their implications for legal and regulatory regimes.

Information is the cornerstone of how legal institutions make decisions. At trial or via decision-making procedures, information is the resource that is manipulated. The identification of stakeholders, their rights and interests are all contingent upon information. Liability and normative requirements are similarly contingent upon information. Information and measurement affect our perception of what is. QIT technologies such as quantum sensing affect what can be known about phenomena in ways that are different from classical devices.

Information processing via quantum computing can similarly affect the types of insights and inferences we can make about the world and decisions predicated upon such information. Quantum communication affects the transfer of information. Keeping information secure is central to economic and social activity. Information affects the reasoning and decision-making. Information is central to the functioning of QIT and the law. The use of QIT affects how information is obtained, how it is processed and how it is disseminated. This in turn has consequences for the information available to stakeholders, participants, regulators and courts among others, influencing and shaping their decisions that are contingent upon such information. Decryption of classified strategic communications represents a change in information state of States, for example, which can mean the difference between prevailing or being defeated in conflict. Information about technological insights or competitor behavior can fundamentally change how agents interact and also the equilibria of systems. QIT may alter the type, scale, and nature of available information, which could potentially influence how participants act. It also changes in some respects the nature of information available to the law when judgments are to be made, or contracts are negotiated.

8.2 Information Is Central to Modern Technology and Economies

We argue that the use of information as an organizing principle according to which technical and regulatory analysis may be conducted is well-motivated. Information is central to modern science, economic activity, social relationships and governance. Within the physical sciences, information theoretic approaches represent increasingly prevalent subdisciplines, such as within life sciences (in the form of bioinformatics). All science, including the life sciences, are information sciences, constituting a set of practices that seek to acquire, process and analyze information. This is particularly true of the sciences due to its vast scope from the atomic and molecular to the organism and population scale. Similarly, much governance technology concerns ensuring scientific procedures for data acquisition, measurement, device design and use are trustworthy, accurate and reliable—all characteristics which ultimately can be framed in information-theoretic terms. The prevalence of information as a conceptual bridge across social, economic and scientific activity fits in a consistent manner with the role of information in the quantum sciences. As we explore below, the concept of quantum information technologies, as the term implies, adopts an information-theoretic approach to classification and dynamics, arising naturally from the combination of classical information and computer science with quantum theory. Doing so enables the synthesis of quantum science beyond traditional quantum mechanics into fields of quantum communication, quantum sensing and quantum computation. We adopt this informational paradigm to explore potential intersectional applications of QIT and their consequences for law and regulatory frameworks.

8.3 Information Enables Comparison of Disparate Domains

We have chosen information as a fulcrum concept in this work as one means of connecting diffuse frameworks, especially in technical fields with import for our chosen areas of jurisprudential focus, being life sciences governance, intellectual property law, information law, property, public international law and communications law. From a technical perspective, adopting information theoretic frame enables us to usefully position quantum information processing, computational and communication use in the broader context of classical information processing upon which the law itself is fundamentally premises. But what exactly does it mean to take an informational or information-theoretic approach to quantum governance? After all, information theory itself is a diverse field, ranging from the highly technical mathematics of information and communication on the one hand, to the qualitative use of informational concepts—such as knowledge, foreseeability and so on—in the law itself.

8.4 Information as Paradigm and Method

Information plays the following roles in our work.

8.4.1 Qualitative (Paradigmatic)

Information serves as a means according to which QIT and legal consequences can be framed paradigmatically. Thus rather than information being measured in the way it is in formal communication theory (which concerns for example the amount of information transmissible by channels), we are focused here on understanding qualitatively the role of an activity or workflow as contingent upon information in order to adequately benchmark how risk and governance changes when components of that process change from classical to QIT-based.

8.4.2 Quantitative

Information-theoretic measures can also be brought to bear in assessing the impacts of QIT. Our work only sketches the technical use of information measures in this work, but we note that measures of information—such as entropy, computational complexity, communication channel capacity—and other technical means of assessing information—arguably could very much play a role in precisely identifying the comparative effects of QIT by comparison with classical counterparts. This may include measures of the quality, reliability and robustness of information extracted from QIT-based simulations, for example. Or it may include technical information regarding the precision and error rates of quantum sensors which in turn may be relevant to their classification for legal purposes under life sciences regulation.

Our adoption of information in this work is focused on the paradigmatic rather than methodological use in order to conceptually address the sui generis implications of QIT. But it is worth noting that technical information-theoretic methods are likely to have direct consequences for QIT governance. Thus, for example, identifying whether two quantum states are in fact identical is something that is of significance across many uses of QIT but also many governance regimes, such as when seeking to provide guarantees as to the robustness of quantum data or quantum computations relied upon in the life sciences, intellectual property or other areas. Comparing quantum states is fundamentally an informational exercise involving measures, such as the Holevo-Helstrom bound, or comparison of distributions of density operators via quantum entropy. And it is also contingent on tomography.

These measures of information—albeit technical—also have consequences for legal regimes dependent upon such information, such as where a claim may be made regarding intellectual property infringement reliant upon comparing quantum states, systems or processes. Another example is the impact or influence of quantum computational simulations can be situated by comparison with current (and emerging, such as in the field of artificial intelligence) classical means of doing so. This is similarly the case with other applications of QIT. In the currently limited cases where QIT extend beyond mere information processing adjunct technology into the realm of corporeal life sciences subject matter, such as being embedded within medical devices (quantum dots), an information-theoretic lens assists in distinguishing what is novel about such use, how existing regulatory responses are or ought to characterize the use of such embedded QIT and ultimately what, if any, recommendations for regulatory reform would be desirable given the objectives of stakeholders.

8.5 *Law and Classical Information Theory*

Information theory can be a useful way of integrating jurisprudential analysis with emerging technologies, and as a means of parsing regulatory theory. As we discuss below, framed in analogous terms to the physical sciences, the law can be construed as a *classical* information processing set of procedures, practices, rules and behaviors. The law does deal with uncertainty and has well-developed, mature and successful ways of resolving uncertainty. But the law proceeds on the basis that uncertainty is epistemic: it might adjudge on the balance of probabilities that some scenario has occurred, but it does not assert or countenance that all or both scenarios actually did occur (or that objects exist ontologically in superposition states for example). In this sense the law relies upon something like a hidden variable theory of information: that phenomena have distinct ontological status, but that any uncertainty in what occurred or what an object is or its properties etc. is epistemic. The extent to which quantum phenomena practically problematize these assumptions is in part what we consider in this work. Nevertheless, we argue that this sort of information theoretic framing is useful precisely because it allows the distinctions and assumptions behind both the law and quantum mechanics to be interrelated.

Various proposals connecting information theory and information processing to governance and regulation have emerged in the literature across several disciplines.[78] Often the use of information theoretic ideas and concepts arises in governance and regulation theory by way of economics and game theory within which information theory, in the modern era, forms a key foundation.[79] Examples of proposals for information-based analysis of regulation and governance include understanding legislative processes in terms of complex systems, understanding governance dynamics in terms of information asymmetries within economics and even the use of classical communication and signaling theory as a means of understanding how regulatory ecosystems function.[80]

Adopting information as our loadstar allows us to adopt a broad scope for our work. It enables us to analyze existing and potential applications of each pillar of QIT—quantum computing, quantum sensing and quantum communication—to activities regulated by or the subject matter of the law. These include research, product design, systems development, clinical trials, commercialization, treatment, use and monitoring of technologies and how these activities are governed. QIT, if realized to its full potential, offers the prospect of a sea-change in economic and social activity because of its informational impacts, opening the door to computational and simulation techniques hitherto unavailable owing to the computational infeasibility or intractability of the problems. Quantum sensing, where quantum devices (such as quantum dots) are utilized to provide high-resolution sensing and measurement apparatuses for devices and laboratories, is already being implemented and utilized in scientific activities. Quantum communication, particularly the use of quantum cryptographic, quantum memory and quantum signaling methods, offers new ways to provide higher degrees of data security over sensitive information, such as bioinformatics and health data, and novel ways for communicating information in secure and faster ways, facilitating collaboration and innovation at heightened scale.

[78] Fromer (2014), Lessig (2000a, b) and Murray (2013).

[79] Akerlof (1970) and Rothschild Stiglitz (1978).

[80] Murray et al. (2019).

Technology governance is mature, highly complex, prescriptive and routinised with implicit and explicit approaches to risk encoded within its structure. It also involves some of the most highly regulated areas of scientific, technological and economic activity, from the extensive requirements surround prototyping, testing and commercialization of devices and products (such as devices and pharmaceuticals), to the complex regulatory networks governing information acquisition, processing and dissemination, such as in healthcare and clinical trials or in how economic markets are regulated. QIT governance is, by contrast, undeveloped, with the primary emerging areas of governance being those focused upon cybersecurity, intellectual property and dual-use considerations. How to square the circle so to speak such that experimental and untested quantum technologies—and the higher degree of risk this entails—may be applied usefully to economic and scientific activity with their fine-grained management of risk is important to both fields. Addressing this dilemma drives our approach to mapping the raft of regulatory regimes to which the applications of QIT will be subject and to understand the consequences of using QIT under existing legislative, regulatory and policy governance regimes. Similarly, as regulation of QIT gathers apace, understanding how that governance ought to take shape in order to realize the benefits in an applied context is crucial.

8.6 Information Taxonomies and Ontologies

As flagged above, to connect the ecosystems of QIT, economic activity and governance instruments (from law, to regulation, to policy and other forms), we approach quantum governance through an information processing lens. Information processing is a broad term encompassing the acquisition, manipulation and utilization of data, such as by way of example direct embeddings of sensors within devices or external diagnostic tools. It also encompasses the use of data in research or product design. QIT can be situated within information processing as a means of acquiring, storing or processing data in ways that are technically distinct from classical technologies and which give rise to novel outcomes that are not possible (or feasible given resource constraints) using classical technologies. We focus on information processing effects of QIT (and the consequences thereof) in order to distinguish QIT from the general role of quantum mechanics in other areas of economic activity. All physical processes are fundamentally grounded in the laws of quantum mechanics, yet the specifically quantum effects have specific significance when used in a QIT context only in specific ways. This is the case across technology stacks.

For example, quantum effects such as quantum tunnelling, chemical structure, composition and evolution, all are essential to physical phenomena. But the incidental involvement of quantum processes does not constitute their use as a *technology* per se. To be a quantum technology, at least in our framing, requires some aspect of the *techné* of quantum mechanical phenomena as a directed or controlled tool or resource. Quantum particles exist all around us in superposition states, but it is not until they are the subject of control, use or deployment that we would regard them as a form of technology. Similarly classical technologies leverage quantum mechanical effects in a variety of ways—such as MRI machines and scanners. And while second generation quantum technologies identified above could reasonably be framed in information-theoretic terms, we distinguish them from QIT in that QIT concerns the direct engineering of quantum systems in order to leverage quantum information effects as is the case when manufacturing quantum circuits, quantum sensing devices or quantum teleportation devices.

To this end we propose a simple but versatile information taxonomy according to which the functionality of QIT (and information systems generally can be based), that of input-process-output but framed in terms of information acquisition (measurement), information processing and information output.

8.6.1 Information Input/Measurement

This first element of information processing concerns the acquisition of data. We analogize the formal theory of measurement described below. Measurement occurs via interaction of a device with the environment in some way. By this process of measurement, data is acquired. This can apply to physical devices, such as quantum dots or quantum sensors, but also in principle to the devices or means by which evidence is gathered (that process effectively constituting the gathering of data). We use input/measurement interchangeably to encompass the case where data is input into a device (which in principle can be construed in measurement formalism), such as when data is input into a quantum computer, or into a quantum communication device.

8.6.2 Information Processing

Information processing then concerns the recombination of data or its functional processing in some way that transforms the data. This might be the identity transformation (so the data remains raw measurement data), but it may also involve constructing statistics from data. A quantum computer takes input data and processes them according to computational parameters (e.g. a Hamiltonian or quantum circuit). A quantum sensor even may transform raw signal data it receives into a particular form. A quantum measurement device is concerned with, for example, eigenstates of the measurement device. In the legal context, information processing can be abstractly but usefully framed in terms of reasoning or other ways in which input data or evidence is transformed as part of the information procedures that constitute legal institutional practices.

8.6.3 Information Output

This concerns the output of a device or process, so concerns information from the device to the environment. The output of classical information procedures often differs from their quantum counterparts, where outputs are ostensibly measurement statistics rather than information repeated extracted from a system unperturbed by the act of measurement itself.

8.7 Levels of Abstraction

How we describe information processing matters. The level of abstraction and discourse according to which information processing is described has important jurisprudential consequences. The way in which computation or algorithms are described forms an important part of computational governance more broadly, relevant to questions of patentability in intellectual property, or technical specifications for technology product disclosure. For example (as we expand upon below), the FDA's Artificial Intelligence and Machine Learning in Software as a Medical Device guidance sets out advice for how manufacturers using artificial intelligence or machine learning (in medical device contexts) describe what changes through computational learning protocols and how algorithms learn while remaining safe and effective. Changing the nature of computation to incorporate quantum computing algorithms or quantum computational techniques will therefore impact how algorithms are described and detailed for the purposes of such regulatory processes. For example, it is commonplace to describe quantum algorithms using both quantum circuit formalism which aligns closely with computational science, but also Hamiltonian formalism which is more commonplace in physics. The extent to which a particular choice of representation of QIT would give rise to any significant consequences or require new responses from a regulatory perspective, or whether existing regimes are adequate for managing QIT in medical devices or other regulated sectors, is an open question. But it is important to keep in mind, because the devil is in the quantum detail so to speak, especially when it comes to precisely distinguishing what is *sui generis* or distinct about QIT and its effects from its classical counterparts.

9 Principles of Quantum Information

Answering the *sui generis* question of quantum governance requires that the impacts of QIT be understood. These impacts may be considered solely with respect to the quantum nature of QIT e.g. superposition and entanglement, the ontologically distinct nature of quantum systems. Or the impact of QIT may be considered indirectly, in terms of how the use of QIT affects the functioning of other components in a process or workflow. In each case, ideally one could quantify the impact of QIT from a risk perspective benchmarked against the equivalent process without QIT, or find something analogous to its coefficient of variation that shows how some particular output varies as a measure of correlation with the use of QIT itself. Doing so in a quantitative manner is of course difficult. Nevertheless, we can still assess QIT impacts using a typical QIT taxonomy that partitions QIT into its three primary divisions of quantum computing, quantum communication and quantum sensing. We consider each application and its implications from the perspective of the law in more detail below.

To understand these impacts, however, it is crucial to have a working familiarity with the quantum mechanical nature of QIT and how its quantum characteristics give rise to such impacts. The quantum characteristics of all QIT stems from their reliance upon and utilization of properties of quantum mechanical systems. Comprehensive reviews of quantum mechanics and quantum information processing may be found throughout the literature,[81] including literature on quantum governance.[82] We set out briefly the key concepts behind quantum information processing below before summarizing the major subsectors of QIT, being quantum computing, quantum communication and quantum sensing. We have aimed to strike a balance between technical specificity and breadth.

9.1 Quantum Mechanics

Quantum computing, quantum sensing and quantum communication are three distinct but overlapping disciplines of quantum information science. The unifying idea behind all three is the study of certain information processing systems, be they in the form of computation, data storage, signaling or detection, which satisfy the postulates of quantum mechanics (see standards texts[83] for an introduction). Quantum information processing is also concerned with abstractions of systems built from composite quantum systems, such as logical qubits, whereby the abstract representation (such as representations of logical qubit states) adhere to quantum as distinct from classical representations. The abstract formalism of quantum information processing is a synthesis elements of quantum mechanics, the formal theory of computation (circuit models) and information theory (such as concepts of channels, registers and so on) (see Watrous (2018)[84] for further detail). Quantum computing, quantum sensing and quantum communication are three interrelated divisions of quantum information. Each is united by the fact that the properties and dynamics of the systems in question, be they computational, mechanical or communicative, satisfy the postulates of quantum mechanics. Quantum information processing represents a means of abstractly reasoning about such systems via axioms and theorems which in turn satisfy the postulates of quantum mechanics. In this way, quantum information processing as a discipline draws upon physics, formal theories of computation and information theory. The key characteristic underpinning of all quantum

[81] Aaronson (2013), Nielsen Chuang (2011), Schuld Petruccione (2021) and Watrous (2018).

[82] Aboy et al. (2022), Hoofnagle Garfinkel (2021), Kop (2021a); Kop et al. (2023, 2024a) and Perrier (2022).

[83] Nielsen Chuang (2011).

[84] Watrous (2018).

information technology that we assess below which renders such technology distinct from its classical analogue is that such technology leverages the unique properties of quantum mechanics. To facilitate our discussion and comparative analyses below, we summarize a few key principles of quantum information processing below, simplifying in certain parts for concision and clarity.

9.1.1 Quantum States

In quantum theory, information is encoded in quantum *states*, denoted in Dirac notation as *kets* $|\psi\rangle$ which represent an information-theoretic abstraction of quantum wavefunctions. States in the abstract are constructed from a vocabulary or alphabet representing the different configurations in which a system may subsist (see Watrous (2018)[85] for a formal exposition). Quantum mechanical states are represented (typically) as a quantization of fields, where quantum systems exhibit discretized (quantized) energy states rather than a continuum of states (however, continuous values can themselves be encoded in probability amplitudes being drawn from the complex field). This quantization (first noticed by early progenitors in physics such as Planck and demonstrated by Einstein) enables quantum systems to represent information in digital-style ways (affording discrete boundaries between a state being valued as 0 or 1). This in turn opens up the space of digital computation. Quantum states are represented as elements of a mathematical vector (Hilbert) space. A central differentiating characteristic of quantum states by comparison with classical states is linearity: if $|0\rangle$ and $|1\rangle$ are quantum (basis) states, then so is a linear superposition of them $|\psi\rangle = a|0\rangle + b|1\rangle$ where $a, b \in C$ are the amplitudes of the possible basis states that the quantum state may be in. This linearity means that any linear combination of basis states (suitably normalised) is also a quantum state, reflecting the phenomenon of quantum superposition (where a state is in more than one state with a certain probability upon measurement). Where the quantum state is two-dimensional, it is denoted a *qubit* (short for 'quantum bit'). Quantum systems may also subsist as composite systems comprising multiple qubits e.g. $|\psi\rangle_a$, $|\psi\rangle_b$. When a quantum system is composed of separable states, it may be represented as a tensor product $|\psi\rangle = |\psi\rangle_a \otimes |\psi\rangle_b$ (a *product state*). Otherwise, the quantum state may be said to be *entangled* such that it cannot be factored into (or separably represented as) a product state. Entangled states are a unique feature of quantum mechanical systems and are a central resource for QIT. They include for example two-qubit Bell states $|\psi\rangle = (|00\rangle - |11\rangle)/\sqrt{2}$ where, as can be seen, measurement outcomes for each qubit are correlated (measuring $|0\rangle$ on the first means it is certain that the second qubit is also in $|0\rangle$, and similarly for $|1\rangle$).Quantum states are often represented in density matrix formalism ρ and may be *pure states* (representing maximal information about the state) or *mixed states* (representing an ensemble of pure states reflecting epistemic uncertainty about the state in question). Density matrices are

[85] Watrous (2018).

analogous to operator representations of probability distributions over states and are a common way of expressing quantum algorithms.

9.1.2 Measurement and Encoding

Information is input into quantum states via encoding protocols[86] (such as via encoding in basis states, relative phases or other forms). Information is extracted from quantum systems via quantum measurement,[87] whereby a measuring apparatus interacts with the system. The measurement of quantum systems occurs via physical interaction of the quantum system with measurement apparatuses (which are distinct from the system itself), sometimes denoted an experiment. Measurement results in a set of classical data that follow particular distributions from which statistics may be drawn, denoted *measurement statistics*. Mathematically, the process of measurement is represented by Hermitian operators acting upon the quantum state, the real eigenvalues of which are measurement outcomes with a probability given by the square of the amplitude of each phase/coefficient. For a quantum state $|\psi\rangle = a|0\rangle + b|1\rangle$ (measured in the appropriate basis), the probability of measuring $|0\rangle$ is $|a|^2$ and $|1\rangle$ is $|b|^2$ (the Born rule). A set of measurement operators that completely characterises the outcomes of an experiment (and is denoted a positive operator-valued measure (POVM)). Measurements are complete in that these POVM specify a set of complete outcomes of the system. Measurement collapses the quantum state post-measurement into a normalised eigenstate of the measurement operator (e.g. a $|0\rangle$ or $|1\rangle$). To obtain data about a quantum state, one must undertake repeated measurement of identically prepared quantum states giving rise to a distribution of measurement outcomes (measurement statistics). Details about the quantum state or its evolution are then reconstructed (using procedures from tomography for example) from this classical set of measurement statistics.

9.1.3 Evolution

The evolution of a closed quantum system (changes in its state) is governed by the Schrödinger equation, a first-order differential equation whose solutions are wavefunctions representative of quantum states and which encode certain symmetry (such as unitary symmetry) and conservation properties (such as conservation of probability or measure) required for quantum characteristics to subsist. Quantum systems interact with the environment (indeed they must in order to be measured) and doing so affects the state of the quantum system reducing that state to classical or tensor states. This is a fundamental distinction with classical systems where ideally measurement does not affect the state of the system in this way. The

---

[86] Schuld Petruccione (2021) and Schuld et al. (2015).

[87] Wiseman Milburn (2010).

environment may include noise or interaction with other specified physical systems. The formalism in which the time evolution of quantum systems is expressed can take a variety of forms (Heisenberg or Schrodinger). Mathematically, an operator denoted the Hamiltonian describes the evolution of quantum systems. The Hamiltonian H, as the generator of time translations, is a Hermitian operator usually expressed in Schrodinger's equation as $\frac{d|\psi}{dt} = -iH|\psi$ where i is the imaginary unit and $\frac{d|\psi}{dt}$ represents the (infinitesimal) change in quantum state over time. Hamiltonians are an important part of the circuit model of quantum computing and quantum control, allowing abstract specification of the unfolding of a quantum computation.

9.1.4 Control

Any use of QIT is dependent—as with any technology—upon the ability to control the system sufficiently for its intended purposes. The control of quantum systems is the subject of the field of quantum control. The types of physical controls that may be exerted upon a quantum system to steer its evolution depend on the physical realization of the system[88] (e.g. trapped ion, superconducting etc). These often physically take the form of electromagnetic pulses or voltages applied to evolve the system in a particular way—or even quantum dots (which are also, as we discuss at length below, the central technology in current quantum sensing devices). Mathematically, these controls are described as functional coefficients of the terms (generators) within the Hamiltonian. The interaction of a quantum system with the environment, be it noise or measurement apparatuses, is similarly expressed via additional terms in the Hamiltonian.

9.1.5 Open and Closed Quantum Systems and Noise

Quantum systems are characterized as closed or open. Closed quantum systems are idealized abstractions where the quantum state evolution is governed by Schrödinger's equation such that the quantum properties of the state, such as superposition or entanglement, remain preserved. More formally, idealized closed quantum systems generally preserve quantum coherence, an important feature of quantum information. Open quantum systems are a way of modelling how a quantum system interacts with its environment. This environment may be classical or quantum in nature. Quantum systems interact with the environment (such as measurement apparatuses) which may be quantum or classical in nature and which may be represented as its own Hamiltonian coupled to that of the quantum system. The Hamiltonian is typically decomposed into a system Hamiltonian H_S (describing the

[88] D'Alessandro (2007).

quantum system evolution), an environment Hamiltonian H_E (describing the environmental evolution) and an interaction Hamiltonian (describing how the system and environment interact). Interactions between the environment and quantum system affect the quantum system's state. This may be by way of the environment causing the quantum state to decohere, or by various types of noise such as T_1 or T_2 noise. Measurement is also a form of interaction that can be modelled in this way. Environmental effects such as noise decohere and affect quantum state evolution. A widely used mathematical formalism to represent open quantum systems, and the effects of noise, are stochastic master equations which model the effects of, for example, environmental noise on quantum systems. Quantum systems are highly sensitive to noise[89] and thus require error correction (such as in the form of error-correcting codes) in order to achieve sufficient fault tolerance, such as fault tolerant quantum computing.[90] Quantum circuit representations of noise are also common within the error correction literature, such as in stabilizer code and surface code formalism (see below).

9.2 Unique Features of Quantum Systems

The fundamental properties of quantum mechanical systems above form the basis for the unique capabilities of quantum computing, quantum communication and quantum sensing. We explore each of these in more detail below and in later chapters link such unique features to capabilities relevant to legal analysis. The postulates of quantum theory listed above also give rise to a number of important consequences which distinguish QIT from classical information processing. These include (i) the *no cloning* theorem[91] (that quantum states cannot be copied), (ii) the fundamental requirement for quantum error correction[92] in order for QIT to function (due to the sensitivity of quantum systems) in fault-tolerant[93] ways, (iii) measurement protocols (requiring identical state preparation or multiple copies produced by an identical quantum process in order to generate measurement statistics rather than having a single quantum state that is repeatedly measured), (iv) quantum ontological phenomena,[94] manifest in contextuality[95] (order of measurement giving rise to different statistics), uncertainty principles and non-local action[96] and (v) that entanglement is a resource. Although we do not focus in-

[89] Gottesman (2010) and Wiseman Milburn (2010).

[90] Aaronson (2013), Preskill (2018) and Preskill (2021).

[91] Wootters Zurek (1982).

[92] Gottesman (1998).

[93] Bennett et al. (1996), Cao et al. (2021), Gottesman (2010) and Kitaev (1997).

[94] Bartlett et al. (2007).

[95] de Silva Barbosa (2019), Harrigan Spekkens (2010) and Kunjwal (2016).

[96] Maudlin (1994).

depth on these consequences, they are both profound and fundamentally distinguish quantum physics from its classical counterpart. It is also not uncommon to compare classical and quantum information processing from an information-theoretic perspective, including comparisons between classical and quantum models of computation, the relationship between classical information theory[97] and its quantum counterpart. We direct the reader to technical discussions in the literature for more detail. Moreover, the extreme sensitivity of quantum systems and the fact that interaction with quantum systems via measurement can effectively decohere or demolish their quantum properties means that verification, auditing and control of such systems varies from classical analogues, a factor relevant to proposals for technical control of such systems and governance regimes (such as international legal standards and protocols).

Near-term quantum devices are still prone to errors, which affect their computational accuracy.[98] Developing noise resilient architectures, either by way of error correcting codes or hardware features, is crucial for achieving scalable fault-tolerant quantum computing in turn required to realize their benefits. Meeting such thresholds is also crucial to meeting data assurance and integrity requirements that are foundational in the QIT applications. Data encoded within a quantum computer may subsist in a quantum state, ultimately data is input and output from quantum systems via classical means such as via encoding classical data in quantum states or extracting data from quantum states via measurement which gives rise to classical measurement statistical distributions. Encoding information within quantum states is a complex process, requiring advanced state preparation techniques and data encoding methods[99] which may operate at different efficiency scales. Moreover, there is often considerable physical qubit overhead required for logical qubits (which represent the data processing aspect) with advances needed in both algorithm design and hardware engineering to reduce qubit usage and improve the efficiency of quantum state preparation.[100] Before summarizing a number of technical features each of the three sectors of quantum computing, quantum communication and quantum sensing relevant to the legal disciplines identified above, we say examine the important topic of quantum ontology and its implications for legal jurisprudence.

[97] Shannon (1948).

[98] Preskill (2021).

[99] Schuld Petruccione (2021).

[100] Bärtschi Eidenbenz (2020) and Plesch Brukner (2011).

10 Quantum Ontology

10.1 Non-locality and Bell's Theorems

Beyond technical implications, the foregoing properties of quantum systems have especially profound implications for how quantum objects are ontologically characterized. This is especially the case with quantum properties of superposition and entanglement. One of the most profound results of twentieth century physics was the theoretical and empirically validated result that quantum systems are ontologically fundamentally distinct from objects described by classical physics. Perhaps the major debate within quantum physics from its inception was whether or not the measurement statistics arising from quantum phenomena—particularly the counter-intuitive results regarding measurement statistics drawn from repeated measurements of identically prepared particles—was merely an artefact of imprecision in measurement as distinct from something ontologically distinct about quantum systems. This question was famously debated by leading foundational theorists of quantum theory, including Einstein. At the heart of the debate was whether the theory of quantum mechanics was a hidden variable theory—that measurement statistical uncertainty (or variance) reflected epistemic rather than ontic uncertainty; and the apparent fact identical particles could seem to have properties, such as spin, momentum, position or other attributes which differed when measured. On one side of the debate, led by Einstein, were hidden variable advocates who famously interred that God does not play dice with the universe, a colloquial expression referring to the fact that uncertainty is epistemic, rather than an inherent property of the universe at the quantum scale. On the other side of the ledger were theorists who contended that the measurement statistics from newly-emergent quantum theory reflected underlying uncertainty at the heart of reality itself.

Debates over the validity of hidden variable theories waxed and waned over the years, until a series of seminal papers by physicist John Bell. In his works that considered then-existing debates,[101] Bell, extending results from Kochen and Specker, showed that local hidden variable theories satisfying certain constraints (local realism and statistical independence) as a class were inconsistent with measurement statistics from entangled quantum particles. Bell showed that any local hidden-variable theory cannot reproduce the correlations predicted and experimentally observed in entangled quantum states. These results highlight a conflict between local realism and quantum correlations. The consequence of Bell's theorems is sometimes described as presenting a Faustian choice as to whether to eschew local realism, or admit that quantum systems exhibited—and that quantum mechanical theories were fundamentally—non-local in character. Hidden-variable approaches typically assume definite values or realism, but they then must allow nonlocal influences or give up other assumptions to match quantum predictions. The consequence of these results is not simply confined to esoteric notions of locality (which have a

[101] Bell (2004), Cavalcanti (2018), Fry Thompson (1976) and Kochen Specker (1967).

precise technical meaning), but to the underlying idea that certain attributes of quantum systems were distinct, fixed and precise. While Schrödinger's cat paradox focuses more on superposition and the measurement problem in a single system, it likewise underscores that quantum measurement can fundamentally alter a system's properties in ways unlike classical physics.

10.2 Epistemic and Ontological Characterization of Quantum States

In modern ontological treatments,[102] such results are often framed in terms of the distinction between ψ-ontic models (where quantum states are part of reality) and ψ-epistemic models (where the quantum state epistemically encodes information about an ontic state). Quantum states are demarcated into pure states and mixed state representations[103] of quantum systems. Epistemic uncertainty about a system's underlying ontic state is captured by mixed-state density operators, while pure states reflect the maximal ontological information about the state. Density operators can be constructed from the outer products of states $|\psi\rangle$ such that $\rho = |\psi\rangle\langle\psi|$. To give an example of what this means, consider the energy state of a quantum particle, consider a quantum state ρ' specified as:

$$\rho' = \frac{|0\,0| + |1\,1|}{2}$$

This state cannot be obtained as an outer product of a single state $|\psi\rangle$, hence it is representative of a mixture of states, in this case a maximally mixed state density operator representation (with diagonal entries only) indicating that the particle is in the basis (such as energy) state $|0\rangle$ with epistemic probability ½ and equivalently for the state $|1\rangle$. For any two-outcome projective measurement (any orthonormal basis), outcomes are 50–50. Hence there is no measurement basis that yields a certain outcome, meaning the uncertainty is not reducible by a change of basis. By contrast, the state:

$$\rho = \frac{1}{2}\left(|0\,0| + |1\,1| + |0\,1| + |1\langle 0|\right)$$

differs from ρ' due to the presence of off-diagonal terms $|0\rangle\langle 1|$ and $|1\rangle\langle 0|$ reflecting quantum coherences. It is representative of the outer product of the state $|\psi = \frac{1}{\sqrt{2}}\left(||0\rangle + ||1\rangle\right)$. In the maximally mixed state, no choice of measurement basis

[102] Bartlett et al. (2007), Harrigan Spekkens (2010) and Leifer Spekkens (2011).
[103] Nielsen Chuang (2011).

yields a definite outcome. By contrast, in the pure superposition state, one can choose a basis (namely the $|+\rangle, |-\rangle$ basis) that yields a definite measurement result for that observable, though other non-commuting observables will remain uncertain.

Although a simplified example, we use it to illustrate ontological impacts of QIT. These arise from the aforementioned unique ontology of quantum systems as established by Bell's Theorems, theories of entanglement and experimental results. By ontological impact, we adopt a jurisprudential approach to consider the types of ontologies that the law adopts. In philosophy, ontology is traditionally the description or statement of what is, of being, and the relations among beings. In computational science, ontology has a related but specific meaning in terms of the taxonomies, classes and relationships that subsist among objects, and is central to establishing programming IDEs, databases and functional interoperability of distributed systems.

10.3 Identifiability of QIT

One of the distinct features of quantum systems as distinct from their classical counterparts lies in how they are identified and individuated. Classically, objects are typically observed through measurement according to which their properties are ascertained. Measurement enables us to form a representation of them. Quantum objects are similarly constructed via measurement statistics. However, as distinct from the classical case where objects are considered to persist in their state and information about them is obtained by measurement in a way that does not fundamentally alter those objects, quantum measurement is different. All measurement in some way disturbs a system via the application of force, but quantum measurement has an additional characteristic by which measurement in effect collapses a quantum state into a classical state (the Copenhagen 'collapse of the wavefunction' interpretation discussed above). In multi-qubit systems, the entire quantum state may remain but the qubit that is measured is decohered into a classical state. These are sometimes described as demolition measurements. And while there are formalisms regarding weak measurements or so-called non-demolition measurement, in effect upon measurement the quantum state is itself collapsed, no longer existing as a quantum system (unless acted upon by a quantum operator to render it in a quantum state again e.g. a Hadamard gate).

This means that while for classical objects repeated measurement implies that *the same* object is repeatedly measured, for quantum systems, this is not the case. We cannot re-measure the same quantum information from the same qubit per se. Instead, information about quantum systems relies upon creating many identical copies of those quantum systems (via identical state preparation procedures). We do not rely upon a *single* quantum system to obtain information in the way that classical ontology assumes something akin to numerical identity when specifying and individuating objects. Instead, we are fundamentally reliant upon the existence of multiple identical copies of quantum states the measurement of which gives rise to sample data from which statistics (measurement statistics) are calculated. And from these measurement statistics, representations of quantum states in terms of chosen formalism are then obtained, such as via quantum state or process tomography. What becomes predicated of the quantum state or quantum system is then contingent upon these measurement statistics. This does not mean that all properties of quantum systems are subject to irreducible uncertainty. It is those operators which do not commute. For example, the mass of an electron is a parameter in quantum theory, while position and momentum are not.

10.4 Consequences of Quantum Ontology

The law relies upon classical ontological concepts in a number of ways. These broad conceptual issues are ones that are relevant to differing degrees to assumptions upon which many legal principles and much reasoning are based. We briefly sketch them out here.

10.4.1 Causality

Quantum mechanics challenges classical assumptions of linear, time-ordered causality by permitting correlations, such as those observed in entangled states, that appear to transcend local causal structure. At a technical level, Bell's theorems demonstrate that no local hidden-variable theory can reproduce the statistical predictions of entangled quantum systems, implying that measurement outcomes can exhibit stronger-than-classical correlations. This non-locality does not allow faster-than-light signaling but disrupts the classical view of causality since outcomes measured on one entangled particle can be instantaneously correlated with outcomes on another spatially separated particle. Consequently, in quantum information protocols (like quantum teleportation), causal links become more nuanced, requiring advanced frameworks of quantum causality[104] (e.g., process matrices in quantum causal modelling) to capture how operations at one node can affect state evolutions at another without violating relativistic constraints.

10.4.2 Ascertainability and Verifiability

Ascertainability and verifiability of information in a quantum context is complicated by superposition and the measurement postulate. Unlike classical systems, which can be freely inspected without fundamentally altering their state, quantum measurement collapses a system into one of the eigenstates associated with the measured observable. This means that certain information about a quantum state

[104] Brukner (2014) and Donoghue Menezes (2020).

(e.g., phase relationships in superposition) is inherently lost upon measurement, limiting the extent to which a state's "true configuration" can be fully ascertained. Techniques such as quantum state tomography address these challenges by collecting statistics from multiple identical quantum states, yet even these methods yield approximations subject to sampling error, noise and resource constraints. As a result, verifiability in quantum systems is probabilistic and partial, hinging on carefully designed measurement protocols and error-correction schemes.

10.4.3 Reproducibility

Reproducibility in quantum experiments confronts unique technical hurdles due to the no-cloning theorem. Classically, scientific reproducibility often presumes the ability to duplicate samples and rerun tests under identical conditions. In quantum mechanics, any attempt to measure or duplicate a state inevitably disturbs it. Researchers rely on preparing multiple identically initialized states—rather than repeatedly measuring the same state—to gather the statistical outcomes needed for verification. Quantum error-correction codes (e.g., surface codes) can mitigate decoherence and other noise sources, but perfect reproducibility remains elusive, with each experiment producing outcome distributions rather than definitive readings of a stable underlying reality.

10.4.4 Interpretability

Interpretability of quantum states and processes is technically constrained by their inherently mathematical representations (e.g., state vectors in Hilbert space or density matrices). While classical systems allow for direct, often intuitive interpretation—like tracking definite positions or trajectories—quantum systems encode information in probability amplitudes and can exhibit entangled relationships across multiple qubits. Interpreting measurement results thus requires understanding interference effects, phase relationships, and entanglement structure, all of which lack direct classical analogues. Advanced computational tools, such as quantum circuit simulators and partial trace operations, help visualize and analyse small-scale quantum algorithms, but the exponential growth of Hilbert space dimension limits direct interpretability for larger systems. Consequently, quantum interpretability relies heavily on abstract mathematical models, approximate visualizations, and carefully designed measurement bases, each carrying potential for misinterpretation if classical intuition is applied too rigidly.

10.4.5 Legal

From a legal standpoint, the unique ontological basis of quantum systems—nonlocal correlations, measurement-induced collapse, irreducible uncertainty, and nocloning— are distinct from the underpinning of many doctrines which are built on classical assumptions of determinism and replicable evidence. For instance, entanglement challenges the conventional view that information is distinctly localized, prompting questions in both public and private law as to how ownership of entangled data or qubits might be defined or transferred. Likewise, evidence regimes grounded in chain-of-custody and reproducible forensic methods may need to adapt to quantum measurement, which necessarily alters the original state under observation (albeit classical audit trails may still be available). Intellectual property protections also face hurdles: quantum algorithms and error-correction codes, being deeply probabilistic and resistant to straightforward disclosure, may motivate adaptation of classical enablement and definiteness requirements (e.g. enablement being met by describing control sequences). Finally, areas such as export control, privacy, and regulatory sandboxes must address the fact that quantum states in general cannot be cloned which may affect how they are audited. In short, the very features that make quantum technologies powerful tools also expose gaps and tensions in laws designed for a world in which objects and information behave classically.

With these concepts in mind, we now examine the particular details of each sector of QIT—quantum computing, quantum sensing and quantum communication. Later chapters draw upon and expand upon these applications in more detail. We begin with quantum computing and quantum simulation.

11 Quantum Computing and Quantum Simulation

11.1 Quantum Computation

Quantum computing[105] is a type of computation and information processing that leverages and is constrained by quantum mechanics. Quantum computing is distinguished from its classical counterpart by way of the existence of certain properties such of superposition, entanglement and quantization noted above. Algorithms which utilize such characteristics, denoted *quantum algorithms*, give rise to computational procedures which are effectively unique and distinct from classical computation (or more formally, which may be simulated by classical computation but only with super-polynomial resource cost).[106] Quantum algorithms vary considerably but are often classified into three broad types based upon the underlying quantum subroutines they leverage. These include (i) *quantum Fourier transforms,*[107] a class of algorithms applying a quantum version of classical Fourier transforms, utilized by Shor's algorithm[108]; (ii) *quantum search algorithms* such as Grover's algorithm[109]

[105] Feynman (1982), Manin (1980) and Nielsen Chuang (2011).

[106] Aaronson (2013).

[107] Browne (2007).

[108] Shor (1994, 1997).

[109] Grover (1996).

for $\sqrt{n}$ speedup of search based on amplitude amplification[110] and (iii) *quantum simulation*[111] which we discuss in more detail below, and which is sometimes classified as an effective use-case of quantum systems rather than a specific subclass of quantum computational methods. The effect of these quantum algorithmic subroutines and methods is to facilitate more efficient computational processes, such as faster or more accurate search and quicker optimization.

11.2 Quantum Simulation

Quantum simulation[112] represents a major prospective use of quantum information systems and computation. It involves utilizing controllable quantum systems to emulate and study the behavior of other, often less accessible or highly complex quantum systems. This approach is particularly valuable in fields such as condensed matter physics, high-energy physics, atomic physics, quantum chemistry, and cosmology, where understanding complex quantum interactions is essential. For companies, simulation of complex dynamical systems such as market behavior may afford them with comparative advantages over competitors. For States, the potential synthesis of chemicals and materials using QIT simulations—or even simulating complex adversarial scenarios—may provide them with a strategic advantage in both peacetime and conflict.

11.3 Quantum Machine Learning

Quantum machine learning (QML)[113] is another cross-over discipline applying principles of machine learning with quantum algorithms which offers potential for significantly enhance the capabilities of machine learning by leveraging quantum algorithm features. QML holds the potential to significantly enhance data-driven research, particularly for tasks where data are intrinsically quantum mechanical (e.g., quantum materials, biochemistry, and high-energy physics). Example QML algorithms include quantum support vector machines[114] and quantum convolutional neural networks[115] (QCNN) and quantum variational algorithms.[116] As with other

---

110 Brassard et al. (2000).

111 Georgescu et al. (2014).

112 Georgescu et al. (2014), Guo Gao (2024) and Sanchez-Palencia (2018).

113 Batra et al. (2021), Benedetti et al. (2019), Biamonte et al. (2017), Cerezo et al. (2021), Ciliberto et al. (2018) and Schuld Petruccione (2021).

114 Cerezo et al. (2021).

115 Cong et al. (2019).

116 Cerezo et al. (2021).

uses of quantum mechanics, the quantum aspect of QML algorithms usually involves some version of the classes of quantum algorithm described above. There are also quantum-specific analogues of classical machine learning algorithms, such as a suite of quantum deep learning algorithms[117] and a variety of hybrid (classical-quantum) algorithms that integrate classical or known prior information with quantum variants. Examples of the latter include quantum geometric machine learning,[118] equivariant[119] quantum neural networks[120] together with quantum neural network analogues.[121]

QML presents an important cross-over discipline between machine learning and AI on the one hand and quantum systems on the other. And while QIT and classical machine learning are distinct, ultimately it is most likely that QIT will be embedded within classical computational systems which involve or are anchored within machine learning systems. Furthermore, given the complexity of the tasks and parameterizations for which QIT is likely to be used—such as quantum simulation—it is likely that the actual use of QIT will involve adaptive computational and information architecture whose optimization strategy or task execution is not fully specified at runtime but is instead learnt over the course of execution. QML may eventually turn out to be a major paradigm within which quantum computing actually takes place.

Despite the promise of QML, its utility faces a number of challenges apart from its reliance on the existence of scalable fault-tolerant quantum computation. Barren plateaus[122] can cause gradients to vanish exponentially in the number of qubits, complicates the training of deeper QML circuits. Noise in quantum devices can also affect the loss landscape, requiring additional resources for optimization. Data embedding also remains an unresolved concern—while classical data can be mapped to quantum states,[123] ensuring that such encoding preserves the relevant structure for learning is nontrivial. Technical responses include designing noise-mitigated algorithms, leveraging symmetries or problem-specific priors, and crafting shallower or more specialized circuit architectures to achieve stable, scalable learning outcomes.

---

[117] Verdon et al. (2018, 2019a, b, c, d).

[118] Perrier (2024) and Ragone et al. (2022).

[119] Larocca et al. (2022).

[120] Nguyen et al. (2024).

[121] Abbas et al. (2021) and Beer (2022).

[122] Cerezo Coles (2021), Cerezo et al. (2022) and Marrero et al. (2021).

[123] Schuld Petruccione (2021).

12 Quantum Communication and Quantum Cryptography

12.1 Quantum Communication

Quantum communication[124] leverages the principles of quantum mechanics to enable secure and efficient transfer of information. It is fundamentally distinct from classical communication as it uses quantum states, such as qubits, to encode and transmit data. Key technologies within quantum communication include quantum key distribution (QKD),[125] quantum networks, and entanglement-based communication protocols,[126] each of which addresses specific challenges and opportunities in secure communication and information sharing. QKD provides a protocol for the secure exchange of cryptographic keys by utilizing features of quantum systems, specifically the no-cloning theorem and the Heisenberg uncertainty principle to detect eavesdropping attempts. Protocols like BB84[127] (prepare and measure) and E91[128] (entanglement) utilize either discrete quantum states (e.g., polarized photons) or entangled particles to securely generate a shared key between two parties, even in non-idealized settings.[129] Any interception of the quantum channel alters the quantum state of the transmitted particles, making eavesdropping detectable. The exchanged key is used in symmetric encryption schemes, such as AES, for secure communication. Entanglement based regimes for communication via quantum teleportation are particularly important for distributed quantum systems relevant to strategic interests. Quantum teleportation[130] enables communication without measurement of an unknown quantum state from one quantum system to another via the use of entanglement, Bell state measurements and EPR channels.[131]

12.2 Quantum Networking

Quantum networking is a major prospective application of quantum communication technologies[132] that utilizes quantum teleportation to enable communication among multiple users across long distances without the need for inter-mediating local networks (albeit quantum repeaters are usually a feature of such systems). Quantum

[124] Bassoli et al. (2021), Cariolaro (2015) and Gisin Thew (2007).

[125] Bennett Brassard (1984) and Lo et al. (2005).

[126] Ekert (1991).

[127] Bennett Brassard (1984).

[128] Ekert (1991).

[129] Scarani et al. (2004).

[130] Bennett et al. (1993), Boschi et al. (1998) and Riebe et al. (2004).

[131] Bouwmeester et al. (1997).

[132] Meter (2014).

networking[133] and quantum teleportation[134] have particular strategic implications as a result of the prospect of a *quantum internet*,[135] representing a network of coupled and linked quantum computational and communication (and even sensing) devices enabling, in the communication context, high-volume and fast information distribution[136] via quantum states transmitted securely and robustly.[137] Such quantum internet proposals are expected to provide enhanced means of using quantum technologies relevant to economic and geopolitical activity subject to a variety of legal regimes, including performing QKD, quantum secure direct communication (allowing confidential information to be distributed without separate key distribution), distributed and used for distributed quantum computing, clock synchronization, and quantum-enhanced communication.

12.3 Post-quantum Cryptography

Post-quantum cryptography (PQC)[138] is a set of cryptographic protocols intended to be secure against adversarial attacks and decryption by adversaries equipped with scalable fault-tolerant quantum computers. PQC is motivated as a way of addressing the strategic threats[139] faced by stakeholders arising from the decryption capabilities of quantum computers identified above which can in principle decrypt public-key systems like RSA, Diffie-Hellman, and elliptic curve cryptography. Classical encryption schemes often rely upon standardized classes algorithm, such as integer factoring or discrete logarithm algorithms.[140] PQC algorithms, by contrast, leverage algorithms and encodings whose decryption is in a higher complexity class i.e. it is hard or intractable for even quantum computers, including lattice-based methods,[141] learning-error based methods,[142] multivariate polynomial systems, or isogeny problems on elliptic curves.[143] In general, PQC algorithms typically generate larger key and ciphers which exceed resources feasibly decode.

133 Simon (2017).

134 Cacciapuoti et al. (2019, 2020).

135 Kimble (2008) and Wehner et al. (2018).

136 Pirandola et al. (2017).

137 Caleffi et al. (2018).

138 Alagic et al. (2022, 2024), Bernstein Lange (2017) and Chen et al. (2016).

139 Joseph et al. (2022).

140 Kumar Pattnaik (2020).

141 Nejatollahi et al. (2019).

142 Bos et al. (2015).

143 Koziel et al. (2016).

13 Quantum Sensing and Quantum Metrology

13.1 Quantum Sensing and Quantum Dots

Quantum sensing[144] in its theoretical and applied forms examines how certain quantum mechanical properties of systems give rise to new and highly sensitive ways of measuring environments, collecting data. Doing so gives rise to finer-grained information about measurement statistics and probability distributions of environmental systems. Quantum sensing also has been shown to improve quantum metrology, often utilizing quantum specific properties of superposition and entanglement, enabling more precise parameter estimation (quantum metrology).[145] One of the more advanced forms of quantum sensing technology are *quantum dots*,[146] types of quantum circuits engineered to confine electrons (or cavities) in particular constrained environments. Quantum dots have a variety of applications and indeed are a candidate component of technology for quantum computational substrates themselves.

The underlying concept of quantum dots is the confinement of single electrons within electromagnetic potentials such that their quantum mechanical state can be effectively tuned or adjusted, such as by way of control architecture involving microwave pulses, magnetic resonance of other methods. By doing so, quantum dots represent a controllable subsystem which may be coupled to an environment in ways that allow *both* for fine-grained control of quantum states (enabling, for example, the implementation of quantum circuit gates) but also enabling their use as a measurement instrument (or apparatus). Intuitively, this is because measurement and control are both interactions with the quantum system: measurement of quantum systems requires that the particular eigenstates and eigenvalues of the measurement device are sufficiently well-defined in order that measurement outcomes are distinguishable and intelligible.

13.2 Quantum Sensing Procedures

Existing quantum sensing devices utilize the sensitivity of quantum systems realized via atomic, ionic, photonic, or solid-state systems for precision measurement. They tend to be classified according to either the quantum system or the target of measurement, with various physical characteristics such as sensitivity, weight, size, power and cost factoring into their use. Quantum sensor technology follows a protocol whereby sensors (i) are initialized, (2) are transformed into a quantum state (e.g. superposition), (3) interact with the environment via coupled

[144] Degen et al. (2017).

[145] Giovannetti et al. (2011) and Tóth Apellaniz (2014).

[146] Belal et al. (2024), Bukowski Simmons (2002) and Jacak et al. (2013).

evolution, (4) transformation into a measurable state (e.g. eigenstate), (5) measured. This process is then repeated sufficiently for measurement statistics to be gathered. Quantum sensors are one of the more advanced forms of QIT with a range of applications that we mention in subsequent chapters below. The study of their use in contexts such as life sciences, national security technology and communications technology provides detail on how QIT integration has fared within existing legal regimes.

14 Quantum Infrastructure Stack

Quantum information technologies can be considered in the abstract, as a form of computational technology with unique effects unavailable to classical technology, or even more abstractly, as an affordance whose effects, rather than technical specificity, is what matters for normative and jurisprudential consideration. Yet such coarse-grained analysis overlooks important technical detail regarding how *quantum infrastructure stack*, within which quantum information systems are and will be necessarily embedded, affects strategic and jurisprudential factors. As foreshadowed above, it is useful to assess this stack both *vertically*, in terms of how layers of classical and quantum architecture are integrated; and *horizontally*, in terms of how quantum and classical infrastructure are distributed and networked. Understanding the technical features of quantum infrastructure stacks can provide greater clarity on how and where stakeholders may actually act (where it the site or locus of their action, at what layer in the stack, its degree of directness and so on) and, as a result, the consequences for the application of international law principles as a result. The two examples we adopt for the purposes of illustrating these technical considerations are (i) a single quantum computer and (ii) a quantum internet, comprising quantum computing nodes networked by either classical or quantum information channels (which might be for example a candidate quantum internet architecture).

14.1 Quantum Computing Stack

The typical qubit-based quantum computing stack can be represented via a layering of features as set out in Table 1. At the base of any quantum computing device is the *physical layer* upon which the quantum computational substrate is constituted, such as photonic, superconducting, trapped ion, topological and other systems. Overlaying the physical layer is the *measurement and control layer* comprising physical infrastructure for exerting fine-grained control over the quantum system, including that required for measurement, such as in the form of microwave pulses and laser signaling. The next layer is the *error correction layer* which encodes

Table 1 A typical quantum computing stack, from the physical quantum computational substrate up through programming languages, compilers, and applications

Layer	Description
Quantum circuit layer	The quantum computational circuit substrate, which includes physical qubits realized using technologies such as photonic systems, superconducting circuits, trapped ions, or topological qubits. This layer involves the physical realization of quantum states and their manipulation
Measurement and Control Layer	Hardware control systems responsible for interacting with the physical quantum layer generating precise signals to manipulate qubits, such as microwave pulses or laser systems. These systems ensure the implementation of quantum gates and readout operations
Error correction layer	Quantum error correction protocols, such as surface codes or concatenated codes, which detect and correct errors arising from decoherence and noise in the quantum system
Logical Qubit layer	Logical qubits formed from physical qubits through error correction, enabling more robust quantum computations by abstracting away the noise at the physical layer
Quantum assembly language	Low-level programming languages designed for quantum computers, specifying quantum operations and circuits in a hardware-specific manner (e.g., OpenQASM (Wesley (2024)))
Quantum compiler	Software tools that translate high-level quantum algorithms into executable instructions for the quantum hardware, optimizing for specific hardware constraints and minimizing error rates
Quantum intermediate representation	Intermediate representations used by compilers to bridge high-level code and hardware-specific assembly instructions, allowing optimizations across different hardware platforms
Quantum programming language	High-level languages used to write quantum algorithms, such as Qiskit and Cirq. These provide abstractions that simplify quantum programming for researchers and developers
Applications layer	End-user applications leveraging quantum algorithms, such as quantum cryptography, optimization, machine learning, and simulation of quantum systems. This layer focuses on domain-specific problems addressed using quantum computing
Classical Interface layer	The interface between classical and quantum systems, managing hybrid computations, data input/output, and pre- and post-processing of results. This includes classical hardware and software integrated with quantum processors

quantum error correction protocols, such as the surface code.[147] The *logical qubit layer* is way of abstracting the logical qubits formed via clusters and interactions of physical qubits (mediated via error correction protocols) and may include quantum memory structures. Logical qubits constitute an element of the logical layer of quantum infrastructure. From the logical qubit layer, there are then effective language and programming layers, such as (i) the *quantum assembly layer*, analogous

[147] Gottesman (2010).

to assembly code layers in classical computers; (ii) *quantum compilers*[148] which enable compilation of development environments and programs; (iii) *quantum intermediate representations* which are ontological representations that mediate between compilers and programming languages; (iv) *quantum programming languages* which are high-level interpretive languages with considerable expressive capacity; (v) the *application layer* for applications and user interfaces and where practically, for example, human interface for the application of quantum computing would apply. In addition, we can also specify a *classical interface layer* such as where quantum systems are encapsulated in classical components, such as classical registers or databases to store measurement statistics, classical specification of algorithms and the like.

14.2 Quantum Network Stack

Quantum networks, whereby QIT systems form distributed systems, are an important prospective QIT use case. A quantum network in simpliciter involves quantum computers as nodes with message passing channels and is thus representable as a graph. The infrastructure requirements for quantum networks are considerable: they include all the required infrastructure for a single quantum computing device, in addition to the complex infrastructure required to support distributed computing and messaging. In Table 2, we set out a number of key features of the quantum network stack. Doing so assists in our analysis in later sections regarding where and how States may interact (cooperatively and adversarially). Our taxonomy is generic but is based upon proposals for a quantum internet.[149] Quantum networks are comprised via *quantum nodes*, being quantum computers or processors that perform information processing and store quantum information.

The nodes are connected via *quantum channels* that link each node and enable information transfer between them. Although these channels may be classical, to leverage the benefits of networked quantum systems, they are quantum channels. Overlaid on top of this core architecture are mechanisms for *entanglement distribution*. These may include a *quantum repeater* layer which extends the range of quantum communication via correcting for errors and amplifying entanglement. Quantum networks also require their own *classical control layer* for managing the network elements of the system (distinct from those at the node level), together with network-specific *quantum memory* for buffering and delayed operations. *Network protocols* represent an abstraction layer over the quantum network setting out how QKD, quantum teleportation and entanglement are managed. There may also be *classical nodes* themselves and a separate network *quantum application* layer for implementation of applications at the network level (such as for distributed

[148] Ge et al. (2024).

[149] Illiano et al. (2022) and Wehner et al. (2018).

Table 2 Elements of a distributed quantum network detailing components and features of a quantum internet, where quantum computers act as network nodes

Component	Description
Quantum nodes	Quantum computers or quantum processors that serve as the computational units in the network. These nodes perform quantum computations and store quantum information using qubits
Quantum channels	Communication links enabling the transfer of quantum states between nodes. Typically implemented using fiber optics, free-space photonics, or satellite-based systems to preserve quantum entanglement
Entanglement distribution	Mechanisms for generating and distributing entangled states across the network, forming the backbone of quantum communication protocols Examples include entanglement swapping and quantum repeaters
Quantum repeaters	Devices that extend the range of quantum communication by correcting errors and amplifying entanglement across long distances. These are essential for large-scale quantum networks
Classical control layer	Classical communication and synchronization layer for coordinating quantum operations, transmitting measurement outcomes, and enabling error correction protocols
Quantum memory	Storage units for preserving quantum states during communication or computation. Quantum memories are critical for buffering entanglement and supporting delayed quantum operations
Network protocols	Protocols governing the operation of the quantum network, including quantum key distribution (QKD), quantum teleportation, and entanglement distribution protocols. These also include hybrid quantum-classical protocols
Classical nodes	Classical systems that interface with quantum nodes to manage control tasks, perform pre- and post-processing, and handle non-quantum computational tasks
Quantum applications	High-level applications running on the network, such as secure communication, distributed quantum computing, clock synchronization, and quantum-enhanced sensing
Security infrastructure	Mechanisms ensuring the security of quantum communication, including QKD systems, eavesdropping detection, and classical cryptographic support for hybrid protocols
Routing and topology management	Management systems that determine the optimal pathways for quantum and classical information, considering the unique constraints of quantum communication such as no-cloning and decoherence
Error correction layer	Quantum error correction protocols to mitigate noise and decoherence in quantum channels, ensuring reliable transmission and storage of quantum states

quantum sensing) together with additional *security infrastructure* to secure the distributed physical infrastructure, *routing and topology management* and other distributed systems optimization processes and of course error correction.

As discussed above, QIT is inevitably situated within classical infrastructure which forms an integral part of the operation and support of QIT. We include a taxonomy of such infrastructure in Table 3. A major and important element are classical control systems, including signal generators and pulse sequence controllers,

Table 3 Classical Infrastructure scaffolding surrounding QIT

Type of Classical Infrastructure	Description
Control systems	Classical control hardware and software used to manipulate qubits, such as signal generators, microwave control systems, and pulse sequence controllers
Classical computing interfaces	Classical computers and servers that interface with quantum computers, managing data processing, initialization, and interaction with quantum systems
Data storage systems	Classical storage solutions for retaining quantum experiment results, intermediate calculations, and large datasets required for hybrid quantum classical computations
Networking equipment	Classical networking devices like routers, switches, and hubs that form the backbone for integrating quantum systems into broader networks, including quantum networks
Error correction systems	Classical processors that implement error detection and correction algorithms for stabilizing quantum computations and communication
Cooling systems	Cryogenic systems required to maintain the operational environment for quantum hardware, such as dilution refrigerators for superconducting qubits
Power supply systems	Reliable power infrastructure ensuring stable and uninterrupted operation of quantum and classical subsystems
Monitoring and diagnostics tools	Classical systems for monitoring the status of quantum systems, including diagnostic tools for noise, stability, and performance analysis
Security systems	Firewalls, intrusion detection systems, and other classical cybersecurity measures to protect quantum infrastructure from unauthorized access
Classical-quantum Interface	Middleware that translates classical commands into quantum instructions and vice versa, enabling seamless operation between classical and quantum systems

which are essential for manipulating qubits and executing quantum operations, such as measurement, encoding of information within quantum systems and classical-quantum hybrid protocols, such as many quantum machine learning systems. Classical computing interfaces are also central to handling data processing, setting initialization specifications, and overall management of QIT. In quantum communication, networking equipment such as classical routers and switches are essential to quantum devices being integrated into larger network architectures, enabling communication across quantum-to-classical and classical-to-quantum channels to subsist. Classical databases and registers are essential to retaining quantum experiment results, measurement statistics and computational datasets.[150] Power supply systems and cooling mechanisms are essential requirements of all candidate physical realizations of quantum systems, including cryogenic refrigerators, in order to ensure the stable operation of quantum hardware under precise, low-noise, environmental conditions.

[150] Perrier (2022).

14.3 Quantum Infrastructure Stack

In addition to surrounding physical infrastructure, classical processors are important components in quantum error correction, implementing syndrome measurements to detect and mitigate errors that arise during quantum computation. Classical systems are also essential to security architecture for QIT, protecting quantum infrastructure through firewalls and intrusion detection, safeguarding sensitive quantum operations. They are critical to monitoring and diagnostic tools used to evaluate the performance of quantum systems, providing real-time insights into noise levels, stability, and efficiency. The classical-quantum interface acts as middleware, translating classical instructions into quantum commands and processing quantum results for classical interpretation. Together, these components form a comprehensive classical infrastructure that supports and enhances the functionality of QIT.

15 Technical Impacts of QIT

15.1 Informational Impacts

We now consider a high-level summary of the key technical informational impacts of QIT relevant to governance. We adopt a specific focus regarding how QIT affects the acquisition, transfer, and use of data. In the subsequent section, we consider how these overall technical effects have consequences for specific legal regimes. As we shall now below, the transition from a classically deterministic to a quantum stochastic model of information affects multiple areas of law, including but not limited to evidence, intellectual property, export controls, data protection, competition policy, and life sciences regulation. We can group QIT's major informational consequences into categories. Each category reflects a shift or expansion in how data are produced and processed, mapping directly onto potential legal and regulatory concerns. These categories are not mutually exclusive—indeed, they often overlap—but they offer a structured lens for understanding QIT's broad effects. The idea of the governance stack is deliberately tied to the ontologies and taxonomies familiar within computational science and engineering in order to precisely and specifically identify where in the technical stack QIT is likely to impact.

This is a particularly important point across each subdivision of QIT: quantum computing, quantum sensing and quantum simulation are fundamentally forms of *information processing*, albeit with particular significance. In keeping our focus on information-related characterization of both QIT and life sciences regulation, we then adopt the following categorical framing of the informational impact of QIT in terms of: (i) its effect upon information, namely the type, quantity, quality, scale and other properties, including how that information is obtained and what information is obtained; (ii) its effect upon information processing, such as by way of enabling computations that would otherwise be intractable, or even simply enabling computations which while technically tractable (within ascertainable complexity classes) are, from the perspective of human timescales, effectively intractable; (iii) control, QIT offers means of interacting with systems and thereby exerting control (to greater or lesser degree) over them. The informational impacts of QIT are extensive but can be classified depending upon the stage or process of information acquisition, storage or processing.

15.1.1 Information Processing Efficiency Impact

By allowing faster, more accurate or improved forms of information processing, QIT can have a significant impact of information efficiency.

15.1.2 Oracular Impact

QIT can impact via enabling new knowledge (and products) which could not (owing to computational constraints or computational intractability) be produced through existing or classical information processing means.

15.1.3 Information Asymmetry Effects

QIT can facilitate the asymmetric distribution of information processing power (such as via some market participants having access to QIT while others do not) in ways that may have consequential impacts upon market stability and regulatory oversight.

15.1.4 Measurement Impacts

QIT already affects measurement protocols. This is primarily in quantum sensing where quantum dot technology which enables higher-resolution and higher-sensitivity measurements is well-advanced beyond the theoretical stage to prototype development.

We set out more detailed analysis on these points in the Appendix. Below we sketch legal implications from the use of QIT across different jurisprudential domains considered to varying degrees in later chapters.

15.2 Enhanced Computational Power

Quantum algorithms (such as Shor's or Grover's noted above) promise exponential or polynomial speedups for certain classes of problems. This can yield a dramatic improvement in processing tasks once deemed computationally infeasible under classical hardware—e.g., factoring large integers (threatening RSA-based encryption) or rapidly simulating complex molecular interactions in drug discovery. On a more incremental level, near-term quantum computers (NISQ devices) can still provide meaningful speed enhancements for specialized tasks, albeit with higher error rates and limited qubit counts. Legal and regulatory issues may include the following.

15.2.1 Data Protection and Security

Faster decryption of classical encryption mechanisms demands urgent revisions in cryptographic standards. Governments and private entities must consider post-quantum cryptography migration, as existing security protocols could become obsolete.

15.2.2 Intellectual Property and Competition

Entities with substantial quantum computing capacity could solve optimization or research-intensive tasks far ahead of competitors, raising questions about market power and the fairness of patent races.

15.3 Oracular Problem-Solving and Intractability

Beyond speedups, quantum computers can act as oracular devices for problems not just difficult but effectively intractable on classical hardware. This includes simulating certain quantum systems, solving high-dimensional optimization tasks, and exploring cryptographic trapdoor functions. The hallmark of oracular QIT is that it generates answers that classical verification cannot always replicate or fully validate, essentially producing outputs from black box processes. Legal and regulatory issues may include the following.

15.3.1 Evidence and Verification

Court systems reliant on replicability and transparent verification may be challenged by black box QIT outputs. For example, if a quantum algorithm suggests a novel drug design, there will be a genuine question as to how regulators or litigants confirm results (especially where verification itself may be too complex for classical verifiers).

15.3.2 Liability and Accountability

For high-stakes use cases (e.g., pharmaceuticals, AI-driven decisions), the lack of transparent explainability might complicate liability assignments if multiple agents are interacting via networked quantum computers to make decisions.

National Security. Oracular QIT capabilities can yield asymmetric advantages in codebreaking or intelligence analysis, intensifying export-control scrutiny or requiring stronger controls.

15.4 Measurement and Ultra-Fine Sensing

Quantum sensing enabling measurement physical quantities—e.g. magnetic fields, molecular structures—at unprecedented resolutions could give rise to legal ramifications or procedural challenges. Devices such as quantum dots enable extreme sensitivity in diagnostics, environmental monitoring, and materials characterization. Unlike classical sensors, quantum sensors can gather data that classical apparatuses either miss entirely or measure only at coarser resolution. Legal and regulatory issues may include the following.

15.4.1 Life Sciences and Medical Devices

Precise quantum diagnostic data may accelerate drug discovery or patient-specific treatments. But regulators may require novel ways of assessing the reliability, calibration, and risk classification for novel quantum-based instruments.

15.4.2 Privacy and Surveillance

High-fidelity measurement can facilitate new forms of invasive data collection—e.g. potentially mapping neural activity in controlled environments or decoding sensitive signals. Data protection laws might need to adapt definitions of personal data if quantum-sensing reveals intimate details not measurable via classical instruments.

15.4.3 Strategic and Security Concerns

Quantum sensors that detect stealth aircraft or submarines could (if developed sufficiently) destabilize military balances, prompting new international law questions around the use of QIT for cyber activities and even arms control considerations.

15.5 Non-clonability and Probabilistic Verification

As noted above, quantum states are subject to the no-cloning theorem i.e. one cannot create an identical copy of an arbitrary unknown quantum state. Additionally, measurement collapses that state, making repeated forensic inspections of the *same* quantum state impossible (note the same physical system may be reinitialized but this is technically a new quantum state). Instead, verification relies on probabilistic sampling from multiple identically prepared states. Error-correction protocols further complicate how original data is defined, as quantum error-correction typically reconstructs logical states from multiple entangled qubits. Legal and regulatory issues may include the following.

15.5.1 Evidentiary Chain-of-Custody

Classical legal systems assume one can replicate data (e.g., forensic data from auditing) for re-analysis. Quantum data cannot be copied or measured repeatedly without altering the underlying states of each instance. Verification cannot occur generally speaking without disturbing the quantum state itself. This may require consideration of how verification can or ought to occur where verification of technical computation or communication, or sensing, is required.

15.5.2 Intellectual Property and Trade Secrets

Patents often require a full written description and enablement. Yet quantum processes that cannot be cloned or fully measured, hence classical disclosure requirements regarding sufficiency may be focused on control regimes instead. Similarly, demonstrating misappropriation of a trade secret stored or used in QIT might prove harder if the state cannot be trivially copied.

15.5.3 Export Controls and Dual Use

Monitoring cross-border quantum information flows is more challenging when intangible quantum entanglement can be established across jurisdictions and data cannot be meaningfully reproducible for inspection.

15.6 Information Asymmetry and Market Concentration

Large-scale quantum infrastructure—be it high-end cryogenic labs for superconducting qubits or specialized photonic networks—demands considerable resources. As a result, a small number of governments or corporations may dominate QIT capabilities. This gives rise to information asymmetry considerations in which only certain actors can decrypt data, optimize complex systems, or innovate at scale with quantum algorithms. In turn, this raises information asymmetry considerations in which only certain actors can decrypt data, optimize complex systems, or innovate at scale with quantum algorithms. Legal and regulatory issues may include the following.

15.6.1 Competition Law

If only a handful of firms (or States) possess robust quantum computing, standard market definitions or anti-collusion frameworks may need rethinking. There's potential for oligopolistic structures around quantum hardware supply chains or specialized quantum-cloud services.

15.6.2 Public International Law and Geopolitics

Strategic asymmetry can motivate competitive dynamics. States with advanced quantum decryption may stand to gain disproportionate intelligence advantages, impacting the global cybersecurity landscape and prospectively motivating anticipatory action (such as preventative strikes) by States before any quantum advantage of their adversaries is crystallized.

15.6.3 Data Protection and Fair Access

Concentrated quantum resources might hamper widespread access to breakthroughs in drug design or climate modelling. This may give rise to considerations regarding how to regulate access to important QIT platforms in order to avoid economic imbalances in information and power.

16 Legal Consequences of QIT

Given the extensive foregoing analysis of how the uniquely quantum mechanical nature of QIT affects information processing and the way in which physical systems evolve, the question from a legal perspective is whether and how we might characterize the implications of QIT from a legal and governance perspective. We sketch a number of primary themes which are expanded upon in later chapters.

16.1 Jurisprudence and Interpretation

In common law jurisdictions, jurisprudential principles derive primarily from a mixture of legal precedent and constitutional sources. Interpretation of the effects of new technologies is usually undertaken against the backdrop of long-standing doctrines which assume a generally classical, deterministic view of the objects and facts coming before courts. Quantum information technologies, by contrast, rest on phenomena such as superposition and entanglement, challenging the classical assumption that legal facts are merely epistemically uncertain. The inherently probabilistic nature of quantum mechanics, evidenced by Bell's Theorems and the no-cloning principle, suggests that some legal concepts—like attributing specific states of affairs to a single, definite cause—may need re-evaluation. Although courts can still apply existing procedural frameworks, future jurisprudential debates might explore how non-locality or irreducible stochasticity alter determinations of causation, responsibility, or factual proof. To prepare, lawmakers and judicial bodies could issue interpretive guidance, emphasizing that quantum phenomena remain justiciable but may require tailored evidentiary or conceptual approaches when entangled processes are at issue.

16.2 Laws of Evidence

Quantum evidence is inherently more fragile due to measurement-induced collapse and the no-cloning theorem, meaning standard chain-of-custody and authentication protocols designed for classical digital data may not apply. To validate or replicate quantum-generated results, one must rely on repeated state preparation and probabilistic output analysis, making the conventional same sample approach impossible. Courts may require specialized procedures—e.g., quantum tomography logs, error-correction records—to establish authenticity under rules similar to evidential rules. Over time, reforms might include quantum forensic methods or guidelines and specialized accreditation for quantum expert witnesses to address the effect, if any, of irreducible stochasticity and reliability of quantum measurements used as evidence in both civil and criminal proceedings.

In the United States, the rules for admitting and authenticating evidence are primarily found in the Federal Rules of Evidence 28 U.S.C. Key provisions which may be affected by QIT include how data is authenticated Rule 901 (authentication) and how information is supplied in an evidentiary fashion Rules 1001–1008 (original writings, recordings, and photographs). There are also open questions regarding how QIT applies to established reliability standards for scientific evidence. In the EU and U.K., rules of evidence largely remain within national civil or criminal procedure codes (for example, the Civil Evidence Act 1995 in the U.K.), but are shaped by overarching principles of fairness and reliability. In each case, how the use of QIT may affect or have consequences for the evidentiary process remains unstudied.

16.3 Intellectual Property

Quantum-specific innovations—like fault-tolerant qubit architectures or entanglement-based protocols—may complicate classical IP doctrines, particularly under Title 35 of the U.S.C. such as specification and enablement (35 U.S.C. § 112) and inventive patentability (35 U.S.C. §§ 101–103), because quantum systems are probabilistic and can in certain cases be difficult to replicate or describe in stable, classical terms. Nevertheless, the fact that a raft of QIT patents have already been awarded indicates that in practice such difficulties may not present a significant barrier. The no-cloning principle may problematize usual assumptions about copying and disclosure, especially in trade secret contexts where courts typically require a showing that proprietary information was copied or wrongfully acquired. Patent examiners and courts may need specialized guidelines for determining how quantum algorithms and hardware meet disclosure, definiteness, and utility requirements. Over time, explicit disclosure standards for quantum mechanical phenomena might be considered to ensure consistent application of law. Case law governing whether computer-implemented or algorithmic claims are deemed abstract ideas[151] is yet to consider questions of quantum algorithms per se, though in principle one ought to expect the same or similar principles to apply. Other relevant laws whose implications may require consideration in terms of QIT include trade secrets are protected under 18 U.S.C. §§ 1831–1839 (relating to economic espionage) and similar legislation. In the EU, patentability is addressed under the European Patent Convention (Arts. 52–57), while trade secrets are harmonized by Directive (EU) 2016/943. The U.K. similarly follows the Patents Act 1977 and common law on breach of confidence.

16.4 Privacy and Confidentiality

Quantum communication and quantum data storage introduce novel issues for data protection regimes, particularly because entangled states and no-cloning may prevent the standard replication and backup processes assumed by regulation. Data localization rules are similarly complicated if quantum data is delocalized or spread across entangled nodes in different jurisdictions. Regulators may need to clarify how unmeasured quantum information (stored in qubits) is classified—for example, ought it count as personal data pre-measurement? As QIT develops, legislators might mandate migration timelines for post-quantum encryption and develop legal definitions or frameworks to handle intangible quantum states under privacy laws. Privacy and data protection laws in the United States are largely sectoral. As QIT expands into realms such as finance and consumer sectors (e.g. a number of financial institutions have quantum computing research divisions currently), existing

[151] Alice Corp. v. CLS Bank Int'l 573 US 208 (2014).

laws may apply to QIT use. Examples include the Health Insurance Portability and Accountability Act (HIPAA), the Gramm-Leach-Bliley Act for financial data, and state-level laws such as the California Consumer Privacy Act. In the EU, data protection is governed by the General Data Protection Regulation (GDPR), Regulation (EU) 2016/679, while the U.K. follows the Data Protection Act 2018 and the U.K. General Data Protection Regulation. The consequences of QIT use under these laws are yet to be fully studied, including in relation to cybersecurity obligations. Similarly, the EU AI Act also has implications for the use of QIT, especially in the context of machine learning and optimization performed using quantum systems.

16.5 Competition Law

Quantum computing's potential exponential speedups and significant capital barriers to development might allow a handful of well-funded entities to dominate essential QIT infrastructures, raising concerns of concentrated market power. Competition authorities may face challenges in defining relevant markets for quantum hardware or quantum software where few substitutes exist. Quantum-secured communications could also limit regulators' ability to detect collusive exchanges if encryption is impervious to standard monitoring. Future reforms might involve specialized merger guidelines covering quantum R&D acquisitions or new approaches to define innovation markets in QIT. International cooperation among competition authorities could help prevent anti-competitive consolidation of quantum IP, particularly where cross-border entanglement or data flows confound traditional jurisdictional rules. This may give rise to implications under U.S. antitrust law such as the Sherman Act, the Clayton Act, and the Federal Trade Commission Act. In the European Union, competition rules come from Articles 101 and 102 of the TFEU, regulating cartels and abuse of dominance, supplemented by the EU Merger Regulation (Council Regulation (EC) No 139/2004). The U.K. Competition Act 1998 and Enterprise Act 2002 govern parallel issues post-Brexit. In each case, the information effect of QIT is one that is at a higher level in terms of governance stacks with regulation indirectly impacting QIT use rather than directed at, for example, the quantum circuit layer.

16.6 Public International Law

Technologies such as quantum decryption and quantum sensing can shift strategic balances, undermining classical cryptographic security used by nation States. To this end, State practice may evolve to interpret the use of force and State responsibility in ways that include quantum-based cyberattacks, particularly if quantum tools cause real-world disruptions or compromise national security systems. Jurisdictional questions also arise if entangled states span multiple territories, making it unclear which State's legal authority or sovereignty is implicated. Over time, new treaties or amendments to existing cybersecurity or arms-control frameworks might explicitly restrict weaponized uses of QIT. Likewise, future versions of the Tallinn Manual could incorporate guidelines on quantum-based espionage, sabotage, or conflict escalation thresholds. Public international law is primarily derived from the UN Charter (1945), customary state practice, and treaties covering security and conflict, such as arms control regimes. Other relevant regimes with consequences for QIT use may include The Budapest Convention on Cybercrime guides certain transnational cyber activities, though it does not yet address QIT specifically. These issues are discussed in depth in a later chapter.

16.7 Dual Use and Export Controls

QIT affordances such as entanglement may blur traditional definitions of transfer as might no-cloning constraints on quantum, which may complicate whether intangible quantum states themselves constitute an export. Entanglement across borders can also serve as a conduit for quantum information without classic data shipment. Existing legislative lists under the Commerce Control List or equivalent EU regulation may need more specific amendments to capture quantum hardware (superconducting chips, ion traps, specialized photonic devices) and relevant software or encryption protocols. Quantum error-correction, which can mask or compress sensitive data, may also frustrate inspection in ways that dual use and export control regimes are yet to countenance. Policymakers might develop specialized licensing regimes for quantum R&D, while multilateral bodies could adopt more detailed categories for QIT to ensure clarity on which exports require prior authorization or are subject to special controls. In the United States, the Export Control Reform Act (50 U.S.C. §§ 4801–4826) and the Export Administration Regulations (EAR) at 15 C.F.R. §§ 730–774 regulate commercial and dual-use exports. Already export controls apply to QIT in the US.[152] The European Union enforces dual-use controls primarily through Regulation (EU) 2021/821, and the U.K. follows its Export Control Act 2002 and subsequent Export Control Orders.

16.8 Life Sciences

Quantum computing promises new avenues for molecular modelling, drug discovery, and precision medicine but raises questions about reproducibility if results rely on probabilistic qubit outputs. Regulators could require documented error rates, noise mitigation protocols, and cross-validation by classical simulations or

[152] Marchant et al. (2024).

lab data. Quantum sensors—particularly quantum dots—offer ultra-precise diagnostics or targeted drug delivery, triggering medical device classifications. Existing regulations might need updated definitions for analytical validity or clinical evaluation when quantum phenomena are employed. Over time, specialized guidance documents could address quantum-based in silico trials, ensuring that results align with Good Clinical Practice or Good Manufacturing Practice standards despite the complexities of entanglement and no-cloning. In the United States, the Food, Drug, and Cosmetic Act and associated FDA regulations govern pharmaceuticals, biologics, and medical devices. The use of QIT may give rise to a number of consequences or motivate legislative responses under these laws. Software as a Medical Device (SaMD) guidelines provide a pathway for algorithm-driven diagnostics, which may conceivably be adapted to cover quantum machine learning depending again on whether the *sui generis* question is answered in the affirmative. In the EU, the key instruments are the Medical Devices Regulation (EU) 2017/745 and the In Vitro Diagnostic Regulation (EU) 2017/746, enforced by national competent authorities. The U.K. relies on the Medicines and Medical Devices Act 2021 and MHRA guidance, reflecting pre- and post-Brexit reforms. In each case, the impact of QIT on life sciences regulation is nascent and limited.

16.9 International Standards

Unlike classical systems, quantum devices exhibit inherent stochasticity, so reliability and error-correction protocols need distinct metrics. Quantum standards[153] provide prospective means for the development of such protocols. Standardizing definitions for fault tolerance or qubit fidelity may help regulators and markets compare hardware from different vendors. Similarly, cryptographic strength must adapt to quantum's ability to break classical keys, prompting standards like those from NIST for PQC and from ISO/IEC for quantum-safe methods. Looking ahead, cooperation among ISO, IEC, IEEE, NIST, and ETSI can prevent fragmentation or conflicting protocols. In practice, new or revised QIT certifications might address quantum error budgets, measurement processes, and interoperability for quantum networks, ensuring robust safety and predictable performance across diverse quantum architectures. ISO and IEC produce international technical standards, many relevant to information and communications technology. In quantum-related areas, ISO/IEC 18033–6 (quantum cryptography) and other prospective standards under the Joint Technical Committee 1 (JTC 1) address quantum-safe cryptography. In the United States, the National Institute of Standards and Technology (NIST) leads the post-quantum cryptography standardization project (as noted above), publishing drafts for quantum-resistant algo-

[153] Aboy et al. (2025).

rithms. Europe's ETSI (European Telecommunications Standards Institute) Industry Specification Group on Quantum Key Distribution (ISG QKD) also develops quantum communication standards.

16.10 Regulatory Sandboxes

As discussed, the unique features of QIT compared with classical technologies—stochastic outputs, no-cloning, entanglement—may complicate standard regulatory approvals, making sandboxes attractive for controlled experimentation. Regulators could waive certain prescriptive requirements temporarily, allowing quantum developers to demonstrate real-world performance while documenting error-correction logs or measurement fidelity. Issues such as liability for unexpected quantum errors or safeguarding personal data (if quantum analytics is used for health or financial data) can be tested with minimal public risk. In the future, specialized quantum sandboxes might include multi-regulator oversight—for instance, involving the export control authority, data protection commissioners, and health regulators—ensuring that unpredictable quantum effects are comprehensively monitored. Through such adaptive testing, policymakers can refine legal definitions and enforcement strategies before QIT is deployed at scale. Regulatory sandboxes typically arise from innovation-oriented agencies rather than a single legislative code. Comparable examples in the United States that might be drawn upon for models of sandboxing QIT include trials run by the Consumer Financial Protection Bureau (CFPB) (e.g. testing the use of quantum computing with sensitive consumer financial data). The U.K. Financial Conduct Authority (FCA) established a sandbox in 2016 to test innovative financial products in a controlled environment, and the Information Commissioner's Office (ICO) runs a data-protection sandbox under the Data Protection Act 2018. Both might be adapted in the case of QIT use in these sectors.

17 Governance Stack Example

17.1 Overview

In this penultimate section, we set out an illustrative example of how a governance stack approach can assist in analysing appropriate regulatory instruments for mapping stakeholder outcomes to technical implementation. As can be seen, the vertically integrated stack (smallest scale at the top) represents a layering of components within a quantum computer scaffolded by an application layer interface. The horizontal stack is designed to illustrate a toy workflow of which QIT is a component.

These two constructs can be used to map governance instruments to the appropriate level in the stack. The idea is that they allow a way to map existing governance instruments to likely QIT use cases. It is a method that can also be used to for risk assessment purposes, and so therefore is useful for analysing any new or novel regulatory responses which may be required to address such risk. Our working toy example is taken from the life sciences where QIT has potential application for chemical drug discovering, quantum sensing and even quantum communication of sensitive data. In this example, we assume QIT is used in a number of places in the horizontal workflow below.

17.2 Horizontal Stack

An example of a horizontal stack technical stack with associated governance instruments is below. We set out a sequence of stages—one involving QIT, one not involving QIT and relevant governance instruments.

For Stage 1, Pharmaceutical drug manufacture starts with a design process which in principle may involve the use of QIT. Already dual use considerations may apply before any life sciences governance considerations arise. For the benchmark case, no quantum dual use considerations would arise (albeit possibly AI or life sciences dual use issues may arise).

At Stage 2, quantum computing QIT may be used for simulation of novel chemicals for which bioinformatics standards under FDA or related guidelines may apply.

At Stage 3 where pharmaceutical products are manufactured, the FDA's Good Manufacturing Process[154] requirements may apply in ways that require adaptation for how QIT operators.

For Stage 4, clinical trials using quantum dot sensing technology may have to comply with both clinical trial rules and nanotechnology regulation in the life sciences.

Finally, in Stage 5, monitoring and distribution of the relevant technology such as to foreign manufacturing hubs may require ways of relating data obtained from monitoring back to QIT processes and consideration of export control consequences. We set out Table 4 below summarizing the workflow process.

At each Stage where QIT is used, we can fashion a vertical stack that identifies where in the stack different governance instruments may be relevant. We use quantum computing in this workflow at Stage 2 as an example and set out in Table 5 below an example of the governance stack.

[154] Good Manufacturing Practice regulations 21 C.F.R. §210–211 (2023).

Table 4 Horizontal stack comparing workflows with and without QIT

Governance Instrument	Dual use requirements	FDA Bioinformatics Standards	FDA Good manufacturing processes	FDA Clinical Trial regulations Nanotechnology regulations	FDA Distribution and monitoring regulations Export controls
Workflow stage without QIT (benchmark)	**Stage 1** Pharmaceutical product design using classical computers	**Stage 2** Limited simulation for chemical synthesis	**Stage 3** Synthesis of pharmaceutical product with classical sensors	**Stage 4** Clinical trials involving classical data processes	**Stage 5** Commercial distribution
Workflow stage with QIT	**Stage 1** Pharmaceutical product design using QIT	**Stage 2** Quantum simulation for chemical synthesis	**Stage 3** Synthesis of pharmaceutical product with quantum sensors	**Stage 4** Clinical trials involving quantum dots	**Stage 5** Commercial distribution

18 Conclusion

In this chapter we have laid the groundwork for understanding the intersection of quantum information technology (QIT) and the law, emphasizing the transformative potential of quantum computing, communication, and sensing while addressing their unique governance challenges. By contextualizing QIT within its historical evolution—from the first quantum revolution's incidental harnessing of quantum effects to the second quantum revolution's engineered utilization of superposition, entanglement, and non-locality—we have delineated the modern state of these technologies, which remain largely prototypical yet poised for profound economic, strategic, and societal impacts. Our contributions are aimed at advancing the discourse on QIT governance in several ways.

First, we conducted a technical jurisprudential analysis, surveying existing legal regimes—such as export controls, post-quantum cryptography standards, and sector-specific regulations—and evaluating how they intersect with QIT's novel affordances, including decryption capabilities and ultra-precise measurements. Second, we explored legal quantum ontologies, revealing how quantum systems' inherent uncertainty, non-locality, and probabilistic nature challenge classical legal assumptions about observability, identity, and determinism, without rendering QIT ungovernable. Third, we introduced and adapted a governance-stack model, integrating vertical (hardware-to-output) and horizontal (workflow) components with information taxonomies to map regulatory instruments precisely to technical layers, facilitating risk assessment and stakeholder alignment. This approach underscores the need for specificity in governance, particularly for strategic and dual-use

Table 5 Governance stack indicating which governance instrument may apply at which level of the vertical technical stack

Layer	Stakeholder Interests/ Obligations	Information Effects	Governance Instrument(s)
Quantum circuit layer	National engineering and quality assurance standards in bioinformatics imposing requirements on circuitry	Information processing in new ways leveraging quantum gates	Technical standards regarding quantum circuitry
Measurement and Control Layer	Stakeholders require levels of control to ensure quantum algorithms are properly implemented and not used for malfeasant purposes	Novel ways in which data is encoded and controlled and measured	International agreements restricting QIT for offensive purposes requiring inspection of QIT scaffolding
Error correction layer	Regulatory authorities require guarantees regarding error correction thresholds for use of QIT in processing high-stakes health or security data	Requirements for fault-tolerant QC may mean homomorphic computation is required distinct from classical	Regulators requiring confirmation of error rates in quantum computation upon which simulation is based
Quantum Programming Language	Developers in integrated workflows require robust CI/CD pipelines and unit testing to assure computational systems involving QIT which may include third-party licensed information	Quantum programming languages (usually classical) may also be utilized	Monitoring systems or copyright instruments governing the use and implementation of code such as open-source licensing
Applications layer	Users utilizing quantum cloud, quantum data or other similar services to store sensitive information in post-quantum cryptographic contexts	QIT may open up avenues for new algorithms e.g. instructions for synthesizing new chemicals or drugs	Legislation requiring robust testing and assurance of post-quantum cryptographic systems
Classical Interface layer	QIT is used by stakeholders for long-range communication for critical infrastructure	QIT enabling scalable computing in ways that overcome thermodynamic limitations	Rules regarding the infrastructure and reliability of quantum networks

technologies, while advocating a risk-centered framework that balances innovation with safeguarding measures.

Unifying these elements through an informational lens (i.e., treating QIT as fundamentally information-processing systems) bridges technical and jurisprudential domains, enabling clearer analysis of impacts on privacy, verification, intellectual property, and geopolitical equilibria. While QIT largely falls under existing frameworks, its *sui generis* qualities may require targeted adaptations to ensure equitable access, mitigate asymmetries, and foster responsible deployment. As QIT matures, future scholarship on its governance can assist policymakers, scholars, and practitioners to proactively shape governance that harnesses QIT's promise while safeguarding against its risks.

Acknowledgement This work was made possible through the generous support of the Novo Nordisk Foundation (NNF) via a grant for the scientifically independent Collaborative Research Program in Bioscience Innovation Law (Inter-CeBIL Program—Grant No. NNF23SA0087056). The opinions expressed are the authors' own and not of their respective affiliations. The authors declare no conflicts of interests.

Appendix A Information Theory

To supplement the discussion above, we briefly set out a short synopsis of the key theoretical and practical characteristics (including software and hardware considerations) of quantum information theory. The focus in this Appendix is upon the informational characterization of quantum technologies. As we touch upon, all technologies can be trivially framed as contingent on quantum mechanics in that all physics relies upon the laws of quantum mechanics. In physics, classical theories about the world are subsets of broader quantum theories (such as field theories and the like)—classical theories are sometimes described as a limiting case of more general quantum theories. At a more granular level, quantum mechanical phenomena are central to life sciences subject matter and related areas, such as organic chemistry, protein and molecular states and synthesis, cellular processes and organism structure and biochemical signaling.

We instead narrow our focus to quantum effects and dynamics in informational terms, where the particular quantum technologies of interest fulfil some information processing role. For quantum computing, this is the processing of data encoded in quantum states and evolved according to quantum mechanical laws, such as in quantum chemistry simulations for drug discovery. For quantum communication this is the use of quantum resources such as entanglement to facilitate communication or to enable cryptographic activities such as quantum key distribution (important to securing life sciences data in a post-quantum scenario) relevant to life sciences. For quantum sensing, this involves how quantum technologies such as quantum dots are used, either by way of being embedded in devices or exogenously, to acquire information via fine-grained measurement. Understanding the theoretical background of quantum information processing is crucial for identifying the relevant quantum technology stack applicable to the use of each form of QIT in life sciences. Importantly, by doing so, we obtain clarity on precisely what is different and what remains the same, from a technical and governance point of view, when QIT are used in life sciences activities. This in turn informs regulatory responses having regard to objectives in mind, be they fostering innovation, improving life sciences outcomes or managing potential downside risks. We begin our theoretical synopsis below with a short summary of key principles of classical information processing theory, followed by a discussion of the distinguishing features of quantum information processing theory.

Classical Information Processing

Principles of Information Processing

Typically, in classical computational science, computation is expressed in a stateful manner, where phenomena of interest are described using states, abstractly considered collections or sets of descriptions, say of certain metrics or even propositions, describing the system of interest. The set of states are assumed to span a space with the potential states in which a system can subsist, or regions in space which that system may occupy, are denoted its configuration space. Computation is then conceptually defined using finite state machines or more fully using Turing machine formalism[155] in order to elucidate the computational process and conditions under which a system will subsist within or change states within the state space. The most general representation of computation in this formalism is that of the universal Turing machine, capable of computing any computable sequence. There exist other representations of computation which can be shown to be essentially equivalent to Turing machine formalism, such as Markov Decision Processes (MDP), an adaptation of Turing machine formalism and which can serve as a general model of computation equivalent to that of a Turing machine. One important representation of computation with direct relevance to quantum computing, especially qubit-based systems, is the *circuit model* of quantum computation where computation consists of inputs and outputs mediated by gates (such as logic gates) that constitutes a functional mapping between one element of the sequence and the next. Both methods can be shown to be equivalent and have utility depending on the context, however the circuit model of quantum computation tends to be more commonly utilized within much quantum computing literature. We address both formalisms briefly in order to connect with the wider quantum information processing landscape.

Turing machine formalism is a stateful model of computation. The stateful representation begins with fundamental abstract concepts of *states* which are usually collections (n-ples) described by elements of an alphabet, which may include coordinates, physical numbers describing phenomenon or more broadly a way of representing a system or object of interest (such as phase or configuration space representations in physics). In classical computing, this is information encoded via bit strings, each of which represents the state of the system (with each bit being a binary-valued variable). The evolution of an information system, how it changes over time, is then usually characterized in terms of transitions (mappings or transition functions) between states or in austere formalism, between bit-strings (or *registers* being sets of bit strings). Usually, a distinction is made between the physical hardware (or realization) of information processing or computational devices and the abstract representation of data or software as a configuration of one or more physical states. In quantum computing contexts, one distinguishes between physical qubits (representing the physical system that acts according to quantum

[155] Sipser (2012).

computational axioms) and abstract logical (informational) qubits which are an abstraction of many qubits, but which behave according to quantum laws.

In formal computational sciences, state transitions are described using *algorithms* which detail how a state evolves given particular inputs. Algorithms represent *effective procedures*, sequences of steps (whose sequential nature allows them to be mapped canonically to the natural numbers). We explicate the formalism in a little more detail than is common in governance contexts in order to draw upon it as a way of characterizing governance further on in information-theoretic terms. The formalization of the theory of algorithms for our purposes can be framed in terms of the Turing model of computation and an equivalent (but distinctly formalized) circuit model of computation. A Turing machine represents an abstraction of the computational process and are formally represented as an *n-tuple* $M = \langle Q, \Gamma, b, \Sigma, \delta, q\_0, F \rangle$ where:

- $Q = \{q_i\}$ is the non-empty set of states with initial state q_0 and a set of final states $F \subseteq Q$
- Γ is a non-zero set of symbols b denoted (the symbolic) alphabet (note combinations of symbols or strings form *words* the set of which is sometimes described as a vocabulary)
- $\Sigma \subset \Gamma$ is the input alphabet, a subset of the alphabet
- $\delta = \frac{Q}{F} \times \Gamma \rightarrow Q \times \Gamma \times \{L,R\}$ is the transition function (with L and R denoting left or right transitions respectively, though this can be dispensed within the generalized form, not to be confused with language below)

The Turing machine described above is a *deterministic* Turing machine, one whose transitions are certain. Turing machines may also be *non-deterministic*, where the transition function is probabilistic (not deterministic) is constructed and the system is said to be stochastic. Often instead other models of computation, such as Markov Decision Processes, are used to model stochastic dynamic systems. Classically the set of functions which a Turing machine may calculate is equated with those computable by an algorithm, hence Turing machines represent a commonplace formalization of the computational process. This statement equating algorithms with Turing machines is in essence the substance of the *Church-Turing Thesis* (see below).

In the theory of computational formal languages, one describes problems (and their algorithmic solutions) in terms of languages L over a collection of symbols (an input alphabet Σ above) being a subset $\Sigma^* \subseteq \Sigma$ of finite symbols known as strings (or words) e.g. for classical bits this is $\Sigma = \{0, 1\}$ with L being the set of sequences of 0 s and 1 s. The solutions to a decision-problem can then be represented as a language L. In Turing machine formalism, a language L is *decidable* if the Turing machine (i.e. the algorithm) enters a state corresponding to yes or no given an input x. Intuitively the formalism then represents decision-problems as classification problems.

In quantum information sciences, it is more commonplace to express computational dynamics using the circuit model of computation. The *circuit model* represents computation via *gates* and *wires*. Gates perform computational tasks (representing functions) while *wires* represent channels that flow information between gates. The circuit model comprises specification of input and output sets and an intermediate sequence of wires and gates which may be in parallel. Logic gates are then expressed functionally as $f: \{0,1\}^m \to \{0,1\}^n$ representing an input of dimension m bits and output of dimension n bits. A variety of gates corresponding to logical operations on bits, such as AND, OR, NAND, XOR and so on form a get set which operates on inputs (or some subset thereof). Circuits are usually characterized also in terms of their *depth* (how 'long' the circuit is) and their *width* (how many parallel computations are occurring at any time step. Circuit depth has important relationships to questions around tractability and computational complexity. In addition to logical bits, the circuit model also envisages the use of *ancilla* bits, essentially spare or additional resources separate from the main circuit enabling for example intermediate computations to be undertaken or data to be stores. Ancilla qubits are an important feature of quantum computation formalism in practice and theory, enabling certain computations to be undertaken more efficiently. The scope of problems that may be computed by a model of computation is denoted its *expressibility* with the ideal case being that the entire gate set available enables arbitrary computations to be performed, denoted *universal computation*. In quantum computation, one is often concerned with whether the gates that can be performed enable universal quantum computation, an important characteristic of fault tolerant architectures. Universal quantum computation can also be expressed in the language of quantum control in terms of rendering a particular computational state (or language) reachable given a set of quantum operations, such as unitary gates. The correspondence between Turing machine formalism and circuit models essentially arises if there exists a Turing machine which can, given inputs, generate a description of the computational circuit in question.

As Turing infamously discovered, certain problems are in fact not computable. So-called *halting problems* exhibit certain recursive or impredicative structure such that they do not halt (at an answer) given an input to the algorithm. Furthermore, there are many problems which are in principle may be computable and even within lower-order complexity classes (such as **P** below), but which in practice exceed the computational resources available or would take such a long time as to render them effectively intractable. It should be noted, as we touch upon below, that problems in quantum complexity classes can in principle be simulated or computed using a classical computer, it is just that the resource cost may be exponential in the inputs. The distinction between classical and quantum computation—and justifications for the use of quantum computing within the life sciences—comes down to the efficiency and tractability benefits that solving problems on quantum computers offer. But what do we mean by these terms? To approach this problem, let us consider in more detail how information processing problems are categorized and the types of problems information processing seeks to solve. Information processing in terms of computation can be subdivided into three distinct questions:

(a) *Is the class of problem computational*? Is the class of problem in question a decision-problem, namely one which can be computed?

(b) *What class of algorithms may solve the class of problems*? Having assumed a problem is computational, the second question becomes whether there exist algorithms which may solve such classes of problems.
(c) *What resources are required to solve the problem optimally*? Assuming one or more algorithms exist to solve the problem, the question then becomes what are the minimal (optimal) resources, in space (energy) or time, to solve the problem.

The first question addresses whether problems of interest can in principle be computed—that is, whether computation can resolve to a solution (accepting a solution language *L*). This threshold question essentially is directed at whether either the problem exhibits some sort of impredicative structure (such that it may reproduce the structure of the halting problem), or whether it may be ill-posed or be insufficiently well-defined so as to bring computational procedures to bear. The second question is ostensibly whether algorithms exist to actually compute an answer. For many problems of interest, the existence of a class of algorithms that even solve the problem is uncertain (such as for the celebrated Navier-Stokes problem or a solution to the Riemann Hypothesis). The third question, which touches upon the computational resources required to solve computational problems, is the domain of *computational complexity*, a subdiscipline of computer science. Even where a problem is computable and a class of algorithms to solve it exist, the resource cost may be prohibitive, growing unsustainably with the input size. In general, the focus of computational technology in the life sciences is only upon computable problems, albeit ones which may be intractable or whose class of algorithms challenging to ascertain. It is this latter question—that of computational complexity—that provides the technical basis for distinguishing between classical and quantum information processing. We provide a short synopsis of the key concepts below.

Computational Complexity

The fundamental distinction between quantum and classical information processing rests on the different computational resources that quantum versus classical algorithms require (in principle) to solve certain classes of problem. In practice, determining necessary computational resources can be a highly challenging problem. At first glance the resources in space, energy and time required to computationally solve an information processing problem are highly contingent on the physical devices used to undertake computation, let alone the algorithmic design and problem specification. Computational complexity science abstracts these technical details away (or within the algorithm itself, such as by choosing multi-tape Turing machines rather than single-tape types) in order to concentrate upon the essential complexity properties of an algorithm. The complexity of an algorithm is represented using *asymptotic notation* (or big 'O') notation which describes, in the abstract, how resource requirements of an algorithm in solving a problem scale as the inputs to the problem increase. Resource requirements are converted into mathematical form, the intuition being that they can be expressed as functions $f(n)$ of input size n—for example given n (bit) inputs, the runtime (expressed in units of time) may be expressed as a function $n \rightarrow f(n)$. Big-O notation describes classically, given n inputs (bits), the upper bound on runtime to receive an answer is expressed as $O(f(n))$. For lower bounds, the notation $\Omega(f(n))$ is used to describe minimal resource costs. Algorithms (up to factors such as constants etc. in which case the notation $\Theta(f(n))$ is used) can then be factored into *classes* based on the functional form of their complexity bounds, hence arises the concept of *complexity classes* and, as a result, the complexity classes into which problems and their algorithms (as solutions to decision problems) are categorized.

This classification is used to describe the *efficiency* of an algorithm as a measure of how the cost of solutions scale with inputs. For example, sometimes there may be a trade-off between the amount of, for example, space and time an algorithm requires (less space but more time), or energy and time (as is common in control theory). The primary distinction in computational complexity science for classifying algorithms is between those algorithms (problems) which (i) may be solved in polynomial functions of input size n (as n increases, the resource cost grows polynomially) and (ii) may only be solved in exponential (or super-polynomial e.g. $n^{\{log\, n\}}$) functions of n. This motivates the important distinction between tractable problems (those for which exists a best possible algorithm generating a solution exists requiring not more than polynomial n resources) and intractable algorithms for which the best possible algorithm requires supra-polynomial or exponential n resources. In computational complexity literature, one also finds synonyms for tractable in terms of feasibility or easiness. We reserve feasible for algorithms which solve problems in timeframes useful to humans rather than the more formal term used in the literature. The distinction between polynomial and exponential resource costs is of direct relevance to one of computer science's foundational propositions, the Extended Church-Turing Thesis which (in its strong form) states that any physically realizable computational model may be simulated or reproduced on a probabilistic Turing machine with at most polynomial (in n) resource increase.

In formal complexity notation, the complexity class is often denoted in capitalized acronyms or abbreviations such as **TIME**(f(n)) where, for example, a problem solvable in polynomial time is denoted **TIME**(n^k) (for finite k). Formally, the set of languages L in **TIME**(n^k) is known as the complexity class $\mathbf{P} = \bigcup_k \mathbf{TIME}\,(n^k)$ for fixed k (such that complexity classes can be framed as set of languages or in our intuitive formulation, sets of solutions to problems). The complexity class **NP** (standing for non-deterministic polynomial time) is then defined as the set of languages whose acceptance can be verified in polynomial time. Alternatively, **NP** has a definition as the set of decision-problems solvable by a non-deterministic Turing machine in polynomial time. **NP**-complete problems are relatedly defined as problems in **NP** to which all other decision-problems in **NP** may be reduced in polynomial time. There is a maze of complexity classes (sometimes called a complexity zoo) such as **PSPACE** (problems solvable with polynomial number of bits rather than space) and **EXP** (decisions solvable in exponential time i.e. $O\left(2^{n^k}\right)$ for k constant) which are believed ordered in a hierarchy.

One of the foundational open problems of computer science remains to formally prove whether **P** $\neq$ **NP** i.e. whether there exist problems in **NP** that are not in **P**. It is the assumption that **P** and **NP** (and other classes) are not equivalent that motivates the quest for quantum computation. One aspect of the use of information processing (classical or quantum) is the extent to which problems can be identifiably classified into one complexity class or another. While it is not necessary to know the complexity class into which an algorithm falls in order to say, for example, attempt to use it for life sciences simulation, complexity analysis is useful as a means of determining what the resource costs are expected to be.

The technical distinction between classical and quantum computers is commonly expressed in terms of probabilistic complexity classes. The probability that a probabilistic (non-deterministic) Turing machine will accept or reject L correctly and output the correct answer with probability of at least 2/3 in polynomial time is denoted as the complexity class **BPP** (bounded-error probabilistic polynomial time). BPP is regarded as a more pragmatic classification of classical computation and classical information processing. In quantum computational settings, the relevant comparative complexity class is **BQP** (bounded-error quantum polynomial time) which is the set of decision-problems solvable using a quantum algorithm in polynomial time with probability 2/3 (or conversely with an error probability of 1/3). BQP can also be defined in terms of *quantum Turing machines* which differ from their classical counterparts.[156] The distinction between quantum and classical computers is in this formulation framed in terms of **BPP** being a proper subset of **BQP**, i.e. that **BPP** $\subset$ **BQP** albeit this is yet to be formally proven. It is this distinction that is often deployed in technical literature as the primary distinction between quantum and classical algorithms. It is also the case that because probabilistic complexity classes tend to be more pragmatically useful, one often sees classes of algorithms framed in terms of 'worst case' or 'average' complexity.

It should be remembered what it means for an algorithm to be so-characterized as quantum: the algorithmic process (the effective procedure) must include steps which are *uniquely* quantum mechanical. Thus, while all quantum algorithms, such as those noted below in terms of search, cryptography and simulation involve classical information processing, it is the specifically quantum informational processing characteristics of those algorithmic classes—their utilization and reliance upon superposition or entanglement for example—which gives rise to their quantum advantage. This is a different but related point as to whether, given a quantum algorithm, there may exist a classical algorithm which efficiently solves the problem. We discuss the importance of algorithmic specification in the context of intellectual property (such as patents) for QIT further on.

[156] Deutsch (1985) and Molina Watrous (2018).

For example, to the extent a patentable method relies upon claims of quantum advantage, then in principle there may be normative arguments that any patent application ought to require specification of these uniquely quantum features that enable such advantage. The complexity class **BQP** represents in effect the working definition of quantum computation by way complexity class (of problems or languages depending on one's chosen formal characterization) formalisation. It is worth noting the hierarchy of classes:

$$\mathbf{P} \subseteq \mathbf{BPP} \subseteq \mathbf{BQP} \subseteq \ldots \subseteq \mathbf{PSPACE} \subseteq \mathbf{EXP}$$

with the inclusions held believed by many (albeit not proven in the certain cases) to be strict proper subsets.[157] On this assumption, the hierarchy shows intuitively that while it is believed quantum computers can in principle tractably solve a wider class of problems than classical computers, there remains a vast swathe of problems that even quantum computers cannot solve or render tractable or feasible. The widely believed distinction between BQP and BPP in turn has implications for the Church-Turing thesis, requiring adjustment (or indeed invalidating it by some viewpoints) by substituting the concept of simulation on a classical computer for a quantum computer. This modification is known as the Church-Turing-Deutsche,[158] potentially problematising its classical counterpart if quantum computers can solve problems that classical computers cannot efficiently solve. We set them out below.

- *Church-Turing Thesis.* Every effectively calculable (algorithmic) function can be computed by a Turing machine
- *Extended Church-Turing Thesis.* Any algorithm may be simulated *efficiently* (with at most polynomial overhead) using a probabilistic Turing machine
- *Quantum Church-Turing-Deutsch Thesis.* A universal quantum computer can simulate any finite physical system i.e. any finite physical system can be efficiently simulated by a quantum computer.

Understanding the conceptual distinctions between classical and quantum information processing is useful for the design of algorithms to solve problems in the life sciences. It is also useful in order to demystify the actual import and effect of quantum information processing technologies in a life sciences context. Having covered the elementary principles of computational theory that motivate the use of quantum information technologies, we present a short synopsis of the principal elements of quantum mechanics and quantum information processing and their relation to QIT.

[157] Bremner et al. (2011).

[158] Deutsch (1985).

Appendix B Informational Impacts

Categorical Effects

Table 6 below sets out a concise mapping of key informational impacts to salient areas of law and governance. This table reiterates points made in preceding subsections but organizes them for quick reference with an emphasis on partitioning QIT into embedded and non-embedded contexts.

In principle, the taxonomy above could be more formally refined by adopting a more fundamental ontology of information processing, such as statistical learning theory, singular learning theory (for deep neural network applications) or quantum analogues. In such cases, the information processing is characterized by certain metrics or properties, such as those related to performance (e.g. accuracy) and generalization, runtime or resource cost (e.g. in terms of time and energy), empirical loss, complexity classes (e.g. classes of problems which may be solved) and so on. Changes to information processing arising from the use of quantum, as distinct from classical, technologies can then be expressed in terms of changes to these metrics.

For example, applying quantum computers to a simulation (say of proteins, chemicals or biological systems) may lead to simulations being run in a more efficient (e.g. faster) way. Or they may enable new computational simulations (such as of interacting molecular effects and evolution) which are currently beyond the reach of classical computational resources. By doing so, one can then estimate the effects of QIT compared to its classical counterparts, allowing the specific differences

Table 6 Categorical effects of QIT

Categorical Effects of QIT	
Non-embedded	
Efficient processing	Use of QIT enables improvement in information processing in life sciences according to key metrics, such as speed, cost, accuracy and so on
Oracular effects	Use of QIT enables information processing currently unable to be done classically (categorically) to be undertaken. Theoretically this is represented by solving or addressing problems in higher-order complexity classes. We group in this class the use of QIT to solve tasks or problems that while classically possible, are computationally infeasible owing to resource costs (e.g. time or energy)
Information asymmetries	Use of QIT could lead to significant information asymmetries among stakeholders affecting economic equilibria. Examples may include QIT technologies allowing asymmetric advantages in cryptography, or optimization, or improvements in technology
Embedded	
Measurement	Use of quantum dots as quantum sensing devices embedded within medical devices or diagnostic tools as measurement (data generating or data gathering) devices
Control	Control mechanisms are different from classical given the stochastic nature of quantum systems. Controllability is probabilistic

between the two to be ascertained. The impact of these differences from a governance perspective can then be studied by reference to existing governance instruments and prospective governance instruments. To this end, we provide a sketch of the germane differences in information processing between quantum and classical technologies as a means of parsing distinctions significant from a governance perspective.

Information Processing

Our focus regarding governance of QIT applications the life sciences is on information processing-related activities, including simulation, data mining, monitoring, measuring and so on. As we discuss below and as is somewhat trite to observe, information, data, storage and processing methods are an important feature of many life sciences divisions. This in turn informs how and where the use of quantum computing in the life sciences is governed. For example, governance frameworks applicable to the life sciences governance impose certain requirements, in both form and substance, on the use, dissemination and character of information. This includes specification and description requirements under intellectual property law, especially patent law; technical detail specifications as part of medical device product approval procedures; disclosures and representations of sufficient scientific testing and processing as part of pharmaceutical design and anticipatory effects of new drugs and medicines, reliability of testing and clinical trial procedures and specifications regarding the nature, quality and reliability of information ascertained from monitoring and surveillance of life sciences applications. Utilization of quantum computing algorithms or devices in, for example, pharmaceutical simulations, drug effect simulations or bioinformatics processing may be become a type of use required to be specified under applicable governance regimes.

Oracular Effects

Moreover, there is what we denote the question of *oracular technology governance* to be considered. In computational science, *oracles* are an artefact, akin to a black box, which can answer a query or solve a decision problem in a single operation, regardless of whether answering is computable or not.[159] In its most general form, it is a black box that outputs a solution to any problem. Drawing upon this by way of analogy, by *oracular technologies*, we mean technologies whose information processing capabilities (such as quantum information processing, machine learning or artificial intelligence) categorically exceed existing classical computational information processing capabilities with some specific impact, in effect being analogous to oracles, in effect black boxes or highly complex (and often non-linear) informa-

[159] Baker et al. (1975), Berthiaume Brassard (1994) and Blum Impagliazzo (1987).

tion processing devices which may solve classes of problem that otherwise could not be solved (in practice or principle).

In practical terms, oracular technology gives rise to what we would assess as a separate class of *risk*, namely *oracular risk*, afforded by for example the generation of knowledge, insights or information which equip those with access to such knowledge a categorically different capacity. The risk is somewhat the topic of AI Safety and AI Risk literature,[160] which analyze counterfactual scenarios in which AI technologies may reach a level of cognitive advancement with high-impact, such as enabling weapons, synthesis of chemicals or even autonomous robotic systems to exhibit significant power. In a life sciences context, this may include the use of AI and QIT to enable synthesis of chemicals, drugs or proteins or engineering designs with particular high-impact effects, such as tailoring of medicines to bioinformatic data of individuals (with positive benefits for treatment but potentially negative hazards for safety), or highly accurate simulations affording highly asymmetric informational advantage.

Moreover, oracular technologies also give rise to the problem of *verification*—how the output of oracles may be verified and trusted. Verification of the information processing and computational procedures and outputs (and by extension their reliability) is an important element across a variety of life sciences governance regimes, including intellectual property, medical device technical disclosures, patent disclosures and elsewhere. The problem of verification is a well-studied and addressed problem for classical information technologies, differences arise in the case of QIT owing to the unique features of quantum information, such as the fact that measurement affects the state of a system and that quantum information cannot be cloned. Verification may occur through tomography, where, for example, being able to verify the state of a quantum system involves repeated measurements upon identical instantiations of that system in a way that enables reconstruction of its state (or evolution) from measurement statistics.

Being unable to verify states or processes renders the system in effect a black box. Yet this is not necessarily problematic: governance methods in life sciences and elsewhere have existing and established means of addressing "black box" information processes where the state or evolution (process) remains inaccessible, or only partially verifiable, in which case other methods (such as statistically assessing outputs which are ascertainable, or simply running trials and dispensing with requirements for specific knowledge about computations per se) may apply.

Information Asymmetry Effects

The information asymmetry effects of potentially oracular technologies, such as AI and QIT, is yet to be fully understood, but represents a significant feature of such information technologies. For example, access to QIT computational technologies

---

[160] Hendrycks (2024).

may provide certain market participants, societies or governments with advantages arising from better drug or medical device design versus competitors with flow-on effects such as better overall health, possibly longer life and other improvements in health and welfare metrics. Better and more accurate simulations from QIT also may lead to further concentration of innovation and invention—and intellectual property—in stakeholders whom have access to sophisticated computational resources. One may see market concentration effects arise due to informational asymmetries that allow oracular-style or highly efficient computational technologies to more rapidly, accurately or broadly generate inventions attracting intellectual property protection.

Clearly—albeit somewhat speculatively—oracular technologies have enormous potential upside, such as in finding cures or preventative strategies regarding disease or other ailments. It is also clear that, as is so often the case in the history of life sciences innovation, it is a few well-resourced participants, such as governments and pharmaceutical companies (or, likely, technology companies) who are at the vanguard of life sciences discovery and product dissemination. There are existing analogical situations upon which to guide governance and responses to the concentration-enhancing effects of resource intensive information processing. And while such effects are not confined to QIT per se, as the development of artificial intelligence technologies, such as Google DeepMind's various Alpha models for protein discovery[161] and the like attest, the combination of resource intensity required for QIT computations and the promise of paradigm-shifting insights from the use of such technology mean that its information asymmetric effects warrant attention and study.

References

Aaronson S (2013) Quantum computing since Democritus. Cambridge University Press, Cambridge

Abbas A et al (2021) The power of quantum neural networks. Nat Comput Sci 1(6):403–409

Aboy M, Minssen T, Kop M (2022) Mapping the patent landscape of quantum technologies: patenting trends, innovation and policy implications. IIC-Int Rev Intellect Property Compet Law 53(6):853–882

Aboy M et al (2025) Quantum technology governance: a standards-first approach. Science 389(6760):575–578

Akerlof GA (1970) The market for "lemons": quality uncertainty and the market mechanism. Q J Econ 84(3):488–500

Alagic G et al (2022) Status report on the third round of the NIST post-quantum cryptography standardization process. National Institute of Standards and Technology, Gaithersburg

Alagic G et al (2024) Status report on the first round of the additional digital signature schemes for the NIST post-quantum cryptography standardization process. National Institute of Standards and Technology, Gaithersburg

[161] Jumper et al. (2021).

Aldred J (2013) Justifying precautionary policies: incommensurability and uncertainty. Ecol Econ 96:132–140

Allen GC, Benson E, Reinsch WA (2022) Improved export controls enforcement technology needed for U.S. National Security. Center for Strategic and International Studies (CSIS), Washington, D.C

Allenby R (2011) Governance and technology systems: the challenge of emerging technologies. In: Marchant G, Allenby B, Herkert J (eds) The growing gap between emerging technologies and legal-ethical oversight. Springer, Cham

Baker T et al (1975) Relativizations of the P=?NP question. SIAM J Comput 4(4):431–442

Bartlett SD et al (2007) Reference frames, superselection rules, and quantum information. Rev Mod Phys 79(2):555–609

Bärtschi A, Eidenbenz S (2020) Grover mixers for QAOA: shifting complexity from mixer design to state preparation. In: Müller H, Byrd G, Culhane C, DeBenedictis E, Humble T (eds) 2020 IEEE international conference on quantum computing and engineering (QCE). IEEE, New York

Bassoli R et al (2021) Quantum communication networks. Springer, Cham

Batra K et al (2021) Quantum machine learning algorithms for drug discovery applications. J Chem Inf Model 61(6):2641–2647

Beer K (2022) Quantum neural networks. arXiv:2205.08154 [quant-ph]

Belal F et al (2024) Recent applications of quantum dots in pharmaceutical analysis. J Fluoresc 34(1):119–138

Bell JS (1964) On the Einstein Podolsky Rosen paradox. Physics Physique Fizika 1(3):195–200

Bell JS (1966) On the problem of hidden variables in quantum mechanics. Rev Mod Phys 38(3):447–452

Bell JS (2004) Speakable and unspeakable in quantum mechanics, 2nd. Cambridge University Press, Cambridge

Benedetti M et al (2019) Parameterized quantum circuits as machine learning models. Quantum Sci Technol 4(4):043001

Bengio Y et al (2024) International Scientific Report on the Safety of Advanced AI. arXiv:2412.05282

Benioff P (1980) The computer as a physical system: a microscopic quantum mechanical Hamiltonian model of computers as represented by Turing machines. J Stat Phys 22:563–591

Bennett CH, Brassard G (1984) Quantum cryptography: public key distribution and coin tossing. In: Proceedings of IEEE international conference on computers, systems and signal processing. IEEE, New York

Bennett CH et al (1993) Teleporting an unknown quantum state via dual classical and Einstein-Podolsky-Rosen channels. Phys Rev Lett 70(13):1895–1899

Bennett CH et al (1996) Purification of noisy entanglement and faithful teleportation via noisy channels. Phys Rev Lett 76(5):722

Bernstein DJ, Lange T (2017) Post-quantum cryptography. Nature 549(7671):188–194

Berthiaume A, Brassard G (1994) Oracle quantum computing. J Mod Opt 41(12):2521–2535

Beyleveld D, Brownsword R (2012) Emerging technologies, extreme uncertainty, and the principle of rational precautionary reasoning. Law Innov Technol 4(1):35–65

Biamonte J et al (2017) Quantum machine learning. Nature 549(7671):195–202

Black-Branch JL, Fleck D (2015) Nuclear non-proliferation in international law: volume II-verification and compliance. Springer, The Hague

Blix H (1992) Verification of nuclear nonproliferation: the lesson of Iraq. Washington Q 15(4):57–65

Blum M, Impagliazzo R (1987) Generic oracles and oracle classes. In: *28th annual symposium on foundations of computer science* (SFCS 1987). IEEE, New York

Bos JW et al (2015) Post-quantum key exchange for the TLS protocol from the ring learning with errors problem. In: *2015 IEEE symposium on security and privacy*. IEEE, New York

Boschi D et al (1998) Experimental realization of teleporting an unknown pure quantum state via dual classical and Einstein-Podolsky-Rosen channels. Phys Rev Lett 80(6):1121–1125

Bouwmeester D et al (1997) Experimental Quantum Teleportation. Nature 390(6660):575–579
Brassard G et al (2000) Quantum amplitude amplification and estimation. arXiv:0005055 [quant-ph]
Bremner MJ et al (2011) Classical simulation of commuting quantum computations implies collapse of the polynomial hierarchy. Proc Royal Soc A Math Phys Eng Sci 467(2126):459–472
Browne DE (2007) Efficient classical simulation of the quantum Fourier transform. New J Phys 9(5):146
Brownsword R (2008) Rights, regulation, and the technological revolution. Oxford University Press, Oxford
Brownsword R et al (2017) The Oxford handbook of law, regulation and technology. Oxford University Press, Oxford
Brukner Č (2014) Quantum causality. Nat Phys 10(4):259–263
Bukowski TJ, Simmons JH (2002) Quantum dot research: current state and future prospects. Critical Rev Solid State Material Sci 27(3–4):119–142
Bureau of Industry and Security (2022) Commerce implements new export controls on advanced computing and semiconductor manufacturing items to the People's Republic of China (PRC). U.S. Department of Commerce, Washington, DC
Cacciapuoti AS et al (2019) When entanglement meets classical communications: quantum teleportation for the quantum internet. IEEE Trans Commun 67(5):3426–3439
Cacciapuoti AS et al (2020) The quantum internet: a vision for the road ahead. IEEE Netw 34(1):142–149
Caleffi M et al (2018) Quantum switch for the quantum internet: noiseless network switching. IEEE J Sel Areas Commun 36(3):292–303
Cao N et al (2021) NISQ: Error Correction, Mitigation, and Noise Simulation. arXiv:2111.02345
Cariolaro G (2015) Quantum communications. Springer, New York
Cavalcanti EG (2018) Classical causal models for Bell and Kochen-Specker inequality violations require fine-tuning. Phys Rev X 8(2):021018
Cerezo M, Coles PJ (2021) Higher order derivatives of quantum neural networks with barren plateaus. Quantum Sci Technol 6(3):035006
Cerezo M et al (2021) Variational quantum algorithms. Nat Rev Phys 3(1):625–644
Cerezo M et al (2022) Challenges and opportunities in quantum machine learning. Nat Comput Sci 2(9):567–576
Chen L et al (2016) Report on post-quantum cryptography. US Department of Commerce, National Institute of Standards and Technology, Gaithersburg
Ciliberto C et al (2018) Quantum machine learning: a classical perspective. Proc Royal Soc A Math Phys Eng Sci 474(2209):20170551
Coenen C, Grunwald A (2017) Responsible research and innovation (RRI) in quantum technology. Ethics Inf Technol 19(4):277–294
Coenen C et al (2022) Quantum technologies and society: *towards a different spin*. NanoEthics 16(1):1–6
Collingridge D (1980) The social control of technology. Frances Pinter, London
Cong I et al (2019) Quantum convolutional neural networks. Nat Phys 15(12):1273–1278
Cortez N (2014) Regulating disruptive innovation. Berkeley Technol Law J 29:173
D'Alessandro D (2007) Introduction to quantum control and dynamics. Taylor & Francis, New York
Daley AJ et al (2022) Practical quantum advantage in quantum simulation. Nature 607(7920):667–676
de Silva N, Barbosa RS (2019) Contextuality and noncommutative geometry in quantum mechanics. Commun Math Phys 365(2):375–429
de Wolf R (2017) The potential impact of quantum computers on society. Ethics Inf Technol 19(4):271–276
Degen CL et al (2017) Quantum sensing. Rev Mod Phys 89(3):035002

Deutsch D (1985) Quantum theory, the church–Turing principle and the universal quantum computer. Proc Royal Soc London A Math Phys Sci 400(1818):97–117
Donoghue JF, Menezes G (2020) Quantum causality and the arrows of time and thermodynamics. Prog Part Nucl Phys 115:103812
Dowling JP, Milburn GJ (2003) Quantum technology: the second quantum revolution. Philos Trans R Soc London, Ser A 361(1809):1655–1674
Ekert AK (1991) Quantum cryptography based on Bell's theorem. Phys Rev Lett 67(6):661
Feynman RP (1982) Simulating physics with computers. Int J Theor Phys 21(6):467–488
Fisher E (2002) Precaution, precaution everywhere: developing a "common understanding" of the precautionary principle in the European Community. Maastricht J Eur Comp Law 9(1):7–28
Flöther F et al (2022) Exploring quantum computing use cases for life sciences. IBM Institute for Business Value, New York
Fromer JC (2014) An information theory of copyright law. Emory Law J 64:71
Fry ES, Thompson RC (1976) Experimental test of local hidden-variable theories. Phys Rev Lett 37:465–468
Ge Y et al (2024) Quantum circuit synthesis and compilation optimization: Overview and prospects. arXiv:2304.03277
Georgescu IM et al (2014) Quantum simulation. Rev Mod Phys 86(1):153
Giovannetti V et al (2011) Advances in quantum metrology. Nat Photonics 5(4):222–229
Gisin N, Thew R (2007) Quantum communication. Nat Photonics 1(3):165–171
Gottesman D (1998) Theory of fault-tolerant quantum computation. Phys Rev A 57(1):127–137
Gottesman D (2010) An introduction to quantum error correction and fault-tolerant quantum computation. Quantum information science and its contributions to mathematics. Proc Symposia Appl Math 63:13–58
Graham J (2004) The perils of the precautionary principle: lessons from the American and European experience. Heritage Foundation, Washington, D.C
Grover LK (1996) A fast quantum mechanical algorithm for database search. In: *Proceedings of the twenty-eighth annual ACM symposium on Theory of computing*. ACM
Guo Y, Gao X (2024) Quantum Simulation of Open Quantum Dynamics via Non-Markovian Quantum State Diffusion. arXiv:2404.10655
Harrigan N, Spekkens RW (2010) Einstein, incompleteness, and the epistemic view of quantum states. Found Phys 40(2):125–157
Harris ED et al (2016) Governance of dual-use technologies: theory and practice. American Academy of Arts and Sciences, Cambridge
Hendrycks D (2024) Introduction to AI safety, ethics and society. Taylor & Francis, Milton-Park
Hoofnagle CJ, Garfinkel S (2021) Law and policy for the quantum age. Cambridge University Press, Cambridge
Illiano J et al (2022) Quantum internet protocol stack: a comprehensive survey. Comput Netw 213:109092
Jacak L, Hawrylak P, Wojs A (2013) Quantum Dots. Springer, Berlin
Johnson WG (2018) Governance tools for the second quantum revolution. Jurimetrics 59(4):487
Johnston EW (2015) Governance in the information era: theory and practice of policy informatics. Routledge, New York
Joseph D et al (2022) Transitioning organizations to post-quantum cryptography. Nature 605(7909):237–243
Jumper J et al (2021) Highly accurate protein structure prediction with AlphaFold. Nature 596(7873):583–589
Kimble HJ (2008) The quantum internet. Nature 453(7198):1023–1030
Kitaev AY (1997) Quantum computations: algorithms and error correction. Russ Math Surv 52(6):1191
Kochen S, Specker E (1967) The problem of hidden variables in quantum mechanics. Indiana Univ Math J 17(1):59–87

Kop M (2021a) Establishing a legal-ethical framework for quantum technology. Yale Law School, Yale Journal of Law & Technology (YJoLT), The Record
Kop M (2021b) Ethics in the quantum age. Phys World 34(12):31
Kop M (2021c) Quantum computing and intellectual property law. Berk Technol Law J 35(3)
Kop M et al (2023) Towards responsible quantum technology. Harvard Berkman Klein Center for Internet & Society Research Publication Series, Cambridge
Kop M et al (2024a) Ten principles for responsible quantum innovation. Quantum Sci Technol 9(3):035013
Kop M et al (2024b) How quantum technologies may be integrated into healthcare, what regulators should consider. Stanford Law School, Stanford
Koziel B et al (2016) Post-quantum cryptography on FPGA based on isogenies on elliptic curves. IEEE Trans Circuits Systems I: Regular Papers 64(1):86–99
Kumar M, Pattnaik P (2020) Post quantum cryptography (pqc)-an overview. In: 2020 IEEE high performance extreme computing conference (HPEC). IEEE, New York
Kunjwal R (2016) Contextuality beyond the Kochen-Specker theorem. arXiv:1612.07250 [quant-ph]
Larocca M et al (2022) Group-Invariant Quantum Machine Learning. arXiv:2205.02261 [quant-ph, stat]
Leifer MS, Spekkens R (2011) Towards a formulation of quantum theory as a causally neutral theory of Bayesian inference. Phys Rev A 88(5):052130
Lessig L (2000a) Code and other Laws of cyberspace. Basic Books, New York
Lessig L (2000b) Code is law. Harvard Magazine 1
Lo HK et al (2005) Decoy state quantum key distribution. Phys Rev Lett 94(23):230504
Maiman TH (1967) Laser applications. Phys Today 20(7):24–28
Manin Y (1980) Computable and Uncomputable. Sovetskoye Radio, Moscow
Marchant GE, Gutierrez CI (2022) Soft law 2.0: an agile and effective governance approach for artificial intelligence. Minn J Law Sci Technol 24:375
Marchant GE, Wallach W (2015) Coordinating technology governance. Iss Sci Technol 31(4)
Marchant GE et al (2024) Learning from emerging technology governance for guiding quantum technology. Rich J Law Tech 31:266
Marrero CO et al (2021) Entanglement-induced barren plateaus. PRX Quantum 2(4):040316
Maudlin T (1994) Quantum non-locality and relativity. Blackwell, Oxford
Meter RV (2014) Quantum networking. Wiley-ISTE, Hoboken
Molina A, Watrous J (2018) Revisiting the simulation of quantum Turing machines by quantum circuits. arXiv:1808.01701 [quant-ph]
Monroe C et al (2019) The US National Quantum Initiative: from act to action. Science 364(6439):440–442
Moses LB (2007) Recurring dilemmas: the law's race to keep up with technological change. Univ Illinois J Law Technol Policy 2007:239
Moses LB (2017) Regulating in the face of sociotechnical change. In: Brownsword R, Scotford E, Yeung K (eds) The Oxford handbook of law, regulation and technology. Oxford University Press, Oxford
Murray A (2013) Information technology law: the law and society. Oxford University Press, Oxford
Murray J et al (2019) Complexity theory and law: mapping an emergent jurisprudence. Routledge, London
Nejatollahi H et al (2019) Post-quantum lattice-based cryptography implementations: a survey. ACM Computing Surveys (CSUR) 51(6):1–41
Nguyen QT et al (2024) Theory for Equivariant quantum neural networks. PRX Quantum 5(2):020328
Nielsen MA, Chuang IL (2011) Quantum computation and quantum information: 10th anniversary edition. Cambridge University Press, New York
Niemeyer I, Dreicer M, Stein G (2020) Nuclear non-proliferation and arms control verification: innovative systems concepts. Springer, New York

Papadimitriou CH (1994) Computational complexity. Addison-Wesley, Boston
Perrier E (2021) Ethical Quantum Computing: A Roadmap. arXiv:2102.00759 [quant-ph]
Perrier E (2022) The quantum governance stack: models of governance for quantum information technologies. Digit Soc 1(3):22
Perrier E (2024) Quantum Geometric Machine Learning. arXiv:2409.04955
Pirandola S et al (2017) Fundamental limits of repeaterless quantum communications. Nat Commun 8(1):15043
Plesch M, Brukner Č (2011) Quantum-state preparation with universal gate decompositions. Phys Rev A 83(3):032302
Preskill J (2018) Quantum computing in the NISQ era and beyond. Quantum 2:79
Preskill J (2021) Quantum computing 40 years later. arXiv:2106.10522
Ragone M et al (2022) Representation Theory for Geometric Quantum Machine Learning. arXiv:2210.07980 [quant-ph]
Rand LE (2023) Schrodinger's technology is here and not: a socio-technical evaluation of quantum sensing implications for nuclear deterrence. University of Maryland, Maryland
Riebe M et al (2004) Deterministic quantum teleportation with atoms. Nature 429(6993):734–737
Riordan M, Hoddeson L, Herring C (1999) The invention of the transistor. Rev Mod Phys 71(2):S336
Rohde PP (2021) The quantum internet: the second quantum revolution. Cambridge University Press, Cambridge
Rothschild M, Stiglitz J (1978) Equilibrium in competitive insurance markets: an essay on the economics of imperfect information. In: Diamond P, Rothschild M (eds) Uncertainty in economics. Academic, New York
Sanchez-Palencia L (2018) Quantum simulation: from basic principles to applications. Comptes Rendus Physique 19(6):357–364
Scarani V et al (2004) Security of quantum key distribution with imperfect devices. Phys Rev Lett 92(5):057901
Schuld M, Petruccione F (2021) Machine learning with quantum computers. Springer, Cham
Schuld M et al (2015) An introduction to quantum machine learning. Contemp Phys 56(2):172–185
Shannon C (1948) A mathematical theory of communication. Bell Syst Tech J 27:379–423
Shor PW (1994) Algorithms for quantum computation: discrete logarithms and factoring. In: Proceedings 35th annual symposium on foundations of computer science. IEEE, New York
Shor PW (1997) Polynomial-time algorithms for prime factorization and discrete logarithms on a quantum computer. SIAM J Comput 26(5):1484–1509
Simon C (2017) Towards a global quantum network. Nat Photonics 11(11):678–680
Sipser M (2012) Introduction to the theory of computation. Cengage Learning, Boston
Ten Holter C et al (2021) Reading the road: challenges and opportunities on the path to responsible innovation in quantum computing. Tech Anal Strat Manag 35(7):844–856
Tóth G, Apellaniz I (2014) Quantum metrology from a quantum information science perspective. J Phys A Math Theor 47(42):424006
Townsend JS (2000) A modern approach to quantum mechanics. University Science Books, Cambridge
Verdon G et al (2018) A Universal Training Algorithm for Quantum Deep Learning. arXiv:1806.09729 [quant-ph]
Verdon G et al (2019a) A quantum algorithm to train neural networks using low-depth circuits. arXiv:1712.05304 [cond-mat, physics:quant-ph]
Verdon G et al (2019b) Learning to learn with quantum neural networks via classical neural networks. arXiv:1907.05415 [quant-ph]
Verdon G et al (2019c) Quantum Hamiltonian-Based Models and the Variational Quantum Thermalizer Algorithm. arXiv:1910.02071 [quant-ph]
Verdon G et al (2019d) Quantum Graph Neural Networks. arXiv:1909.12264 [quant-ph]
Vermaas PE (2017) The societal impact of the emerging quantum technologies: a renewed urgency to make quantum theory understandable. Ethics Inf Technol 19(4):214–246

Watrous J (2018) The theory of quantum information. Cambridge University Press, Cambridge
Wehner S et al (2018) Quantum internet: a vision for the road ahead. Science 362(6412)
Wesley S (2024) LinguaQuanta: towards a quantum Transpiler between OpenQASM and Quipper. In: Phillips I, Hafizur R (eds) International conference on reversible computation. Springer, Cham
Wiseman HM, Milburn GJ (2010) Quantum measurement and control. Cambridge University Press, Cambridge
Wootters WK, Zurek WH (1982) A single quantum cannot be cloned. Nature 299(5886):802–803

IP in Superposition: Patents, Trade Secrets, and Open Innovation in Quantum Information Technology

Gabriela Lenarczyk, Timo Minssen, and Mateo Aboy

Abstract This chapter analyzes the intellectual property (IP) strategies deployed in quantum information technologies (QIT), showing that firms operate in a "superposition" of approaches: selectively combining patents, trade secrets, and open innovation across different layers of the quantum stack. While patent filings have increased significantly, trade secrecy remains important due to the tacit, context-specific nature of key processes and the constraints of export-control regimes. At the same time, openness is a scientific and often strategic lever, enabling interoperability, cumulative research, and ecosystem formation through mechanisms such as open-source frameworks and cloud-access platforms which can lead to competitive advantage through network effects. Using a governance-stack heuristic that links legal instruments to specific technical layers—from hardware and control systems to software and interfaces—the chapter maps how exclusivity, confidentiality, and collaboration are configured in practice. This layered combination, involving the superposition and entanglement of IP and open innovation, shows that QIT competitive strategy depends not on choosing between proprietary and open models, but on calibrating their combination to fit technical, commercial, and policy objectives. The chapter reframes the prevailing debate in quantum innovation: rather than asking whether patents or secrecy are appropriate for quantum technologies, the key question becomes when, where, and in what form each instrument best serves both private incentives and public goals.

Keywords FRAND licensing for quantum technologies · Intellectual property · Know-how in Quantum R&D · Strategic collaboration · Open innovation · Technology policy

G. Lenarczyk (✉) · T. Minssen
Center for Advanced Studies in Bioscience Innovation Law (CeBIL), University of Copenhagen, Copenhagen, Denmark
e-mail: gale@jur.ku.dk

M. Aboy
Centre for Law, Medicine and Life Sciences (LML) and Centre for Intellectual Property and Information Law (CIPIL), University of Cambridge, Cambridge, UK
e-mail: ma608@cam.ac.uk

M. Aboy et al. (eds.), *Quantum Technology Governance I*, Perspectives in Law, Business and Innovation, https://doi.org/10.1007/978-981-95-8371-3_3

1 Introduction

As quantum science transitions from the realm of theoretical possibility to near-term commercial viability, its legal and strategic context sharpens. As Chap. 1 has underscored, quantum information technology (QIT) encompasses a suite of emerging innovations in quantum computing, quantum communication, and quantum sensing, each leveraging unique features of quantum mechanics such as superposition, entanglement, and non-locality to process information in classically unattainable ways.[1] Although these properties defy certain long-standing assumptions of classical ontology and rest on irreducibly probabilistic no-cloning foundations, the accumulating evidence shows that existing IP doctrine absorbs them with little friction.[2]

QIT are *sui generis* in many respects, blending fundamental physics with engineering in a manner that was thought to strain the conventional legal frameworks.[3] QIT harnesses quantum mechanical phenomena such as superposition and entanglement to achieve capabilities that are unattainable with classical systems, including exponentially speedups in computation[4] and unconditionally secure communication.[5] While these principles challenge classical assumptions about information and observability, they have not necessitated fundamental changes to existing IP frameworks. Patent, trade secret, and open innovation regimes have thus far accommodated quantum-specific features without requiring doctrinal overhaul.

Data and patent drafting practice indicate that, while the technology itself certainly is *sui generis*, the existing mix of patent, trade-secret and open-innovation tools proves accommodating enough. Since 2014, the United States Patent and Trademark Office (USPTO) and European Patent Office (EPO) have jointly granted more than 1200 quantum-computing patents, and annual grants exceed 400, yielding a 42% compound annual growth rate over 2014–2021.[6]

The probabilistic nature of quantum technology and the no-cloning theorem,[7] which forbids perfect copying of an unknown quantum state, has been raised as potentially threatening core doctrines of patent law: how can a patentee "enable" others to practice the invention, and how can infringement be proven, if inspecting or duplicating the protected state would collapse it?[8]

[1] Perrier et al. (2025).

[2] Aboy et al. (2022) and Kop et al. (2022).

[3] Perrier (2022), OECD (2025), Balarabe (2025) and Perrier et al. (2025).

[4] Brandão and Horodecki (2013) and Ekert and Renner (2014).

[5] Ekert (1991).

[6] Aboy et al. (2022). The study documents quantum computing patent growth showing a compound annual growth rate of 42% from 2014–2021, based on USPTO and EPO data using CPC classification codes. See also EPO (2023).

[7] Wootters and Zurek (1982).

[8] Consider the issue of infringement proof for quantum claims. To prevail, a patentee must still show that the defendant "puts the teaching of the patent into practice" for *every* claim element (Art

While concerns have been raised, in our view this is not insurmountable in practice. We argue the enablement requirement is met, for instance, by disclosing a repeatable state-preparation protocol[9] along with the technical details necessary to reproduce the invention. Depending on the nature of the invention, this may include the specification of materials, circuit architecture, device design, fabrication methods, or control algorithms. If a quantum processor can be sufficiently defined to allow its physical construction, then it can also be described in a patent. Similarly, if a quantum algorithm can be implemented on available quantum hardware, then it can be disclosed in executable or schematic form. Infringement, while not always directly observable due to quantum measurement constraints, can often be shown through indirect means such as statistical sampling, analysis of classical control files, or device-independent self-tests.[10] These approaches indicate that, although quantum technologies pose epistemic challenges, they do not preclude compliance with patent law's core requirements of disclosure, enablement, and enforceability.

Initially, however, companies defaulted to trade secrecy: prior to 2014, patenting activity in quantum technologies was essentially flat,[11] most firms relied on trade secrecy, keeping experimental results and process know-how outside the patent system. The landscape began to change in the mid-2010s, as the risk of exclusion by rivals' portfolios triggered a defensive rise in filings aimed at securing freedom to operate. Nonetheless, trade secrecy continues to play a pivotal role in safeguarding the tacit expertise[12] that underpins daily quantum R&D.

Bridging a fault-tolerant quantum processor online—or stabilizing a quantum-key-distribution link—demands tuning, materials handling and noise-mitigation routines that live in lab notebooks and muscle memory rather than in peer-reviewed

---

64 of the Convention on the Grant of European Patents (European Patent Convention, EPC) of 5 October 1973, as revised). But no EPO Board of Appeal, national court, or UPC rule has yet said *what* evidence suffices when the element is intrinsically non-classical - e.g., generation of a specified multi-qubit entangled state that collapses on direct measurement. See, generally, Rantala and Giardini (2024).

[9] Courts and patent offices accept a *state-preparation recipe* in lieu of the state itself. The disclosure requirement is therefore satisfied once the patent teaches a reproducible protocol, even though quantum mechanics forbids handing over a perfect copy. See, e.g., USPTO Patent Trial and Appeal Board, *Ex parte Yudong Cao*, Appeal No. 2022–005123 (6 Feb 2024) (accepting a pulse-schedule recipe under 35 U.S.C. § 112); EPC Guidelines F-III 3.1. (April 2025 edition, available at: https://www.epo.org/en/legal/guidelines-epc, accessed 22 July 2025).

[10] An often-cited example of such measurement-based verification is the tamper-indicating quantum seal: entangled photons reveal any intercept-resend attack with >99.99% confidence, converting measurement disturbance into proof of tampering. Williams et al. (2016).

[11] Aboy et al. (2022), p. 854.

[12] The terms *tacit knowledge*, *tacit know-how* and *embedded expertise* used throughout this Chapter draw on Michael Polanyi's classic distinction between knowledge that we can articulate and the "knowing that is in doing." Polanyi uses *tacit knowledge* to describe information that is understood or enacted without being readily verbalized or codified, typically appearing as skilled practice or expert intuition. See Polanyi (1966). Building on Polanyi, Harry Collins shows that much scientific and technical competence resides in forms of expertise that are inseparable from the local contexts of use, apprenticeship and experiment in which they are cultivated. See Collins (2010).

articles.[13] This reality tests the practical workings of the patent system's core disclosure bargain. European patent law requires that an invention be disclosed "in a manner sufficiently clear and complete for it to be carried out by a person skilled in the art",[14] yet in cutting-edge quantum fields, meeting this enablement (or "sufficiency of disclosure") requirement can be challenging. A patent on, say, a particular quantum error-correction method might describe the theoretical protocol, but reproducing the invention could require months of laboratory calibration or proprietary engineering methods not explicitly in the patent text. Indeed, it has been noted in the literature that the ontological ambiguities of quantum systems—e.g., the fact that qubit states are described probabilistically and cannot be directly observed without collapse—prompt fresh questions about classical disclosure assumptions.[15] That said, we argue that when inventions can be clearly specified—such as well-defined hardware designs, fabrication processes, or executable quantum algorithms—nothing in the physics prevents them from being fully disclosed in a manner that satisfies legal requirements; the challenge lies less in principle than in practice.

Because some of this knowledge is difficult to codify and even harder to reverse-engineer, the innovation calculus tilts toward secrecy. Trade secret protection demands no enabling detail, imposes no twenty-year sunset and, in a cloud-based delivery model, can be effectively shielded indefinitely from competitors. For quantum developers the regime is attractive: dilution refrigerators, ion-trap vacuum systems and cloud-access interfaces create natural barriers to inspection[16]; secrecy lasts for as long as the information is kept confidential, matching the long development horizon of fault-tolerant architectures; and the doctrine covers everything from negative experimental data to calibration curves that would not meet patentability thresholds.

The cost, however, is a contraction of the public domain.

Consider the fact that quantum science grew out of an academic culture steeped in Mertonian norms of openness,[17] and that its future—algorithms to benchmark, devices to inter-operate, standards to agree—still depends on cumulative enquiry. Motivated by a blend of objectives—including averting knowledge silos, securing freedom to operate, and cultivating platform network effects—the quantum community has begun to experiment with hybrid governance. IBM's Qiskit and Xanadu's PennyLane open-source high-level tool-chains while reserving

[13] See, e.g., Quantum Machines and Rigetti (2024) and Adkoli (2025).

[14] EPC, Art. 83.

[15] Aboy et al. (2022), p. 854.

[16] Consider the following: a superconducting processor sits at $\sim$10 mK inside a dilution refrigerator that costs $\approx$ US \$0.5–three million and cannot be opened without lengthy thermal cycling, so third parties seldom get physical sight of the chip or its microwave control hardware; Ion-trap devices are sealed in ultra-high-vacuum ($\approx 10^{-11}$ mbar) chambers where any attempt at inspection would break confinement and decohere the qubits; finally, most commercial quantum computers are offered exclusively as remote "black-box" cloud services; users run circuits through an API and never gain direct physical control of the underlying electronics.

[17] Merton (1942).

pulse-level controls as proprietary know-how; cloud programs operated by Amazon Web Service (AWS,) Google and European initiatives such as Quantum Inspire grant external researchers time on otherwise opaque hardware; pre-competitive foundries like the UK National Quantum Foundry pool clean-room capacity; and industry proposals for FRAND (Fair, Reasonable and Non-Discriminatory)-based patent pools on quantum error-correction seek to pre-empt licensing thickets. Chapter 1's governance-stack heuristic, which links legal instruments to distinct layers of the technical stack, provides a lens through which these experiments can be mapped: secrecy dominates at the physical and control layers, patents retain residual value at the interface layers, and open innovation and collaborative mechanisms flourish at the scientific and where ecosystem network effects are strongest.

Our analysis proceeds in four steps. Section 2 analyses the quantum-patent landscape and explains how European and U.S. practice has thus far absorbed quantum inventions without apparent doctrinal strain. Section 3 examines the persistent attraction of trade and state secrecy for classes of know-how such as fabrication recipes and calibration software and draws parallels with biotechnology and artificial-intelligence practice. Section 4 surveys the sector's open-innovation measures: open-source frameworks, cloud testbeds, shared foundries, FRAND patent pools and ISO/IEC (International Organization for Standardization/International Electrotechnical Commission) standardization. At the end, we conclude that no single instrument is decisive; rather, each firm assembles a bespoke *superposition* of patents, guarded know-how and selective openness aligned with its resources, business model and platform ambitions.

2 Quantum Technologies and Patent Law

Quantum innovation spans a remarkable spectrum from foundational physics and algorithm design to the engineering of scalable processors and cryogenic infrastructure. As such, it traverses conceptual terrains often regarded as legally sensitive: abstract mathematical formulations, physical phenomena, and experimental prototypes not yet fully realized in practice. One might therefore expect quantum technologies to test the limits of patent law's subject-matter boundaries or strain its disclosure and enablement doctrines. Yet, surprisingly, the opposite appears true. As with many other emerging technologies, the patent systems have proven adaptable so far, absorbing quantum inventions without doctrinal rupture and—at least thus far—without the need for a *sui generis* framework. This section traces the emerging patent landscape in QIT, situating recent empirical trends within the doctrinal architecture of contemporary patent law. In doing so, it offers an empirically grounded account of patent activity in the sector, paying particular attention to questions of subject-matter eligibility, strategic behavior, and disclosure quality, and laying the groundwork for a discussion of the relationship between patenting, trade secrecy, and openness in quantum research.

Under both the European Patent Convention (EPC) and U.S. patent law, certain abstract categories—such as mathematical methods, algorithms, and scientific theories—are excluded from protection unless they are tied to a concrete technical implementation or make a technical contribution.[18] On this view, a quantum algorithm understood purely as a mathematical construct (e.g., Shor's algorithm for factoring, or quantum error-correcting codes) is *prima facie* unpatentable. However, patent eligibility turns not on abstraction *per se*, but on whether the claimed subject matter produces a technical effect or is implemented in a way that solves a concrete technical problem.[19]

In practice, quantum inventions have cleared this threshold with increasing ease. Patent offices apply conventional eligibility doctrines: the European "technical character" test and the U.S. *Alice/Mayo* framework.[20] Quantum algorithm claims that are embedded in a physical implementation—such as their integration with a quantum processor or use in controlling a physical quantum system—are routinely held patentable, and indeed a number of patents on quantum algorithms and software have been granted.[21] Examples include claims directed to the operation of superconducting qubit arrays, quantum key distribution protocols, or machine learning architectures implemented on quantum circuits. The grant of such patents suggests that quantum information technologies do not so much strain the eligibility doctrines as they affirm their continuing relevance.

The empirical data corroborates this assessment. Between 2001 and 2021, a total of 1892 patents related to quantum computing were granted globally. Of these, 1224—or 64.7% —were granted in the three-year period from 2018 to 2021 alone. Analysis of granted claims reveals that the quantum patent landscape encompasses a diverse range of subject matter, generally falling into four broad clusters: physical

[18] EPC Art. 52(2)–(3); EPC Guidelines Part G-II, 3.3 (Mathematical methods) & 3.6 (Computer-implemented inventions) (2025); See also See *Alice Corp. Pty. Ltd. v. CLS Bank Int'l*, 573 U.S. 208, 217–18 (2014) (confirming that claims "directed to" an abstract idea—such as a mathematical algorithm implemented on a generic computer—are not patent-eligible under 35 U.S.C. § 101 unless they contain an "inventive concept" that transforms the idea into a patent-eligible application).

[19] EPO BoA T 641/00 *Comvik* (2002) (only claim features that contribute to a *further technical effect* count toward inventive step); EPC Guidelines G-II, 3.6 (2025) (requiring a technical solution to a technical problem).

[20] See EPO (2023); *Alice v. CLS* (2014); *Mayo Collaborative Servs. v. Prometheus Labs.*, 566 U.S. 66 (2012) (two-step test for abstract ideas and laws of nature).

[21] Aboy et al. (2022), p. 860.

realization and quantum hardware,[22] applied quantum algorithms and methods,[23] quantum error correction,[24] and application level quantum inventions.[25]

It has further been observed that the claim formats used in these patents closely mirror those found in classical computing and semiconductor domains.[26] While quantum systems do rest on non-classical principles, the operative quantum behavior *can* be conveyed through classical artefacts. Ontological discontinuity has not, thus far, translated into an epistemic barrier. In fact, the required disclosures—quantum circuit diagrams, Hamiltonians, calibration sequences—tend to *exceed* the minimal threshold of sufficiency.[27] This is in part because many quantum patents are filed by academic physicists or engineers with deep domain expertise, who bring a high degree of technical specificity to their drafting. Compared to patents in artificial intelligence and machine learning, which have often been criticized for vague, functional, or speculative disclosures, quantum filings tend to exhibit a markedly higher level of descriptive rigor. One of this chapter's key claims is that, despite the epistemic and ontological peculiarities of quantum systems, there is no structural incompatibility between quantum technologies and the core requirements of patent law—particularly disclosure and enablement. In practice, quantum inventions can be and are being disclosed with sufficient clarity and completeness to satisfy legal thresholds. When the subject matter is a quantum processor, enablement may involve specifying the materials, qubit architecture, control hardware, and fabrication processes needed to reproduce the device. If the invention lies in an applied quantum algorithm, disclosure typically includes executable circuit diagrams, gate sequences, or mathematical descriptions tied to specific computational tasks. Even phenomena governed by the no-cloning theorem or measurement-induced collapse do not preclude patentability, as long as the invention is defined by repeatable preparation procedures and verifiable classical parameters. Enforcement, while sometimes indirect due to the non-observability of quantum states, can still be achieved through statistical testing, audit of classical control code, or device-independent self-verification protocols.

This is not merely theoretical. A growing corpus of granted patents—including disclosures of Hamiltonians, quantum error-correction routines, and qubit calibration protocols—shows that quantum inventions, when properly specified, can be

---

[22] Superconducting qubit systems, ion trap architectures, quantum repeaters, and cryogenic control hardware. Aboy et al. (2022), pp. 864–865.

[23] Where the claim is directed not to the abstract algorithm, but to a method implemented using quantum logic gates or producing a concrete technical effect (e.g., a quantum machine learning classifier deployed in a photonic processor). Aboy et al. (2022), pp. 864–865.

[24] Patents covering stabilizer codes, surface codes, and other techniques for mitigating decoherence and fault propagation. Aboy et al. (2022), pp. 864–865.

[25] Covering methods for compiling or optimizing quantum circuits, quantum instruction sets, and intermediate representations used to bridge high-level programming languages and hardware layers. Aboy et al. (2022), pp. 864–865.

[26] Aboy et al. (2022), p. 869.

[27] Aboy et al. (2022), p. 869.

captured through classical representations that meet the legal standard. What matters is not the quantum nature of the invention *per se*, but the degree to which it has been stabilized, formalized, and codified in a way that supports reproducibility. In this respect, for the purposes of patent law quantum technologies differ less from classical ones than often assumed: where the technical maturity exists, legal enablement follows. The supposed ontological discontinuity between quantum and classical systems does not amount to a doctrinal rupture in IP law—it can be, and already is being, bridged through precise and technically rich disclosures.

This rise is both a function of maturing science and a reflection of a shift in industry behavior. As quantum technologies began attracting significant venture capital and public funding, patent portfolios became critical signaling instruments, particularly for new entrants. Startups such as Rigetti and D-Wave used early patent grants to secure funding and market visibility,[28] while incumbents like IBM and Google escalated filings to secure freedom to operate and guard against encroachment.

Empirical evidence also suggests a rapid turnover of quantum patents. One study found that roughly 50% of all quantum technology patent disclosures from the last 20 years are already in the public domain, either expired or abandoned.[29] Over 4500 granted quantum patents have lapsed, and nearly 15,000 published applications never resulted in grants, serving instead as public disclosures of technical knowledge.[30]

The temporality of patent rights is often raised in the quantum context as a potential argument against their appropriateness[31]: a patent's life is finite—typically 20 years from filling[32]—and front-loaded in time: applications are published 18 months after filing, long before most quantum technologies will be commercially mature. In classical, fast-paced industries (like smartphones), a 20-year term is often more than sufficient to exploit an invention. Quantum technology, by contrast, is still nascent and may require long development horizons. Many quantum inventions being patented today are proofs-of-concept or components for systems that might only achieve full utility a decade or two in the future (well within or just beyond patent terms).

Yet faced with competitive market dynamics, this concern has not slowed the rise of quantum patenting activity. On the contrary, the sector has witnessed a marked increase in filings and grants, as firms—particularly new entrants—deploy patents both as strategic signals and as instruments of exclusion or negotiation. On the one hand, this rapid infusion of quantum know-how into the public sphere is creating an

[28] This is not to say that patents are the only—or even primary—IP lever for early-stage firms. Start-ups in both software and hardware fields frequently rely on trade secrets because they are cheaper to maintain, can last indefinitely, and offer broader legal certainty than copyright (which protects only expression) or patents. See Levine and Sichelman (2019).

[29] Aboy et al. (2022), p. 870.

[30] Aboy et al. (2022), p. 871.

[31] See, e.g., Kop (2021).

[32] TRIPS Agreement, 1869 U.N.T.S. 299, 33 I.L.M. 1197 (1994), Art. 33.

emergent "quantum information commons",[33] on the other, it underscored that many early quantum patents have not translated into enduring proprietary advantages for their owners, either because the inventions proved premature or because firms strategically published via patents without pursuing full exclusivity. Rather than exposing a structural misfit between quantum innovation and the patent system, this dynamic suggests that temporal constraints have been offset—or indeed co-opted—by the strategic imperatives of a competitive and fast-evolving field.

3 Strategic Secrecy in Quantum R&D

In light of Sect. 2's account of a flourishing patent landscape, it is perhaps unsurprising that trade secrecy has risen to prominence as a complementary IP strategy in QIT. A trade secret be *any information*—experimental data, fabrication techniques, software source, even a compiled quantum circuit—that confers a competitive advantage by virtue of not being publicly known, so long as its holder takes reasonable steps to keep it confidential.[34] Unlike patents, trade secrets confer no formal monopoly against independent discovery or reverse-engineering, but they also have no fixed expiration date. The protection lasts as long as secrecy is maintained. In practice, this makes them particularly attractive in sectors where the full commercial value of innovation may not be realized with patent lifespans.

In the quantum sector, several factors make trade secrets, and, depending on the context, state secrecy, particularly attractive.

The first is epistemic: much of the most valuable quantum know-how is either processual or tacit, embedded in laboratory routines, calibration workflows, and tuning sequences that are difficult—if not impossible—to reduce to writing. These are often decisive in determining whether a quantum system performs stably or collapses under noise.

Second, many quantum systems are architecturally complex and physically inaccessible to outsiders. Cloud-based quantum computing platforms, such as those offered by IBM, IonQ, or Alibaba, provide users with a quantum programming interface but no direct visibility into the underlying hardware, calibration protocols, or firmware stack. This model of "black-box computing" makes reverse-engineering prohibitively difficult, particularly when system performance depends on an integrated stack of cryogenic control, error mitigation, and proprietary compilation pathways. Where physical access is limited, de facto secrecy is structurally embedded into the platform architecture.

[33] Aboy et al. (2022), p. 878.

[34] Directive (EU) 2016/943 of the European Parliament and the Council of 8 June 2016 on the protection of undisclosed know-how and business information (trade secrets) against their unlawful acquisition, use and disclosure, OJ L 157, 15.6.2016, p. 1–18, Art. 2. The Directive, implemented across Member States, provides a uniform definition of trade secrets and remedies against misappropriation.

Third, secrecy in QIT is often a strategic response to geopolitical risk and investor expectation. Quantum technologies are widely understood to have military and intelligence applications, from quantum radar and sensing to post-quantum cryptographic resilience. These dual-use characteristics have led many national governments to impose export controls, classification regimes, or institutional firewalls around certain classes of quantum R&D.[35] Secrecy, in such contexts, is mandated.

Finally, secrecy is also a function of the distinctive material and infrastructural demands of quantum innovation. Quantum devices must be physically constructed, housed, and operated within high-specification environments, such as cryogenic dilution refrigerators, superconducting circuits, and ultra-high vacuum chambers. These facilities are expensive to build, difficult to access, and often require custom materials and tightly integrated control systems. Moreover, the knowledge required to operate quantum hardware effectively is deeply tacit, residing within specialized engineering teams and iterative lab routines. As a result, even in the absence of formal legal protections, QIT is naturally resistant to observation, duplication, and reverse engineering. This stands in marked contrast to sectors like pharmaceuticals, where the cost of developing a new compound is also extremely high, but once the product is on the market, its composition can often be reverse engineered with relative ease. That asymmetry underpins the strong reliance on patent protection in the life sciences: exclusivity must be legally constructed because secrecy is difficult to maintain. In QIT, the inverse holds. The high barriers to inspection and replication enable firms to rely more heavily on trade secrecy, even for innovations that would otherwise be patentable. This structural opacity makes quantum technologies uniquely amenable to secrecy-based strategies, especially in early-stage development, where firms may prefer to defer disclosure or avoid it altogether.

Trade secret law, however, also embodies policy trade-offs. Most obviously, it slows the pace of cumulative science. Unlike patents, which are published and accessible and thus incentivize disclosure, trade secrets by definition keep information out of the public domain. Critical basic research in quantum science has historically been conducted in open academic settings with rapid publication and data sharing: a turn to corporate secrecy could slow the diffusion of scientific knowledge or even impede standards development. Trade secret protection, by design, channels inventive effort into "the suppression of information".[36] The bargain may be efficient when it merely prevents free-riding, but it also deprives peer scientists of the negative results, calibration data and laboratory routines that form the invisible infrastructure of cumulative inquiry. It exacerbates structural asymmetries.

[35] See, e.g., the U.S. Export Administration Regulations; Bureau of Industry and Security, "Implementation of Controls on Quantum Computing and Other Advanced Technologies", Interim Final Rule, 89 Fed. Reg. 56,437 (5 Sept 2024); Regulation (EU) 2021/821 of the European Parliament and of the Council of 20 May 2021 setting up a Union regime for the control of exports, brokering, technical assistance, transit and transfer of dual-use items (recast), PE/54/2020/REV/2. Both regimes restrict cross-border disclosure of calibration software or high-coherence devices absent a license. See in more detail Davis et al. (2025).

[36] Thomas (2014).

Maintaining secrecy requires not only technical sophistication but also organizational infrastructure: secure cleanrooms, access protocols, employee vetting, legal compliance. These are costs that scale with the size of the firm. Major players—AWS, Google or Alibaba—can amortize that overhead across billion-dollar research budgets, but a seed-stage spin-out cannot.[37] Start-ups are left on the wrong side of an information asymmetry: they must license black-box access to hardware they cannot inspect, while simultaneously courting investors who demand IP collateral they cannot disclose. The result is a self-reinforcing cycle of market concentration, chilling the contestability delivered by open science in the first quantum revolution.[38]

Opacity can hinder interoperability and standards formation. Many performance metrics in quantum computing—gate fidelity, decoherence time, qubit connectivity—are not easily independently verifiable without access to raw data and protocols. When firms claim technical superiority based on proprietary benchmarks, it becomes difficult to establish shared criteria for comparison. This complicates procurement decisions, academic research partnerships, and regulatory oversight. Hidden methods may also frustrate formal verification, certification, or export control review, particularly in sensitive cross-border collaborations.

These policy tensions are not left unaddressed in quantum innovation. Rather, they are met with a parallel set of strategic instruments which achieve collaboration and foster openness, sometimes within strategic limits that focus on certain coalitions or regions. This multi-modal configuration reflects the architecture of quantum systems themselves: stacked, interdependent, and sensitive to context. The following section turns to this architecture directly, examining how collaborative mechanisms are being deployed across distinct technical layers of the quantum stack.

4 Collaborative Mechanisms Across the Governance Stack

Open innovation, in Chesbrough's seminal definition, is the purposeful orchestration of knowledge flows across firm boundaries so that both outside ideas and outside paths-to-market accelerate technology development.[39] Once regarded as radical, the model is now a compelling paradigm in sectors as diverse as automotive (e.g.,

[37] On top of firm-size asymmetries, recent policy studies warn of emerging *geographical* "quantum divide." Building and operating quantum computers demands specialized hardware, cryogenics and skills that few countries can marshal. With the exception of Singapore and India, no G-77 economy currently possesses its own quantum-computing system, which could limit the socio-economic gains these technologies might deliver and heighten digital-security exposure in the Global South. See AWO (2024), pp. 15–17.

[38] Aspect (2024), pp. 7–14.

[39] Chesbrough (2003) and Chesbrough and Bogers (2014).

the BMW–Toyota Z4/Supra co-development)[40] and biotechnology.[41] The EU is notably championing it in its policy discourse,[42] developing framework programs that explicitly promote knowledge sharing, standardization efforts, and joint development of foundational quantum infrastructure.[43]

In the context of QIT, despite (or in parallel to) the momentum behind secrecy, open innovation manifests in multiple ways. We see it in public-private research consortia (a hallmark of the EU's Quantum Flagship program) where academic institutions and companies pool expertise and share interim findings, each benefiting from the collective push forward. We see it in the proliferation of open-source quantum software and hardware standards. For example, IBM famously open-sourced its Qiskit quantum programming framework and provided cloud-based access to real quantum processors for developers worldwide. This strategy catalyzed a global community of over 450,000 users and 1700 publications built on IBM's platform.[44]

IBM's example shows how openness at the interface layer can be sustained precisely because exclusivity is preserved deeper in the stack.[45] Put differently, open innovation does not imply the absence of IP rights. Rather, it reconfigures their use. Patents in an open innovation model may be used more selectively: for instance, to secure a firm's defensive position or enable cross-licensing, rather than to block broad areas of research. Trade secrets may still protect truly core proprietary processes, but firms might willingly share other insights in open forums to set industry standards or attract partners.[46] Patent pledges—voluntary public commitment made by a patent holder to refrain from exercising some or all its rights in one or more patents—embody this same logic, signaling openness to collaboration while preserving leverage over indispensable assets.[47] The growing popularity of the instrument in other high-technology areas[48] suggests they could, in due course, serve a

[40] Bortolini (2023).

[41] Fujiwara (2015) and Kunz (2020).

[42] European Commission (2015).

[43] See, e.g., the European Quantum Industry Consortium (EURO-QIC), available at: https://www.euroquic.org. Accessed 22 July 2025.

[44] Data accurate as of 9 January 2023. See IBM (2023).

[45] Although Qiskit remains fully open-source, IBM ring-fences the layers below it. Direct pulse-level control of the company's superconducting qubits, once available to a handful of advanced users—was removed from the Qiskit SDK in February 2025 (see the old version here: https://quantum.cloud.ibm.com/docs/en/api/qiskit/0.24/pulse. Accessed 22 July 2025). The detailed calibration parameters that keep those devices within specification are never exposed. At the same time, the firm is steadily expending a patent portfolio on context-aware noise-correction and other low-level control techniques, such as its April 2025 US filing on "contextually calibrating quantum hardware by minimizing contextual cost functions" (Rubio-Licht, 2025).

[46] Bogers et al. (2018), p. 10.

[47] Lenarczyk et al. (2024) and Contreras (2015).

[48] Lenarczyk et al. (2024) and Contreras (2015).

similar gap-filling role in QIT: an option worth keeping in view as this governance stack continues to evolve.

This section examines how a layered open innovation ecosystem, structured through private ordering, i.e., the contractual and consortial rule-systems that private actors devise to supplement public law,[49] has begun to complement and counterbalance the formal IP regime's tilt toward proprietary secrecy.

Five key open innovation mechanisms, spanning from software to hardware to intellectual property governance, illustrate a countervailing trend against quantum knowledge enclosure. These mechanisms—(1) open-source development kits, (2) cloud-based testbeds, (3) pre-competitive fabrication hubs, (4) FRAND-oriented patent pools, and (5) standards collaborations—are analyzed below in turn, situated in the context of European IP governance and contemporary quantum physics developments. The *layered* approach aligns with Chap. 1's idea that effective QIT governance will be multi-tiered: technical and legal measures reinforcing each other at different levels.

Before turning to the five mechanisms, it is worth flagging a background trend: intensifying geopolitical competition is beginning to shape what "openness" can realistically mean for quantum R&D. Tightening export-control schedules and security-cleared consortia risk producing a "tragedy of the anticommons," in which fragmented or gated rights slow collective progress.[50] Consequently, *openness* increasingly bifurcates into two concentric rings: inner club-based openness among trusted jurisdictions that share devices and data under reciprocal licenses, and an outer, standards-based global openness where interface specifications and permissively licensed code remain accessible to all. The latter aspires to a truly global commons, where interface standards and permissive OSS licenses invite worldwide uptake, irrespective of geopolitical blocs.

The matrix in Table 1 distils the core insight of this section: openness in QIT is layer-specific and contractually choreographed. The subsections that follow (§4.1–§4.4) unpack each mechanism in turn, showing how their legal design choices reinforce both competitive advantage and ecosystem coherence.

[49] Private ordering in legal theory generally refers to the self-created systems of rules or arrangements by which private actors govern their own relationships, as distinct from rules imposed by public law or the state. In other words, individuals and organizations create and enforce their own governance arrangements—for example, through contracts, corporate bylaws, or industry norms—rather than relying solely on statutes or public regulation. See Contreras (2017) on private ordering in the context of standards-setting and Dusollier (2007) on open licensing schemes' reliance on private ordering.

[50] Heller (1998).

Table 1 Open innovation in QIT

Instrument	Layer (stack)	Example	Governance features
Open-source SDK (Qiskit, PennyLane)	Complier/ application	Qiskit (IBM) (As of 8 May 2025, the Qiskit Python package recorded 519,646 downloads in the preceding month, according to PyPI statistics. See https://pypistats.org/packages/Qiskit? Accessed 22 July 2025), PennyLane (Xanadu)	Permissive license (Apache 2.0), includes royalty-free patent grants Contributor-license agreements (CLAs) ensure inbound rights; out-bound licenses allow proprietary add-ons while obliging preservation of notices Open APIs become *de-facto* circuit/ pulse standards, yet hide lower-level calibration IP
Cloud test-beds with grant programs	Classical interface/ cloud access layer	IBM quantum experience & academic "open" tier, Amazon Braket research credits, Microsoft azure quantum grants	Click-wrap terms bar hacking, reverse-engineering and export-controlled experiments; providers may suspend accounts Granular metering (shots, queue priority) ("Metering" refers to how usage of quantum services is measured and controlled. For example, Amazon Braket charges users per task and per "shot" (quantum circuit execution) and IBM offers a certain number of executions for free without queueing, while premium users or hub members get prioritized access.)
Shared fabrication hubs and open hardware	Hardware/ fabrication	Qu-pilot (EU chips JU)	Framework partnership agreements allocate EU funding, require cost-sharing and open access slots Background IP stays with contributors; foreground process know-how shared royalty-free within the consortium End-use screening and NDAs satisfy EU dual-use controls
Patent pools and standards	All layers	China quantum patent Alliance (CQPA)	First dedicated quantum-computing patent pool (2023), aggregating prospective SEPs in seven domains (incl. QEC) Specific licensing terms not yet public

4.1 Open-Source Software Development Kits

The first layer of the stack comprises a growing array of open-source software development kits (SDKs) and algorithms. Leading frameworks such as IBM's Qiskit[51] and Xanadu's PennyLane[52] are both released under the permissive open-source Apache 2.0 license,[53] openly available to anyone.[54] These SDKs allow researchers and developers worldwide to write quantum programs, simulate quantum circuits, and even run code on actual quantum processors. Here, the trade-secret paradigm is inverted at the software layer, which has strategic and governance significance. Open code seeds a global developer community and a common knowledge base, aligning the community on common interfaces and representations. In turn, the data structures and APIs (Application Programming Interfaces) embedded in these toolkits—Qiskit's formats for quantum circuits and PennyLane's integration of quantum machine learning libraries—can become as *de facto* standards.[55] What is more, by providing a common open infrastructure for writing quantum programs, such SDKs dramatically lower barriers to entry and accelerate knowledge diffusion in the field.

Licensing choices play an important role in the SDKs success. The Apache 2.0. license used by Qiskit allows proprietary and open integration alike, requiring only preservation of copyright notices and otherwise imposing minimal restrictions. It also includes an express patent grant from contributors, meaning anyone who contributes code also grants users a royalty-free license to any patent claims that would be infringed by using that contribution.[56] Thus, commercial firms can incorporate the open-source quantum SDK into their workflows or products without risking IP conflicts, and academic developers can build upon it knowing their work will remain openly available and protected.

Contributor models and governance structures accompany these licenses. Major open-source quantum projects typically require contributors to sign Contributor License Agreements (CLAs) or similar agreements, formalizing the contributor's acceptance of the license terms and the grant of rights to their contributions. For instance, IBM's CLA for Qiskit explicitly asks contributors (including corporate

---

[51] IBM, Qiskit, available at: https://www.ibm.com/quantum/Qiskit. Accessed 22 July 2025.

[52] XANADU, PennyLane, https://www.xanadu.ai/products/pennylane/. Accessed 22 July 2025.

[53] Qskit license available at: https://github.com/Qiskit/qiskit-tutorials/blob/master/LICENSE. Accessed 22 July 2025.

[54] See also Quantum Open Source Foundation, "Awesome Quantum Software," GitHub repository, available at: https://github.com/qosf/awesome-quantum-software. Accessed 22 July 2025. The curated list currently indexes more than 350 open-source quantum-software projects across 18 functional categories - from full-stack SDKs and simulators to compilers, control libraries and post-quantum cryptography.

[55] Similarly to OpenQASM 2's quantum assembly language (developed in Qiskit) having influenced cross-platform instruction standards. See Cross et al. (2022).

[56] Apache 2.0 Qiskit, para 3.

contributors) to grant IBM and downstream users a license to both the copyright and any patents covering their contributed code.[57]

As observed in other Information and Communication Technology (ICT) domains, an open-source implementation promotes wide deployment of a standard, interoperability, and avoids lock-in effects.[58] In the quantum context, having multiple hardware vendors and research groups coalesce around common SDKs means programs written for one system can often be run on another with minimal changes.

4.2 Cloud Testbeds with Grant Programs

Connecting software to physical hardware is the cloud testbed layer. Because quantum processors are expensive, scarce, and require specialized environments, direct hardware access is limited. In response, companies like IBM, Amazon, and Google have made their quantum processors available via cloud services, often with special access programs for academia and public research. IBM Quantum Experience, launched in 2016, was the first public quantum cloud: it enabled anyone to run algorithms on a 5-qubit superconducting device over the internet.[59] Since then, IBM has grown a network of cloud-accessible quantum processors, joined by others (e.g., Amazon Braket providing access to multiple companies' quantum chips,[60] Microsoft Azure Quantum[61] or the European Quantum Inspire platform).[62]

This open-access hardware model has dramatically lowered entry barriers. By 2018 IBM reported 80,000 users had run over three million experiments on its cloud quantum machines and by 2020 the free IBM Quantum program had a community of over 200,000 registered users who collectively executed *millions* of experiments and published hundreds of papers.[63]

Open hardware strategies democratize access to an otherwise tightly controlled resource, addressing equity and dissemination goals.[64]

These programs frequently offer free tiers or special academic programs (e.g., the U.S. Oak Ridge National Lab's Quantum Computing User Program.[65] This

---

[57] IBM's Software Grant and Corporate Contributor License Agreement, available at: https://docs.quantum.ibm.com/open-source/qiskit-corporate-cla.pdf. Accessed 22 July 2025.

[58] Gamalielsson et al. (2024).

[59] Quantum Zeitgeist (2023).

[60] Amazon Web Services, *Amazon Braket*, available at: https://aws.amazon.com/braket, Accessed 22 July 2025.

[61] Microsoft, https://azure.microsoft.com/en-us/solutions/quantum-computing. Accessed 22 July 2025.

[62] Quantum Inspire, https://www.quantum-inspire.com. Accessed 22 July 2025.

[63] Quantum Zeitgeist (2024).

[64] See, generally, Powell (2012). In the quantum context, see Shammah et al. (2023).

[65] Oak Ridge National Laboratory, QCUP Access, available at: https://docs.olcf.ornl.gov/quantum/quantum_access.html. Accessed 22 July 2025. See also AWS Bracket's AWS Cloud Credit for Research program or Microsoft's Azure Quantum Credits program.

reflects a pre-competitive cost-sharing philosophy: companies and governments share the high upfront costs of quantum machines so that the whole community can learn and innovate, creating a rising tide that will eventually lift all boats. From the perspective of IP, while users run algorithms openly, the hardware's design and operation often remain proprietary—the cloud APIs expose a controlled interface (gates, circuits) but not the trade-secret details of calibration or noise mitigation behind the scenes. They are a key part of the QIT governance stack because they serve as a quasi-regulatory mechanism: by setting terms of use and requiring users to abide by certain policies (for example, no hacking the system or export-controlled experiments),[66] cloud providers fill a governance role in real time, even as formal regulations for quantum computing are still nascent.

4.3 Shared Fabrication Hubs and Open Hardware

At the hardware layer, QIT faces resource and knowledge barriers: fabricating quantum devices (qubits, quantum sensors, etc.) requires state-of-the-art clean-rooms, exotic materials, and deep expertise. To avoid duplicating these efforts in silos, the quantum community has begun establishing shared fabrication hubs and open hardware initiatives. These can be thought of as the quantum equivalent of collaborative foundries or multi-project wafer services in classical semiconductor research.[67]

For example, the U.S. has launched academic and government-supported foundries (the UCSB Quantum Foundry,[68] the LPS Qubit Collaboratory,[69] the MonArk Quantum Foundry)[70] aimed at providing researchers and startups access to cutting-edge fabrication for superconducting, photonic, or other qubit technologies. Europe is following suit: the Qu-Pilot program, launched in 2024 under the EU Chips Joint Undertaking, will finance two cross-border pilot lines, one focused on high-stability superconducting/photonic chips, and another on trapped-ion devices.[71] Each line will be covered by a multi-year Framework Partnership Agreement. EU funds cover tool upgrades and baseline process qualification, while participating Small and Medium-Sized Enterprises (SMEs), start-ups and universities buy "wafer tickets" at marginal run cost, ensuring access for actors that could never afford a full clean-room stack.[72]

---

[66] See, e.g., IBM Quantum End User Agreement, art. 9(b) and (h), available at: https://quantum.ibm.com/terms. Accessed 22 July 2025.

[67] See, e.g., Wu and Lin (2005).

[68] UCSB Quantum Foundry, https://quantumfoundry.ucsb.edu. Accessed 22 July 2025.

[69] LPS Qubit Collaboratory, https://www.qubitcollaboratory.org. Accessed 22 July 2025.

[70] MonArk Quantum Foundry, https://www.monarkfoundry.org. Accessed 22 July 2025.

[71] Rantala and Giardini (2024).

[72] Qu-Pilot, https://qu-pilot.eu/open-call/. Accessed 22 July 2025.

These open fabrication hubs pool the high fixed costs of quantum device R&D and allow multiple stakeholders to benefit from advanced infrastructure that no single startup or university lab could afford alone. They operate on a cost-sharing model that lowers entry barriers while preserving strategic IP: background IP remains with each contributing organization; foreground process improvements generated on shared runs are licensed royalty-free within the consortium and may be offered to external users on fair reasonable terms. Horizon-Europe open-science guidance encourages deposit of process data and reference designs, permitting an embargo where necessary to protect IP, reinforcing the public knowledge base without immediate loss of competitive edge.[73] Finally, sensitive steps—such as sub-10 mK cryogenics or ion-trap electrode machining—are vetted under EU Dual-Use Regulation, with end-use screening and NDAs protecting export-controlled know-how.[74]

4.4 Patent Pools and Standards

At the top of the governance stack (and cutting across all technical layers) sit collaborative IP arrangements: patent pools and standards-setting organizations (SSOs), whose members pledge to license essential technology on FRAND terms. As quantum technologies mature and companies are amassing patent portfolios, there is a concern that a patent thicket or exclusive control of fundamental quantum techniques could slow down the field.[75] One proposed solution, drawing from other industries, is the formation of quantum patent pools. Patent pools are consortia where multiple patent holders agree to cross-license or bundle their patents, typically to provide easier access for third parties on standard terms. In March 2023 Baidu and the Beijing Academy of Quantum Information Sciences launched the China Quantum Patent Alliance (CQPA) and, with it, the country's first quantum-computing patent pool, open to new members and already aggregating several dozen patents. The pool explicitly targets seven strategic areas—including quantum error correction—and operates under a dedicated Standards & IP working group that will position any future standard-essential patents for FRAND licensing.[76]

---

[73] Horizon-Europe Model Grant Agreement, available at: https://ec.europa.eu/info/funding-tenders/opportunities/docs/2021-2027/horizon/agr-contr/unit-mga_he_en.pdf; REA Open Science Q&A, available at: https://rea.ec.europa.eu/open-science_en. Accessed 22 July 2025.

[74] All Horizon Europe and Chips JU pilot-line projects must implement an Internal Compliance Programme (ICP) for export controls. See Commission Recommendation (EU) 2021/1700 of 15 September 2021 on internal compliance programmes for controls of research involving dual-use items under Regulation (EU) 2021/821 of the European Parliament and of the Council setting up a Union regime for the control of exports, brokering, technical assistance, transit and transfer of dual-use items, OJ L 338, 23.9.2021, p. 1–52.

[75] Kop et al. (2022).

[76] Unitalen (2023).

Quantum error correction (QEC) is widely acknowledged as a linchpin for scalable quantum computing: numerous groups are inventing codes and control techniques to detect and fix qubit errors. This has led to a flurry of patent filings on QEC methods, from topological surface codes to ingenious error mitigation algorithms.[77] Scattered ownership of these filings risks impeding interoperability or making it prohibitively expensive for any entrant to build a fault-tolerant processor. A QEC-focused patent pool—of the kind CQPA is already curating—would pre-empt that danger by gathering the key patents and licensing them as a single package on FRAND terms. Contributors receive royalties and reciprocal access to the rest of the pool, extending the same non-discriminatory offer to outsiders. The model mirrors the wireless 4G and MPEG pools in which no single company can veto market entry by withholding essential IP.[78]

The risk is that a thicket of scattered QEC patents could impede interoperability or make it prohibitively expensive for any new entrant to build a fault-tolerant quantum computer.[79] The patent pool would aim to pre-empt this problem by gathering key QEC patents and licensing them as a package under FRAND terms. In practical terms, companies contributing their patents to the pool agree to license them to *all* implementers (including competitors) for a fair royalty and likewise get access to the others' patents: a form of cross-licensing that also extends to outsiders on equal terms. This follows the approach long used in industries like telecommunications, where no one company controls the standard's essential IP.[80]

Should a dominant QEC scheme be adopted as an industry standard, EU law would likely treat those patents as standard-essential, triggering obligations to license on FRAND terms under ETSI (European Telecommunications Standards Institute)/ISO rules. By voluntarily pooling patents now, the quantum industry is essentially self-imposing a pro-competitive regime that regulators encourage. Europe is already preparing the ground: the Commission's 2020 Action Plan on Intellectual Property urges rapid, voluntary patent pooling in high-tech fields to avoid "winner-takes-all" outcomes, while the Quantum Flagship's 2024 IP guidelines recommend pooling and FRAND as default tools for quantum standard.[81]

Pooling also amplifies knowledge dissemination: when patents are pooled and published, it actually reinforces the public domain of technical knowledge.[82] Patent disclosures teach the community about new QEC techniques, contributing to an emerging "quantum information commons" of ideas, while the pool ensures those ideas remain accessible for use.[83] Without a pool, companies might be inclined to

[77] Rubio-Licht (2025).

[78] See, e.g., Baron and Pohlmann (2015) and Lerner and Tirole (2004).

[79] Dominant portfolios can chill follow-on research and SME commercialization because "the cost of accessing those patents, through either royalties or legal battles, may simply be too high for small firms to sustain." See Gallini and Hollis (2019).

[80] Lemley and Shapiro (2007), p. 1148.

[81] European Commission (2020), p. 5; Rantala and Giardini (2024), pp. 39–40.

[82] Aboy et al. (2022), p. 854.

[83] Aboy et al. (2022).

keep their QEC breakthroughs as internal know-how (since disclosing them via patent could enable competitors). But the pool creates a middle ground: patent and share the innovation for mutual benefit, rather than hide it. A patent pool uses the patent system's disclosure function and a contractual sharing arrangement to balance the incentive to invent (each contributor still gets a slice of license revenue) with the need to disseminate critical technology widely. If successful, it could set a precedent for other quantum subfields (e.g., quantum cryptography or sensing) to form similar collaborative IP platforms.

A recurring policy question, however, is who may join. More precisely, whether the pool should limit participation (or voting rights) to entities from jurisdictions that share common export-control, security-review, and rule-of-law standards.

Finally, standards-setting organizations (SSOs) and working groups are playing a vital role in aligning the quantum industry toward openness and interoperability. Bodies such as the ISO/IEC Joint Technical Committee on Quantum Technologies and the European CEN-CENELEC JTC 22 on Quantum Technologies are convening experts from academia, industry, and government to develop common standards for quantum computing interfaces, data formats, terminology, and protocols.[84] Standards development is intrinsically open innovation: participants must share enough detail about their approaches to build consensus. A contemporary illustration is OpenQASM, the *de facto* assembly language adopted by hardware and software vendors alike. The EU's Quantum Flagship roadmap emphasizes that early standards "prevent vendor lock-in and encourage a competitive supply base"[85]; they also dovetail neatly with patent pools, because pooled patents can be designated as SEPs and automatically offered on FRAND conditions.

Standardization initiatives in quantum technology serve as an upper-layer framework tying together the open innovation ecosystem: they build on open-source software (which often gets adopted into standards), rely on pooled IP (with FRAND commitments), and incorporate broad input (through consortia and working groups).

4.5 *Strategic Coordination Across Layers: The Architecture of Quantum Openness*

Taken together, these five mechanisms constitute the privately-ordered, multi-layer open-innovation ecosystem introduced at the start of this section: an ecosystem built on contractual and consortial rule-systems that temper quantum R&D's natural drift toward trade-secret opacity. Each mechanism targets a different chokepoint in the innovation pipeline: open-source SDKs inject transparency and sharing at the software and algorithm level; cloud testbeds widen access to otherwise secluded

[84] CENELEC, https://www.cencenelec.eu/areas-of-work/cen-cenelec-topics/quantum-technologies/. Accessed 22 July 2025.

[85] Rantala and Giardini (2024), p. 21.

hardware; shared foundries and hubs spread know-how in building the physical backbone; patent pools unclog the intellectual property space; and standards ensure the entire ecosystem speaks the same language. This multi-pronged approach reflects what innovation scholars term “innovation policy pluralism”: a recognition that a mix of collaborative and competitive strategies yield the best outcome in nascent high-tech fields.[86]

5 Patterns, Incentives, and the Logic of Disclosure

Empirically, the intellectual property landscape in quantum information technology (QIT) is entirely continuous with broader patterns documented in the last decade. Innovators are increasingly relying on trade secrets to protect early-stage, high-stakes R&D, especially when products are physically inaccessible and difficult to dissect.[87] Classical innovation theory anticipated exactly this configuration. Where imitation costs are high, capital outlays lumpy and commercial lead-times compressed, rational firms bank on perpetual confidentiality.[88] Disclosure typically follows later, when driven by the demands of IP defense and cross-licensing, interoperability, funding, or strategic signaling.

QIT follows this logic. Across the industry, we observe a layered IP architecture that reflects both the integration complexity of quantum systems and the epistemic opacity of their operation. Trade secrecy and patenting have both proven useful: the former protects integration-sensitive and hard-to-reverse-engineer processes, while the latter facilitates investment, interoperability, and strategic positioning. In some cases, national-security classifications or government contracting obligations impose a fourth layer: the state secret. At the same time, the discipline's academic roots, from Dirac's Cambridge lectures to the open-access pre-print culture of arXiv, have instilled disclosure norms that offset proprietary instincts. Each instrument of private ordering described in this Chapter channels the long-standing “reveal and collaborate” culture into IP architectures—patent pools, FRAND licensing—that law can readily accommodate.

Firms rarely innovate in isolation. They often need collaborators, adopters, and standards. Secrecy does not generate ecosystems. As a results QIT developers increasingly engage in selective openness: withholding sensitive know-how while patenting key inventions to pre-empt rivals' broad filings and attract investment.[89] IBM exemplifies this approach. While it guards key aspects of the design of its

---

[86] Hemel and Ouellette (2019); On the open architecture of the Internet, see Zittrain (2006).

[87] The 2012 Community Innovation Survey found that 52% of product- or process-innovating firms relied on trade secrecy, while only 32% deployed patents. See Wajsman and Garcia-Valero (2017), Table 4. Sectoral regression shows the ratio widening to two-to-one for process and service innovations—exactly the loci in which quantum computing today is most active.

[88] Anton and Yao (2004) and Levin et al. (1987).

[89] Aboy et al. (2022).

quantum processors through secrecy, it patents extensively and provides open access to its quantum cloud platform and developer tools.[90] The intended objective of this is strategy is to catalyze external innovation on IBM's stack, ultimately reinforcing the company's market position and leadership in the field.

6 Conclusion

Quantum information technologies do not seem to require *sui generis* IP regimes. Instead, existing legal instruments and frameworks have proven sufficiently adaptable when applied with attention to the distinctive features of the field. As this chapter has shown, firms engage in a "superposition" of IP strategies that vary depending on their position within the quantum stack, their stage of development, funding environment, and business model. A startup seeking venture capital may emphasize patent filings to attract investors, while a large, well-resourced firm may rely more heavily on trade secrecy and controlled openness to protect core capabilities and shape standards.

The governance-stack heuristic offers a useful framework for understanding how different legal tools align with specific technical layers: from hardware and control systems to software and user interfaces. Rather than posing a binary between proprietary and open models, the chapter emphasizes the importance of calibrated combinations that shift over time and across contexts. The key policy question is not whether patents or secrecy are inherently suitable for quantum innovation, but how, where, and under what conditions each mode of protection contributes to both private incentives and broader public value. In this layered and heterogeneous landscape, the interplay of exclusivity and openness is not a contradiction but a defining feature of effective innovation strategy.

Acknowledgement This work was made possible through the generous support of the Novo Nordisk Foundation (NNF) via a grant for the scientifically independent Collaborative Research Program in Bioscience Innovation Law (Inter-CeBIL Program—Grant No. NNF23SA0087056).

References

Aboy M, Minssen T, Kop M (2022) Mapping the patent landscape of quantum technologies: patenting trends, innovation and policy implications. IIC–Int Rev Intellect Property Compet Law 53(6):853–882

Adkoli VR (2025) Test and Measurements of Quantum Chips, More Than Just Technology. https://www.electronicsforu.com/tech-zone/test-and-measurements-of-quantum-chips-more-than-just-technology. Accessed 22 Jul 2025

[90] Gil (2023).

Anton J, Yao D (2004) Little patents and big secrets: managing intellectual property. RAND J Econ 35(1):1–22

Aspect A (2024) Einstein and the quantum revolutions. University of Chicago Press, Chicago

AWO (2024) Quantum Computing and the G-77. https://www.ivir.nl/new-report-quantum-computing-and-the-global-south/. Accessed 22 Jul 2025

Balarabe K (2025) Quantum computing and the law: navigating the legal implications of a quantum leap. Eur J Risk Regulation 16(2):794–813

Baron J, Pohlmann T (2015) The Effect of Patent Pools on Patenting and Innovation—Evidence from Contemporary Technology Standards. https://wwws.law.northwestern.edu/research-faculty/clbe/innovationeconomics/documents/baron_pohlmann_effect_of_patents.pdf. Accessed 22 Jul 2025

Bogers M, Chesbrough H, Moedas C (2018) Open innovation: research, practices, and policies. Calif Manag Rev 60(2):5–16

Bortolini L (2023) Open Innovation in the Automotive Industry: How it Affects MNCs' Businesses…, Master's thesis, LUISS University. https://tesi.luiss.it/36334/1/735501_BORTOLINI_LUCA.pdf. Accessed 22 Jul 2025

Brandão FGSL, Horodecki M (2013) Exponential quantum speed-ups are generic. Quantum Inf Comput 13(11–12):901–924

Chesbrough H (2003) Open innovation: the new imperative for creating and profiting from technology. Harvard Business School Press, Boston

Chesbrough H, Bogers M (2014) Introduction. In: Chesbrough H, Vanhaverbeke W, West J (eds) New Frontiers in open innovation. Oxford University Press, Oxford

Collins H (2010) Tacit and explicit knowledge. University of Chicago Press, Chicago

Contreras JL (2015) Patent pledges. Arizona State Law J 47(3):543–608

Contreras JL (2017) From private ordering to public law: the legal frameworks governing standards-essential patents. Harv J Law Technol 30(Symposium):211–272

Cross A et al (2022) OpenQASM 3: a broader and deeper quantum assembly language. ACM Trans Quantum Comp 3(3):1–50

Davis PAE et al (2025) EU Cybersecurity regulation. In: Aboy M, Corrales Compagnucci M, Minssen T (eds) Quantum technology governance: law, policy and ethics in the quantum era. Springer, Cham

Dusollier S (2007) Sharing access to intellectual property through private ordering. Chi-Kent Law Rev 82(3):1391–1435

Ekert A (1991) Quantum cryptography based on bell's theorem. Phys Rev Lett 67(6):661–663

Ekert A, Renner R (2014) The ultimate physical limits of privacy. Nature 507(7493):443–447

EPO (2023) Quantum computing—insight report. European Patent Office, Munich. https://link.epo.org/web/epo_patent_insight_report-quantum_computing_en.pdf. Accessed 22 Jul 2025

European Commission (2015) European Commission: Directorate-General for Research and Innovation, open innovation, open science, open to the world—a vision for Europe. Publications Office, Brussels. https://op.europa.eu/en/publication-detail/-/publication/3213b335-1cbc-11e6-ba9a-01aa75ed71a1/language-en. Accessed 22 Jul 2025

European Commission (2020) Making the most of the EU's innovative potential—An intellectual property action plan to support the EU's recovery and resilience, COM/2020/760 final

Fujiwara T (2015) Option games analysis on biotech open innovation mediated by start-ups. In: 2015 IEEE International Conference on Engineering, Technology and Innovation/ International Technology Management Conference (ICE/ITMC), Belfast, UK, pp. 1–6. Available at: https://ieeexplore.ieee.org/document/7438644. Accessed 22 Jul 2025

Gallini N, Hollis A (2019) To Sell or Scale Up: Canada's Patent Strategy in a Knowledge Economy. Montréal: Institute for Research on Public Policy. https://irpp.org/research-studies/to-sell-or-scale-up-canadas-patent-strategy-in-a-knowledge-economy/. Accessed 22 Jul 2025

Gamalielsson J et al (2024) Open source software reference implementations for standards issued by different standards setting organisations: availability, perceptions and practices. J Standardisation 3(2):1–33

Gil D (2023) Why IBM is no longer interested in breaking patent records, Fortune (17 Jan 2023). https://fortune.com/2023/01/06/ibm-patent-record-how-to-measure-innovation-open-source-quantum-computing-tech/. Accessed 22 Jul 2025
Heller MA (1998) The tragedy of the Anticommons: property in the transition from Marx to markets. Harv Law Rev 111(3):621–688
Hemel D, Ouellette LL (2019) Innovation policy pluralism. Yale Law J 128(3):544–614
IBM (2023) How do you measure innovation? IBM Research Blog (9 Jan 2023). https://research.ibm.com/blog/Ibm-innovation-2022. Accessed 22 Jul 2025
Kop M (2021) Quantum computing and intellectual property law. Berk Technol Law J 35(3):101–115
Kop M, Aboy M, Minssen T (2022) Intellectual property in quantum computing and market power: a theoretical discussion and empirical analysis. J Intellect Property Law Practice 17(8):613–628
Kunz R (2020) The Adoption and Adaption of Open Innovation: Empirical Evidence from the Biotechnology Industry. PhD Thesis London South Bank University School of Business. https://openresearch.lsbu.ac.uk/item/94997. Accessed 22 Jul 2025
Lemley M, Shapiro C (2007) Patent holdup and royalty stacking. Texas Law Rev 85:1991–2049
Lenarczyk G, Minssen T, Aboy M (2024) The nature, scope and validity of patent pledges. J Intellect Property Law Practice 19(11):805–808
Lerner J, Tirole J (2004) Efficient patent pools. Am Econ Rev 94(3):691–711
Levin RC et al (1987) Appropriating the returns from industrial R&D. Brook Pap Econ Act 18(3):783–832
Levine DS, Sichelman T (2019) Why do start-ups use trade secrets? Notre Dame Law Rev 94(2):751–820
Merton RK (1942) The Normative Structure of Science. https://www.panarchy.org/merton/science.html. Accessed 22 July 2025
OECD (2025) A quantum technologies policy primer. OECD digital economy papers no. 371. OECD Publishing, Paris
Perrier E (2022) The quantum governance stack: models of governance for quantum information technologies. DISCO 1(22)
Perrier E et al (2025) Quantum information technology, governance and the law. In: Aboy M, Corrales Compagnucci M, Minssen T (eds) Quantum technology governance: law, policy and ethics in the quantum era. Springer, Cham
Polanyi M (1966) The tacit dimension. Doubleday, Garden City, NY
Powell A (2012) Democratising production through open-source knowledge: from open software to open hardware. Media Culture Soc 34(6):691–708
Quantum Machines & Rigetti (2024) Joint press release (10 Dec 2024). https://investors.rigetti.com/news-releases/news-release-details/quantum-machines-and-rigetti-announce-successful-ai-powered. Accessed 22 Jul 2025
Quantum Zeitgeist (2023) IBM Quantum Computer Timeline: From 5 to 1,121 Qubits, Big Blue accelerates its Quantum Efforts (5 Dec 2023). https://quantumzeitgeist.com/ibm-quantum-computer-timeline/. Accessed 22 Jul 2025
Quantum Zeitgeist (2024) IBM quantum cloud (22 May 2024). https://quantumzeitgeist.com/ibm-quantum-cloud/. Accessed 22 Jul 2025
Rantala J, Giardini C (2024) IP Guidelines for Quantum Technologists. Quantum Flagship, https://qt.eu/media/pdf/IP_Guidelines_for_Quantum_Technologists_2024.pdf. Accessed 22 Jul 2025
Rubio-Licht N (2025) IBM continues quantum quest with noise-correction patent, The Daily Upside (14 Apr 2025). https://www.thedailyupside.com/technology/big-tech/ibm-continues-quantum-quest-with-noise-correction-patent/. Accessed 22 Jul 2025
Shammah N et al (2023) Open hardware in quantum technology. *arXiv* 2309.17233
Thomas JR (2014) The Role of Trade Secrets in Innovation Policy. SSRN 5156805. https://papers.ssrn.com/sol3/papers.cfm?abstract_id=5156805. Accessed 22 Jul 2025
Unitalen (2023) China's First Quantum Computing Patent Pool Established in Beijing (6 May 2023), https://unitalen.com/html/report/23050269-1.htm? Accessed 22 Jul 2025

Wajsman N, García-Valero F (2017) Protecting innovation through trade secrets and patents: determinants for European Union firms. EUIPO Observatory, Alicante
Williams B et al (2016) Tamper-indicating quantum seal. Phys Rev Appl 5:014001
Wootters WK, Zurek WH (1982) A single quantum cannot be cloned. Nature 299(5886):802–803
Wu MC, Lin RB (2005) Multiple project wafers for medium-volume IC production, Proceesings-IEEE International Symposium on Cicuits and Systems. https://ieeexplore.ieee.org/document/1465688?arnumber=1465688. Accessed 22 Jul 2025
Zittrain JL (2006) The generative internet. Harv Law Rev 119(7):1974–2040

Mapping the Patent Landscape of Quantum Technologies: Evolving Patenting Trends and Policy Implications (2025 Update)

Mateo Aboy, Cristina Crespo, and Timo Minssen

Abstract Recent advancements in quantum science highlight the potential transformative capabilities of second-generation (2G) quantum technologies, such as quantum computing, quantum communications, and quantum sensing. Patenting trends in such technologies serve as key indicators of innovation pace at the invention stage. Empirical analyses of real-world patenting activity offer essential evidence to evaluate and inform policy proposals on intellectual property rights, innovation, and governance in quantum technologies. Building upon the insights gained from our earlier 2022 study mapping the patent landscape of quantum technologies, this chapter reports the results of an updated study incorporating data up to October 2025. We assess patenting trends over the period from 2001 to 2025 to determine: (1) the growth of quantum technology patents, (2) the technology breakdown and classification of patenting activity, (3) the choice of priority patent office, (4) the types of patent claims and strategies, (5) the subject matter of recently awarded patents, (6) the top patent owners, (7) the dominant patent portfolios, and (8) the geographical distribution of this activity. Drawing on this landscape analysis, we critically evaluate the impact of patents in the field of quantum technologies, ranging from their significance in incentivising innovation to their private value effects. Our findings show how patent disclosures are contributing to an emerging quantum information commons, progressively enriching the public domain. Furthermore, we explore the innovation and policy implications of these results within the broader framework of quantum innovation initiatives, market competition dynamics, the patent-trade secret interface, and the governance of quantum technologies, emphasizing the role of patents in fostering disclosure amid rapid commercialization and geopolitical shifts.

M. Aboy (✉) · C. Crespo
Centre for Law, Medicine and Life Sciences (LML) and Centre for Intellectual Property and Information Law (CIPIL), University of Cambridge, Cambridge, UK
e-mail: ma608@cam.ac.uk

T. Minssen
Center for Advanced Studies in Bioscience Innovation Law (CeBIL), University of Copenhagen, Copenhagen, Denmark

M. Aboy et al. (eds.), *Quantum Technology Governance I*, Perspectives in Law, Business and Innovation, https://doi.org/10.1007/978-981-95-8371-3_4

Keywords Quantum technologies · Quantum computing · Quantum patent landscape · Quantum innovation landscape · Quantum innovation policy

1 Introduction

Recent advancements in quantum science have spotlighted the immense promise of second-generation (2G) quantum technologies, encompassing domains such as simulation, sensing and metrology, computation, and communication. Notable milestones, including demonstrations of quantum advantage with programmable processors utilizing superconducting qubits,[1] illustrate this progress. The applications span from simulating complex quantum systems to advance foundational knowledge and practical uses (e.g., accelerating drug discovery through chemical process modeling), to enabling superior precision in measurements via quantum sensing and metrology, tackling intractable computational challenges with quantum algorithms on quantum computers, and establishing ultra-secure communication networks.[2]

These developments captivate academia, industry, and policymakers alike, owing to their ramifications for fundamental research, diverse sectors like information technology and pharmaceuticals, and national security considerations.[3] Innovation in quantum technologies typically arises from collaborations among academic institutions, corporations, and market dynamics, including competitive pressures, new entrants, alternative technologies, and stakeholder bargaining power. Governments are pivotal, shaping incentive structures and regulatory environments, while often serving as primary customers, particularly for defense-related applications.

Governmental strategies include both push mechanisms—such as research grants that fuelled the first quantum revolution and technology transfer initiatives propelling the second quantum revolution,[4] exemplified by the European Quantum Technologies Flagship Programme[5]—and pull incentives like patent protections to encourage invention disclosure in exchange for limited exclusivity. Push incentives aim to propel technologies from early proof-of-concept stages (e.g., Technology Readiness Level 3) toward prototype validation in relevant settings (TRL 6-7), while pull mechanisms, including intellectual property rights (IPRs), facilitate commercialization once risks are mitigated (TRL 8-9).

In anticipation of quantum technologies' integration into practical products, scholars, officials, and analysts have voiced apprehensions and advanced recommendations for governance, standardization (e.g., via ISO/IEC/IEEE), and

[1] Arute et al. (2019), pp. 505–510.

[2] Acín et al. (2018).

[3] See also, Acín et al. (2018).

[4] Dowling and Milburn (2003), pp. 1655–1674.

[5] Riedel et al. (2017).

regulation.[6] These often target incentives, IPRs, and broader oversight. To evaluate such ideas effectively, they must be grounded in empirical insights for evidence-informed policymaking. For example, earlier scholarship has flagged risks of excessive IP protection in quantum fields and suggested patent system adjustments.[7] Yet, does contemporary evidence as of 2025 support claims of overprotection?

What patterns emerge in quantum technology patenting over the past quarter-century? Which nations and entities dominate this activity? What claim structures and strategies prevail, and in which venues are protections sought? Absent robust, data-driven IP analyses addressing these queries, policymakers risk ill-advised modifications to existing regimes, especially in high-stakes, capital-intensive areas like quantum technologies that demand overcoming formidable scientific and engineering hurdles.[8]

Underprotection is conventionally seen as stifling incentives in emerging fields, where patents and other IPRs are vital to secure investments for risky R&D. Conversely, overprotection might erect market barriers, undermining competition and open innovation. Patents signal innovation dynamics at the inventive phase, making empirical patent studies invaluable for appraising policies on IPRs, innovation, and regulation. The significance of empirical studies in these areas is further highlighted by current geopolitical tensions and increasing calls for using IPRs and regulation as one instrument in the toolbox to increase resilience and so-called "technological sovereignty" in strategically crucial areas, such as AI- and quantum technologies.

Existing patent analyses in this domain, however, are limited: many lack peer review,[9] concentrate on narrow reviews,[10] or methodological innovations,[11] or are outdated.[12] This chapter presents an updated mapping of the quantum technologies patent landscape, building on our prior study published in the *International Review of Intellectual Property and Competition Law.*[13] Incorporating four additional years of data through October 2025, we analyze trends from 2001 onward to ascertain: (1) patent growth in quantum technologies, (2) technological categorizations and breakdowns, (3) preferred priority offices, (4) claim types and approaches, (5) content of recent grants, (6) leading owners and their profiles, (7) influential portfolios via forward citations, and (8) global geographic patterns. These findings allow us to scrutinize assertions of patent over- or underprotection in applied quantum technologies at the current technological frontier. We further dissect the innovation and

[6] Kop (2020).

[7] Kop (2022).

[8] Córcoles et al. (2020), pp. 1338–1352.

[9] Alex (2021).

[10] Haney (2021).

[11] Jiang and Chen (2021), pp. 1317–1331.

[12] Chang (2005), pp. 1177–1181; Bachmann (2011), pp. 926–931; Winiarczyk et al. (2013).

[13] Aboy et al. (2022), pp. 853–882.

policy ramifications in the context of quantum initiatives, competitive markets, the patent-trade secret nexus, and quantum governance.

2 Defining Quantum Technologies

Defining quantum technologies accurately is essential, particularly in the context of intellectual property protection, as it delineates the boundaries of what inventions are considered "quantum" for patenting within this emerging field. A precise definition helps determine classification under systems like the Cooperative Patent Classification (CPC), as well as any quantum-specific guidance related to subject-matter eligibility, written description and enablement requirements, and scope of protection, while avoiding overreach into established classical technologies. This clarity is important for policymakers considering guidance or reforms, such as potential sui generis regimes for quantum IP, to prevent distortions in innovation incentives and maintain harmony with international standards like TRIPS, which mandate technology-neutral patent availability. Misdefinitions could lead to either underprotection, deterring investment in high-risk R&D, or overprotection, creating barriers to entry and stifling collaborative progress in a domain increasingly intertwined with national security and global competition.

As we previously noted,[14] it may seem natural to define a quantum technology as one whose operation is governed by the laws of quantum mechanics. However, such a definition is problematic since technically the laws of quantum mechanics govern the behaviour of all physical phenomena at a fundamental particle level. Even narrower definitions such as technologies whose operation exploit the principles of quantum mechanics would include the semiconductor devices used in the latest classical processors, since the channel length of the transistors used are currently in the 2 nm scale which means that quantum mechanical effects must be considered in the design and development of these electronic devices. Thus, quantum technologies are often classified into two generations, and the term is typically reserved for those belonging to the second generation (2G).[15]

First-generation (1G) technologies include transistors, lasers, and other devices whose design and operation are based on the principles of quantum mechanics (i.e., devices that directly leverage the scientific discoveries from the first quantum revolution). These 1G devices have resulted in computing and communication technologies that have transformed entire industries and society since the introduction of the first semiconductor integrated circuit (IC). The initial patent on ICs (US Patent No. US3138743A, filed in 1959 and granted in 1964) stated:

[14] See also, Aboy et al. (2022).

[15] Dowling and Milburn (2003).

> [...] principal object of this invention [is] to provide a novel miniaturised electronic circuit fabricated from a body of semiconductor material [...] wherein all components of the electronic circuit are completely integrated into the body of semiconductor material.

Miniaturisation through ICs led to the computer and information technology revolution. As an illustration, the Intel 8008 processor introduced in 1974 contained 2500 transistors and used a MOS process of 10,000 nm, the 2005 Intel Pentium 4 contained 169 million transistors (90 nm), the 2017 Intel Xeon contained 8 billion transistors (14 nm), the 2021 Apple M1 Max had 57 billion transistors (5 nm), and the 2025 NVIDIA Blackwell B200 features 208 billion transistors (4 nm), with 2 nm processes entering production in late 2025. This miniaturisation has enabled the industry to increase the number of transistors in a chip (i.e., increasing the computational power and functionality of ICs) and their speed, while reducing the cost of production. A consequence of this scaling is that the classical devices used in "classical computers" exhibit quantum mechanical effects that need to be taken into account as part of the design and development of processors (CPU) and graphical processing units (GPU) for our current computing devices (e.g., phones, tablets, laptops, computers). In other words, quantum physical phenomena become unavoidable at the nanometre scale. For instance, at deep submicron and nanometre scales, MOSFETs exhibit quantum mechanical tunnelling from source to gate oxide due to the thickness of the oxide layers (approximately 2 nm), quantum mechanical tunnelling from source to drain when the channel lengths are less than 10 nm, and energy quantization.

Second generation (2G) quantum technologies are technologies currently being developed that directly harness the unique quantum mechanical phenomena such as superposition, entanglement, tunnelling, and quantization as their underlying principle of operation (i.e., devices whose operation directly exploits quantum phenomena) to achieve advantages over our current state-of-the-art technologies. These include quantum computing, quantum communications, and quantum sensing.

3 Patent Search Strategy

To address the research questions outlined above, we employed a refined search strategy that promotes consistency and transparency in patent landscaping,[16] while adhering to established guidelines for quality and reproducibility in patent landscape reports.[17] This approach is tailored specifically to our study's objectives rather than offering a comprehensive overview. Comparable methods have previously

---

[16] Bubela et al. (2013), pp. 202–206.

[17] Smith et al. (2018), pp. 1043–1047.

Table 1 Quantum technologies patented in the US (USPTO) and Europe (EPO)

ID	Search Concept	Search Term	Applications	Granted
S1	Quantum related patents	"quantum" (& QT keywords)	344,541	238,303
S2	Quantum patents (TAC)	S1 & TAC:Quantum	49,894	29,701
S3	Quantum claims	ACLM: Quantum	43,704	27,131
S4	Q. Independent claims	ICLM: Quantum	22,546	15,448
S5	Quantum computing	CPC: G06N10	6685	2879

Source: USPTO & EPO patent application and grant data from 2001-01-01 to 2025-10-15 (search conducted by MA on 2025-10-15). CPC class G06N10 is devoted to "Quantum computing, i.e. information processing based on quantum-mechanical phenomena" (with a total of 2879 patents granted by the USPTO and EPO across all dates)

been applied to map patent landscapes in areas such as gene patents,[18] drug repurposing,[19] and medical AI.[20]

Our strategy spans from broad, high-sensitivity searches (Table 1, Search ID: S1) to more targeted, high-specificity queries aimed at reducing false positives (Table 1, Search ID: S4). Specifically, it captures: 1) all patent documents loosely associated with "quantum" concepts (S1), 2) essential quantum technology patents (S2), 3) patents featuring claims focused on "quantum"-related inventions (S3), and 4) patents where independent claims pertain to quantum technologies (S4). S1 prioritizes inclusivity, encompassing any document with keywords like "quantum" or related terms (e.g., qubit, entanglement) to establish an upper limit for broadly defined quantum-related patents. In contrast, S2-S4 enhance precision by limiting results to instances where the keyword appears in the title, abstract, or claims (TAC) for S2, solely in the claims for S3, and within the independent claims for S4.

To further boost specificity, we restricted results to Cooperative Patent Classification (CPC) categories designated by the USPTO and EPO for quantum-specific inventions. This method capitalizes on expert manual classifications by patent examiners at these offices, blending automated searches with human oversight. The CPC, an expansion of the WIPO's International Patent Classification (IPC), is co-managed by the USPTO and EPO to standardize classifications and enhance search efficiency across jurisdictions. We utilized CPC classes to segment patents into key quantum areas: quantum devices (S5), quantum optics (S6), quantum information processing (S7), quantum computing (S8), quantum cryptography (S9), and quantum communication (S10). Subsequent analysis of these documents examined annual growth in quantum technology patenting, patent legal statuses, preferred priority offices, activity by CPC class, claim language and inventive concepts, leading owners in quantum computing, forward citation metrics, and worldwide geographic distributions. The search encompasses patent applications and grants published from January 1, 2001, to October 15, 2025 (conducted on October 15, 2025).

[18] Aboy et al. (2016), pp. 1119–1123.

[19] Aboy et al. (2021), pp. 1336–1343.

[20] See also, Aboy et al. (2021).

4 Patent Landscape Results

Having laid out the search strategy, this section presents the empirical results of the patent landscape analysis. We first describe the size and composition of the dataset across our search sets (S1–S5) and key CPC classes, before examining annual patenting activity, legal status, technological specialisation, office preferences, claim structures, ownership patterns, citation dynamics, and geographical distributions. Throughout, particular emphasis is placed on quantum computing patents, which provide a focal lens on developments in a strategically important subfield.

4.1 *Patent Search Results*

Table 1 presents the outcomes of our search for patent applications and granted patents pertaining to quantum technologies, published between 2001 and 2025 at the USPTO and EPO. The methodology varies from high-sensitivity searches (S1) to high-specificity ones (S2–S5) to reduce false positives. Our findings reveal 344,541 quantum-related patent applications and 238,303 grants since 2001 (S1). However, most of these are only peripherally linked to quantum technologies, making S1 a broad upper limit for inclusively defined quantum-related patents.

The S2–S5 searches refine the focus to pinpoint core quantum technology patents and categorize them by subfield. We identified 29,701 granted patents where "quantum" is central, appearing in the title, abstract, or claims (TAC) (S2). Among these, 27,131 include at least one claim with "quantum" as a limitation (S3), and 15,448 have independent claims directed to quantum-related inventions (S4). Our study will particularly focus on patents related to quantum computing (i.e., those belonging to CPC class G06N10), of which there are a total of 2879 granted patents since 2001.

4.2 *Annual Quantum Technology Patenting Activity and Legal Status*

Figure 1 shows the annual patenting activity for quantum technologies at the USPTO and EPO (S2). The figure shows the current legal status (active or expired) of granted patents published each year since 2001.

The results show a five-fold increase in the number of patents granted per year in the last 10 years, from approximately 500 in 2004 to over 2500 in 2024, corresponding to a compound annual growth rate (CAGR) of 17.5%. This growth has not happened at a constant rate over the entire period, but rather the graph shows a period of relative stability (e.g., virtually no increase in number of granted patents per year) between 2003 and 2008, followed by a 10-year period of rapid increase until 2019, and then another

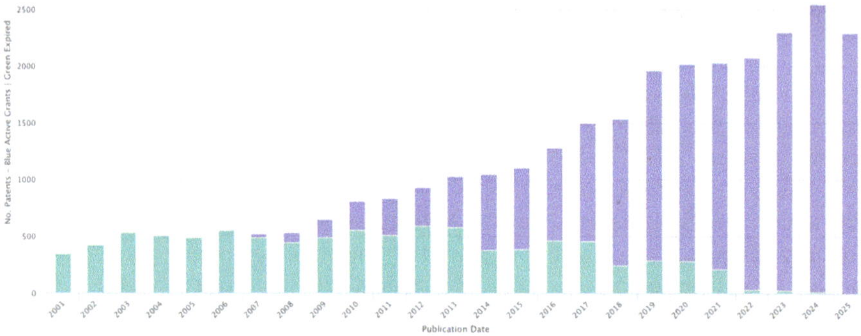

Fig. 1 Annual patenting activity for quantum technologies at the USPTO and EPO (Search ID: S2) and current legal status (active or expired) sorted by publication date of the patent (2001-01-01 to 2025-09-30)

period of growth stagnation from 2019 to 2022 (possibly impacted by restrictions during the COVID-19 pandemic) before another period of rapid growth starting in 2023.

The graph also shows that around 25% of the patents granted since 2001 have expired and thus entered the public domain. This number does not include applications that may have been rejected or abandoned, which also contribute to the volume of public disclosure in the field of quantum technologies.

4.3 Technology Breakdown

Table 2 shows the top CPC classes by number of patents granted, their description, and the corresponding patents granted for each class by the USPTO and EPO. Our results show that B82Y* classes related to nanostructures and their applications (e.g., quantum optics, quantum computing, single electron logic) have the highest number of patents (*n* > *6000)*, followed by G06N10 quantum computing (*n* = 3295) and cryptography (n = *1742*).

4.4 USPTO vs EPO Quantum Technology Patent Activity

Figure 2 shows the number of published patent documents (published patent applications and granted patents) on quantum technologies segregated by patent office (USPTO versus EPO). Our results indicate that the USPTO has been the patent office of choice over the last 25 years, with the number of patents granted by the USPTO consistently exceeding 75% of the overall number of patents granted by the USPTO and EPO combined. Although the overall number of patents for both offices has been steadily increasing over the last 10 years, the proportion of patents granted by each has remained relatively stable over time. In 2024 out of the overall 6823 USPTO/EPO patent cohort, 5172 (75.8%) were granted by the USPTO and 1651 (24.2%) by the EPO.

Table 2 USPTO and EPO quantum-related patents classified by CPC class

CPC	Cooperative Patent Classification (CPC) Class Description	Patents
B82Y20	SPECIFIC USES OR APPLICATIONS OF NANOSTRUCTURES; MEASUREMENT OR ANALYSIS OF NANOSTRUCTURES; MANUFACTURE OR TREATMENT OF NANOSTRUCTURES > Nanooptics, e.g. **quantum optics or photonic crystals**	4047
G06N10	COMPUTING ARRANGEMENTS BASED ON SPECIFIC COMPUTATIONAL MODELS > **Quantum computing, i.e. information processing based on quantum-mechanical phenomena**	3295
B82Y10	SPECIFIC USES OR APPLICATIONS OF NANOSTRUCTURES; MEASUREMENT OR ANALYSIS OF NANOSTRUCTURES; MANUFACTURE OR TREATMENT OF NANOSTRUCTURES > Nanotechnology for information processing, storage or transmission, e.g. **quantum computing or single electron logic**	2724
H04L9	TRANSMISSION OF DIGITAL INFORMATION, e.g. TELEGRAPHIC COMMUNICATION > Cryptographic mechanisms or cryptographicarrangements for secret or secure communications; Network security protocols	1742

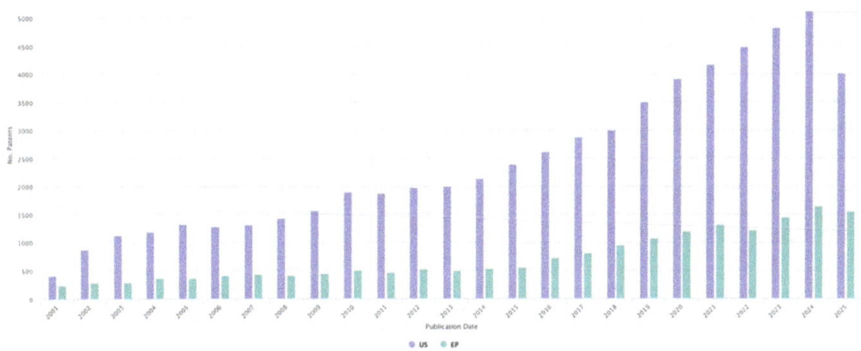

Fig. 2 Choice of patent office (USPTO vs. EPO) for quantum technologies (Search ID: S2)

4.5 Patents Claiming Quantum Technologies

Figure 3 shows the prevalence of (a) patents broadly related to quantum technologies (S1), (b) core quantum patents (S2), (c) patents with claims directed to a quantum concept (S3), and (d) patents with independent claims (broadest claims) directed to a quantum concept (S4). Since the S1 search captures any patent including the keyword "quantum" and related concepts (e.g., qubit, entangl* and superposit*) anywhere in the patent document, it is highly sensitive but not specific (i.e., in addition to the core quantum technology patents, it includes related applications that mention "quantum" or related terms anywhere in the specification). Therefore,

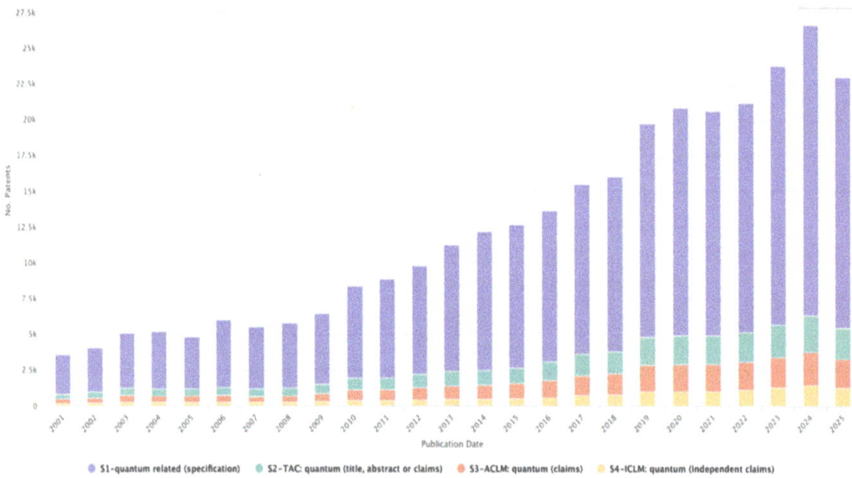

Fig. 3 Relative prevalence of (a) patents broadly related to quantum technologies (S1), (b) core quantum patents (S2), (c) patents with claims directed to a quantum concept (S3), and (d) patents with the independent claims related to a quantum concept (S4)

our landscape results are based on more specific searches where quantum technology is core to the patent and accordingly the quantum keywords are used in the TAC (S2), claims (S3) and independent claims (S4). We also focus more closely on patents belonging to CPC class G06N10, which relates to quantum computing (S5).

Figure 3 shows that over 90% of patents that use the "quantum" keyword in the title or abstract (S2) also have claims directed to a "quantum" inventive concept (S3). Additionally, in over 50% of the S2 patents, the quantum inventive concept is claimed in the broadest claims of the patent (i.e., independent claims). Since 2020 there have been over 2000 patent publications per year (S2), with over 1800 patent publications per year containing claims directed to a quantum concept (S3) and over 1000 yearly patent publications with the broadest claim including a quantum feature or limitation (S4).

Figure 4 shows the relative prevalence of USPTO and EPO quantum technology patents with claims related to (a) quantum circuits, (b) quantum computing, (c) quantum communication, and (d) quantum algorithms. Over the last 25 years, patents including claim limitations related to quantum circuits (ACLM: quantum and circuit*) and quantum communications (ACLM: quantum and communic*) have been the most prevalent, with a close match between the number of patents in each of the two categories. However, in the last 5 years quantum computing patents have taken over as the most prevalent type. Patents containing claim limitations directed to quantum "algorithms" have been lagging significantly behind the other three types. Patent attorneys may have intentionally avoided the use of the word "algorithm" in the claims to overcome subject matter eligibility restrictions related to the patent ineligibility of "abstract ideas" (*Bilsky* and *Alice*). Nevertheless, Fig. 4 shows

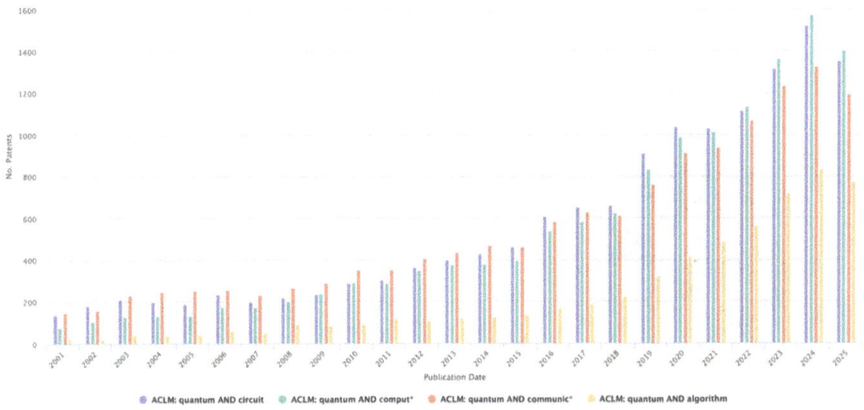

Fig. 4 Relative prevalence of USPTO and EPO quantum technology patents with claims directed to (**a**) quantum circuits, (**b**) quantum computing, (**c**) quantum communication, and (**c**) quantum algorithms

a significant and consistent increase in patents related to quantum algorithms (ACLM: quantum and algorithm) in the last 5 years.

Figure 5 shows the concept landscape for quantum computing patents (S5). The graph was generated using automatic text analysis of the abstract, title, and claims to identify frequently used terms and cluster them by category. Our results indicate that the patents are clustered in six main areas, namely, (1) quantum circuits, (2) quantum processors, (3) quantum gates, (4) qubit modalities, and (5) error correction. The second layer includes additional details regarding the terms used to describe and claim the respective inventive concepts. Some of these overlap across the primary groups. For instance, "quantum bits" (qubits) are both in patents related to "quantum states" and "quantum computing". Similarly, the terms "quantum processor" and "quantum control" are part of the "quantum circuits" and "quantum computing" clusters of S2 patents.

Figure 5 can be thought of as a summary of the technical terms used in the title, abstract, and claims of the 3732 quantum computing patents (CPC G06N10) that have been granted across all dates. That said, this information is highly compressed and it is not a substitute for direct analysis of the actual claim language to examine the claim drafting strategies and scope of protection.

Review of patent grants in G06N10 (i.e., the CPC class for quantum computing) reveals that patent claims are directed to: (1) physical realisations of building blocks for quantum computers (e.g., quantum processors and components for manipulating qubits such qubit control), (2) quantum error correction (e.g., detection and prevention of errors using surface codes, magic state distillation, etc), (3) models quantum circuits and universal quantum computers, (4) applications of quantum algorithms (e.g., quantum optimisation, applied quantum Fourier or Hadamard transforms, etc), and (5) platforms for accessing, simulating, and programming quantum

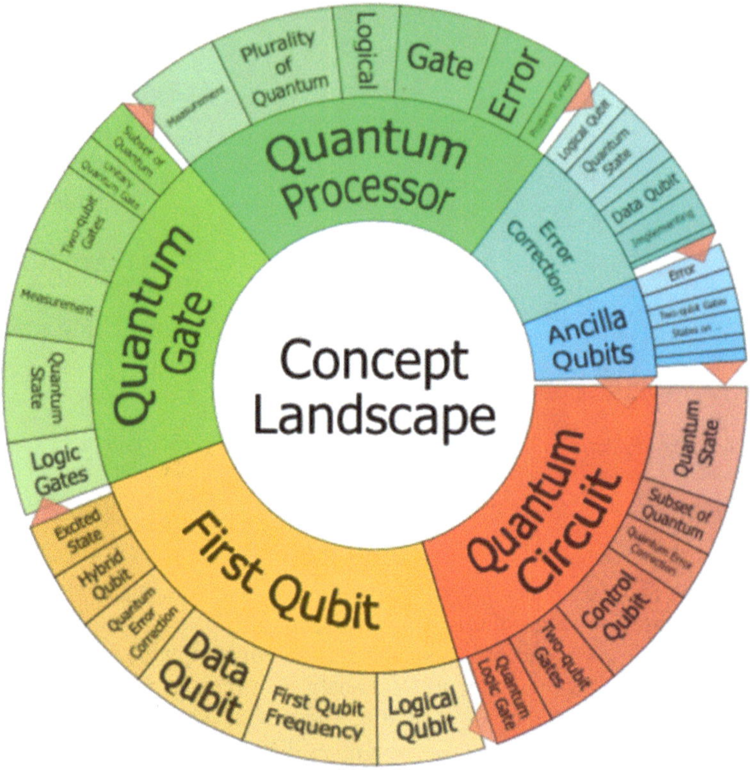

Fig. 5 Concept landscape for quantum computing patents (CPC: G06N10)

computers (e.g., cloud-based computing, platforms for simulating quantum systems, quantum programming interfaces).

In particular, the top subclasses within the CPC G06N10 quantum computing class in terms of granted patents by the USPTO and EPO are:

- G06N10/40-"Physical realisations or architectures of quantum processors or components for manipulating qubits, e.g. qubit coupling or qubit control" with 2312 granted patents.
- G06N10/20-"Models of quantum computing, e.g. quantum circuits or universal quantum computers" with 1408 granted patents.
- G06N10/60-"Quantum algorithms, e.g. based on quantum optimisation, quantum Fourier or Hadamard transforms with 993 granted patents.
- G06N10/70-"Quantum error correction, detection or prevention, e.g. surface codes" with 828 granted patents.
- G06N10/80-"Quantum programming, e.g. interfaces, languages or software-development kits for creating or handling programs capable of running on

quantum computers; Platforms for simulating or accessing quantum computers, e.g. cloud-based quantum computing|" with 535 granted patents.

4.6 *Recently Granted Quantum Computing Patents*

Table 3 lists the titles of the most recent quantum computing patents granted in the month preceding the search date and their respective assignees. According to 37 CFR 1.72 "The title of the invention may not exceed 500 characters in length[...]" and pursuant to MPEP 606.01 if "the title is not descriptive of the invention claimed, the examiner should require the substitution of a new title that is clearly indicative of the invention to which the claims are directed". Accordingly, the titles can be considered brief (<500 characters) summaries of the claimed inventions. These patents, granted between September and October 2025, help illustrate the focus and range of subject matter of recent patents in quantum computing.

Table 3 Titles of the 40 most recent quantum computing patents (CPC: G06N10) granted and published by the USPTO and their respective ultimate patent owners

Title	Assignee Ultimate	Grant Date
Method for executing quantum program and method for compiling quantum program	SHENZHEN TENCENT COMPUTER SYSTEMS CO; INST OF SOFTWARE CHINESE ACADEMY OF SCIENCE	2025-10-07
Probabalistic amplification and attenuation of quantum errors using a single dataset	IBM	2025-10-07
Performance analysis of quantum programs	CLASSIQ TECH LTD	2025-10-07
Methods, systems, and apparatus for enabling and managing quantum networks	INTERDIGITAL TECH CORP	2025-10-07
Thermal transition filter for a superconducting circuit system	NORTHROP GRUMMAN CORP	2025-10-07
Combined classical/quantum predictor evaluation	IBM	2025-10-07
Electro-optomechanical quantum transduction	IBM	2025-10-07
Identifying severe hook faults of stabilizer channel	MICROSOFT CORP	2025-10-07
Methods and apparatuses for AOD crosstalk mitigation	IONQ INC	2025-10-07
Combined classical/quantum predictor evaluation with model accuracy adjustment	IBM	2025-10-07
Linear-optical encoded GHZ measurements and fault-tolerant quantum computation and communication	ORCA COMPUTING LTD	2025-10-07
Baseband filter for current-mode signal path	IBM	2025-10-07
Phase-accurate generation of quantum-computing control signals	ZURICH INSTRUMENTS AG	2025-10-07
Systems and methods for providing a nearest neighbors classification pipeline with automated dimensionality reduction	CAPITAL ONE FINANCIAL CORP	2025-10-07
Information processing apparatus, arithmetic device, and information processing method	HITACHI VANTARA LTD	2025-10-07
Noise reduced circuits for trapped-ion quantum computers	IONQ INC	2025-10-07
Methods and systems for providing quantum computer interface	CALIFORNIA INST OF TECH UNIV	2025-10-07
Systems and methods for efficient photonic heralded quantum computing systems	SOUTHERN METHODIST UNIV INC	2025-10-07
Systems and methods for using distributed quantum computing simulators	JPMORGAN CHASE BANK NA	2025-10-07
Quantum computing decoder and associated methods	RIVER LANE RES LTD	2025-10-07
Accelerated molecular dynamics simulation method on a computing system	UNIV SYSTEM OF MARYLAND	2025-09-30
Generating DC offsets in flux-tunable transmons with persistent current loops	IBM	2025-09-30
Quantum computing system with secured multi-source cloud application programming interface	BANK OF AMERICA	2025-09-30
Methods and apparatuses for doppler cooling	IONQ INC	2025-09-30
Methods and apparatuses for trap-door loading	IONQ INC	2025-09-30
Systems and methods for quantum tomography using an ancilla	ALPHABET INC	2025-09-30
Quantum sensing and computing using cascaded phases	UNIV COLORADO	2025-09-30
Tuning storage devices	PURE STORAGE INC	2025-09-30
Classical processor for quantum control	QM TECH LTD	2025-09-30
Motional mode configuration for implementation of entangling gates in ion trap quantum computers	IONQ INC	2025-09-30
Quantum computing service with quality of service (QoS) enforcement via out-of-band prioritization of quantum tasks	AMAZON TECH INC	2025-09-30
Error mitigation in a quantum program	IBM	2025-09-30
Selection of pauli strings for variational quantum eigensolver	IBM	2025-09-30
Maximum-likelihood decoding of quantum codes	IBM	2025-09-23
Computing device of Ising model	NIPPON TELEGRAPH & TELEPHONE	2025-09-23
Verified quantum phase estimation	ALPHABET INC	2025-09-23
Non-contact thermal radiation shield interface	IBM	2025-09-23
Managing workloads in a container orchestration system	IBM	2025-09-23
Electrode fabrication and die shaping for metal-on-glass ion traps	IONQ INC	2025-09-23

4.7 Top Quantum Computing Patent Owners

Figure 6 lists top patent owners of quantum computing patents in the last 25 years. In the top 10 with more than 25 quantum computing patents, we find US global technology companies focused on hardware and software platforms (IBM, Google, Microsoft, Intel), a US defence technology company (Northrop Grumman), and quantum-specific companies (IonQ, Rigetti, D-Wave). Among the top university portfolios in quantum computing are U. Maryland, MIT, Yale, Duke, Harvard, Caltech, and Tech. Univ. Delft.

4.8 Citation Analysis and Dominant Patent Portfolios

Figure 7 shows the forward citation analysis of patent portfolios on quantum computing by assignee (ultimate patent owners). Forward citations are a measure of private value and a proxy for the potential social value of inventions. Patents without established market values (e.g., in the absence of licensing agreements with negotiated royalty rates) are often valued based on forward citations and related valuation metrics. The patent portfolios with the highest number of forward citations are IBM, Google, Microsoft, and IonQ (Fig. 7).

4.9 Global Geographical Distribution

Figures 8 and 9 show top patent offices of issuance for quantum technology patents (Search ID: S2). The US and China are the top countries of issuance, followed by Japan, EPO, Australia, South Korea and Canada. While the US continues to lead the field of quantum computing, China is arguably becoming the leader in

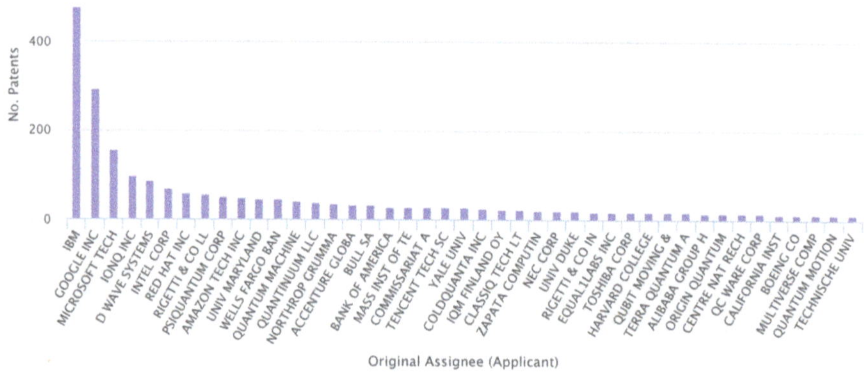

Fig. 6 Top patent owners of quantum computing patents (G06N10) in the USPTO and EPO

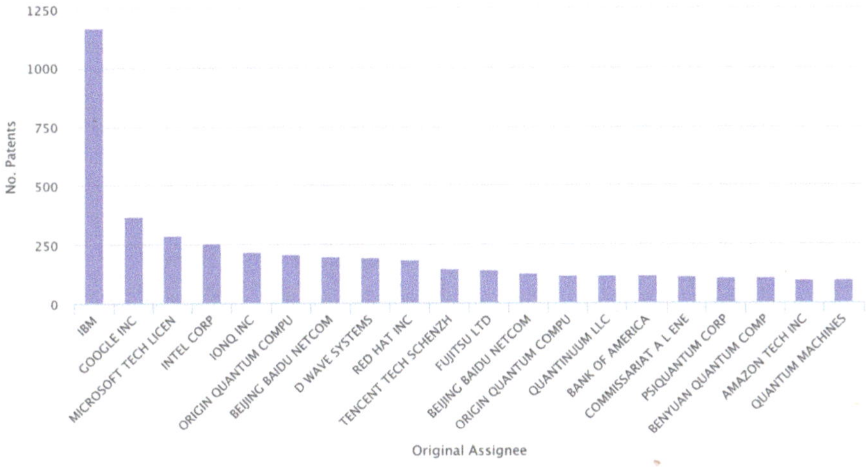

Fig. 7 Forward citation analysis of patent portfolios on quantum computing (S8) by assignee

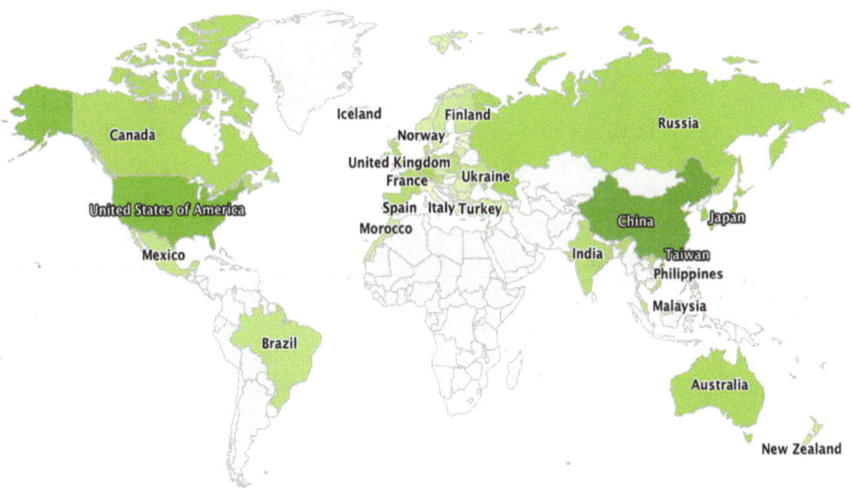

Fig. 8 Top patenting countries of issuance for quantum technology patents (Search ID: S2) across all jurisdictions within the PCT

quantum communications. This is remarkable since most of this Chinese growth in secure quantum communications has taken place in the last 5 years. Thus, it is expected that Chinese quantum networking and communications devices will soon be present in the global markets. As of 2021, China is now a close second to the US, with close to 3x the number of patents as Japan, and over 5x that of the EPO (Fig. 9).

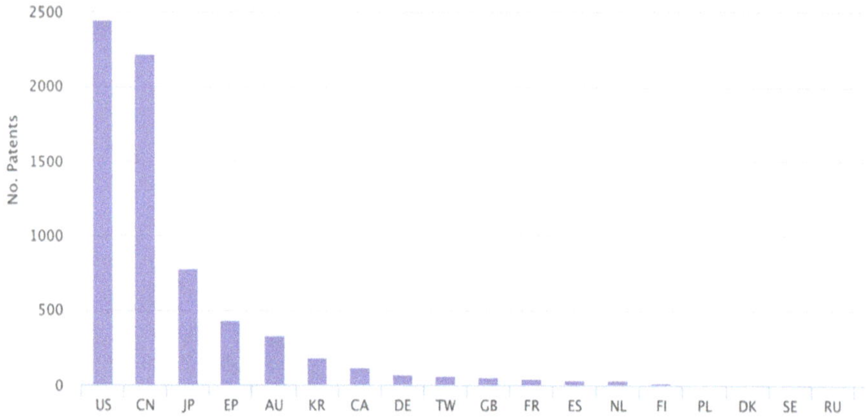

Fig. 9 Top patenting countries for quantum computing (CPC G08N10). As of 2021, China is now second ahead of Japan, Europe, and Australia

5 Policy Considerations

Building on our 2022 analysis in the *International Review of Intellectual Property and Competition Law,*[21] which examined quantum patent trends up to 2021 and emphasized the role of patents in promoting disclosure amid concerns of over-protection, this updated examination through October 2025 confirms the continuation of key patterns while highlighting amplified growth. The post-2014 acceleration in patenting activity has persisted without deviation, driven by increased commercialization, geopolitical investments (e.g., in quantum computing and secure communications), and integration with emerging technologies like AI. However, the data reveals no new evidence of patent thickets or barriers; instead, the expanding public domain and diverse ownership reinforce the innovation incentives identified previously, with fresh implications for antitrust in a maturing market.

5.1 Growth of Quantum Technology Patents

The results of our updated landscape study indicate that the USPTO and EPO are now jointly granting approximately 2500 patents related to quantum technologies per year (S2), up from the ~2000 annual grants observed in our previous analysis for 2021. A total of 29,701 patents were granted from 2001 to 2025, reflecting an overall compound annual growth rate (CAGR) of around 14.5% over the past 24 years—a slight adjustment from the 15.23% CAGR to 2021, but indicative of sustained

[21] Aboy et al. (2022), pp. 853–882.

momentum. Notably, more than 40% of these patent grants have occurred in the last 4 years, extending the trend of rapid expansion post-2014 after the relative stagnation between 2003 and 2013 (CAGR $\approx$ 4.05%) noted in our prior work. This continued surge aligns with global quantum initiatives, such as expanded funding under the EU Quantum Flagship and US National Quantum Initiative, without introducing unexpected shifts.

5.2 *Patent Disclosures in the Public Domain Versus Trade Secrets*

From a public policy perspective, it is noteworthy that approximately 54% of the patent disclosures published over the past 24 years are now in the public domain, a modest increase from the ~50% reported in our 2022 study. This includes an estimated 7697 previously granted patents that have expired (up from 4536), as well as the 21,676 patent applications that did not result in a grant (up from 14,830). The teachings in these public disclosures remain freely available for societal use, continuing to elevate the patentability threshold for subsequent applications as we previously highlighted—preventing the patenting of these inventions and narrowing the scope of protection for follow-on claims. Unlike trade secrets, these dynamics persist in benefiting open innovation, with no new trends toward increased secrecy despite the field's maturation. To meet novelty and non-obviousness requirements, applicants often claim priority to earlier disclosures, effectively shortening the patent term (20 years from the priority date). For instance, among the quantum technology patents granted in 2025, a substantial portion—estimated at around 80% based on historical patterns—have priority dates ranging from 2005 to 2021, consistent with the continuity observed in our earlier findings.

5.3 *Continuum from Classical to Quantum Technology*

The majority of quantum technology patents granted over the past 24 years (S2) pertain to nanostructures, solid-state devices, and their applications (e.g., sensing and metrology), with claims and drafting practices that closely resemble those in semiconductor patents fueling the information technology revolution over the last 60 years—a pattern unchanged since our 2022 analysis. Transistor density in integrated circuits has continued to follow Moore's law trends, with miniaturization pushing boundaries further: As illustrated, the Intel 8008 (1974) had 2500 transistors at 10,000 nm, the Pentium 4 (2005) 169 million at 90 nm, the Xeon (2017) 8 billion at 14 nm, the Apple M1 Max (2021) 57 billion at 5 nm, and the NVIDIA Blackwell B200 (2025) 208 billion at 4 nm, with 2 nm processes now in production. This scaling has made quantum effects even more integral to classical device design, intensifying the blur between classical and quantum technologies noted previously, without resolving the definitional challenges for IP regimes.

5.4 Defining Quantum Technology Patents

The growing overlap between classical (e.g., sub-5 nm transistors in current CPUs and GPUs) and quantum technologies poses the question: What constitutes a quantum technology patent? This ambiguity, first raised in our 2022 study, continues to challenge proposals for sui generis quantum patent regimes, as defining the field's scope risks claim "draftsmanship" or misalignment with international standards like TRIPS, which require technology-neutral patents and a 20-year patent term. Our updated results show the USPTO remains the preferred office (accounting for ~75% of S2 patents), and unharmonized reforms could still distort filing choices, with no new developments alleviating this concern amid rising global filings.

5.5 Growth in Quantum Computing Patents

Our search (S5) identified 6685 quantum computing patent applications, resulting in 2879 granted patents classified under CPC G06N10 ("quantum computing based on quantum-mechanical phenomena")—a substantial increase from the 3042 applications and 1603 grants in our 2022 analysis. The field remained niche from 2001 to 2014 (<48 grants/year), but has since accelerated consistently: Grants rose from 37 in 2014 to 435 in 2021 (CAGR $\approx$ 42.2%), and have continued growing robustly through 2025, with an estimated average of over 300 grants annually from 2022 to 2025, yielding a revised CAGR of approximately 35% in recent years. This trajectory extends the heightened R&D investment and interest highlighted previously, with no slowdown, potentially fueled by advancements in error-corrected qubits and hybrid quantum-classical systems.

5.6 Top Quantum Computing Patent Owners

Examination of top patent owners reveals less concentration than in classical computing markets, a finding that holds from our 2022 study. Alongside established firms (IBM, Microsoft, Alphabet/Google, Intel), universities, and startups feature prominently, with portfolios expanding ~80% overall since 2021. Strong patents remain crucial for new entrants and quantum-focused SMEs compared to incumbents. Well-capitalized incumbents fund R&D internally, while new-entrants rely on IP for fundraising—Rigetti and IonQ hold top-10 portfolios, exemplifying the enduring IP leverage for SMEs noted earlier.

5.7 *IP and Antitrust Implications*

Quantum patent trends raise antitrust considerations, as concentration in key portfolios could limit access to essential technologies—a potential risk flagged in our 2022 analysis that has grown more relevant with 2025's commercialization wave (e.g., quantum cloud services). However, the current diversity among owners mitigates thicket risks, promoting competition without major new concentrations emerging. Policymakers should continue monitoring the more dynamic aspects of (innovation) competition and the patent-trade secret balance to avoid monopolies in strategic areas like national security, with the updated data showing no shift toward dominance but increased geopolitical fragmentation (e.g., China's expanded portfolios).

6 Discussion

Our updated general patent landscape study, extending our 2022 analysis,[22] confirm the persistence of key trends while highlighting amplified growth over the additional 4 years through October 2025. Specifically: (1) the USPTO and EPO are now jointly granting approximately 2500 patents per year related to quantum technologies (S2), up from ~2000 in 2021; (2) the overall CAGR over the 24 years from 2001 to 2025 has been around 14.5% reflective of sustained acceleration; (3) over 50% of the patent disclosures published in this period are already in the public domain progressively enriching the quantum information commons as anticipated; (4) the majority of granted quantum computing patents relate to physical realisations of building blocks for quantum computers, quantum error correction, quantum circuits and applications, with no shift in dominance; (5) the nature of claims and drafting practices remains nearly indistinguishable from those in semiconductor and computing patents that drove the information technology revolution, underscoring the ongoing continuum between classical and quantum tech; (6) the increasing overlap between classical and quantum technologies persists as a challenge for proposals advocating *sui generis* quantum patent regimes; (7) following the limited activity from 2001–2014 noted previously, quantum computing has seen continued substantial growth, with granted patents rising; (8) concentration among top quantum computing patent owners remains lower than in classical computing and IT markets, with diversity holding steady; (9) in addition to well-known large-cap companies, specialized quantum new ventures, universities, and government entities feature among top assignees, with SMEs leveraging IP for growth as before; and (10) the USPTO continues as the preferred office, accounting for ~75% of granted quantum technology patents by the EPO and USPTO.

[22] Aboy et al. (2022), pp. 853–882.

The updated data also reinforce our 2022 conclusion that the patent system continues to incentivize public disclosure in quantum computing and related fields, in settings where trade secrecy might otherwise be expected to dominate given the early-stage character of the technologies, their market structures, and business models such as quantum cloud-computing "as a service." Across the 2001–2025 period, approximately 57% of quantum-related patent disclosures are now in the public domain (up from about 50% in 2021) including over 6000 granted patents that have expired. This expanding "quantum information commons" raises the novelty bar and narrows claim scope over time, mitigating concerns about overprotection or blocking positions. Nearly all 2879 quantum-computing patents in our dataset will have entered the public domain by the time the quantum-computing market reaches a scale comparable to today's cloud-computing industry, suggesting that, from a temporal perspective, a substantial body of codified technical knowledge will be freely available at the point of broader commercial maturity.

Consistent with our prior analysis, the additional 4 years of data show no emergence of patent thickets or new structural barriers to entry. Patenting activity has accelerated as anticipated, but without any observable shift toward systemic overprotection. Allowance rates remain stable, and the increase in grants classified under CPC G06N10 since 2021 aligns with recent technological developments such as Google's Willow chip, the Quantum Echoes algorithm, Microsoft's Majorana 1 chip, and NIST's advances in quantum nanofabrication. These breakthroughs appear to have stimulated additional filing activity while remaining compatible with a competitive and relatively unconcentrated patent landscape.

At the same time, our earlier observations on the interaction between patents, trade secrets, and state secrecy continue to hold, though with notable asymmetries across technologies. Some important innovations in quantum computing occur in conditions of secrecy, particularly in strategic government R&D programs where non-disclosure is required by national security considerations. However, unlike in certain AI domains, the updated data do not indicate a structural pivot away from patents. In quantum hardware in particular, high capital requirements, specialized facilities, and complex supply chains make patents comparatively more attractive: for new entrants and SMEs, patenting costs remain small relative to R&D expenditures, and quantum's capital intensity amplifies the value of patents as both appropriation and signaling devices. In contrast to AI's relatively low entry barriers and code-centric innovation cycles, the quantum sector as observed through 2025 continues to rely on patents rather than trade or state secrets as its primary formal IP channel, even as secrecy remains significant at the frontier.

That said, it has not escaped our notice that geopolitical dynamics have intensified since our 2022 analysis, adding further context to these IP patterns. Updated studies such as the MIT Quantum Index Report 2025 indicate that China's quantum patent filings increased significantly from 2014 to 2024, showing top 3 global leadership in quantum technology patents (including quantum-computing) and narrowing the gap with the United States, with some projections suggesting a possible overtaking by 2027. This development extends our earlier observations of China's rapid ascent in quantum communications into a broader assertion of strength across multiple quantum domains. The result is a more complex competitive landscape in which patents, trade secrets, and state secrets are deployed as instruments of industrial policy, technological leadership, and strategic autonomy. These trends also give rise to nascent competition law questions, as breakthroughs such as Google's Willow chip and the Quantum Echoes algorithm signal a transition from primarily experimental implementations toward more practical and commercially relevant applications. The evolving interplay between technological breakthroughs, concentrated data or infrastructure, and strategic portfolios of quantum-related patents will likely shape future enforcement and regulatory priorities.

From a public-policy perspective, the updated empirical record thus refines our earlier assessment of how the patent system interacts with quantum innovation. For instance, our 2022 study flagged the risks of ill-advised IP reforms in capital-intensive sectors and highlighted the distributional dimension of patent policy, whereby large-cap incumbents with strong market positions may rationally prefer weaker patent rights, whereas new quantum entrants and SMEs typically rely on robust patent protection to attract investment and credibly participate in global markets.

The 2025 evidence is consistent with this framing: sustained growth in grants, stable allowance rates, and the expansion of the quantum information commons all point to a system that continues to foster disclosure and support innovation in quantum technologies rather than to one that systematically obstructs it. However, the amplified geopolitical and competition-law dimensions observed in the updated data underscore that future debates on quantum governance and IP design should be grounded in empirically informed assessments of these dynamics, rather than in speculative fears about either overprotection or under-incentivization.

7 Conclusion

The results of this updated patent landscape study reaffirm our 2022 conclusion that the patent system is incentivizing public disclosure in quantum computing and related fields, serving the public interest where trade secrets might otherwise prevail due to the technologies' early-stage nature, market structures, and business models (e.g., quantum cloud-computing as a service). No new evidence of overprotection has arisen; instead, the amplified growth and expanding public domain mitigate barriers, while geopolitical shifts—such as China's substantial increase in patent filings—add layers to global competition. From a public policy perspective, large-cap incumbents with leading positions may favor weaker patent rights (as they do not need these patents to secure funding and the technology can be protected through trade secrets), whereas new quantum entrants benefit from stronger protections to secure investment funding.

This updated analysis of the quantum technologies patent landscape from 2001 to October 2025 reveals a robust and accelerating innovation ecosystem, characterized by a double digit compound annual growth rate in grants, predominantly at the

USPTO, and a diverse array of top owners ranging from tech companies like IBM, Google, and Microsoft to startups and universities. With over 50% of disclosures now entering the public domain (including 25% of the granted patents), the patent system continues to foster an expanding quantum information commons, countering trade secrecy and state secrecy risks and elevating the novelty and non-obviousness/inventive step threshold for future inventions without evidence of overprotection or thickets.

At the same time, geopolitical shifts such as China's rapid ascent in quantum computing and quantum communications, as well as increasing calls around the globe for employing IPRs and regulation to increase resilience and so-called "technological sovereignty" in strategically crucial areas, such as AI- and quantum technologies, underscore the need for evidence-based policies. Policmakers should see it as a primary task to balance IP incentives with competition law considerations, standardization efforts,[23] and global collaboration to sustain open innovation amid commercialization and national security imperatives.

In sum, this updated analysis of the quantum technologies patent landscape from 2001 to October 2025 reinforces our 2022 findings: patents drive disclosure and innovation without posing major "overprotection" problems, but geopolitical shifts and potential concentration risks reinforce the need for evidence-based quantum innovation policy.

Acknowledgement This work was made possible through the generous support of the Novo Nordisk Foundation (NNF) via a grant for the scientifically independent Collaborative Research Program in Bioscience Innovation Law (Inter-CeBIL Program—Grant No. NNF23SA0087056). The opinions expressed are the authors' own and not of their respective affiliations. The authors declare no conflicts of interests.

References

Aboy M, Liddell K, Liddicoat J et al (2016) Myriad's impact on gene patents. Nat Biotechnol 34:1119–1123. https://doi.org/10.1038/nbt.3719

Aboy M, Liddell K, Liddicoat J et al (2021) Mapping the European patent landscape for medical uses of known products. Nat Biotechnol 39:1336–1343. https://doi.org/10.1038/s41587-021-01104-1

Aboy M, Minssen T, Kop M (2022) Mapping the patent landscape of quantum technologies: patenting trends, innovation and policy implications. IIC - Int Rev Intellect Prop Compet Law 53:853–882. https://doi.org/10.1007/s40319-022-01209-3

Aboy M, Gasser U, Cohen IG, Kop M (2025) Quantum technology governance: a standards-first approeach. Science 389(6760):575–578

Acín A et al (2018) The quantum technologies roadmap: a European community view. New J Phys 20:080201. https://doi.org/10.1088/1367-2630/aad1ea

Alex M (2021) arXiv preprint 2102.04552. 10.48550/arXiv.2102.04552

[23] Aboy et al. (2025)

Arute F, Arya K, Babbush R et al (2019) Quantum supremacy using a programmable superconducting processor. Nature 574:505–510. https://doi.org/10.1038/s41586-019-1666-5

Bachmann S (2011) The big five—patent filings reveal the hottest upcoming areas in nanotechnology commercialization. In: 2011 11th IEEE international conference on nanotechnology (NANO), Portland, OR, pp 926–931. https://doi.org/10.1109/NANO.2011.6144609

Bubela T, Gold E, Graff G et al (2013) Patent landscaping for life sciences innovation: toward consistent and transparent practices. Nat Biotechnol 31:202–206. https://doi.org/10.1038/nbt.2521

Chang M (2005) Quantum computation patent mapping—a strategic view for the information technique of tomorrow. In: ICSSSM 2005 International Conference on Services Systems and Services Management, vol 2, Chongqing, China, pp. 1177–1181. https://doi.org/10.1109/ICSSSM.2005.1500183

Córcoles AD et al (2020) Challenges and opportunities of near-term quantum computing systems. Proc IEEE 108(8):1338–1352. https://doi.org/10.1109/JPROC.2019.2954005

Dowling JP, Milburn GJ (2003) Quantum technology: the second quantum revolution. Phil Trans R Soc A 361:1655–1674. https://doi.org/10.1098/rsta.2003.1227

Haney BS (2021) Quantum machine learning: a patent review. Case Western Reserve J Law Technol Internet 12(1) https://scholarlycommons.law.case.edu/jolti/vol12/iss1/6

Jiang SY, Chen SL (2021) Exploring landscapes of quantum technology with patent network analysis. Tech Anal Strat Manag 33(11):1317–1331. https://doi.org/10.1080/09537325.2021.1928056

Kop M (2020) Regulating transformative technology in the quantum age: intellectual property, standardization & sustainable innovation. Stanford–Vienna Transatlantic Technology Law Forum, Transatlantic Antitrust and IPR Developments, Issue 2/2020. https://ssrn.com/abstract=3653544

Kop M (2022) Quantum computing and intellectual property law. Berkeley Technol Law J 35(3):101–115. https://btlj.org/2022/02/quantum-computing-and-intellectual-property-law/

Riedel MF, Binosi D, Thew R, Calarco T (2017) The European quantum technologies flagship programme. Quantum Sci Technol 2:030501. https://doi.org/10.1088/2058-9565/aa6aca

Smith J, Arshad Z, Trippe A et al (2018) The reporting items for patent landscapes statement. Nat Biotechnol 36:1043–1047. https://doi.org/10.1038/nbt.4291

Winiarczyk R et al (2013) Analysis of patent activity in the field of quantum information processing. Int J Quantum Information 11(1):1350007. https://doi.org/10.1142/S021974991350007X

EU Cybersecurity Regulation in the Quantum Age

Peter Alexander Earls Davis, Mateo Aboy, Lee Andrew Bygrave, Timo Minssen, Urs Gasser, and Marcelo Corrales Compagnucci

Abstract This chapter explores the intersection of quantum computing and European Union (EU) cybersecurity law. It examines to what extent cybersecurity regulation in the EU is fit-for-purpose to deal with the challenges of quantum computing. Two key challenges are identified: (i) harvest now, decrypt later (HNDL) attacks, and (ii) the accelerated development of quantum computers outpacing current cybersecurity measures. The chapter argues that concepts like "state of the art" and "appropriate technical and organizational measures" characteristic of EU cybersecurity law fail to sufficiently account for cybersecurity threats anticipated to materialize in the future, but impacting networks and information systems today. Proposed solutions include enhancing judicial clarity of technical cybersecurity requirements, increasing policy focus on post-quantum cryptography, adopting firmer cybersecurity requirements in hard law, and shifting towards alternative terms that properly account for future cybersecurity uncertainties. The chapter concludes by advocating for proactive regulatory approaches anchored in anticipatory governance and multi-layered strategies to safeguard against the quantum threat.

Keywords Encryption · Cybersecurity · Post-quantum cryptography · Quantum key distribution · Security-by-design · Anticipatory governance · Technology governance · Privacy · Security

---

P. A. E. Davis (✉) · T. Minssen · M. C. Compagnucci
Center for Advanced Studies in Bioscience Innovation Law (CeBIL), University of Copenhagen, Copenhagen, Denmark
e-mail: paed@jur.ku.dk

M. Aboy
Centre for Law, Medicine and Life Sciences (LML) & Centre for Intellectual Property & Information Law (CIPIL), University of Cambridge, Cambridge, UK
e-mail: ma608@cam.ac.uk

L. A. Bygrave
Norwegian Research Center for Computers and Law (NRCCL), University of Oslo, Oslo, Norway

U. Gasser
Technical University of Munich (TUM), Munich, Germany

M. Aboy et al. (eds.), *Quantum Technology Governance I*, Perspectives in Law, Business and Innovation, https://doi.org/10.1007/978-981-95-8371-3_5

1 Introduction

Quantum computers promise to excel at tasks traditional computers struggle with, heralding a paradigm shift across numerous fields. Whilst the precise nature and scope of these tasks remain uncertain, the current period of development—often referred to as the "Noisy Intermediate-Scale Quantum" (NISQ)[1] era—reflects the technology's limited practical applications at present. Nevertheless, a growing body of research and development, coupled with increasing confidence in its progress and a few concrete recent successes,[2] suggests quantum advantage is near.

Unfortunately for cybersecurity experts, one of the most promising fields of application for quantum computers is in the field of cryptography. Shor's algorithm stands to undermine the mathematical principles upon which much of our digital infrastructure is secured, with Gartner forecasting that "by 2029, advances in quantum computing will make asymmetric cryptography unsafe and by 2034 fully breakable."[3] Although such predictions are notorious for being overly optimistic, many actors are already working systematically to ameliorate quantum-based security challenges, with various inter-disciplinary projects in post-quantum cryptography (PQC) at advanced stages, and PQC beginning to be implemented across various products and services.

Whilst the European Union (EU) has been investing in projects relating to quantum computing,[4] and indeed quantum cryptography,[5] its substantial recent efforts in the regulation of cybersecurity through secondary legislation have failed to flag the quantum threat specifically.[6] This chapter examines the risks of this neglect, and suggests possible pathways for closing legislative gaps.

The chapter is structured as follows. Section 2 first gives a primer on the nature of the threats posed by quantum computing to cybersecurity and identifies two key cybersecurity issues that may affect organizations today and in the future. These issues are (i) harvest now, decrypt later (HNDL) attacks, and (ii) the more general threat of quantum computers outpacing current cybersecurity measures. Thereafter, the current EU cybersecurity regulatory regime is analyzed in Sect. 3, revealing a reliance on several heuristics and assumptions that are vulnerable in light of quantum threats. Section 4 of the chapter then examines policy options available for the EU to pursue in order to mitigate the potential harms of quantum computers, and ameliorating the shortcomings of the current approach to cybersecurity. Section 5 concludes that the EU is uniquely situated, as an actor with relatively high

[1] Preskill (2018); Brooks (2019).

[2] See, e.g., Panizza et al. (2024); Aghaee et al. (2025); Ghazi Vakili et al. (2025).

[3] Horvath (2024).

[4] European Commission (2018).

[5] European Commission (2019).

[6] Though see the policy action described below at Sect. 4.2.

regulatory capacity,[7] to taking a leading role in developing regulatory mechanisms in this space.

2 The Quantum Threat to Cybersecurity

Whether, and the extent to which, quantum computing will revolutionize the information age remains to be seen. In today's NISQ era, quantum computers are characterized by processors with tens to hundreds of quantum bits (qubits) with significant error rates.[8] Despite the immense hype surrounding them, for the most part, quantum computers can so far only solve "toy models" to provide proof of concept, rather than offering appreciable advantages. At present (i.e., July 2025, when this chapter was finalized), there are decidedly few problems that the scientific community believes, with some confidence, quantum computers will have a significant advantage solving over their classical counterparts.[9]

2.1 *Shor's Algorithm and Asymmetric Encryption*

Shor's algorithm is one of the oldest and most researched quantum algorithms, which in principle has a "devastating impact"[10] on the most widely deployed asymmetric encryption algorithms. This means that encryption of data *in transit*, which overwhelmingly relies upon asymmetric cryptography for key exchange and authentication, is vulnerable to attack by a fault-tolerant quantum computer of sufficient qubits. These "asymmetric" algorithms, most notably Rivest–Shamir–Adleman (RSA) and Elliptic-curve cryptography (ECC), rely on mathematical problems that are easy to solve when encrypting data with the public key but infeasible for classical computers to reverse when trying to decrypt the data without the private key.[11] Shor's algorithm has been proven to efficiently solve these mathematical problems, thereby breaking the security of these encryption methods should a quantum computer of sufficient qubits and stability be built.

The practical implications of Shor's algorithm, if they materialize, are vast. A wide variety of digital infrastructure in myriad industries would be affected. The sharing of government secrets, banking information, healthcare data, transactional data related to e-commerce and a multitude of other day-to-day communications would be markedly more vulnerable to access by unauthorized parties.

---

[7] Bradford (2023).

[8] Chen et al. (2023).

[9] See Jordan (2025); Montanaro (2016).

[10] Bernstein and Lange (2017).

[11] Mavroeidis et al. (2018).

Other types of cryptosystems may also be weakened due to quantum computing, for instance, due to a novel quantum algorithm being developed that poses additional threats beyond Shor's algorithm. Indeed, other quantum algorithms, such as Grover's algorithm, do stand to impact symmetric cryptography, but current research indicates that these are able to be mitigated by simply increasing the key-size.[12] Since Shor's algorithm affects the very fundaments of contemporary asymmetric cryptography, a new cryptographic approach entirely is likely needed to account for the threat.

2.2 *Post-Quantum Cryptography (PQC)*

Whilst quantum key distribution (QKD) is emerging as a means of cyber defense,[13] PQC presents the most realistic solution to combat the threat of quantum computing for most situations given there is no need for specialized hardware.[14] PQC refers to cryptographic algorithms designed to be secure against quantum attacks. These algorithms are being developed and standardized to replace or supplement current encryption methods vulnerable to quantum computing. As put by Bernstein and Lange, "[t]he central challenge in post-quantum cryptography is to meet demands for cryptographic usability and flexibility without sacrificing confidence."[15] The US-based National Institute of Standards and Technology (NIST) has led efforts to standardize PQC since 2016 when it called for PQC submissions for consideration as part of a competition. It recently issued three "winning" PQC standards that leverage quantum-resistant cryptographic algorithms.[16]

However, the transition to PQC is complex, involving not only the development of new algorithms but also their integration into existing systems and protocols. Legacy systems, for instance, may have technical limitations that make the implementation and interoperability of PQC difficult or impossible. Moreover, even though the NIST competition involved robust testing of the winning PQC algorithms, they are not as battle-hardened as ubiquitous classical standards like RSA, and their ultimate resilience against future quantum attack is still uncertain.[17] This is all to underscore that time, i.e., chronological co-ordination, is of the essence in preparing for the quantum threat, despite its precise event horizon and nature being as-yet unknown.

---

[12] Hoofnagle and Garfinkel (2022), pp. 315–319.

[13] Korzh et al. (2015); Liao et al. (2017).

[14] Rodríguez (2025), pp. 4–5; Xu et al. (2023).

[15] Bernstein and Lange (2017).

[16] See further below at Sect. 3.3.3.

[17] Indeed, one of the final selected algorithms was proven vulnerable by a classical computer employed by researchers: see Savage (2023).

2.3 Future Threats, Today's Risks

Quantum threats to cybersecurity depend on several variables, such as the type of actor that has access to quantum computing (e.g., public or private; civilian or military; friendly or non-friendly nation-state).[18] Moreover, threats can be conceived from a variety of perspectives including from upstream and downstream in the cybersecurity value chain. For instance, a lack of confidence as to encryption's efficacy in securing information across public networks could impact medical research that relies on efficient and secure transmission of sensitive information. There is little imaginative limit, with quantum computing being uniquely suited to doomsday prophesizing in the cybersecurity field.[19]

To focus discussion, two types of threats are given specific attention in this chapter. These are selected since both can be mitigated through actions taken today, including by regulators. First, are HNDL attacks, being the practice of intercepting and storing encrypted data sent over public networks with the intention of decrypting it once quantum computers become powerful enough to break current encryption methods.[20] Second, are the risks associated with insufficient "cryptographic agility", i.e., shortfalls in the adoption of quantum-resistant algorithms, which may leave some systems vulnerable during the transition period to PQC and other mitigation measures.[21]

Arguably, these risks make the quantum threat ripe for regulatory intervention, and indeed NIST's considerable PQC coordination work as a key "soft law" regulator in the field is indicative of the importance of regulatory agencies (broadly understood) to mitigate the quantum threat. Moreover, as elaborated below at Sect. 4.1, organizations are unlikely to adequately respond to the risks without appropriate regulatory (dis)incentives, leading to considerable negative externalities if left unregulated.

2.4 Global Quantum and Cybersecurity Governance

Whilst this contribution analyses the EU regulatory approach to the threat of quantum computers, the complexity of the issue, within the context of global cybersecurity governance, should be emphasized at the outset. Cybersecurity is a critical challenge for organizations of all kinds and sizes, and myriad stakeholders are increasingly recognizing it as a priority—from the C-suite, to heads of government, civil society, and individuals. These stakeholders often have diverging approaches and interests, and significant imbalances in power inhere within and between them.

[18] Hoofnagle and Garfinkel (2022), pp. 308 ff.

[19] See, e.g., Taddeo et al. (2024).

[20] Barker et al. (2021), p. 2.

[21] Ott and Peikert (2019); Savage (2023).

Quantum computing further challenges an already strained problem space by introducing unprecedented risks to critical and ubiquitous security tools.

Accordingly, the EU's regulatory response in and of itself is, and will be, far from sufficient to comprehensively deal with the issues raised by the possibilities of quantum computers. The potential problems are global, multi-dimensional, and deal with the ramifications of cutting-edge technologies of which we are far from a complete understanding. Nevertheless, so far as the EU sees itself as a leader in the global cybersecurity—and indeed quantum technology—ecosystem, it does have a role to play, however modest. The following section describes what role it is currently playing.

3 EU Cybersecurity Regulation

EU cybersecurity regulation is a far-flung, complex and somewhat confusing system of rules, making generalized pronouncements about its reach and (attempted) effect difficult.[22] Moreover, it presents a moving target due to the speed of adoption of new laws and policies, and the "plasticity"[23] of the concept of cybersecurity itself. Despite this, there exists a growing body of literature directed towards examining the emerging logic and scope of EU cybersecurity law and policy.[24] This literature makes it unnecessary for this chapter to conduct a comprehensive appraisal or assessment of EU cybersecurity law. Rather, the chapter synthesizes and assesses those attributes of EU cybersecurity law that are especially relevant to the challenges posed by quantum computing.

This section proceeds as follows. First, key cybersecurity "hard law" instruments are analyzed, revealing a tendency for the EU legislature to rely on the term "state of the art" rather than instituting specific technical, operational and organizational security requirements. Second, the concept of state of the art is discussed, and the importance of soft law in fleshing out that concept is introduced. Third, the chapter analyses influential industry guidelines on state of the art, revealing a lack of consideration of the threat to cybersecurity posed by quantum computing.

3.1 EU Cybersecurity Instruments

The EU has developed a multitude of secondary law instruments to enhance the security of networks and information systems within different contexts. In addition, particular cybersecurity requirements also inhere in primary law—notably in respect of personal data, the security of which constitutes part of the "essence" of the

[22] See further Bygrave (2025b).

[23] Porcedda (2022), p. 67.

[24] Porcedda (2022); Wessel (2015); Papakonstantinou (2022); Fuster and Jasmontaite (2020); Bygrave (2025b).

fundamental rights to privacy and data protection. enshrined in, respectively, Articles 7 and 8 of the EU Charter of Fundamental Rights.[25] There is no omnibus instrument that covers cybersecurity regulation across different domains; somewhat underwhelmingly,[26] the Cybersecurity Act[27] merely establishes a certification mechanism and strengthens the European Union Agency for Cybersecurity (ENISA) with a permanent mandate. Instead, a patchwork of sector- and domain-specific instruments contain rules as to the technical, operational and organizational measures required to be taken by regulatees (i.e., the entities that are subject to the instruments) across different, often overlapping, contexts.

Three such instruments are worth highlighting in this respect: the General Data Protection Regulation[28] (GDPR), the Cyber Resilience Act[29] (CRA), and the updated Network and Information Systems Directive[30] (NIS 2). These are not the only instruments with a cybersecurity remit, but they are arguably the most central due to their relatively broad ambit. They regulate, respectively, personal data protection, internet-connected products (including internet-of-things (IoT) devices) and the security of critical infrastructure. Each of them contains provisions requiring regulatees to implement "appropriate" security measures to manage cybersecurity risks.[31] The specific measures required are not conclusively listed in each instrument—and nor could or should they be, considering the near-endless number and variety of possible measures, and the desirability of formulating rules with a significant degree of technological neutrality.

---

[25] See, e.g., the EU Court of Justice Grand Chamber judgments in Joined Cases C-293/12 and C-594/12, *Digital Rights Ireland Ltd v Minister for Communications, Marine and Natural Resources and Others* and *Kärntner Landesregierung and Others* (at para. 40), and Case C-817/19, *Ligue des droits humains v Conseil des ministers* (at para. 120).

[26] Bygrave (2025b), p. 7.

[27] Regulation (EU) 2019/881 of the European Parliament and of the Council of 17 April 2019 on ENISA (the European Union Agency for Cybersecurity) and on information and communications technology cybersecurity certification and repealing Regulation (EU) No 526/2013 (Cybersecurity Act) OJ L 151, 7.6.2019, pp. 15–69.

[28] Regulation (EU) 2016/679 of the European Parliament and of the Council of 27 April 2016 on the protection of natural persons with regard to the processing of personal data and on the free movement of such data, and repealing Directive 95/46/EC (General Data Protection Regulation), OJ L 119, 4.5.2016.

[29] Regulation (EU) 2024/2847 of the European Parliament and of the Council of 23 October 2024 on horizontal cybersecurity requirements for products with digital elements and amending Regulations (EU) No 168/2013 and (EU) 2019/1020 and Directive (EU) 2020/1828 (Cyber Resilience Act), OJ L, 2024/2847, 20.11.2024. Note that most provisions of the CRA will not apply until 11 December 2027.

[30] Directive (EU) 2022/2555 of the European Parliament and of the Council of 14 December 2022 on measures for a high common level of cybersecurity across the Union, amending Regulation (EU) No 910/2014 and Directive (EU) 2018/1972, and repealing Directive (EU) 2016/1148 (NIS 2 Directive) OJ L 333 27.12.2022.

[31] GDPR Art. 32 (see also Art. 25); CRA Art. 13 & Annex I, Part I; NIS 2 Directive Art. 21.

More specifically, the GDPR states in Article 32(1):

> Taking into account the state of the art, the costs of implementation and the nature, scope, context and purposes of processing as well as the risk of varying likelihood and severity for the rights and freedoms of natural persons, the controller and the processor shall implement appropriate technical and organisational measures to ensure a level of security appropriate to the risk, including inter alia as appropriate:
>
> a) the pseudonymisation and encryption of personal data;

Similarly, the CRA mandates manufacturers of products with digital elements to design, develop and produce these in accordance with "essential cybersecurity requirements",[32] which demand manufacturers to "ensure an appropriate level of cybersecurity based on the risks."[33] Amongst the requirements is that IoT products must:

> protect the confidentiality of stored, transmitted or otherwise processed data, personal or other, such as by encrypting relevant data at rest or in transit by state of the art mechanisms, and by using other technical means…[34]

NIS 2 uses similar language, requiring so-called "essential and important entities"[35] to "take appropriate and proportionate technical, operational and organisational measures to manage the risks posed to the security of network and information systems",[36] those measures being determined by "[t]aking into account the state-of-the-art and, where applicable, relevant European and international standards, as well as the cost of implementation".[37] The instrument refers to "policies and procedures regarding the use of cryptography and, where appropriate, encryption"[38] as being one of the necessary measures required of essential and important entities.

Each of these three EU instruments specifically refers to encryption as a measure that may, or must, be implemented as "appropriate", albeit without explicit guidance as to which encryption schemes may be appropriate in a given setting. They are not the only instruments to flag encryption specifically. For instance, the European Electronic Communications Code does so as well.[39] The pertinent question for this chapter is whether security requirements in EU cybersecurity law, given present legal and technological conditions, could be properly construed to require the use of PQC in certain contexts.

In some instances covered by these instruments, PQC will never conceivably be appropriate. For example, in the case of the GDPR which regulates a broad

---

[32] CRA Art. 13(1).

[33] CRA Annex I, Part I(1).

[34] CRA, Annex I, Part I(2)(e).

[35] See NIS 2, Art. 3.

[36] NIS 2, Art. 21(1).

[37] NIS 2, Art. 21(1).

[38] NIS 2, Art. 21(2)(h).

[39] See recital 97 in the preamble to Directive (EU) 2018/1972 of the European Parliament and of the Council of 11 December 2018 establishing the European Electronic Communications Code (Recast), OJ 2018 L 321/36.

spectrum of personal data processing, including on physical media such as paper,[40] there may be instances where any form of encryption, let alone PQC, is not appropriate to the level of risk. For the purposes of this chapter, however, it is asked whether PQC could *ever* be a legal requirement according to the proper interpretation of the above provisions. In the case of the GDPR, that may be in the context of a processing operation with high risks to data subjects' fundamental rights, such as the transfer of sensitive medical data or critical financial information.

The key criterion in determining this question is whether PQC falls within the "state of the art". As put by Bygrave, EU cybersecurity law exhibits "widespread legislative use of generic functional requirements rooted in 'state of the art'".[41] Schmitz conceives of state of the art in cybersecurity as a "protection goal"[42] implemented by the EU legislature for organizations to meet. At minimum, it requires regulatees to "take account of the current progress in technology"[43] in determining which cybersecurity measures, including which cryptographical methods, may be appropriate. Thus, in the context of advancements in quantum computing, the concept requires careful consideration.

3.2 *State of the Art*

As noted by Schmitz, whilst the concept of state of the art is commonly used in EU instruments, including in cybersecurity, neither EU nor national legislators have formally defined it.[44] Nor, since its apparent inception in the 1985 Product Liability Directive,[45] has the Court of Justice of the European Union (CJEU) found opportunity to elaborate on what the concept actually means.[46] In the absence of EU legislative or judicial proclamation, interpretation by commentators has relied on German jurisprudence on the concept (formulated as "Stand der Technik" in German)[47] and guidance from regulatory agencies like the European Data Protection Board (EDPB) and ENISA.[48]

---

[40] GDPR Art. 2(1).

[41] Bygrave (2025b), p. 6.

[42] Schmitz (2022), p. 25.

[43] European Data Protection Board, Guidelines 4/2019 on Article 25 Data Protection by Design and by Default, Version 2.0, Adopted on 20 October 2020, p. 8.

[44] Schmitz (2022), p. 25.

[45] Council Directive 85/374/EEC of 25 July 1985 on the approximation of the laws, regulations and administrative provisions of the Member States concerning liability for defective products OJ L 210, 7.8.1985, pp. 29–33.

[46] Bygrave (2025a), p. 69.

[47] German Federal Constitutional Court (Second Senate) (*Bundesverfassungsgericht*), decision of 8 August 1978 ('Kalkar'), BVerfGE, pp. 49, 89.

[48] Bygrave (2025a), pp. 68–70.

In this vein, German organization TeleTrust, in collaboration with ENISA,[49] has created (and continues to update) their own published guidelines that comprehensively deal with the state of the art under the GDPR.[50] This publication relies considerably on the decision of the German Federal Constitutional Court in the *Kalkar* case[51] when conceptualizing 'state of the art', situating the concept in between "existing scientific knowledge and research" and "generally accepted rules of technology".[52] This is depicted in the below graphic from the document (Fig. 1):

Within this construct, it is questionable whether PQC has reached the status of the "state of the art" or is presently within the state of "existing scientific knowledge and research". The document states that:

> Technical measures at the "existing scientific knowledge and research" stage are highly dynamic in their development and pass into the "state of the art" stage when they reach market maturity (or at least are launched on the market).[53]

The maturity of PQC is difficult to adjudicate in this sense. On the one hand, PQC is only just beginning to reach mainstream adoption, with Apple[54] and Signal[55] being early movers in adding PQC to their popular messaging applications. As a further example, a recent collaborative effort by the Banque de France and the Monetary Authority of Singapore involving the application of PQC to certain email

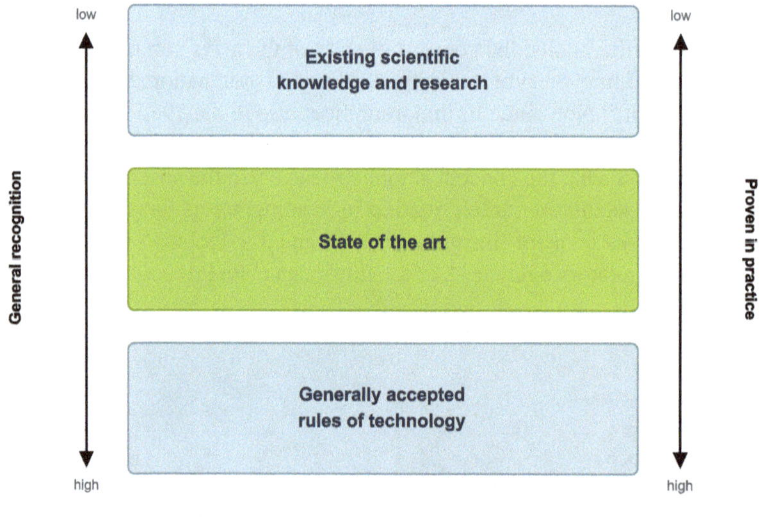

Fig. 1 Depiction of "state of the art" under German law (Adapted from: Teletrust/ENISA 2023)

[49] ENISA (2019).

[50] TeleTrust and ENISA 2023.

[51] TeleTrust and ENISA 2023, p. 11.

[52] TeleTrust and ENISA 2023, p. 11.

[53] TeleTrust and ENISA 2023, p. 12.

[54] Apple Security Engineering and Architecture (SEAR) 2024.

[55] Kret (2023).

communications[56] was heralded as 'ground-breaking'.[57] Notable in each of these instances is that PQC comprises an *additional* protection on top of classic cryptography. The hybrid cryptographic approach is indicative of the nascence of PQC and the uncertainty of its protective benefits—especially given the lack of a quantum computer capable of robustly testing the algorithms. These considerations weigh against the "proven in practice" factor in Teletrust/ENISA's conceptualization and hence indicate that PQC is not yet "state of the art".

On the other hand, the TeleTrust/ENISA guidance suggests that mere entry into the market means that a measure has reached the state of the art stage.[58] Clearly, certain types of PQC have reached some level of mainstream adoption and have, in this sense, entered the market. Indeed, even cutting-edge quantum key distribution using specialized hardware and software, like that offered by Swiss company ID Quantique, are currently available. This would suggest that, despite the nascence of PQC, and the cautious way in which it is being implemented by certain organizations, PQC should properly be considered as within the state of the art.

However, it bears emphasis that the *Kalkar* approach, as interpreted in the Teletrust/ENISA document, is not decisive for the proper interpretation of the state of the art criterion in EU law.[59] Further, Bygrave cogently argues that more factors are probably relevant to consider: "the criterion likely requires security measures to conform not only with the current state of technological advancement, but also with contemporary practices, standards and other norms for technical and organizational management that are generally regarded as offering the best degree of security at the time."[60] Thus, mere entry to market does not mean that a measure necessarily rises to the state of the art for the purposes of EU law.

Bygrave points to the role that soft law standards play in fleshing out the notion, with Data Protection Agencies (DPAs) referencing output from ISO, NIST and ENISA in decisions involving cybersecurity breaches.[61] Bygrave's—and indeed Teletrust/ENISA's—analysis is limited to the meaning of state of the art under the GDPR. Looking at EU cybersecurity law more generally, the argument that standards are critical in determining appropriate security measures is more straightforward. As aforementioned, NIS 2 explicitly refers to "state-of-the-art and, where applicable, relevant European and international standards".[62] The CRA, as a product safety law based on the New Legislative Framework, allows regulatees to rely on harmonized standards to presumptively demonstrate conformity to the

[56] Margaine and Goh (2024).

[57] Hall (2024).

[58] TeleTrust and ENISA (2023), pp. 11, 12.

[59] Bygrave (2025a), p. 69.

[60] Bygrave (2025a), p. 69.

[61] Bygrave (2025a), p. 69. See also Bygrave (2021), pp. 140–141.

[62] NIS 2, Art. 21(1). See also Art. 25(1), requiring Member States to 'encourage the use of European and international standards and technical specifications relevant to the security of network and information systems'.

rules.[63] Work is ongoing by the European Commission's Joint Research Centre (JRC) and ENISA on mapping existing standards to the essential requirements under the CRA, including as regards cryptography.[64]

It is clear, therefore, that standards from organizations like ISO, NIST and ENISA (including the Teletrust/ENISA document) are critical for determining the state of the art and more fundamentally "appropriate" security measures under EU cybersecurity law. Accordingly, the present treatment of PQC within soft law promulgated by these entities necessitates consideration.

3.3 *PQC in Soft Law*

Currently, there is no clear normative priority between different standards instruments within EU cybersecurity regulation. This may change once harmonized standards have been adopted under, for example, the CRA (see particularly Articles 13(14) and 27 of the latter). Harmonized standards are a special hybrid of 'soft law' and 'hard law'. They are drafted by the three official European standards organizations: the European Telecommunications Standards Institute (ETSI), the European Committee for Standardisation (CEN) and the European Committee for Electrotechnical Standardisation (CENELEC)) at the request of the European Commission and in accordance with the procedure laid out in Regulation (EU) 1025/2012. When published in the Official Journal, such standards become formally part of EU law.[65] However, in the absence of such standards having been adopted in the cybersecurity field, we find regulatory bodies referencing a range of other relevant standards. This is evidenced both in the treatment of cybersecurity standards by DPAs under the GDPR[66] and the cybersecurity mapping exercise conducted by the JRC and ENISA, which has regard to several standards organizations.[67] It is logical to suggest that European standards[68] possess greater normative force than international standards,[69] which in turn possess greater normative force

---

[63] CRA, Art. 27.

[64] EC Joint Research Centre and ENISA 2024, pp. 15–17.

[65] See Case C-613/14, *James Elliott Construction Limited v Irish Asphalt Limited*, judgment of 27 October 2016 (ECLI:EU:C:2016:821), para 40; Case C-185/17, *Mitnitsa Varna v SAKSA OOD*, judgment of 22 February 2018 (ECLI:EU:C:2018:108), para 39; Case C-588/21 P, *PublicResourceOrg, Inc and Right to Know CLG v European Commission*, judgment of 5 March 2024 (Grand Chamber) (ECLI:EU:C:2024:201), paras 70, 74 and 89.

[66] Bygrave (2025a), p. 69.

[67] EC Joint Research Centre and ENISA (2024), p. 3.

[68] E.g., by ENISA, the European Telecommunications Standards Institute (ETSI), the European Committee for Standardisation (CEN) and the European Committee for Electrotechnical Standardisation (CENELEC).

[69] E.g., by ISO, the International Electrotechnical Commission (IEC) and International Telecommunication Union (ITU).

than non-European domestic standards.[70] Indeed, this appears to be the approach taken by the JRC and ENISA in their mapping exercise, with the publication "giving precedence to European and international standardisation organisations."[71] Whilst US-based NIST is not formally identified as a "relevant" standards organization, its output is referenced several times throughout the document, indicating its strong influence on cybersecurity standards globally. In the PQC cryptography realm, it is clear that NIST is leading standardization efforts, a fact recognized by key European organizations such as ENISA[72] and ETSI.[73] Therefore, the work of European standards organizations on PQC and the 'state of the art' is considered, before analyzing output from international standards organizations and thereafter NIST.

3.3.1 European Guidelines and Standards

Post-quantum standardization work in Europe is best described as preparatory. ETSI has produced Technical Reports (TRs) to contribute to NIST's PQC process,[74] in addition to TRs that lay the groundwork to a migration to PQC.[75] However, ETSI TRs simply contain "explanatory material"[76] and are distinct from (and often precursory to) European Standards and Technical Specifications that more concretely specify requirements. Tellingly, CEN-CENELEC output notes "a lack of standards for quantum key management and integration of quantum keys with encryption technologies like PQC."[77]

ENISA's work is also preliminary. A 2022 report points to EU Member State agency work, including the French Agence nationale de la sécurité des systèmes d'information (ANSSI),[78] which "cautions about the immaturity of post-quantum algorithms, saying that they are still in the research phase."[79] The ENISA/Teletrust

[70] E.g., by NIST.

[71] EC Joint Research Centre and ENISA (2024), p. 3.

[72] Bernstein et al. (2022), p. 25: "While we recognise NIST's leading role in standardising cryptographic systems we recommend that all stakeholders—governments, industry, and data-protection officers as well as other standardisation bodies—acquire sufficient understanding of post-quantum cryptography to make informed decisions." See also IETF Hybrid PQC-TLS (RFC 9180, "Hybrid Key Exchange"), acknowledging the importance of NIST's PQC project.

[73] Antipolis (2021).

[74] Antipolis (2021).

[75] ETSI TR 103966 V1.1.1 (2024-10); ETSI TR 104 016 V1.1.1 (2024-10).

[76] ETSI (2025).

[77] CEN-CENELEC Focus Group on Quantum Technologies 2023, p. 19.

[78] ANSSI (2022).

[79] Bernstein et al. (2022), p. 25. Note also that the German Federal Office for Information Security has commented similarly on PQC standards (German Federal Office for Information Security (BSI) 2021, p. 33), however, recognises three PQC schemes in its Technical Guideline, *Cryptographic Mechanisms: Recommendations and Key Lengths* BSI TR-02102-1 (Version 2025-1), 31 January 2025.

document on the state of the art under the GDPR appears to suggest that organizations storing data in the cloud should, at present, be prepared to switch to PQC at some unspecified future point, but stops short of making this a requirement:

> With a view to the future, an encryption gateway should be selected which allows the user organisation to freely exchange the encryption algorithms used (Crypto Agility). With the progressive development of extremely powerful quantum computers, procedures that are classified as secure today may become obsolete in the near future. Therefore, a solution that is already compatible with algorithms of post-quantum cryptography (PQC) is ideal.[80]

This indicates that implementing PQC is not currently considered a state of the art technical and organizational measure that is required in any of the many contexts examined in the document.

3.3.2 International Standards

Work by international standards bodies on PQC is in a similar place to that of European organizations. ISO has released standards relating to quantum key distribution,[81] and has made an amendment to its standard on identification cards to allow for interoperability for interchange of security operations using PQC.[82] At present, ISO is currently considering PQC-related amendments to ISO/IEC 18033–2 on asymmetric encryption algorithms.[83] Interestingly, the algorithms selected for identification cards, and currently being considered for more general asymmetric cryptography application, include those that were selected in the final rounds of NIST's PQC contest, but were ultimately not selected.[84]

In January 2023, the Internet Engineering Task Force (IETF) established the working group Post-Quantum Use In Protocols (PQUIP),[85] which is positioned to support the work of other organizations such as NIST and has various PQC-related documents in draft stages.[86] The International Telecommunications Union (ITU),

---

[80] TeleTrust and ENISA (2023), p. 38. See also at p. 24: "With increasing technical development and the resulting increase in computing power, there is a danger that the secret key information will be determined and thus the procedures used so far will be broken… This is exactly what is expected in connection with the now legendary quantum computers. It is expected that as soon as quantum computers are available, the methods used up to now will be broken or their effectiveness at least halved."

[81] ISO/IEC 23837-1:2023.

[82] ISO/IEC 7816-8:2021/Amd 1:2023.

[83] GSM Association (2024), p. 15.

[84] Specifically, Classic McEliece and FrodoKEM: see ISO/IEC 7816-8:2021/Amd 1:2023(en) Identification cards—Integrated circuit cards—Part 8: Commands and mechanisms for security operations—AMENDMENT 1: Interoperability for the interchange of security operations using quantum safe cryptography, 3.9 and 3.18.

[85] Gross (2023).

[86] IETF (2025).

whose work is focused on telecommunications infrastructure, perhaps unsurprisingly has focused its efforts on QKD (Quantum Key Distribution) rather than PQC.[87]

3.3.3 NIST

As already alluded to, NIST is clearly the organization leading standard-setting efforts of post-quantum cryptographic protocols. This is an extension of its historical role in setting classical cryptographic algorithm standards,[88] a role not without controversy due to alleged involvement by national security agencies.[89]

Between December 2016 and March 2025,[90] NIST held a competition designed to find the most suitable PQC algorithms for general asymmetric encryption and digital signatures for authentication.[91] In August 2024, Federal Information Processing Standard (FIPS) 203 was specified, using the Module-Lattice-Based Key-Encapsulation Mechanism (ML-KEM), being derived from the CRYSTALS-KYBER submission.[92] FIPS 204 and 205 relate to post-quantum digital signature algorithms for secure authentication. In March 2025, additional PQC algorithms were identified as further selected algorithms, including HQC as an additional key encapsulation mechanism.[93]

Officially, NIST's cybersecurity and cryptography standards are mandatory for US federal agencies in specific contexts, in which only approved cryptographic algorithms can be used by these agencies.[94] However, NIST standards are influential in US and global industry, with US agencies like the FTC[95] and European agencies such as the EDPB[96] or national DPAs[97] often referring to NIST standards as indicative of industry practice or appropriate security measures. Reflecting the broader importance of NIST's PQC competition is the diversity of countries and institutions from which the designers of finalists were based.[98]

Despite the official recognition of PQC algorithms as FIPS, it should be emphasized that NIST expects migration to PQC to take some time. In this sense, the mere

---

[87] European Commission (2024c). See also ITU-T XSTR-SEC-QKD, Technical Report: Security considerations for quantum key distribution network (March 2020).

[88] Lorenzo Hall (2014).

[89] NIST 2014; Bernstein et al. 2016; On alleged ongoing involvement in the PQC standards process, see Bernstein 2022.

[90] Alagic et al. (2025), p. 2.

[91] Genkina (2024).

[92] Moody et al. (2024), p. 4.

[93] Alagic et al. (2025), p. 10.

[94] Barker (2020).

[95] See, e.g., *In the Matter of Henry Schein Practice Solutions, Inc., a corporation* (Docket No. C-4575), 2016.

[96] E.g., European Data Protection Board (2021), p. 30.

[97] E.g., CNIL (2024), p. 50.

[98] See, e.g., Lundgreen (2024); INRIA (2023).

fact that there exist PQC algorithms recognized by NIST (or any other standards bodies) does not automatically entail that their use is required by US federal agencies. There remains significant work in specifying further protocols for the implementation of PQC into different settings.[99] NIST is currently targeting 2030 for classic algorithms to be "deprecated" (i.e., allowed, but cautioned against) and 2035 for them to be "disallowed"[100] for use. It is also apparent that European and international standards organizations were waiting for the outcome of NIST's PQC competition before deciding on their own approach to standardization and road mapping of the migration to PQC.[101] Thus, the recognition in itself is a critical yet insufficient step towards more holistic adoption of PQC.[102] To the extent that NIST's soft law standards are capable of 'hardening' under EU cybersecurity regulation, this would suggest that the selected PQC standards are not yet within the 'state of the art'.

3.4 Is EU Cybersecurity Regulation Fit-for-Purpose?

In the absence of explicit reference to the quantum threat in secondary EU law, one must rely on a fairly tortuous interpretive exercise to conclude that, at present, EU cybersecurity law probably does not require the use of PQC. This is due to the lack of acknowledgment of PQC in European standards, the nascence of the NIST PQC algorithms, and the considerable work ahead to ensure PQC can be robustly implemented across different products.

Within the context of the foregoing discussion, two observations are striking. First, rightly or wrongly, EU cybersecurity law leans heavily on the work of standards organizations, a process over which it may have zero-to-little influence. This gives rise to concerns such as legitimacy described in more detail elsewhere in this volume[103] and a lack of control by EU regulators. Nevertheless, standards organizations are critical actors within global cybersecurity governance. As discussed below at Sect. 4.3, the EU is best advised to work with and within this construct, rather than against it.

Second, and relatedly, is that the "widespread legislative use of generic functional requirements rooted in 'state of the art'"[104] by the EU entails a sharp focus on the present state of technology. The presentist approach taken by the EU legislator

[99] Moody et al. (2024), p. 11.

[100] Moody et al. (2024), pp. 11–14.

[101] See, e.g., GSM Association (2024), p. 51.

[102] Soutar et al. (2024).

[103] Smith et al. (2025).

[104] Bygrave (2025b), p. 6.

here probably reflects the tort law origins of the state of the art notion[105] based on the premise that one cannot be expected to account for, and defend against, unknown defects or outcomes. To be sure, the concept of the state of the art is a "dynamic, fluid criterion necessitating regular revisiting of security practices".[106] This means, in principle, that organizations should be adaptable to emerging threats like quantum computing. However, the concept presumes that adopting state of the art measures is all that can be asked of organizations seeking to protect networks and information systems. There is no explicit requirement (though it is arguably latent within the concept) for organizations to look beyond the current state of the art and towards the future. Significantly, this completely disregards the HNDL threat—systems are vulnerable now to a threat against which state of the art measures are insufficient. Moreover, it is doubtful whether EU cybersecurity law requires organizations to be ready, if the quantum threat materializes imminently, to pivot to PQC systems. One can ask whether this should be made clearer by the EU regulator. In this sense, EU cybersecurity law currently does not account for the possibility of a paradigm shift in cybersecurity, as quantum computing may entail.

4 The Path Forward

The question that follows is whether EU cybersecurity regulation needs to change, and if so, how? EU cybersecurity law is justified on the basis that it protects the internal market, and/or fundamental rights,[107] depending on the instrument.[108] So far as quantum computing presents an existential threat to these interests and rights, an adequate response is necessary. Given the EU, and its Member States, are investing heavily in quantum computing due to the significant opportunities afforded by the technology, it is logical that its risks should also be accounted for.

From a high-level strategic perspective, the quantum threat is arriving at a time of other significant policy challenges confronting the EU—not least of all within the technological domain. Once a global leader in technology, Europe now finds itself increasingly reliant on rapidly evolving external technologies, putting its economic strength, political coherence, and global influence in jeopardy.[109] Recent scholarship emphasizes that the EU must go beyond fragmented national strategies to forge a coherent, long-term framework that enhances European digital autonomy.[110] Thus, the EU's PQC strategy must not be treated in isolation, but rather as a component of

[105] Schmitz (2022), p. 26.

[106] Bygrave (2025a), p. 70.

[107] Bygrave (2025b), pp. 2–4.

[108] See, e.g., GDPR Art. 1(1), rec. 13; CRA rec. 4 & 13; NIS 2 Art. 1(1).

[109] Zenner et al. (2025).

[110] Zenner et al. (2025); Vogiatzoglou (2025).

its broader quantum and cybersecurity strategies. The quantum era is not only a technical challenge and economic opportunity, but a test of the EU's capacity to act as a coherent and sovereign digital power. Meeting that challenge could further secure its place as a sovereign digital power.[111]

From a more concrete perspective, if EU cybersecurity law is not fit-for-purpose to tackle the quantum threat, a variety of levers are available for regulators to pull. Responsibility for meeting the quantum threat can also be placed on a range of actors within the EU cybersecurity regulatory framework, from industry to standards organizations to lawmakers and the judiciary. Likely, a combination of the regulatory tools discussed in this section comprise the most appropriate response, rather than any single approach. These are roughly graded from lightest touch to most heavy-handed response, ranging from a light-touch market-driven approach to a complete rethinking of cybersecurity norms as conceived in the EU cybersecurity *acquis*.

4.1 Laissez-Faire: Industry-led Approach

There is some evidence to suggest that private industry is moving ahead with the PQC transition despite the absence of any formal legal requirement to do so. As alluded to in the previous section, PQC is already offered seamlessly and by-default within many popular products and cryptographic protocols such as instant messaging and banking. This would suggest the existence of market incentives to transition to PQC promptly—e.g., out of genuine fears arising from quantum computing or to give the appearance of being on the cutting-edge of cybersecurity.

However, leaving the PQC transition in the hands of industry and market forces would be foolhardy. Cybersecurity is arguably a "market of lemons" considering the incentives against investing in robust (and expensive) tools and personnel that appear as a cost on the balance sheet and considering the numerous security breaches of private sector systems.[112] Given the uncertain and largely theoretical threat of quantum computing, expecting companies *en masse* to expend scarce resources on nascent and complex PQC is unrealistic. Moreover, market incentives do not directly apply to public entities, which control (albeit often in tandem with private industry) some of the most societally important and vulnerable systems. Finally, whilst industry adoption of PQC may pick up for current and future products and services, there is less incentive to protect older or legacy systems.

Ultimately, the vast majority of the work in implementing PQC falls on the shoulders of private industry, which is responsible for key digital infrastructure, including that behind public goods and services. However, it is unrealistic and

[111] Zenner et al. (2025).

[112] Bygrave (2025b), p. 2; Bygrave (2021), pp. 150–151.

irresponsible to leave the task of PQC migration to market whims. The migration to PQC ought to be more forcefully incentivized.

4.2 Policy Action: Executive-led Approach

Whilst there has not yet been explicit hard law recognition of the quantum threat to cybersecurity, there is a growing recognition at the executive level. The European Commission notes in a recent White Paper that it is "important to encourage Member States to develop a coordinated and harmonized approach, ensuring consistency in the development and adoption of EU PQC standards across Member States."[113] It has also released a Recommendation regarding a roadmap to PQC that finds similarly,[114] as does its recent Quantum Europe Strategy, published on 7 July 2025.[115] The importance of a harmonized approach is critical in light of Member State cybersecurity agencies publishing their own reports regarding the PQC transition.[116] These instruments underline a recognition, though lack of affirmative action in responding to the quantum threat to cybersecurity.[117]

To this end, Rodríguez argues that the Commission should take a more active role in coordinating responses by Member States and key portfolios such as DG CONNECT and ENISA.[118] A briefing to the European Parliament[119] indicates that EU and Member State action is fragmented, with significant attention on the outcome of the NIST PQC standards competition.

Related to efforts within standardization agencies (discussed below), agencies like ENISA[120] and the EDPB have a significant role in outputting soft law relevant to interpretation and practice of EU cybersecurity law. Rodríguez also points to certification under the Cybersecurity Act as a potential avenue for encouraging PQC adoption.[121] One advantage of the EU's current "grey box"[122] approach to cyberse-

[113] European Commission (2024b).

[114] European Commission (2024a).

[115] European Commission (2025), p. 9.

[116] De Luca and Marcelin (2024), p. 5.

[117] Though note European Commission (2025), in which the EU Commission in June 2025 launched a Call for proposals related to the PQC transition, including "Integration of privacy-by-design at the core of software and protocol development processes, with attention to ensure that cryptographic building blocks and implementations of privacy-enhancing digital signatures and user-authentication schemes are crypto-agile and modular, to facilitate a transition towards post-quantum cryptographic algorithms."

[118] Rodríguez (2025), p. 11.

[119] De Luca and Marcelin (2024). See also German Federal Office for Information Security (BSI) (2021), p. 34.

[120] See, e.g., NIS 2 Art. 25.

[121] Rodríguez (2025), p. 12.

[122] Bygrave (2025b).

curity regulation, wherein key concepts like "state of the art" are underdetermined, is that it leaves considerable room for these executive agencies to interpret and enforce the law in a way that is responsive to novel cybersecurity threats. Thus, the arguably presentist interpretation of "state of the art" could be expanded through administrative guidance to include future threats associated with quantum computing.

For examples, ENISA, in contrast to its co-publication with TeleTrust,[123] could guide entities more forcefully and expediently towards PQC, or at least encourage organizations to consider quantum-related risks. The EDPB, too, could release guidelines outlining when PQC may be appropriate to implement—for instance, in high-risk processing operations, or international transfers. Further, considering the threat posed by HNDL, guidance may require regulatees to consider whether sensitive or high-risk data is appropriate to transfer over public networks at all, and seek alternatives to asymmetric encryption. These approaches would, in principle, negate the need for more fulsome hard law amendments to EU cybersecurity regulation and enable the EU to respond more promptly to the PQC threat when compared with other alternatives.

4.3 Standards Organizations-led Approach

Related to, but distinct from guidance documents from organizations such as ENISA and EDPB are the output of standards organizations such as those discussed above at Sect. 3.3. A light touch approach to regulation would leave the shaping of norms concerning PQC up to standards organizations. Arguably, this has been the approach largely taken by the EU so far by leaving much of the PQC algorithm standard-setting to NIST, albeit with some support from its agencies.[124]

Regardless of whether it was appropriate for the European regulators and standards organizations to lean heavily on a US entity-led standardization process in deciding on the selection of PQC algorithms, the conclusion of the NIST competition provides the EU with an opportunity to forge a path in alignment with its own interests. In this sense, it should be emphasized that the EU has different relationships with, and differing degrees of influence over, key international and European standards organizations. Standards are beginning to play a more significant role in technology regulation, particularly through its New Legislative Framework approach under the CRA and Artificial Intelligence Act (AI Act).[125] Noting that the

[123] See above at Sect. 3.3.

[124] De Luca and Marcelin (2024), p. 25.

[125] Regulation (EU) 2024/1689 of the European Parliament and of the Council of 13 June 2024 laying down harmonised rules on artificial intelligence and amending Regulations (EC) No 300/2008, (EU) No 167/2013, (EU) No 168/2013, (EU) 2018/858, (EU) 2018/1139 and (EU) 2019/2144 and Directives 2014/90/EU, (EU) 2016/797 and (EU) 2020/1828 (Artificial Intelligence Act) PE/24/2024/REV/1 OJ L, 2024/1689, 12.7.2024.

work of European standards organizations on PQC is at an early stage,[126] the EU could direct standards agencies to prioritize work on the PQC transition. For instance, within the context of the CRA[127] (or other Union harmonization legislation such as the AI Act), the European Commission could request CEN, CENELEC or ETSI to draft European standards pertaining to PQC. The AI Act provides precedent of the EU Commission whipping along the standards-making process in areas it deems important.[128]

There are drawbacks to relying on this approach, and indeed to pushing European standardization of nascent PQC implementations. For one, significant time is required to draft appropriate standards. As discussed above at Sect. 2.3, the threat from quantum computers may materialize imminently. Secondly, it is questionable whether the EU's involvement would have any material beneficial impact on the current global efforts around PQC standardization, given the highly complex and specialized nature of cybersecurity and PQC research. Thirdly, and relatedly, given the global interoperability of networks and information systems, the EU attempting to take a more active role in standardization may undesirably fragment or even weaken the security of global digital infrastructure.[129] Thus, whilst the PQC transition is time-critical, the current path towards PQC standardization and adoption may be optimal considering what is presently known about the quantum threat.

4.4 *Clarity of Hard Law Requirements: Judiciary-led Approach*

As described above at Sect. 3.1, EU cybersecurity law is subject to an extreme paucity of judicial decisions on its key instruments. Bygrave explains that:

> The lack of case law construing legal cybersecurity requirements with a fair degree of precision also means that they remain grey boxes in another sense—that is, as opaque, underdetermined norms, especially when they rely on slippery criteria, such as reasonableness, appropriateness, proportionality and 'state of the art'. Such criteria are not only nebulous on their face; they are prone to generating woolly decisions informed by relatively subjective notions of propriety.[130]

Judicial clarity over key concepts like state of the art would be desirable in many more contexts than quantum. In principle, pronouncement by the CJEU as to what types of technical, operational and organizational measures may be appropriate in

126 See above at Sect. 3.3.

127 CRA Art. 27(1).

128 Soler Garrido et al. (2024).

129 See, e.g., German Federal Office for Information Security (BSI) 2021, p. 34: "A 'proliferation' of international standards would both hamper interoperability and reduce the market opportunities of crypto producers. In addition, a splitting of personnel and research resources would lead to a lower evaluation quality for those algorithms that are ultimately selected".

130 Bygrave (2025b), p. 7.

given cases could provide valuable context for how to interpret EU cybersecurity law in light of the quantum threat. As described above at Sect. 3.4, EU cybersecurity law is currently ill-prepared to deal with future threats like HNDL. The "slippery"[131] criteria used by the European legislator could be construed in such a way that future threats must be robustly considered by regulatees. Doing so would shift from the presentist approach of current EU cybersecurity law, as has been argued herein.

This hope, however, is perhaps unrealistic considering the nascence of many key cybersecurity instruments (e.g., CRA, NIS 2) and the lack of existing case law on comparatively well-established instruments (e.g., GDPR[132]). The chance that an appropriate case arrives that gives the CJEU opportunity to opine on appropriate or state of the art security measures, and the CJEU takes that opportunity, is slim. In its single case so far involving the interpretation of Article 32 of the GDPR (on security measures), the CJEU offered "precious little detail on the actual security measures required by Article 32".[133] At the same time, it would be unreasonable to expect the judiciary to provide an abundance of such detail given that they are not domain experts. Judges will likely (indeed, ought to) defer to the views of cybersecurity specialists, and when these views are underdeveloped, the judicial pronouncements will (and ought to) err on the side of generality. Thus, case law is unlikely to provide lawyers, engineers and other practitioners with timely requisite clarification of PQC-era requirements.

4.5 Firmer Cybersecurity Requirements in Hard Law: Legislator-led Approach

A heavier-handed regulatory response would involve amending the EU cybersecurity *acquis* to better account for the evolving nature of cybersecurity threats like PQC. Writing in 2016 on EU law regarding communications security, Arnbak was critical of the way that the EU legislator has unimaginatively re-used terms from other instruments relating to cybersecurity:

> The EU regulatory framework contains, in sum, a large amount of legislative arrangements on communications security, but both a coherent vision on part of the lawmaker as well as a clear view of what laws exist and how to apply them is lacking. Legal uncertainty permeates EU communications security law […]. A legislative habit seems to exist in which "security" conceptualizations are copied from previous documents, with little argumentation and elaboration on what impact a particular conception of "security" has on the actual policies furthered in these instruments.[134]

[131] Bygrave (2025b), p. 7.

[132] Porcedda (2022), Chap. 5.

[133] Bygrave (2025a), p. 71, referring to Case C-340/21, *VB v Natsionalna agentsia za prihodite*.

[134] Arnbak (2016), p. 50.

The above analysis[135] of newer EU instruments (i.e., NIS 2 and CRA) suggests that this "legislative habit" is alive and well, despite the requirements being more detailed and prescriptive than earlier instruments (e.g., GDPR). Arguably, as suggested by Arnbak, the tendency to recycle provisions across instruments means that lawmakers do not think critically as to what risks and threats regulatees should be attuned to.

As other contributions to this book suggest, the unique dynamics of quantum technologies may prompt a broader legal disruption than just within cybersecurity. If this disruption occurs, one can expect that many more legal instruments than those discussed herein will need to be revisited by legislators. However, in the case of cybersecurity, that may come too late. The potential problems are somewhat distinct in that actions taken *today* can help to mitigate the effects of future threats. In this sense, explicit legislative recognition that organizations cannot in all cases rely on currently available 'state of the art' measures to protect networks and information systems may be worthwhile adding alongside existing functional requirements. Such an approach would, in principle, require organizations to consider HNDL attacks. Moreover, legislation (rather than, as discussed above, executive agencies or courts) may more explicitly (rather than, at present, latently) require organizations to be more agile to respond to emerging threats like quantum computing.

Realistically, however, EU digital instruments are rarely amended on a piecemeal basis. This would require amendments across the many different instruments that require cybersecurity requirements. That political capital may best be spent elsewhere, especially given the unknown nature of the threat. Legislative change may be nice, but is perhaps an unrealistic hope and potentially not impactful in practice—at least on its own.

4.6 *Re-Conceptualization of Cybersecurity Norms: All-Hands Approach*

At its most reductive, cybersecurity pertains to maintaining the confidentiality, integrity and availability of networks and information systems (i.e., the "CIA triad").[136] EU cybersecurity law frequently alludes to this foundational model. For instance, NIS 2 defines "security of network and information systems" as "the ability of network and information systems to resist, at a given level of confidence, any event that may compromise the availability, authenticity, integrity or confidentiality of stored, transmitted or processed data or of the services offered by, or accessible via, those network and information systems".[137]

---

[135] See Sect. 3 above.

[136] See further Urgessa (2020), pp. 3–5.

[137] NIS2 Art. 6(2); see also CRA Art. 3(44) and Art. 32(2) GDPR.

A variety of principles, strategies and concepts exist that supplement and support the CIA triad, some of which are reflected in EU law. For instance, security by design involves the embedding of security principles into the development process of products and services from the outset, rather than as an afterthought.[138] This is referred to in the Cybersecurity Act[139] and is embodied in the GDPR as data protection by design.[140] Cyber resilience, which refers to an organization's ability to prevent, withstand, and recover from cybersecurity incidents is a further concept that manifests itself strongly in the CRA.

None of these directly demand or even encourage regulatees of EU cybersecurity regulation to think about nascent, emerging threats like quantum computing. This begs the question of whether new concepts must be developed and eventually emerge within EU cybersecurity regulation that adequately cover such threats. The notion of cryptographic agility is gaining some purchase as a concept within cybersecurity discourse, with one definition offered as "the ability to migrate to new cryptographic algorithms and standards in an ongoing way."[141] There is reference to this concept in the ENISA/Teletrust publication on the state of the art,[142] indicating some regulatory recognition. This concept could certainly prove useful in readying organizations to migrate to PQC in a timely fashion.

However, as mentioned by Ott et al., the concept is young:

> …there is an important need to develop a principled science of cryptographic agility; one that broadens and expands the scope of agility to that of developing secure frameworks that enable ongoing cryptographic advancements in a wide variety of system, protocol, and application contexts.[143]

Simply placing such a requirement in hard or soft law would be insufficient to bring it to life; an all-hands, interdisciplinary approach is required. Prematurely incorporating a requirement for organizations to maintain "cryptographic agility" would, at present, amount to a vapid catch-cry of little concrete regulatory value. Moreover, cryptographic agility does not sufficiently mitigate the threat of HNDL attacks. Arguably, for HNDL attacks to be covered by cybersecurity regulation and practice, a re-thinking of cybersecurity would be required that encourages or mandates organizations to think beyond the present or near-term.

One possibility is the incorporation of a greater degree of anticipatory governance within the EU cybersecurity regime. Anticipatory governance refers to the capacity of institutions to foresee, prepare for, and shape future developments in a proactive and inclusive manner. It arose to prominence in STS scholarship on nanotechnology. In that context, anticipatory governance treats "the prospects" of

---

138 OECD (2002), p. 8; Bygrave 2021.

139 Cybersecurity Act rec. 12, 13, 41.

140 GDPR Art. 25; see further Bygrave (2021).

141 Ott and Peikert (2019), p. 4.

142 See above at Sect. 3.

143 Ott and Peikert (2019), p. 4; see further Näther et al. (2024).

nanotechnology as "fundamentally uncertain".[144] Such an approach is eminently well-suited for informing the (re)rigging of the EU cybersecurity regime as it looks ahead to the challenges of quantum computing. As the above discussion makes clear, this regime should not be locked into a complacent worldview that fails to take account of the likelihood of rapid and unexpected turns of events. Rather, it needs to be premised on a view that does justice to the frequently inchoate, unpredictable and "emergent" character of technological change. Regulatees must be encouraged to develop a mindset that is able continually to reassess assumptions about the technological-organizational landscape, including the threats that gather on the horizon. As put by Mandel,

> A legal system that realizes the unpredictability of new issues, that is flexible and adaptable, and that recognizes that new issues produced by technological advance may not fit well into pre-existing legal constructs, will operate far better in managing technological innovation than a system that fails to learn these lessons.[145]

Building on the need for anticipatory governance, recent developments within the EU cybersecurity landscape suggest a growing—albeit still nascent—recognition of the importance of forward-looking regulatory frameworks. More general recent EU-level discourse identifies anticipatory governance as increasingly important for navigating the risks and opportunities posed by disruptive technologies.[146] Although not explicitly referring to anticipatory governance, the recent ENISA Report on the State of Cybersecurity in the Union promotes "a forward-leaning legislative approach [that] could bring additional benefits for the EU"[147] in light of novel cyber threats like AI and quantum computing.

Whilst this acknowledgment is promising, significant work remains to translate this recognition into concrete legal and institutional mechanisms. There is a significant challenge in cultivating a regulatory culture that is agile, reflective, and capable of evolving in tandem with the technologies it seeks to govern. This requires input and buy-in from many actors in the cybersecurity value chain, from those at the coal-face, to academics, security experts, and private sector. Time will tell if this is achievable before current asymmetric encryption techniques are threatened. However, given the cybersecurity industry will inevitably encounter other existential threats ahead, it is nonetheless a worthy pursuit.

---

[144] Barben et al. (2008).

[145] Mandel (2017), pp. 243–244.

[146] European Commission et al. (2024).

[147] ENISA (2024), p. 58.

5 Conclusion

This chapter has explored the extent to which the EU's cybersecurity regulatory framework is prepared to address the transformative challenges posed by quantum computing. Whilst the EU has made significant strides in developing a comprehensive body of cybersecurity law—including instruments such as the GDPR, NIS 2 Directive, and the Cyber Resilience Act—this analysis suggests that important gaps remain in the ability of these frameworks to anticipate and respond to quantum-related threats.

At the heart of this issue lies the reliance on legal concepts such as "state of the art" and "appropriate technical and organizational measures." Whilst these terms offer flexibility and technological neutrality, they also risk being overly focused on present conditions and may not sufficiently incentivize forward-looking risk management. This is particularly relevant in the context of emerging threats like harvest now, decrypt later attacks, which create vulnerabilities today based on the anticipated capabilities of quantum computers in the future.

Although PQC has emerged as a leading technical solution, its incorporation into regulatory expectations remains limited. Current EU instruments do not explicitly require the use of PQC, in part due to the nascent status of relevant standards and the absence of clear guidance from European regulatory bodies. Additionally, the EU has to date played a more observational role in the global standardization process, particularly relying on the outcomes of the US-based NIST PQC initiative. This reflects a broader challenge for the EU in asserting normative leadership in an area where it does not currently dominate the technological frontier.

At the same time, the EU has at its disposal a range of tools that could be more assertively employed to address these challenges. Agencies such as ENISA and the EDPB are well-placed to develop soft law instruments—such as interpretive guidance or certification schemes—that promote proactive responses to quantum threats. However, these efforts remain underdeveloped and somewhat fragmented. The judiciary and the legislature also play key roles, though judicial engagement with cybersecurity requirements has so far been minimal, and legislative processes often unfold at a pace that struggles to match rapid technological change.

Beyond specific legal instruments, this chapter has identified a broader conceptual issue. Much of EU cybersecurity regulation remains rooted in traditional models of security, such as the CIA triad. Yet the evolving threat landscape arguably demands a more anticipatory and adaptive regulatory mindset—one that embraces concepts like cryptographic agility and is capable of responding to uncertain but potentially systemic risks. Whilst these ideas are beginning to appear in EU-level discourse, they have yet to be operationalized in a meaningful way.

Table 1 encapsulates the key findings of this contribution.

In light of these findings, this chapter concludes that whilst the EU's cybersecurity framework provides a valuable foundation, further evolution is necessary to ensure resilience in the quantum era. The development of more explicit guidance, clearer standards, and future-oriented legal tools—coupled with enhanced

Table 1 Summary of key findings

Key Finding	Summary
EU Cybersecurity Law Is Ill-Prepared for Quantum Threats	Existing laws rely on vague terms like "state of the art" which do not account for future risks such as quantum computing.
Post-Quantum Cryptography (PQC) Adoption is Lagging	EU laws do not clearly mandate PQC, due to unclear status in standards and limited regulatory push.
Standards Bodies Drive Regulation, but the EU Lacks Control	EU is dependent on external standards (especially NIST), limiting its ability to lead globally.
Soft Law Tools Are Underutilized	Agencies like ENISA and EDPB could encourage PQC adoption but have yet to do so decisively.
Judicial and Legislative Pathways Offer Limited Relief	Courts have not clarified cybersecurity expectations; legislative changes are slow and politically challenging.
Conceptual Gaps Exist in Current Frameworks	Current cybersecurity law lacks forward-looking concepts like cryptographic agility and anticipatory governance.
Urgent Need for Proactive and Coordinated Response	A combined approach involving law, standards, policy, and governance is needed to address the quantum threat.

coordination among institutional actors—would help position the EU to more effectively address the quantum challenge. As a global regulatory reference point, the EU is well-placed to lead in shaping responses to emerging technologies, but doing so will require a more deliberate engagement with the uncertainties and complexities that lie ahead.

Acknowledgments This work was made possible through the generous support of the Novo Nordisk Foundation (NNF) via a grant for the scientifically independent Collaborative Research Program in Bioscience Innovation Law (Inter-CeBIL Program—Grant No. NNF23SA0087056).

References

Aghaee M et al (2025) Interferometric single-shot parity measurement in InAs–Al hybrid devices. Nature 638:651–655

Alagic G et al (2025) Status report on the fourth round of the NIST post-quantum cryptography standardization process. NIST Internal Report 8545. Available at: https://csrc.nist.gov/pubs/ir/8545/final. Accessed 4 June 2025

ANSSI (2022) ANSSI views on the Post-Quantum Cryptography transition. Available at: https://cyber.gouv.fr/en/publications/anssi-views-post-quantum-cryptography-transition. Accessed 4 June 2025

Antipolis S (2021) ETSI releases two Technical Reports to support US NIST standards for post-quantum cryptography. Available at: https://www.etsi.org/newsroom/news/1981-2021-10-etsi-releases-two-technical-reports-to-support-us-nist-standards-for-post-quantum-cryptography. Accessed 4 June 2025

Apple Security Engineering and Architecture (SEAR) (2024) iMessage with PQ3: The new state of the art in quantum-secure messaging at scale. Available at: https://security.apple.com/blog/imessage-pq3/. Accessed 4 June 2025

Arnbak A (2016) Securing private communications: protecting private communications security in eu law, fundamental rights, functional value chains, and market incentives. Wolters Kluwer Law International B.V., Alphen aan den Rijn

Barben D et al (2008) Anticipatory governance of nanotechnology: foresight, engagement, and integration. In: Hackett E et al (eds) The handbook of science and technology studies, 3rd edn. MIT Press, Cambridge

Barker E (2020) Guideline for using cryptographic standards in the federal government. NIST Special Publication 800-175B Revision 1

Barker W et al (2021) Getting ready for post-quantum cryptography: exploring challenges associated with adopting and using post-quantum cryptographic algorithms. NIST Cybersecurity White Paper

Bernstein D (2022) NSA, NIST, and post-quantum cryptography: Announcing my second lawsuit against the U.S. government. Available at: https://blog.cr.yp.to/20220805-nsa.html. Accessed 5 June 2025

Bernstein D et al (2016) Dual EC: a standardized back door. In: Ryan P, Naccache D, Quisquater JJ (eds) The new codebreakers. Springer, Berlin

Bernstein D et al (2022) Post-quantum cryptography integration. ENISA Integration Study

Bernstein DJ, Lange T (2017) Post-quantum cryptography Nature 549(7671) 188–194. https://doi.org/10.100710.1038/nature23461

Bradford A (2023) Digital empires: the global battle to regulate technology. Oxford University Press, New York

Brooks M (2019) Beyond quantum supremacy: the hunt for useful quantum computers. Nature 574(7776):19–21

Bygrave L (2021) Security by design: aspirations and realities in a regulatory context. Oslo Law Rev 8(3):126–177

Bygrave L (2025a) Article 32. In: Kuner C, Bygrave L, Docksey C (eds) Compilation from the EU General Data Protection Regulation: a commentary, 2nd edn. Oxford University Press, Oxford

Bygrave L (2025b) The emergence of EU cybersecurity law: a tale of lemons, angst, turf, surf and grey boxes. Comput Law Secur Rev 56(106071):1–8

CEN-CENELEC Focus Group on Quantum Technologies (2023) Quantum technologies use cases. Focus Group on Quantum Technologies

Chen S et al (2023) The complexity of NISQ. Nat Commun 14(1):6001

CNIL (2024) Security of personal data. Practice Guide GDPR: Version 2024

De Luca S, Marcelin T (2024) Cryptographic security: critical to Europe's digital sovereignty. European Parliament Briefing PE 766.237

EC Joint Research Centre and ENISA (2024) Cyber resilience act requirements standards mapping. Publication Office of the European Union

ENISA (2019) What is "state of the art" in IT security? Available at: https://www.enisa.europa.eu/news/enisa-news/what-is-state-of-the-art-in-it-security. Accessed 5 June 2025

ENISA (2024) 2024 Report on the state of the cybersecurity in the union

ETSI (2025) Types of standards. Available at: https://www.etsi.org/standards/types-of-standards. Accessed 5 June 2025

European Commission (2018) Quantum Technologies Flagship kicks off with first 20 projects. Available at: https://ec.europa.eu/commission/presscorner/detail/en/ip_18_6205. Accessed 5 June 2025

European Commission (2019) The future is quantum: EU countries plan ultra-secure communication network. Available at: https://digital-strategy.ec.europa.eu/en/news/future-quantum-eu-countries-plan-ultra-secure-communication-network. Accessed 5 June 2025

European Commission et al (2024) Embedding anticipatory governance in Europe's transitions. Publications Office of the European Union

European Commission (2024a) Commission Recommendation on a Coordinated Implementation Roadmap for the transition to Post-Quantum Cryptography. Commission Recommendation C(2024) 2393 final

European Commission (2024b) How to master Europe's digital infrastructure needs? White Paper COM(2024) 81 final

European Commission (2024c) Rolling Plan for ICT standardisation, Quantum Technologies. Available at: https://interoperable-europe.ec.europa.eu/collection/rolling-plan-ict-standardisation/quantum-technologies-rp2024. Accessed 5 June 2025

European Commission (2025a) European Funding & Tenders Portal, Privacy Enhancing Technologies, HORIZON-CL3-2025-02-CS-ECCC-03. Available at: https://ec.europa.eu/info/funding-tenders/opportunities/portal/screen/opportunities/topic-details/HORIZON-CL3-2025-02-CS-ECCC-03?isExactMatch=true&status=31094501,31094502,31094503&order=DESC&pageNumber=2&pageSize=50&sortBy=startDate. Accessed 7 Aug 2025

European Commission (2025b) Quantum Europe strategy. Available at: https://digital-strategy.ec.europa.eu/en/library/quantum-europe-strategy. Accessed 7 August 2025

European Data Protection Board (2021) Recommendations 01/2020 on measures that supplement transfer tools to ensure compliance with the EU level of protection of personal data Version 2.0 (adopted on 18 June 2021). EDPB Recommendation

Fuster GG, Jasmontaite L (2020) Cybersecurity Regulation in the European Union: the digital, the critical and fundamental rights. In: Christen M, Gordijn B, Loi M (eds) The ethics of cybersecurity. Springer, Cham

Genkina D (2024) NIST Announces Post-Quantum Cryptography Standards. Available at: https://spectrum.ieee.org/post-quantum-cryptography-2668949802. Accessed 5 June 2025

German Federal Office for Information Security (BSI) (2021) Quantum-safe cryptography – fundamentals, current developments and recommendations. BSI-Bro21/01

Ghazi Vakili M et al (2025) Quantum-computing-enhanced algorithm unveils potential KRAS inhibitors. Nat Biotechnol:1–6

Gross G (2023) IETF launches post-quantum encryption working group. Available at: https://www.ietf.org/blog/pquip/. Accessed 5 June 2025

GSM Association (2024) Post Quantum Cryptography – guidelines for telecom use cases (version 1.0). Official Document PQ.03

Hall I (2024) Central banks hail 'ground-breaking' post-quantum cryptography experiment. Available at: https://www.globalgovernmentfintech.com/banque-de-france-singapore-quantum-cryptography-resilience/. Accessed 5 June 2025

Hoofnagle CJ, Garfinkel SL (2022) Law and policy for the quantum age. Cambridge University Press, Cambridge

Horvath M (2024) Begin transitioning to post-quantum cryptography now. Available at: https://www.gartner.com/en/articles/post-quantum-cryptography. Accessed 5 June 2025

IETF (2025) Post-quantum use in protocols (pquip). Available at: https://datatracker.ietf.org/wg/pquip/documents/. Accessed 5 June 2025

INRIA (2023) NIST Chooses Falcon as Standard for Post- Quantum Cryptographic Signature. Available at: https://www.inria.fr/en/nist-algorithm-falcon-post-quantum-cryptographic. Accessed 5 June 2025

Jordan S (2025) Quantum Algorithm Zoo. Available at: https://quantumalgorithmzoo.org. Accessed 5 June 2025

Korzh B et al (2015) Provably secure and practical quantum key distribution over 307 km of optical fibre. Nat Photonics 9(3):163–168

Kret, E. (2023) Quantum resistance and the signal protocol. Available at: https://signal.org/blog/pqxdh/. Accessed 5 June 2025

Liao SK et al (2017) Satellite-to-ground quantum key distribution. Nature 549(7670):43–47

Lorenzo Hall J (2014) Our comments on NIST's cryptographic standards review process. Available at: https://cdt.org/insights/our-comments-on-nists-cryptographic-standards-review-process/. Accessed 5 June 2025

Lundgreen U (2024) SPHINCS+ digital signature algorithm becomes post-quantum cryptography standard – SDU professor is co-creator. Available at: https://www.sdu.dk/en/om-sdu/institutter-centre/imada_matematik_og_datalogi/nyt_fra_imada/sphincs. Accessed 5 June 2025

Mandel G (2017) Legal evolution in response to technological change. In: Brownsword R, Scotford E, Yeung K (eds) The Oxford handbook of law, regulation and technology. Oxford University Press, Oxford
Margaine N, Goh E (2024) Securing digital communications between the Banque de France & the Monetary Authority of Singapore. Quantum-Safe Experiment Report
Mavroeidis V et al (2018) The impact of quantum computing on present cryptography. arXiv preprint arXiv:1804.00200: 1–10
Montanaro A (2016) Quantum algorithms: an overview. NPJ Quantum Inf 2(1):1–8
Moody D et al (2024) Transition to post-quantum cryptography standards. NIST Internal Report 8547
Näther C et al (2024) Toward a common understanding of cryptographic agility – a systematic review. arXiv preprint arXiv:2411.08781
NIST (2014) Cryptographic standards and guidelines development process. NISTIR 7977
OECD (2002) OECD guidelines for the security of information systems and networks: towards a culture of security. OECD Publishing
Ott D, Peikert C (2019) Identifying research challenges in post quantum cryptography migration and cryptographic agility. arXiv preprint arXiv:1909.07353
Panizza V et al (2024) Protein design by integrating machine learning and quantum-encoded optimization. PRX Life 2(4):043012
Papakonstantinou V (2022) Cybersecurity as praxis and as a state: the EU law path towards acknowledgement of a new right to cybersecurity? Comput Law Secur Rev 44(105653):1–15
Porcedda MG (2022) Cybersecurity, privacy and data protection in EU Law: a law, policy and technology analysis, 1st edn. Hart Publishing, London
Preskill J (2018) Quantum computing in the NISQ era and beyond. Quantum 2(79):1–20
Rodríguez A (2025) A quantum cybersecurity agenda for Europe II: enabling policy and investment options for the quantum transition. European Policy Centre - Discussion Paper
Savage N (2023) Keeping secrets in a quantum world. Nature 623(7985):S1–S3
Schmitz S (2022) Conceptualising the legal notion of 'state of the art' in the context of IT security. In: Friedewald M, Krenn S, Schiering I, Schiffner S (eds) Privacy and identity management: between data protection and security. Springer, Cham
Smith HL, Aboy M, Davis PAE, Minssen T (2025) Quantum governance in the making: why standards matter. https://papers.ssrn.com/sol3/papers.cfm?abstract_id=5853722
Soler Garrido J et al (2024) Harmonised standards for the European AI Act. Joint Research Centre Publication JRC139430
Soutar C et al (2024) Why the new NIST standards mean quantum cryptography may just have come of age. Available at: https://www.weforum.org/stories/2024/10/quantum-cryptography-nist-standards/. Accessed 5 June 2025
Taddeo M et al (2024) Consider the ethical impacts of quantum technologies in defence—before it's too late. Nature 634(8035):779–781
TeleTrust and ENISA (2023) IT Security Act (Germany) and EU General Data Protection Regulation: Guideline "State of the Art" – Technical and Organisational Measures, Version 2_2023-05 EN. TeleTrust Guidelines
Urgessa WG (2020) Multilateral cybersecurity governance: divergent conceptualizations and its origin. Comput Law Secur Rev 36(105368):1–8
Vogiatzoglou P (2025) The EU's quest for digital sovereignty: a matter of quantum innovation? Digit Soc 4(1):1–19
Wessel R (2015) Towards EU cybersecurity law: regulating a new policy field. In: Tsagourias N, Buchan R (eds) Research handbook on international law and cyberspace. Edward Elgar Publishing, Cheltenham
Xu G et al (2023) An overview of quantum-safe approaches: quantum key distribution and post-quantum cryptography. In: 2023 57th Annual conference on information sciences and systems (CISS)
Zenner K et al (2025) The European way. A blueprint for reclaiming our digital future. Available at SSRN: https://ssrn.com/abstract=5251254. Accessed 5 June 2025

Regulatory Challenges and Opportunities of Export Controls on Quantum Computing

Peter Alexander Earls Davis, Mateo Aboy, and Timo Minssen

Abstract Quantum technologies are emerging as strategic assets with the potential to confer significant economic, technological, and security advantages to governments and corporations that achieve early leadership. As quantum innovations become strategically vital, export controls on these technologies introduce complex legal and policy dilemmas, including tensions between innovation, collaboration, and national security. Quantum computing, in particular, presents unique regulatory challenges due to its layered technological stack and dual-use potential. This chapter offers an in-depth analysis of recent export control measures on quantum computing adopted by the United States and selected European Union Member States. It maps the scope and structure of these controls, examines how they target specific elements of the quantum supply chain, and highlights the shift toward plurilateral regulatory approaches outside traditional multilateral frameworks. Furthermore, it identifies key governance challenges—such as regulating intangible assets, avoiding fragmentation, and adapting to novel quantum paradigms—and provides a forward-looking framework for regulators to design more coordinated and adaptive export control strategies.

In addition to analyzing constraints, the chapter identifies a range of quantum-specific enforcement opportunities that are uniquely tied to the physical, architectural, and access-layer characteristics of the technology. These include the physical footprint and centralization of large-scale infrastructure, the potential of cloud-based access models for dynamic and differentiated control, and the modular nature

P. A. E. Davis (✉)
Center for Advanced Studies in Bioscience Innovation Law (CeBIL), University of Copenhagen, Copenhagen, Denmark
e-mail: paed@jur.ku.dk

M. Aboy
Centre for Law, Medicine and Life Sciences (LML) & Centre for Intellectual Property & Information Law (CIPIL), University of Cambridge, Cambridge, UK
e-mail: ma608@cam.ac.uk

T. Minssen
Center for Advanced Studies in Bioscience Innovation Law (CeBIL), University of Copenhagen, Copenhagen, Denmark

M. Aboy et al. (eds.), *Quantum Technology Governance I*, Perspectives in Law, Business and Innovation, https://doi.org/10.1007/978-981-95-8371-3_6

of hardware that allows for granular, component-level restrictions. Rather than offering a normative assessment, the chapter distills emerging patterns and strategic considerations likely to shape the future of quantum technology governance. It assesses that there are certain opportunities and challenges of export controls with regard to quantum computers that may inform regulators' strategies in this space and help guide the design of adaptive, forward-compatible regulatory approaches.

Keywords Export controls · Quantum computing · Quantum technologies · Multilateral gridlock · Wassenaar Arrangement · Emerging technologies · Semiconductors · Plurilateralism · Unilateralism

1 Introduction

Export controls serve as a legal and policy instrument utilized by governments to limit adversaries' access to advanced technologies.[1] The heightened rivalry among China, the US, and the EU has brought the regulation of emerging and breakthrough technologies into sharp relief.[2] Since 2022, multiple jurisdictions across multiple iterations have increased restrictions on the export of technologies directly and indirectly related to the research and production of quantum computers,[3] amongst other high technologies with "known unknown"[4] impacts on economic and national security.[5]

The rationale for and efficacy of export controls as a regulatory tool, in a broad sense, depends on several factors. These include the level of international cooperation, the robustness of enforcement mechanisms, the clarity of regulations, and the ability of regulators to adapt to technological advancements.[6] Arguably under-examined in the literature,[7] however, is the effect that the subject matter of export controls may be more or less amenable to restrictions depending on the nature of the technology, its research and development pipeline, and supply chain.

Quantum computers[8] represent a frontier technology underpinned by highly complex and interdependent supply chains. Their development and deployment require not only specialized quantum hardware and software, but also advanced

[1] Brockmann (2019), pp. 13–15; Bonarriva et al. (2009); Kazeki and Kleitz (2003).

[2] Palmer (2023a).

[3] Sparkes (2024); Sparkes (2025).

[4] Taddeo et al. (2024).

[5] Note that national security and economic security are intrinsically intertwined notions: see further Nanto (2011).

[6] Rasser (2020); Palmer (2023a).

[7] For an earlier analysis, see Flamm (1996). Arguably, however, any legal or policy matter is under-examined by the literature such is the dearth of commentary: see further Alter (2024).

[8] For the purposes of this chapter, non-computing technologies such as quantum sensing, and post-quantum encryption and quantum key distribution are excluded from consideration.

enabling infrastructure—such as cryogenic systems, cleanroom facilities, and precision fabrication tools—as well as highly specialized expertise across multiple scientific and engineering disciplines. These are also technologies that currently lack explicit governance under multilateral export controls,[9] making quantum computers an ideal example through which to examine the opportunities and limitations of export controls on advanced technologies.

This chapter makes four key contributions to the scholarly and policy discourse on quantum technology export controls. First, it provides a detailed comparative legal and regulatory mapping of recent US and selected EU Member State export controls specific to quantum computing—highlighting their technical scope, national variations, and underlying geopolitical drivers. Second, it presents a structured breakdown of the quantum computing 'stack'—from hardware and materials to software and enabling infrastructure—thereby offering a framework for understanding how export controls interact with the layered and modular nature of this frontier technology. Third, it identifies and critically analyzes emerging regulatory trends, such as the shift toward plurilateral coordination outside traditional multilateral frameworks like the Wassenaar Arrangement, and their implications for harmonization, enforcement, and compliance. Fourth, the chapter details a series of nuanced governance challenges—including definitional ambiguity, technology diffusion, and the difficulties of regulating intangible assets like know-how and software—in light of the rapidly evolving and internationally diffuse quantum ecosystem.

In addition to these core contributions, the chapter draws attention to strategic enforcement opportunities that arise from the physical and architectural characteristics of quantum computing. These include the physical footprint of quantum hardware infrastructure, the centralized control afforded by cloud-based access models, and the potential for targeted restrictions on enabling components within quantum systems. Taken together, these features create a regulatory landscape in which selective, technically grounded measures can be both feasible and impactful—especially at this early stage in the field's commercialization.

In doing so, the chapter contributes both conceptual clarity and practical insight to an area where policy is evolving faster than legal or academic consensus, and provides a foundation for more coordinated, adaptive, and effective regulatory responses. It underscores the importance of aligning export control design not only with national security concerns but also with the specific technological affordances and governance possibilities presented by the quantum computing domain.

The stakes are high, and the risks are real. Optimistically, export controls may promote and facilitate strategic and regional collaboration amongst geopolitical allies.[10] However, export controls could (if they do not already) discourage legitimate, lawful and desirable international collaboration on quantum computers while

---

[9] Nousiainen and Keski-Rahkonen (2024), p. 37. See further Seskir et al. (2023); U.S. Government Accountability Office (2021); Johnson (2019), p. 508.

[10] European Commission (2022).

simultaneously being ineffective in achieving the outcome sought. It is therefore critical for policymakers to understand the challenges associated with implementing export controls on certain types of technologies.

Before proceeding, a disclaimer must be made regarding the scope of this chapter. The politics and policy around export controls are complex and opaque, as well as under-examined in academic literature.[11] This chapter does not aim to provide a comprehensive policy analysis or normative evaluation of export controls. Instead, it examines the current export control frameworks governing quantum computing technologies in the US and its strategic allies in the EU and identifies certain opportunities and challenges in light of the quantum computing "stack" and broader supply chain. Finally, this chapter's analysis is restricted to quantum computing, not other quantum technologies such as quantum communications or sensing (except so far as those applications overlap with computing).

2 Logic and Scope of Export Controls

Export controls[12] may be implemented for a variety of reasons, from crisis response and resource management to environmental protection and protecting human rights. In the case of emerging technologies such as quantum computers, these controls are often justified on national or regional security grounds, even if maintaining a technological edge over economic competitors is the dominant concern.[13] Moreover, export controls can also be regarded as a prerequisite to enable, support and justify strategic regional collaboration and for protecting supply chains.[14] Of course, economic prosperity and security are increasingly intertwined concepts.[15] However, in the case of controls on emerging technologies, the legal justification is often directly related to defense, with many jurisdictions placing quantum computers on "dual-use" lists of technologies with military and civilian applications.

Therefore, quantum computers appear alongside nuclear hardware, biotechnologies, and satellites as warranting governmental restriction and oversight due to their potential military use by geopolitical adversaries. This approach is based on the

[11] For a recent appraisal of US law and policy on export restrictions, see Alter (2024), reviewing Daniels and Krige (2022) and Meijer (2016).

[12] By export controls, it is meant herein regulatory methods aimed specifically at restricting or preventing export between jurisdictions. It does not include regulatory measures that may incidentally restrict export, such as tariffs or currency controls.

[13] Palmer (2023b).

[14] Bauer and Pandya (2024).

[15] Steinberg and Wolff (2024); Nanto (2011).

various "known unknowns"[16] that quantum computers may herald, from risks to global cybersecurity[17] to use in computerized weapons systems.[18]

While these risks are significant and warrant mitigation, they should not overshadow other motivations for restricting quantum computer exports, such as economic protectionism.[19] Given the early stage of quantum computing and its substantial potential, being a first mover offers considerable advantages for both private companies and the nations where they operate. Crucially, there is significant downside risk for those who fail to establish themselves in the quantum computing arena. The quantum computing industry could become highly influential, with far-reaching impacts on downstream sectors like biomedical research, artificial intelligence, logistics, and finance.[20] The economic moats[21] erected in other frontier technology industries such as semiconductors and graphical processing units (GPUs) may similarly appear in the quantum computing sector, wherein one or a few dominant companies or regions disproportionately benefit from the technology.

The ultimate aims of export controls can be difficult to deduce, making the measure of their success somewhere near impossible. In the case of emerging technologies, it would be fair to assume that one of the primary objectives is to slow, if not completely stop, geopolitical rivals from enjoying technological progress in the area regulated. For instance, US restrictions on Chinese access to advanced semiconductors on 7 October 2022 were explicitly aimed at "restrict[ing] the PRC's ability to obtain advanced computing chips, develop and maintain supercomputers, and manufacture advanced semiconductors."[22] The US Bureau of Industry and Security's announcement outlines several expected downstream effects of these controls as policy rationales. These include military implications (such as autonomous weapons systems), economic impacts (like China's growing AI industry that relies on advanced chips), and human rights concerns (such as AI's role in enhancing China's citizen surveillance capabilities).[23]

These controls have reportedly succeeded in limiting China's access to advanced GPUs used in AI training.[24] However, they have also spurred China to intensify its

---

[16] Taddeo et al. (2024), p. 781.

[17] See Davis et al. (2026).

[18] Taddeo et al. (2024), p. 781.

[19] See, e.g., Draghi (2024), p. 90, calling for amendment to the EU Chips Act to "Support European consolidation and leadership in semiconductor manufacturing equipment (lithography, depositions, etc.) as a pillar of the EU long term strategy in semiconductors as well as a geopolitical negotiation strategy for partnerships with third countries to boost the EU's value chain autonomy. Increasingly manage export controls at the EU level and defend EU interests in equipment and materials from third-countries' export restrictions."

[20] See further Danish Business Authority and Danish Quantum Community (2024).

[21] Watts et al. (2024).

[22] Bureau of Industry and Security (2022), p. 1.

[23] Bureau of Industry and Security (2022), p. 1.

[24] Palmer (2023a).

efforts in domestic semiconductor production.[25] In fact, some tech analysts have argued that such controls may only offer a temporary advantage, as they can accelerate indigenous R&D, encourage supply chain decoupling, and motivate the emergence of alternative ecosystems beyond the reach of US or allied jurisdictions. For example, the rapid progress of Chinese firms' AIs like DeepSeek, which recently developed and released a domestic large language model (LLM) reportedly trained without access to top-tier NVIDIA chips, highlights how constraints can stimulate parallel development, algorithmic innovation, and accelerate self-reliance.[26] It can be argued that allowing continued but constrained access to US platforms—such as NVIDIA's GPU infrastructure or US cloud-deployed systems—could have locked competitors into US-controlled ecosystems, where usage could be monitored, throttled, and strategically governed over time.

Therefore, whether these developments constitute a net policy "win" or failure is difficult to determine.[27] When combined with the inherent uncertainty of quantum computing, they underscore the challenge of anticipating the long-term effects of export controls. Moreover, the success, competitiveness, and sustainability of innovation ecosystems also depend on scientific collaboration and well-governed open innovation at the precompetitive stage. This highlights the need to navigate delicate trade-offs between sometimes conflicting values and interests. Striking the right balance—such as between "as open as possible and as closed as necessary" and its inverse—is no easy task. Alongside factors such as reciprocity, political values, trust, and dual-use risk levels, export and import controls play a crucial role in calibrating this balance and identifying a viable "sweet spot."

3 Unilateral and Multilateral Export Control Instruments

Internationally, export controls often take the form of multilateral agreements and unilateral instruments. Multilateral agreements in this context are cooperative frameworks involving multiple countries that agree to implement common export control policies. The primary objective of these agreements is to prevent the proliferation of weapons of mass destruction and other technologies with associated national security concerns.[28] Most relevantly for emerging technologies, the Wassenaar Arrangement focuses on controlling the export of conventional arms and dual-use goods and technologies, promoting transparency and greater responsibility in transfers of dual-use items with the aim of enhancing regional and international

[25] Davidson (2025).

[26] Villasenor (2025).

[27] See further Davidson (2025).

[28] See, e.g., Regulation (EU) 2021/821 of the European Parliament and of the Council of 20 May 2021 setting up a Union regime for the control of exports, brokering, technical assistance, transit and transfer of dual-use items *OJ L 206, 11.6.2021,* recitals 4–5 & Annex I; Section 1758 of the Export Control Reform Act of 2018 (ECRA) 50 USC § 4811(a) (2018).

security.[29] Wassenaar Arrangement signatories include the US, all EU countries, Japan and Russia. Its provisions are, however, voluntary and require domestic implementation.[30]

Unilateral instruments, on the other hand, are export control measures implemented by individual countries independently of multilateral agreements. Nations may adopt unilateral controls to address specific national security concerns, protect economic interests, or respond to geopolitical developments that are not (yet) covered by multilateral agreements.

Both have advantages and shortcomings. Finding multilateral agreement can be cumbersome and slow, and in many cases (including the non-binding Wassenaar Arrangement) the rules must be implemented domestically by each signatory. Multilateralism may also face gridlock; the geopolitical tensions prompted by Russia's invasion of Ukraine make updating the Wassenaar export list difficult.[31] In the US, the first Trump presidency strongly favored unilateralism,[32] and his second presidency appears only further in that direction.[33]

While unilateral controls can be more flexible and responsive to immediate national interests, they may also lead to tensions with other countries and have unpredictable impacts on global supply chains. The lack of coordination through multilateral frameworks can result in inconsistencies and potential conflicts between national policies, and to "forum shopping" by regulated entities seeking to avoid burdensome regulation.[34]

As is illustrated below, there has been a recent flurry of export controls on quantum computing technologies by Wassenaar signatories, albeit outside of official Wassenaar channels.[35] Some of these efforts can be described as plurilateral[36] since they have clearly arisen from multi-jurisdictional collaboration,[37] but outside of an established framework like the Wassenaar Arrangement. These measures may increase fragmentation, and risk making more difficult the challenge of balancing national security concerns with the benefits of international cooperation and supply chains.

[29] See also Australia Group on chemical and biological weapons, the Missile Technology Control Regime (MTCR) on anti-proliferation of missile and unmanned aerial vehicle technology and the Nuclear Suppliers Group (NSG).

[30] Brunel (2023), p. 9.

[31] Bennink et al. (2025), p. 96; European Commission (2024), p. 2; Bureau of Industry and Security (2024a); Junusova and Reinsch (2024).

[32] Bown (2019), p. 286.

[33] McFaul (2025).

[34] Brunel (2023), p. 13.

[35] Bennink et al. (2025), p. 96.

[36] Bennink et al. (2025), p. 96.

[37] Sparkes (2025).

4 European and US Export Controls Relevant to Quantum Computing

The US, the EU, and certain EU Member States each have implemented export controls that specifically or incidentally affect quantum computing and its supply chains.[38] This section describes the currently implemented rules relating to quantum computers. It first examines the Wassenaar Arrangement, describing the lack of quantum computing specific controls. It then reviews recent US controls that target quantum computing, and European controls that are drafted in similar terms. It is noted that the EU presently lacks a significant role; hence, Member States have implemented a "patchwork"[39] of controls at a national level that reflect the US rules to varying degrees.

4.1 Wassenaar Arrangement

The Wassenaar Arrangement lists nine categories of dual-use goods and technologies, ranging from materials processing to aerospace and propulsion. Within these categories, controls are organized into five sections, namely:

A—Systems, Equipment, and Components
B—Test, Inspection, and Production Equipment
C—Materials
D—Software
E—Technology

The Wassenaar Arrangement does not directly address quantum computers. Its only explicit references to quantum technologies are to quantum-related cryptography[40] and quantum sensing.[41]

Certain classical computer hardware and software are in-principle restricted by the Wassenaar Arrangement. On hardware, Categories 3 and 4, Electronics and Computers, have historically applied a wide range of components including types of "microprocessor microcircuits" and "electro-optical" and "optical integrated circuits".[42] It is conceivable that some of these may be relevant to the research or development of quantum computers. However, most of the generally applicable

[38] Nguyen (2025).

[39] European Commission (2024), p. 8.

[40] Wassenaar Arrangement, Item 5.A.2.c; 5.A.2.a (Technical Note 2(c)). See further Bureau of Industry and Security (2019).

[41] Wassenaar Arrangement, Item 6, especially 6.A.2.a.3.

[42] Wassenaar Arrangement, Category 3.A.1.a.3, 3.A.1.a6.

controls on computers have been relaxed[43] or removed,[44] and the Wassenaar Arrangement does not apply to technology or software in the public domain, or to basic scientific research.[45]

The Wassenaar Arrangement does restrict the export of certain cryogenic refrigerators and systems. However, these are in its munitions list[46] and apply only to liquid rocket propulsion systems.[47] Cryogenic refrigeration systems commonly used in superconducting qubit quantum computers[48] are not covered.

Hence, while the Wassenaar Arrangement does regulate, or has historically regulated, technologies adjacent to quantum computers and supporting infrastructure, it does not specifically target quantum computers. It has been reported that the recent plurilateral controls on quantum computers discussed below arose "on the sidelines"[49] of the annual Wassenaar Arrangement meeting in 2023.[50] This would imply that several countries have recently sought to have quantum computing technologies added to the control list in the Wassenaar Arrangement, which self-evidently failed, leading to the current fragmented approach. Ultimately, such conclusions are speculative given the secrecy of national security discussions on sensitive technologies.[51] It suggests, however, appetite to regulate quantum computers within the Wassenaar framework, which would enhance the legitimacy and coordination of the controls.

4.2 *United States*

The US approach to export controls distinguishes between dual-use items and those specifically designed for military applications.[52] Dual-use technologies are regulated under the Export Administration Regulations (EAR) by the Bureau of Industry and Security (BIS). These technologies have both commercial and military applications, with export controls aiming to prevent adversaries from enhancing their military capabilities while still promoting commercial innova-

43 Wassenaar Arrangement Secretariat 2015, 106.

44 Wassenaar Arrangement, Category 4 Note 3.

45 Wassenaar Arrangement, p. 3.

46 The Wassenaar Arrangement distinguishes between the Munitions List and Dual-Use List: see Evans 2014, 22.

47 Wassenaar Arrangement, Item 9.A.6.

48 See below at Sect. 4.5.3.

49 Hmaidi and Groenewegen-Lau (2024).

50 Stewart (2024).

51 See Sparkes (2024).

52 Technologies specifically designed for military use are regulated under the International Traffic in Arms Regulations (ITAR) by the Directorate of Defense Trade Controls (DDTC) within the Department of State. Given their direct implications for national security, ITAR controls are more stringent and less flexible compared to dual-use controls.

tion and trade. The US employs licensing requirements and end-use checks to ensure that these dual-use technologies do not fall into the hands of restricted countries.

The US export control regime categorizes countries into different groups (A to E[53]) based on their level of cooperation with US export control policies and their adherence to international non-proliferation norms. This categorization determines whether licensing exemptions may apply. Country A groups consist of traditional US allies that enjoy the most favorable treatment.[54] Country Group D includes countries of concern, such as those with a history of proliferation or those subject to US sanctions, including China and Russia. Exports to these countries are comparatively restricted and often require specific licenses. In addition to restrictions on export to specific countries based on lists of items, US export controls may also target specific end-users (e.g., Chinese technology companies) and end-uses (e.g., for use in weapons).[55]

In September 2024, the US Department of Commerce announced[56] export controls in the form of an Interim Final Rule[57] on several emerging technologies, including quantum computers, semiconductor manufacturing, advanced computing and items related to their manufacture. Following the Wassenaar Arrangement categories, the restricted items appear in Category 3 (Electronics) and Category 4 (Computers). These controls build upon previously implemented export controls on semiconductors in October 2022 and October 2023, in a series of policy maneuvers known as the "chip wars",[58] which focus predominantly on US concerns that it will lose its competitive advantage in artificial intelligence (AI) on China.[59] As has been noted,[60] the controls are similar to those implemented by geopolitical allies such as

[53] Note that Group C is undefined and held in reserve for future use. See Supplement No 1 to Part 740, Title 15 Code of Federal Regulations (2025).

[54] §§ 740.11, 740.16 and 740.20, Title 15 Code of Federal Regulations (2025).

[55] For a summary, see Allen and Goldston (2025).

[56] Bureau of Industry and Security (2024c).

[57] Commerce Control List Additions and Revisions; Implementation of Controls on Advanced Technologies Consistent With Controls Implemented by International Partners (Bureau of Industry and Security, Interim Final Rule, 6 September 2024) 89 Fed Reg 72, 926.

[58] Allen and Goldston (2025).

[59] Allen and Goldston (2025).

[60] Sparkes (2024); Sparkes (2025); Nguyen (2025).

the Netherlands,[61] United Kingdom,[62] Spain,[63] France,[64] Australia[65] and Japan[66] implemented within a year either side of the US rules. The September 2024 controls signify the US expansion of the "chip wars" directly into the realm of quantum computing, with restrictions placed on "quantum computers, related equipment, components, materials, software, and technology that can be used in the development and maintenance of quantum computers."[67]

The controls contain licensing exemptions for exports to countries that have implemented similar export restrictions, including the United Kingdom, Norway, the Netherlands, Australia and Japan.[68] Interestingly, the controls allow organizations to share technologies to foreign nationals within the US. These are typically regarded as "deemed exports" and thus subject to the licensing regime. The Interim Final Rule notes that "this hardship would be devastating to the continued progress of future developments in the quantum field, which depends on foreign person employees from these destinations."[69] Thus, as reported, "the rule permits sharing with foreign nationals working in the US, even if they are from countries identified by the government as posing national security concerns or subject to arms embargoes".[70] Instead, the rules impose record-keeping requirements on organizations that share controlled quantum technologies to those of certain nationalities; it is reported that this is likely a government-led information gathering exercise to potentially ratchet up controls in the future.[71]

The items added to the control list do not apply to all quantum computers and their enabling infrastructure. Rather, the items are targeted towards the development

---

[61] Regeling van de Minister voor Buitenlandse Handel en Ontwikkelingshulp van 11 oktober 2024, nr. BZ2405833 houdende invoering van een vergunningplicht voor de uitvoer van producten die niet zijn genoemd in bijlage I van Verordening 2021/821 (Regeling aanvullende controlemaatregelen op de Verordening producten voor tweeërlei gebruik).

[62] Export Control (Amendment) Regulations 2024, SI 2024/346.

[63] Compilation of national control lists under Article 9(4) of Regulation (EU) 2021/821 of the European Parliament and of the Council of 20 May 2021 setting up a Union regime for the control of exports, brokering, technical assistance, transit and transfer of dual-use items, (C/2023/441) 4A1901 & 4E1901, referencing Annex III.5 of the Royal Decree 679/2014 of 1 August 2014, with entry into force on 7 June 2023.

[64] Arrêté du 2 février 2024 relatif aux exportations vers les pays tiers de biens et technologies associés à l'ordinateur quantique et à ses technologies habilitantes et d'équipements de conception, développement, production, test et inspection de composants électroniques avancés.

[65] Defence and Strategic Goods List 2024; see Customs (Prohibited Exports) Regulations 1958 (Cth) & Customs Act 1901 (Cth), s 112(2A)(aa).

[66] Kobayashi (2024).

[67] Bureau of Industry and Security (2024c).

[68] License Exception Implemented Export Controls (IEC) Eligible Items and Destinations', incorporated by reference in § 740.24, Title 15 Code of Federal Regulations (2025), last modified 2 December 2024. Available at https://www.bis.gov/iec. Accessed 11 June 2025.

[69] § 742.6, Title 15 Code of Federal Regulations (2025).

[70] Zhang (2024).

[71] Zhang (2024).

of quantum computers of certain performance thresholds. Most directly, Export Control Classification Number (ECCN) 4A906, *Quantum computers and related "electronic assemblies" and "components"*, restricts quantum computers with more than 34 qubits of certain levels of coherence. The possible rationale for the 34-qubit cutoff is discussed below at Sect. 4.5.1.

Item 4A906 also encompasses components specifically related to the controlled quantum computers. In parallel, ECCNs 4D906 and 4E906 have been added to include software and technology that are specially designed or modified for the development or production of such systems. Together, these provisions aim to comprehensively regulate not only the quantum computers themselves but also the critical supporting hardware, software, and technical know-how required to build systems that meet or exceed the specified performance thresholds.

Along with these restrictions on quantum computers as a reasonably broad category, the Interim Final Rule also targets specific raw materials and items that are perceived as being on the cutting edge of the development of quantum computing hardware. These include certain cryogenic cooling systems and cryogenic probing equipment (ECCNs 3A904 & 3B904) as well as materials related to silicon and germanium (ECCNs 3C907, 3C908, 3C909) that contain valuable properties for certain types of quantum computers. These controls are further analyzed below at Sect. 4.5.

Table 1 summarizes the main ECCNs relevant to quantum computing.

Table 1 US ECCNs relevant to quantum computing under the Interim Final Rule

ECCN	Description	Explanation
3A901	Cryo-CMOS and signal amplifiers	Future technology designed to operate at ≤4.5 K; relevant for scalable quantum computing.
3A904	Certain cryogenic cooling systems and components	Supports large-scale quantum systems with many physical qubits.
3B904	Cryogenic wafer probing equipment	Enables rapid testing of quantum chips at cryogenic temperatures.
3C907	Epitaxial materials with specified compositions	Materials used in quantum device fabrication.
3C908	Fluorides, hydrides, chlorides of Si/Ge with specified materials	Materials for spin-based qubit development.
3C909	Si, SiO_2, Ge, GeO_2 with specified dopants	Materials supporting semiconducting qubit platforms.
4A906	Quantum computers >34 qubits or equivalent, and related components	Includes full systems, qubit arrays, and control/measurement devices. Unclear why 34 bits is the threshold.[a]
4D906	Software for development/production of 4A906.b or .c items	Targets software for advanced quantum systems.
4E906	Technology for development/production/use of controlled items	Applies to technical data or know-how related to 4A906 and related ECCNs.

[a]Sparkes (2024)

4.3 European Union

The role of the EU in export control regulations has been historically complex,[72] due to the EU's (in principle[73]) limited competence in areas of national security.[74] To oversimplify the present regime (one that is comprehensively unpacked by Bennink et al.[75]), dual-use items are presently regulated by the EU through Regulation (EU) 2021/821 (the "Dual-Use Regulation").[76] The Dual-Use Regulation requires authorization for the export of dual-use items listed in its Annex I,[77] which reproduces the texts of the Wassenaar Arrangement and other multilateral regimes through which the EU and/or its Member States are signatory to.[78] Unlike the US "deemed export" rules, the Dual-Use Regulation does not apply to foreign nationals accessing controlled items within the EU.[79]

As noted in an EU Commission White Paper, the EU "does not have the necessary legal provisions to adopt at EU level uniform export controls independently from what is adopted in the multilateral regimes, except in very limited areas."[80] Thus the EU cannot, in the context of quantum computing, impose export restrictions beyond what is already contained within multilateral regimes like the Wassenaar Arrangement.[81] It follows that there are presently no quantum computing specific export restrictions imposed by the EU.

Instead, EU Member States have taken to implementing their own controls at a national level. The Dual-Use Regulation provides for this possibility in its Chapter II. Article 4 allows export controls on items not listed in Annex I that "are or may be intended" for use in weapons of mass destruction. Article 5 provides similarly for cyber-surveillance tools. Article 9 gives room for Member States to impose restrictions on a broad variety of items, "for reasons of public security, including the

---

[72] von der Dunk (2009).

[73] de Witte (2017).

[74] Art. 4(2), Treaty on European Union (TEU); see also Art. 36, Treaty on the Functioning of the European Union (TFEU).

[75] Bennink et al. (2025).

[76] Regulation (EU) 2021/821 of the European Parliament and of the Council of 20 May 2021 setting up a Union regime for the control of exports, brokering, technical assistance, transit and transfer of dual-use items (recast) PE/54/2020/REV/2 OJ L 206, 11.6.2021, pp. 1–461.

[77] Art. 3(1) Dual-Use Regulation.

[78] Dual-Use Regulation, Annex I; see further European Commission 2024, 2; Bennink et al. (2025), p. 96.

[79] Commission Recommendation (EU) 2021/1700 of 15 September 2021 on internal compliance programmes for controls of research involving dual-use items under Regulation (EU) 2021/821 of the European Parliament and of the Council setting up a Union regime for the control of exports, brokering, technical assistance, transit and transfer of dual-use items C/2021/6636, OJ L 338, 23.9.2021, pp. 1–52, Appendix 2.

[80] European Commission (2024), p. 6.

[81] Art. 15 Dual-Use Regulation; European Commission (2024), p. 12.

prevention of acts of terrorism, or for human rights considerations."[82] Member States must notify the EU Commission of measures adopted under Article 9,[83] with the Commission being tasked with iteratively publishing a compilation of these measures.[84] As noted by Bennink et al., this latter requirement does not apply to items restricted under Article 4 or 5,[85] which makes it difficult to track Member State rules that go beyond the Dual-Use Regulation Annex I.

In its White Paper on Dual-Use, the EU Commission notes that recent multilateral gridlock and the pace of new controls implemented outside of multilateral regimes effectively sidelines the EU, and renders coordination amongst Member States problematic. It outlines several means of ameliorating the present circumstances in its White Paper, and a recent Recommendation suggests Member States coordinate and information-share regarding national control lists.[86] These actions sit alongside broader EU-led efforts in facilitating quantum computing innovation in its Chips Act, which calls for the coordinated development of quantum chip value chains.[87] However, at present, it remains that the EU has no formal role in restricting exports of items relating to quantum computers.

4.4 EU Member States

Several EU Member States have implemented quantum computing export controls in national control lists. Among these are the Netherlands, Spain, France, Italy, Germany and Finland,[88] along with European Economic Area (EEA) country Norway,[89] some of which are discussed below. As of finalizing this chapter in August 2025, the Compilation of national control lists maintained by the EU Commission under Article 9(4) of the Dual-Use Regulation[90] only refers to select controls implemented by France and Spain. For the most part, the controls are made in near-

[82] Art. 9(1) Dual-Use Regulation.

[83] Art. 9(3) Dual-Use Regulation.

[84] Art. 9(4) Dual-Use Regulation.

[85] Bennink et al. (2025), p. 94.

[86] Commission Recommendation (EU) 2025/683 of 8 April 2025 on coordination of national control lists, C/2025/2113 OJ L, 2025/683, 16.4.2025.

[87] Art. 5(c) & rec. 17, Regulation (EU) 2023/1781 of the European Parliament and of the Council of 13 September 2023 establishing a framework of measures for strengthening Europe's semiconductor ecosystem and amending Regulation (EU) 2021/694 (Chips Act) (Text with EEA relevance) PE/28/2023/INIT OJ L 229, 18.9.2023, pp. 1–53.

[88] Ministry for Foregin Affairs of Finland (2024).

[89] Vigmostad and Meldahl (2024).

[90] Compilation of national control lists under Article 9(4) of Regulation (EU) 2021/821 of the European Parliament and of the Council of 20 May 2021 setting up a Union regime for the control of exports, brokering, technical assistance, transit and transfer of dual-use items PUB/2024/770 OJ C, C/2024/5880, 27.9.2024 (Control List Compilation 2024).

identical terms to the US Interim Final Rules discussed above. However, perhaps owing to the different times at which these rules were implemented, and the degree to which Member States are concerned with the quantum computing industry, not all the US export restrictions are implemented by all the Member States that have adopted restrictions on quantum computing technologies. Once again, due to the secrecy behind these measures, the rationale behind similarities and differences is difficult to ascertain.[91]

Table 2 illustrates the measures implemented by Spain, France, the Netherlands, Italy, and Germany as of writing. These are benchmarked against the equivalent ECCNs in the US Control List. As indicated in the table, the Netherlands and Italy have effectively fully adopted the same controls as the US. However, Spain has only adopted the equivalent of ECCN 4A906 on quantum computing hardware above 34 qubits and related components.

The similarity of controls between these Member States and the US (amongst others) suggests a degree of cooperation between international partners—likely "on the sidelines"[92] of Wassenaar Arrangement discussions.[93] However, not all EU Member States have implemented restrictions on quantum computing, and those who have differ somewhat in their approach. Moreover, the fact that only Spain and France's controls specific to quantum computing have appeared in the Control List Compilation managed by the EU Commission suggests issues with the coordination of national control lists that the Dual-Use Regulation envisages for the EU Commission. These issues would be avoided, or at least mitigated, in a functioning multilateral arrangement—a fact noted by many calling for a "Wassenaar Minus One"[94]—or at least better coordination amongst EU Member States—as noted by the EU Commission.[95]

4.5 Analysis of Quantum Computing Specific Controls

To date, the US, several EU Member States, and other Wassenaar Arrangement signatories such as Australia and the UK have implemented export controls targeting two of the nine dual-use categories—Computers and Electronics. These controls span all five technical sections (A through E), though they were enacted outside formal Wassenaar channels. The inclusion of items from every section suggests a broad regulatory intent to cover the entire quantum computing supply chain. Among the jurisdictions examined, the only common measure is the restriction of specific quantum computing hardware, indicating that quantum computers themselves are

[91] Sparkes (2024).

[92] Hmaidi and Groenewegen-Lau (2024).

[93] Sparkes (2024).

[94] Junusova and Reinsch (2024).

[95] European Commission (2024).

Table 2 Export restricted items relevant to quantum computing by select EU Member States

US ECCN	Description	Spain[a]	France[b]	Netherlands[c]	Italy[d]	Germany[e]
3A901	Cryo-CMOS and signal amplifiers		3A1901.a.15	3A901.a.15	3A901.a.15	3A1901a15
3A904	Certain cryogenic cooling systems and components			3A904	3A904	3A1904
3B904	Cryogenic wafer probing equipment			3B904	3B904	3B1904
3C907	Epitaxial materials with specified compositions			3C907	3C907	
3C908	Fluorides, hydrides, chlorides of Si/Ge with specified materials			3C908	3C908	
3C909	Si, SiO_2, Ge, GeO_2 with specified dopants			3C909	3C909	
4A906	Quantum computers >34 qubits or equivalent, and related components	4A1901	4A1906	4A906	4A906	4A1906
4D906	Software for development/ production of 4A906.b or .c items		4D1901.b.3	4D901.b.3.	4D901.b.3	4D1901b3
4E906	Technology for development/ production/use of controlled items		4E1901	4E901.b.3.	4E901.b.3	4E1901b3

[a]Control List Compilation 2024; Annex III.5 of the Royal Decree 679/2014 of 1 August 2014, with entry into force on 7 June 2023

[b]Control List Compilation 2024; Order of 2 February 2024 on exports to third countries of goods and technologies associated with quantum computers and their enabling technologies, and of equipment to design, develop, produce, test and inspect advanced electronic components; Arrêté du 2 février 2024 relatif aux exportations vers les pays tiers de biens et technologies associés à l'ordinateur quantique et à ses technologies habilitantes et d'équipements de conception, développement, production, test et inspection de composants électroniques JORF n°0034 du 10 février 2024, texte n° 8

[c]Regeling van de Minister voor Buitenlandse Handel en Ontwikkelingshulp van 11 oktober 2024, nr. BZ2405833 houdende invoering van een vergunningplicht voor de uitvoer van producten die niet zijn genoemd in bijlage I van Verordening 2021/821 (Regeling aanvullende controlemaatregelen op de Verordening producten voor tweeërlei gebruik). Available at: https://zoek.officielebekendmakingen.nl/stcrt-2024-33838.html. Accessed 11 June 2025

[d]Control List Compilation 2024; Italian Decree of 1 July 2024 establishing the National Control List for dual-use goods and technology not listed in Annex I to Regulation (EU) 2021/821; Decreto del Vice Ministro degli Affari Esteri e della Cooperazione Internazionale n. 1325/BIS/371 del 1 Luglio (2024). Available at: https://www.esteri.it/wp-content/uploads/2024/07/allegato-A.pdf. Accessed 11 June 2025

[e]Einundzwanzigste Verordnung zur Änderung der Außenwirtschaftsverordnung (30 Aug. 2024). Available at: https://dserver.bundestag.de/btd/20/126/2012685.pdf. Accessed 11 June 2025

Table 3 Qubit range and error rates thresholds for application of export controls to quantum computers

Category	Qubit Range	C-NOT Error Rate
a.1	34–99	$\leq 10^{-4}$
a.2	100–199	$\leq 10^{-3}$
a.3	200–349	$\leq 2 \times 10^{-3}$
a.4	350–499	$\leq 3 \times 10^{-3}$
a.5	500–699	$\leq 4 \times 10^{-3}$
a.6	700–1099	$\leq 5 \times 10^{-3}$
a.7	1100–1999	$\leq 6 \times 10^{-3}$
a.8	2000+	N/A

viewed as the most critical concern for regulators. This item (US ECCN 4A906) is therefore considered first in this section, before continuing to an analysis of the other quantum computing-relevant items. To simplify discussion, the below analysis refers to the US ECCNs unless otherwise stated.

4.5.1 Quantum Computers

Acknowledging that there are many different quantum computing paradigms with differing levels of performance based on the quality of qubits, item 4A906 defines eight performance categories. In simple terms, quantum computers of less than 34 qubits are not controlled, and all computers of greater than 2000 qubits are controlled. Computers between 34 and 1999 qubits may be covered by the rules, depending on the number of qubits and average Controlled NOT (C-Not) gate error rate of the computer. This approach follows the wisdom that quantum computers with greater physical qubits but high error rates will have comparable performance to lesser qubit machines with lower error rates. The different categories are reflected in the Table 3:

It is unclear why these specific performance thresholds have been arrived at by regulators. However, it has been suggested that the 34-qubit threshold approximates the level at which quantum computers can no longer be simulated by classical computers.[96] By setting the threshold at this level, regulators appear to be targeting systems that cross a meaningful boundary in computational capability, while still allowing academic and industrial research on less capable systems to continue without restriction. A note by the US Bureau of Industry and Security (BIS) in the Interim Final Rule states that:

> BIS has determined that a near-term generation of quantum computers will support 34 or more "fully controlled", "connected" and "working" "physical qubits" at the specified error rates, and that this number of qubits and error rate represents a high level of technological sophistication warranting national security, regional stability, and anti-terrorism controls.[97]

[96] Sparkes (2024).

[97] Bureau of Industry and Security (2024b).

Table 4 Qubit count for select, currently available quantum computers

Company	System	Qubits
IBM	Osprey	433
IBM	Eagle	127
IBM	Heron	156
IBM	Condor	1121
Intel	Tunnel Falls	12
IonQ	Forte	36
Google	Sycamore	~53
Google	Willow	105
Microsoft	Majorana 1	8
Quantinuum	H2	56
QuEra	Aquila	256
Rigetti	Aspen-M3	80

Finding concrete and accurate numbers on average error rate of currently available quantum computers is difficult, especially given the tendency for companies to position their advances in quantum computing in the most favorable light. This makes the determination of whether specific current examples of quantum computers are subject to the controls difficult. Indeed, a side-effect of these export controls may be to discourage inflated performance numbers to avoid being captured by the new rules. Table 4 illustrates the Qubit count of a selection of quantum computers announced by several companies. As the table suggests, many of these items will be restricted by export controls unless average C-NOT error rate is above the relevant threshold.

In identifying the number and type of qubits to be counted according to the rules, item 4A906 only applies to fully controlled, connected, working, physical qubits. These four terms are elaborated in the Technical Note accompanying item 4A906. The Technical Note confirms that physical qubits are treated as distinct from logical qubits, "in that logical qubits are error-corrected qubits comprised of many 'physical qubits'."

Finally, two further Notes are relevant to Item 4A906.a. Note 1 confirms that the controls only apply to gate-based and measurement-based quantum computers, not adiabatic (or annealing) quantum computers which are primarily designed for solving optimization problems rather than for universal quantum computation.[98] Note 2 specifies that "physical qubits" may not be permanently present, and the rule covers computers with qubits that are generated during operation (e.g., photonic schemes). These notes also appear in other countries' equivalents to US ECCN 4A906. They reveal an appreciation of the nuance that must be applied to properly capture technologies that regulators wish to restrict—yet portend the potential for "creative compliance" by quantum computing hardware companies to avoid restrictions

[98] Yarkoni et al. (2022).

through quantum computing paradigms that might slip through the cracks of the rules.[99]

4.5.2 Quantum Computing Components, Software and Technology

Along with restrictions on certain quantum computers above the 34-qubit threshold are the individual components and supporting software which are "specifically designed" for restricted quantum computers. Item 4A906.b covers qubit devices and circuits being, respectively, the physical components that implement qubits (e.g., superconducting circuits, trapped ions, photonic systems) and integrated systems or chips that host multiple qubits and allow them to interact. Item 4A906.c restricts control components, which include electronics and systems that manage qubit operations (e.g., microwave generators and pulse modulators) and measurement devices (e.g., single photon detectors). These, in effect, ensure that disparate physical components of a quantum computer that reaches the thresholds in item 4A906.a are covered, and not just entire quantum computers.

Item 4D906 also restricts software that is "specifically designed" or modified for the development or production of qubit devices, qubit circuits, quantum control components or quantum measurement devices described in 4A906.b and 4A906.c. This means that the software restrictions do not apply to quantum computing software as a broad category (i.e. algorithms designed for quantum computers of a certain performance threshold). Rather, the controls are narrowly focused on software that enables the physical realization of quantum hardware. In practical terms, this includes software used to design, fabricate, calibrate, or test the physical infrastructure of a quantum computer such as chip layout tools, control signal generators, or measurement automation. Software that is used to develop quantum algorithms, simulate quantum systems, or run applications on quantum processors is not restricted under 4D906, unless it is also specifically designed for the development or production of the aforementioned hardware. This distinction ensures that general-purpose quantum software development remains largely unrestricted under the controls.

Finally, item 4E906 is aimed at controlling "technology" related to the development and production of the abovementioned quantum computing components and software, and additionally technology for the *use* of software controlled in 4D906. Technology, as defined under the Wassenaar Arrangement,[100] refers to "Specific information necessary for the development, production or use of a product", which takes the form of "Technical data" and "technical assistance". This includes technical know-how, design methodologies, manufacturing processes, documentation, and other forms of intangible knowledge that enable the creation or application of controlled quantum hardware and software. As such, 4E906 endeavors to ensure

[99] See further below at Sect. 5.2.

[100] Wassenaar Arrangement, Definitions.

that not only the physical items and software are controlled, but also the underlying expertise that could be transferred to replicate or enhance those capabilities in restricted countries.

4.5.3 Cryogenic Equipment

Many quantum computers must operate at extremely low temperatures (often slightly above absolute zero) in order to maintain the delicate quantum states of their qubits. This applies to systems based on superconducting qubits or spin qubits, which require cryogenic environments to minimize thermal noise and decoherence.[101] In this context, 3A904 imposes export controls on cryogenic cooling systems and components that are capable of delivering cooling power of 600 μW or more at or below 0.1 Kelvin (−273.05 C) for over 48 h. The US Interim Final Rule points out that cryogenic systems with greatest cooling power are generally required for more advanced quantum computers, rationalizing the threshold chosen as being "on items that are relevant for research on quantum systems with a larger quantity of physical qubits".[102]

Complementing this item, ECCN 3B904 imposes export controls on certain cryogenic wafer probing equipment which is used to test and characterize quantum devices, such as solid-state qubits, at cryogenic temperatures. According to the US Interim Final Rule, these tools are particularly important for scaling up quantum computing, as they enable faster and more comprehensive testing of qubit devices by collecting high volumes of data under operational conditions. Thus, this control targets anticipated advancements in research and design pipelines of certain quantum computing paradigms.

ECCN 3A901 introduces export controls on cryogenic electronics that, according to the US Interim Final Rule, are critical to the development of advanced quantum systems. In particular, the Rule notes that "CMOS designs are currently being developed that are suitable for operating around 4K temperatures or below for the purposes of quantum computing",[103] with current CMOS temperature limits reported as being around −40 C (233 K). Hence, 3A901.a restricts cryo-CMOS designed to operate at these extreme low temperatures. In a similar vein, 3A901.b covers signal amplifiers which are used to read out weak qubit signals with very low noise at extremely low temperatures. The addition of these items reflects the anticipated strategic importance of cryogenic electronics in enabling scalable, high-performance quantum computing.

[101] Bureau of Industry and Security (2024b).

[102] Bureau of Industry and Security (2024b).

[103] Bureau of Industry and Security (2024b).

4.5.4 Quantum Computing Materials

The export controls introduced under ECCNs 3C907, 3C908, and 3C909 and their equivalents in other jurisdictions are designed to regulate access to specific enriched materials. These materials, as explained in the Interim Final Rule, are perceived as critical for the development of spin-based quantum computers. Spin-based quantum systems use the spin of electrons or nuclei, often in silicon or germanium atoms, to represent qubits.[104] Because certain isotopes of silicon and germanium have no nuclear spin, they create a much quieter quantum environment, reducing interference and allowing qubits to retain their state for longer periods.[105] This makes spin-based quantum computing a promising platform for building scalable, high-fidelity quantum processors.

Item 3C907 controls layered materials made from silicon or germanium that include a high percentage of specific isotopes. Item 3C908 applies to certain chemical compounds of silicon or germanium that also contain these isotopes. Item 3C909 covers bulk forms of silicon, silicon dioxide, germanium, and germanium dioxide with similar isotopic enrichment. Together, these controls operate further upstream in the quantum computing stack by restricting access to the specialized materials that form the foundation of certain quantum hardware, thereby endeavoring to limit the ability to develop advanced quantum systems before they can even be built.

4.6 Strategic Implications of Current Plurilateral Quantum Computing Controls

4.6.1 Summary of Current Controls and Prevailing View

So far, this section has examined the measures that have arisen from the "mysterious quantum export deal"[106] between the US and certain of its allies. Likely, these represent just the first wave of controls targeted at quantum computing technologies, given the ongoing "chip wars" between, *inter alia*, the US and China. From this examination, three main points can be deduced.

First, there is an obvious lack of harmonization compared to if these controls would have come through the traditional multilateral approach under the Wassenaar Arrangement. That is not to say that such an approach would provide a panacea for uniform adherence to the rules. As argued by Brunel in the context of semiconductor regulation, "the voluntary approach of the Wassenaar Arrangement has plainly failed".[107] However, the current patchwork of rules leads to significant uncertainty.

---

[104] Sarma et al. (2005); Giordano et al. (2021).

[105] Giordano et al. (2021).

[106] Sparkes (2024).

[107] Brunel (2023), p. 3.

Second, the most comprehensive set of controls (i.e. those implemented by the US, Italy and the Netherlands of countries examined) are clearly concerned with a broad range of the quantum computing stack and supply chain. Controls include not just quantum computers and their physical components, but also materials used to develop hardware, and less- or intangible items such as software and "know-how" (or "technology" in Wassenaar Arrangement terms).

Third, the measures appear less concerned with restricting the export of existing quantum technologies and more focused on shaping the future trajectory of development. This is evident in the 34-qubit cutoff and the targeting of emerging technologies such as spin-based quantum materials and cryo-CMOS. Rather than disrupting current commercial and academic efforts, regulators seem intent on pre-emptively delineating the boundaries of acceptable technological dissemination—focusing on capabilities that could significantly accelerate quantum advantage.

4.6.2 Strategic Implications and Counter-Arguments

The emergence of plurilateral quantum computing export controls—developed and implemented outside traditional multilateral mechanisms like the Wassenaar Arrangement—marks a significant evolution in how states govern access to frontier technologies. While such arrangements may appear *ad hoc* or fragmented, they reflect a deliberate strategic shift: one aimed not merely at containment of adversarial capabilities but at shaping the long-term development of the global quantum ecosystem.

A common critique of plurilateralism[108] is that it fragments export control regimes, creates compliance asymmetries, and invites forum shopping. These risks are real—particularly for global firms navigating inconsistent ECCN adoptions and varying national interpretations. However, this view may underestimate the structural and technological realities of quantum computing. Given the field's rapid evolution, scientific opacity, and lack of standardized metrics,[109] a conventional multilateral model may be ill-suited to its governance. In this light, the emerging plurilateral approach can be seen not as a deficiency but as a pragmatic response—one that allows for tailored, domain-specific coordination among states with shared risk thresholds, industrial capabilities, and intelligence insights. Rather than fragmentation, this may reflect the early contours of a *sui generis* governance regime more appropriate to quantum technologies' complexity and unpredictability.

Crucially, the scope of current controls—targeting not only complete quantum computers but also cryogenic infrastructure, enriched materials, and specialized software—suggests a shift from reactive regulation to anticipatory containment. As alluded to above, by focusing on enabling technologies and performance thresholds

[108] See, e.g., Basedow (2018); Dimitropoulos et al. (2025).

[109] See further Smith et al. (2026).

(such as the symbolic 34-qubit cutoff), regulators appear to be drawing a strategic line in the sand: restricting downstream potential without unduly impeding upstream academic and industrial research. This forward-looking posture, aimed at shaping trajectories rather than reacting to milestones, underscores the exceptionalism of quantum in the export control domain.

Yet the long-term strategic endgame of these measures remains under-articulated. Is the goal to slow adversarial progress, protect domestic industry, foster trusted supply chains, or incentivize international norms? In practice, it is likely a combination of all these objectives. Rather than choosing a single path, policymakers appear to be pursuing a strategy of flexibility and optionality—creating overlapping, modular controls that can be dialed up, coordinated, or recalibrated as geopolitical, technological, and commercial dynamics evolve. From this perspective, a deliberately plurilateral, adaptive approach may offer a more resilient framework than rigid multilateralism, especially given the uncertain direction and impact of quantum breakthroughs.

Ultimately, the plurilateral controls now taking shape should not be seen merely as stopgap measures or symptoms of gridlock. They may in fact represent the early architecture of a more fit-for-purpose export control regime—one that balances security and openness, containment and collaboration, and legal enforceability with technical nuance. If strategically maintained, this regime could serve not only as a bulwark against proliferation but as a scaffold for shaping the responsible and secure evolution of quantum technologies.

5 Challenges and Opportunities of Export Controls

As this chapter has so far illustrated, export controls on quantum technologies are becoming increasingly central to national and international efforts to manage emerging security and economic risks. Comprising a particularly sensitive and fast-evolving subset of the broader quantum technology landscape, quantum computing poses unique regulatory challenges due to its wide-ranging dual-use potential and the uncertain pace and potential of technological breakthroughs. The ability of quantum computers to disrupt existing cryptographic systems, accelerate materials discovery, or simulate complex biological systems gives rise to both considerable strategic value and profound governance dilemmas.

However, the opportunities and challenges of applying export controls to quantum computing are not simply a subset of broader debates about controlling the export of emerging technologies. Rather, as this section illustrates, issues also stem from the distinctive characteristics of quantum computing itself, such as its scientific foundations, hardware dependencies, and global research ecosystem.

5.1 Opportunities

While export controls on quantum computing technologies present significant regulatory challenges, they also offer important opportunities to shape the global development of this transformative field. Carefully designed controls can foster responsible innovation by encouraging transparency, security-conscious research practices, and international collaboration on shared norms. They can also serve as a catalyst for multilateral dialogue, helping to align national strategies and avoid regulatory fragmentation. Moreover, export controls provide a mechanism for anticipating and managing future risks, allowing policymakers to adapt to technological advances while promoting trust and stability in global quantum research and commercial ecosystems. The following discussion focuses on selected factors considered critical for realizing the opportunities that well-calibrated export controls can offer.

5.1.1 Timing

Quantum computing is at an earlier stage of development than more mature technologies like semiconductors that form the core of the ongoing "chip wars". Since the infrastructure, supply chains, and talent pools for quantum computing are still forming, export controls can shape the ecosystem early on. In contrast to mature technologies, where controls often struggle to keep pace with widespread diffusion, early-stage controls in quantum computing can potentially shut out economic rivals before the technology and expertise becomes ubiquitous.[110]

This is reflected in the controls already implemented, whereby certain advanced quantum computing technologies, or technologies with perceived high potential, are subject to restriction. In particular, the item related to cryogenic wafer probing[111] reflects an intention not just to restrict finished products, but items that can be used to further develop quantum technologies.

On the other hand, the early stage of development means that restricted countries may have the time, and incentive, to invest heavily in domestic quantum capabilities, potentially accelerating their own programs. Export controls, while limiting access to cutting-edge systems, will doubtless further encourage the indigenization of quantum technologies in countries with the capacity to do so (like China), which may increase focus on building self-reliant quantum computing ecosystems encompassing hardware, software, and talent development.[112] As noted by Nguyen, China

[110] This dynamic is often framed through the "Collingridge dilemma", which highlights the difficulty of regulating emerging technologies: early in their development, the consequences are uncertain, but once the consequences become clear, the technologies are often too entrenched to control effectively.

[111] See above at Sect. 4.5.3.

[112] Shivakumar et al. (2025).

has already announced its own breakthroughs in quantum computing since the imposition of export controls by the US.[113]

5.1.2 Physical Footprint of QC Infrastructure

As reported in the New York Times, "[o]ne problem with trying to control the global flow of semiconductors is that they're very small, lightweight and valuable."[114] In contrast, many quantum computers are large, bulky systems that require specialized infrastructure, including dilution refrigerators, cryogenic systems, vibration isolation, and electromagnetic shielding. These machines are not only physically substantial but also highly sensitive to environmental conditions, making them difficult to transport, replicate, or conceal. This physicality offers an advantage towards export control efforts: much of the hardware required to build advanced quantum computers is inherently less portable and more traceable than, for instance, microchips. The complexity and visibility of the supporting infrastructure thus create natural chokepoints for monitoring and regulation.

The size and specialized nature of quantum computing infrastructure also enable a highly targeted regulatory approach. Since these systems can only operate in environments with ultra-stable temperatures, shielding, and precision engineering, their use is confined to specialized laboratories and institutional actors—typically national labs, research universities, and major industrial R&D centers. This centralization of capability makes it easier for authorities to implement licensing, inspection, and compliance schemes that focus on a manageable number of actors, while also reducing the risk of proliferation to unsanctioned users or jurisdictions.

Importantly, this infrastructure-heavy phase of quantum development supports component-level export controls that can be both surgical and strategic. Rather than restricting full systems, regulators can focus on critical enabling technologies—such as cryogenic cooling units, wafer-scale probing equipment, or cryo-CMOS electronics—which are essential to performance but not widely used outside of quantum. Because these items are not broadly commercialized, their restriction imposes minimal collateral friction while delivering maximum strategic impact. In this way, physical infrastructure enables a more granular and effective export control regime tailored to the quantum computing domain.

Furthermore, the scale and visibility of quantum installations strengthen enforcement through observability and deterrence. Unlike small-scale or software-based technologies that may operate clandestinely, quantum computers are difficult to build or operate discreetly. Their physical footprint and environmental dependencies make them more transparent to both regulators and intelligence services, facilitating national assessments of technological maturity and compliance. This

---

[113] Nguyen (2025), p. 74.

[114] Palmer (2023b).

visibility, in turn, can act as a strategic signaling tool—deterring adversarial development and reinforcing collective oversight among allied states.

Finally, the foreseeable trajectory toward miniaturized, deployable quantum systems—enabled by photonic chips, integrated control electronics, and neutral atom platforms—provides regulators with a critical window for anticipatory action. By identifying and locking down key enabling technologies early in the development curve, export control frameworks can evolve ahead of these advancements. The current infrastructure-intensive nature of quantum computing is therefore not just a constraint—it is a strategic asset. It offers both an immediate locus for enforcement and a predictive opportunity to shape the technological future before systems become modular, portable, and harder to control.

5.1.3 Cloud and API Access

Another factor enhancing the viability of export restrictions in quantum computing is the increasing reliance on cloud-based access models. Unlike traditional computing hardware, which is often sold and shipped to end-users, many of the world's most advanced quantum systems are now accessed remotely, providing a point of control that regulators can leverage for enforcement. Cloud-based quantum computing, and remote access through Application Programming Interfaces (APIs), offer regulators a rare advantage in the export control landscape: centralized access infrastructure.

Unlike traditional exports, which involve one-time shipments and *post hoc* enforcement, quantum cloud services provide a persistent point of control through which user activity can be actively governed, monitored, and—if necessary—revoked. Access can be geo-fenced or restricted based on user location, affiliation, or other factors. To avoid circumvention of these controls through technical measures like Virtual Private Networks (VPNs), providers can implement robust identity verification, contractual agreements, usage monitoring, and access controls to ensure that users in sanctioned jurisdictions or entities of concern are not given access. This dynamic control model allows for real-time restriction of access to specific capabilities, updates, or performance tiers, providing a level of granularity and responsiveness that is difficult to replicate in physical trade regulation.

Moreover, the cloud model facilitates a new form of public-private enforcement partnership. Quantum cloud providers—typically large, well-regulated technology firms—are positioned to become frontline actors in ensuring compliance with national security requirements. Governments can engage with these firms through licensing frameworks, export control clauses, and cooperative audit protocols to ensure consistent application of restrictions across jurisdictions. This integration of regulatory oversight into platform architecture enables a scalable and adaptive model for controlling access to sensitive quantum capabilities.

Finally, the ability to tier or segment access in the cloud opens opportunities for precision diplomacy and norm-setting. Regulators and service providers can distinguish between academic users, commercial developers, and state-affiliated entities, tailoring access controls accordingly. For example, limited-functionality access can be provided to trusted research institutions, while more advanced features are withheld from strategic competitors. This flexibility supports a more calibrated export control posture—one that encourages responsible innovation and scientific collaboration among allies, while denying advanced capabilities to potential adversaries. As quantum computing matures, cloud access will not only serve as a technical enforcement mechanism but also as a strategic policy tool, aligning access privileges with broader diplomatic, scientific, and security objectives.

5.2 *Challenges*

Despite the strategic opportunities presented by export controls on quantum computing, their implementation is fraught with both longstanding and emerging challenges. Export control regimes have historically struggled to keep pace with rapidly evolving technologies, and quantum computing intensifies many of these difficulties. The field's rapid development, scientific opacity, and dual-use potential make it difficult to define what constitutes a controllable capability. This is further complicated by the open and collaborative nature of quantum research, which complicates efforts to monitor knowledge flows without stifling innovation.

Additionally, unilateral or poorly coordinated controls risk creating regulatory fragmentation, encouraging workarounds, or disadvantaging domestic industries. Striking the right balance between security and scientific openness is further complicated by uncertainties about the pace and direction of quantum breakthroughs, making timely and proportionate regulation particularly difficult to achieve.[115] The following discussion examines several key issues that illustrate the distinctive obstacles facing export control regimes in the domain of quantum computing. It also discusses potential upsides to these challenges, and ways of mitigating their downsides.

5.2.1 International Ecosystem

One of the most significant challenges to effective export controls in quantum computing is the deeply international nature of the knowledge ecosystem and supply chain.[116] Unlike the semiconductor industry, where the US, Taiwan, South Korea, and the Netherlands dominate key segments of the value chain, quantum innovation is widely distributed across academic institutions, startups, and national labs in dozens of countries, including the US, China, Canada, Germany,

---

[115] See further Smith et al. (2026) and Lenarczyk et al. (2026).

[116] Parker (2023); Greinert et al. (2024).

the UK, Denmark, France and Australia. There is no single dominant country or company that controls the full quantum stack, from materials and fabrication to software and algorithms. This means that no single country can unilaterally impose effective controls without isolating themselves from the global quantum community, stifling local innovation.

This isolation may manifest itself in multiple ways. For example, the recent export controls on raw materials discussed above at Sect. 4.5.4 aim to restrict geopolitical rivals from accessing certain key hardware inputs for advanced quantum systems. However, China has significant capacity to adapt and respond to these restrictions. As noted in a press release from the EU Parliament following a resolution on the topic,[117] "China has a quasi-monopoly on the export of critical raw materials, rare earth elements and permanent magnets."[118] Given its own recent export controls in retaliation to the US,[119] China can similarly withdraw raw materials from the US and its allies.[120]

Moreover, many Western quantum companies and research programs rely on international talent pipelines,[121] with researchers trained or collaborating across borders, not least of all from China.[122] The recent quantum computing export controls apply to "technology" (i.e. US ECCN 4E906), which broadly includes "[s]pecific information necessary for the development, production or use of a product".[123] However, given the US exemption on "deemed exports" to foreign citizens,[124] the controls do not currently apply to knowledge transfer facilitated by natural persons.[125] This is theoretically possible to amend, and there are other mechanisms to help reduce such knowledge transfer such as visa restrictions.[126] Such an approach, though, risks excluding international expertise to a disproportionate extent, and discouraging legitimate cross-border collaboration that may be encumbered by bureaucratic red tape.[127]

---

[117] European Parliament resolution of 10 July 2025 on tackling China's critical raw materials export restrictions (2025/2800(RSP)).

[118] European Parliament (2025).

[119] Baskeran and Schwartz (2024).

[120] Swayne (2025).

[121] See National Science and Technology Council (2021); Kaur and Venegas-Gomez (2022).

[122] Nguyen (2025), pp. 74–75; Moscioni (2025).

[123] Wassenaar Arrangement, Definitions. See above at 0.

[124] See above at 0.

[125] Nguyen (2025), pp. 74–75.

[126] See, e.g., Moscioni (2025).

[127] Nguyen (2025), p. 75. The US Interim Final Rule notes that "...there is a global shortage of quantum computing expertise, with demand currently outstripping supply. This has led to a substantial world-wide competition to attract the top talent. Academia and industry have described the talent bottleneck as one of the largest impediments to acceleration."

5.2.2 Fragmentation and Duplicative Efforts

While export controls aim to prevent adversarial access to sensitive quantum technologies, they can also strain collaboration among allies, leading to fragmentation of research efforts and duplicative investments. The recent erosion of multilateralism and move to national or plurilateral regimes has led to divergent control regimes, as described in Sect. 4. This may prompt even close partners to pursue parallel quantum development tracks out of caution or strategic necessity, to the detriment of collective advancement of allies.[128]

This fragmentation can result in redundant infrastructure (e.g., multiple countries building similar quantum hardware platforms), inefficient allocation of talent and funding, and barriers to cross-border collaboration, even among trusted partners. Such outcomes not only slow collective progress but also undermine the very security goals that export controls are meant to serve. The global quantum ecosystem could become siloed, with reduced interoperability, fewer shared standards,[129] and diminished scientific exchange.

This issue may be mitigated through more coordinated multilateral controls, such as the abovementioned "Wassenaar Minus One"[130] strategy. At a regional level, coordinated EU controls as suggested by the EU Commission[131] that go beyond international agreements like the Wassenaar Arrangement could prevent intra-European forum shopping.

However, it is also possible to view fragmentation as a strategic feature rather than a flaw, especially given the early, uncertain, and geopolitically sensitive stage of quantum technology development. Diverse national approaches can serve as experiments in regulatory design, allowing states to pilot tailored control frameworks suited to their industrial base, security posture, and technological strengths. Moreover, strategic duplication of capabilities across allied countries can provide supply chain resilience, reduce single points of dependency, and enhance collective deterrence. In an environment where consensus is slow and geopolitical alignment is partial, fragmentation may enable flexibility, optionality, and responsiveness—potentially making it a pragmatic stepping stone toward longer-term coordination rather than an outright obstacle.

5.2.3 Forum Shopping, Regulatory Arbitrage and Strategic Compliance

A further complication in enforcing quantum export controls is the risk of forum shopping. Given, as described above at Sect. 5.2.1, the internationally diffuse quantum value chain, companies or researchers seek out jurisdictions with the weakest

---

[128] Moscioni (2025).

[129] See Lenarczyk et al. (2026).

[130] Junusova and Reinsch (2024).

[131] European Commission (2024).

regulatory oversight to access restricted technologies or collaborate more freely, thus undermining the purpose of controls.

Relatedly, as for semiconductors, "the onus of compliance will fall largely on private companies",[132] which are economically incentivized to comply with regulations to the lowest possible extent. Export controls endeavor to remove potentially lucrative markets from corporate actors. The economically rational decision may be to relocate, to ignore export restrictions, or to circumvent them (for instance, by selling to intermediaries with less onerous restrictions, which can on-sell to restricted countries).

That said, differentiated national approaches may also introduce productive regulatory competition that allows for policy experimentation and refinement. Jurisdictions with thoughtful, well-calibrated controls could emerge as trusted nodes within an international framework, attracting talent and investment while maintaining alignment with broader security goals. In this sense, what may appear as "forum shopping" could also reflect a form of strategic alignment-seeking, where companies and institutions migrate toward environments that balance national security concerns with scientific openness and legal clarity. Rather than eroding controls, such dynamics—if transparently governed—can support adaptive compliance ecosystems and stimulate innovation in how export regimes are implemented and improved.

5.2.4 Novel Quantum Computing Paradigms and Pace of Development

A further challenge for export control regimes is the emergence of novel quantum computing paradigms that do not fit neatly into the currently decided-upon regulatory framework. The core of the abovementioned controls focuses predominantly on gate-based quantum computers, measured by qubit count and error rate, but there is a diverse and rapidly evolving landscape of alternative architectures.[133]

These systems may not use traditional qubits or CNOT gates, making it difficult to apply standard performance thresholds. For example, a photonic quantum computer[134] might achieve high computational power without ever crossing a qubit count threshold,[135] while a neutral atom system[136] could be reconfigured dynamically, blurring the line between hardware and software and making benchmarking difficult. It is conceivable that future quantum computing platforms could further challenge regulatory definition.

This diversity creates the potential for regulatory blind spots, where powerful systems may fall outside the scope of current controls simply because they use

---

[132] Palmer (2023b).

[133] Parker (2024), p. 3.

[134] Aghaee et al. (2025).

[135] Note 2 of US ECCN 4A906 does endeavor to cover this possibility.

[136] Evered et al. (2023).

novel metrics or architectures. Moreover, as quantum advantage may arise from algorithmic or architectural breakthroughs, and not just raw hardware performance, controls based solely on physical specifications may quickly become outdated. As described elsewhere in this volume,[137] regulators confront the Collingridge dilemma, where early intervention in emerging technologies is difficult due to limited understanding of their future impact, yet delaying regulation until the consequences are clear often means the technology has become too entrenched to control effectively.

The common catch cry that the pace of rulemaking is outstripped by the pace of innovation rings true in the quantum space, which is often marked by sudden, transformative breakthroughs. This juxtaposition is even more apparent when one considers multilateral controls, which are arguably more desirable in order to increase harmonization and coordination, yet are typically slower than national regulatory processes due to the need to build consensus amongst a large bloc of nation-states with varying strategic interests and technological capabilities. In this way, the complexity of the technology and geopolitical dynamics can, together, frustrate timely and effective governance.

5.2.5 Difficulty of Controlling Intangible Items

The newly introduced controls on quantum computing apply to both tangible items like raw materials and computing hardware, and non-tangible items such as software and "technology". Controlling the flow of these elements presents distinct challenges.

Unlike physical goods, software and digital items can be transmitted instantaneously across borders via digital means, often without leaving a clear trace. Source code, design files, and technical documentation can be shared through encrypted channels, cloud platforms, or even informal communication in academic or professional settings. This makes enforcement far more difficult, especially when the boundaries between open research and controlled technology are blurry. The "Crypto Wars" of the 1990s provides a stark illustration of this dynamic, wherein export controls on robust encryption algorithms ultimately failed,[138] as the underlying knowledge and software could spread through academic publications, open-source communities, and academic and commercial institutions from countries with less restrictive controls. This hampered academic and commercial development in countries that maintained stricter controls (i.e. the US), leading to their ultimate relaxation.

Quantum computing faces a similar dilemma. The global and collaborative nature of quantum computing research means that much of the relevant knowledge is developed in open academic environments, where norms of transparency and information sharing prevail. Efforts to restrict the dissemination of intangible items

[137] See Lenarczyk et al. (2026).

[138] See Porsdam Mann et al. (2026); Levy (2001).

risk clashing with these norms, potentially chilling international collaboration or affecting compliance by regulatees.

6 Conclusion

The governance of quantum technologies through export controls presents a delicate and increasingly urgent policy challenge. As this volume explores, quantum technologies—particularly quantum computing—hold immense transformative potential, but they also raise serious national security, digital sovereignty, economic, and ethical concerns. At a time of increasing geopolitical tensions and competition, export controls have emerged as a key tool in managing these risks, aiming to prevent the proliferation of sensitive capabilities. Yet their implementation also exposes tensions within existing regulatory regimes, particularly for jurisdictions like the US, the EU, and its member states that have strong commitments to innovation, economic competitiveness, and international scientific collaboration.

At the same time, export controls offer opportunities to shape the development of quantum technologies responsibly. They can serve as mechanisms for promoting transparency, encouraging early adoption of security-aware research practices, and fostering international dialogue around emerging norms and fundamental values. If designed with adaptability and global coordination in mind, export controls can strike a balance between security and openness—mitigating risks without unduly constraining progress.

One of the key insights of this chapter is that quantum computing presents a unique set of structural features that lend themselves unusually well to targeted export controls. The scale, complexity, and infrastructure-dependence of current quantum hardware create natural chokepoints for enforcement—unlike other dual-use technologies such as semiconductors or AI models. Similarly, the rise of cloud-based access models offers a persistent and centralized platform for real-time control, geo-fencing, and differentiated access. These features provide rare advantages in both traceability and policy responsiveness, enabling a more adaptive and layered approach to governing access to the nascent technology.

In considering the shift away from traditional multilateral regimes, the chapter has also outlined the potential strategic logic behind emerging plurilateral frameworks. While fragmentation and forum shopping are often viewed as risks, differentiated national approaches can support regulatory experimentation, build supply chain resilience, and offer strategic optionality in a fluid geopolitical landscape. Rather than signaling disorder, this emerging architecture may reflect a more nimble and fit-for-purpose model—especially in the absence of consensus in legacy export control forums.

Finally, the move toward controlling not only tangible goods but also enabling technologies, intangible know-how, and pre-commercial capabilities points to a broader evolution in export control philosophy. States are no longer merely reacting to proliferation risks—they are beginning to shape the global research environment proactively. This anticipatory posture, if balanced with transparency and due process, could play a central role in steering quantum innovation in directions that are secure, collaborative, and strategically sustainable.

Acknowledgments This work was made possible through the generous support of the Novo Nordisk Foundation (NNF) via a grant for the scientifically independent Collaborative Research Program in Bioscience Innovation Law (Inter-CeBIL Program—Grant No. NNF23SA0087056).

References

Aghaee M et al (2025) Interferometric single-shot parity measurement in InAs–Al hybrid devices. Nature 638(8051):651–655

Allen G, Goldston I (2025) Understanding U.S. allies' current legal authority to implement AI and semiconductor export controls. Available at: https://www.csis.org/analysis/understanding-us-allies-current-legal-authority-implement-ai-and-semiconductor-export. Accessed 25 Aug 2025

Alter, K.J. (2024) US export controls across time: knowledge, technology and China. iCourts Working Paper Series, no. 356

Basedow R (2018) The WTO and the rise of plurilateralism—what lessons can we learn from the European Union's experience with differentiated integration? J Int Econ Law 21(2):411–431

Baskeran G, Schwartz M (2024) China imposes its most stringent critical minerals export restrictions yet amidst escalating U.S.-China Tech War. Available at: https://www.csis.org/analysis/china-imposes-its-most-stringent-critical-minerals-export-restrictions-yet-amidst. Accessed 25 Aug 2025

Bauer M, Pandya D (2024) Time to rethink export controls for strengthened US-EU cooperation. European Centre for International Political Economy - Policy Brief No. 07/2024

Bennink S et al (2025) EU export controls on dual-use items: recent developments and emerging trends. Glob Trade Cust J 20(2):89–99

Bonarriva J et al (2009) Export controls: an overview of their use, economic effects, and treatment in the global trading system. US International Trade Commission, Office of Industries Working Paper

Bown C (2019) Export controls: America's other national security threat. Duke J Comp Int Law 30(2):283–308

Brockmann K (2019) Challenges to multilateral export controls: the case for inter-regime dialogue and coordination. Stockholm International Peace Research Institute

Brunel A (2023) A proposal for a semiconductor export control treaty. J Bus Technol Law 19(1):1–52

Bureau of Industry and Security UDoC (2019) Implementation of certain new controls on emerging technologies agreed at Wassenaar Arrangement 2018 Plenary. Available at: https://www.federalregister.gov/documents/2019/05/23/2019-10778/implementation-of-certain-new-controls-on-emerging-technologies-agreed-at-wassenaar-arrangement-2018. Accessed 25 Aug 2025

Bureau of Industry and Security UDoC (2022) Commerce implements new export controls on advanced computing and semiconductor manufacturing items to the People's Republic of China (PRC). Available at: https://www.bis.doc.gov/index.php/documents/about-bis/newsroom/press-releases/3158-2022-10-07-bis-press-release-advanced-computing-and-semiconductor-manufacturing-controls-final/file. Accessed 25 Aug 2025

Bureau of Industry and Security UDoC (2024a) BIS's 2024 update conference on export controls and policy. Available at: https://www.bis.gov/speech/assistant-secretary-commerce-export-administration-thea-d.-rozman-kendler-biss-2024-update-conference-export. Accessed 25 Aug 2025

Bureau of Industry and Security UDoC (2024b) Commerce control list additions and revisions; implementation of controls on advanced technologies consistent with controls implemented by international partners (interim final rule). Available at: https://www.federalregister.gov/documents/2024/09/06/2024-19633/commerce-control-list-additions-and-revisions-implementation-of-controls-on-advanced-technologies#print. Accessed 25 Aug 2025

Bureau of Industry and Security UDoC (2024c) Department of Commerce implements controls on quantum computing and other advanced technologies alongside international partners. Available at: https://www.bis.gov/press-release/department-commerce-implements-controls-quantum-computing-other-advanced-technologies-alongside. Accessed 25 Aug 2025

Daniels M, Krige J (2022) Knowledge regulation and national security in Postwar America. University of Chicago Press, Chicago

Danish Business Authority and Danish Quantum Community (2024) 16 Danish quantum use cases: practical insights into applications of quantum technologies across industries. Danish Quantum Community Report

Davidson H (2025) US chip export controls are a 'failure' because they spur Chinese Development, Nvidia boss says. Available at: https://www.theguardian.com/technology/2025/may/21/us-chip-export-controls-a-failure-spur-chinese-development-nvidia-boss-says. Accessed 25 Aug 2025

Davis PAE et al (2026) EU cybersecurity regulation in the quantum age. In: Aboy M, Corrales Compagnucci M, Minssen T (eds) Quantum technology governance: law, policy & ethics in the quantum era. Springer, Cham

de Witte B (2017) Exclusive member state competences: is there such a thing? In: Garben S, Govaere I (eds) The Division of Competences between the EU and the Member States: reflections on the past, the present and the future. Hart Publishing, Oxford

Dimitropoulos G et al (2025) Plurilateralism: a new form of international economic ordering? The Journal of World Investment & Trade 26(1–2):1–30

Draghi M (2024) The future of European Competitiveness: in-depth analysis and recommendations. Publications Office of the European Union, Luxembourg

European Commission (2022) EU-US Joint Statement of the Trade and Technology Council. Available at: https://ec.europa.eu/commission/presscorner/detail/en/statement_22_7516. Accessed 25 Aug 2025

European Commission (2024) WHITE PAPER on Export Controls. COM(2024) 25 final

European Parliament (2025) Commission must tackle China's export restrictions on rare earth elements. Available at: https://www.europarl.europa.eu/news/en/press-room/20250704IPR29456/commission-must-tackle-china-s-export-restrictions-on-rare-earth-elements. Accessed 25 Aug 2025

Evans S (2014) Revising export control lists. Flemish Peace Institute

Evered SJ et al (2023) High-fidelity parallel entangling gates on a neutral-atom quantum computer. Nature 622(7982):268–272

Flamm K (1996) Controlling the uncontrollable: reforming U.S. export controls on computers. Brookings Rev 14(1):22–25

Giordano S et al (2021) The germanium quantum information route. Nat Rev Mater 6(10):926–943

Greinert F et al (2024) Advancing quantum technology workforce: industry insights into qualification and training needs. EPJ Quantum Technol 11(1):82

Hmaidi A, Groenewegen-Lau J (2024) China's long view on quantum tech has the US and EU playing catch-up. Available at: https://merics.org/en/report/chinas-long-view-quantum-tech-has-us-and-eu-playing-catch. Accessed 25 Aug 2025

Johnson W (2019) Governance tools for the second quantum revolution. Jurimetrics 59(4):487–522

Junusova A, Reinsch WA (2024) Rethinking the Wassenaar Minus One Strategy. Available at: https://www.csis.org/analysis/rethinking-wassenaar-minus-one-strategy. Accessed 25 Aug 2025

Kaur M, Venegas-Gomez A (2022) Defining the quantum workforce landscape: a review of global quantum education initiatives. Opt Eng 61(8):081806

Kazeki J, Kleitz A (2003) Analysis of non-tariff measures: the case of export duties. OECD Papers Working Party of the Trade Committee TD/TC/WP(2003)7/FINAL
Kobayashi S (2024) Japan's export control on quantum technology. Available at: https://fsi.stanford.edu/sipr/japan-qt. Accessed 25 Aug 2025
Lenarczyk G et al (2026) IP in superposition: patents, trade secrets and open innovation in quantum information technology. In: Aboy M, Corrales Compagnucci M, Minssen T (eds) Quantum technology governance: law, policy & ethics in the quantum era. Springer, Cham
Levy S (2001) Crypto: how the code rebels beat the government - saving privacy in the digital age. Viking, New York
McFaul M (2025) Foreign policy: where is trump going? Available at: https://www.hoover.org/research/foreign-policy-where-trump-going. Accessed 25 Aug 2025
Meijer H (2016) Trading with the enemy: the making of US Export Control Policy toward the People's Republic of China. Oxford University Press, Oxford
Ministry for Foregin Affairs of Finland (2024) United States liberalises export of high technology products to Finland. Available at: https://um.fi/international-technology-policy. Accessed 25 August 2025
Moscioni, B. (2025) Another technology race: US-China quantum computing landscape. Available at: https://www.belfercenter.org/research-analysis/another-technology-race-us-china-quantum-computing-landscape. Accessed 25 Aug 2025
Nanto D (2011) Economics and national security: issues and implications for U.S. Policy. Congressional Research Service 7-5700
National Science & Technology Council (2021) The role of international talent in quantum information science. A report by the Subcommittee on Economic and Security Implications of Quantum Science and Committee on Homeland and National Security
Nguyen A (2025) Export controls as innovation marketing? Sociotechnical imaginaries in the ring-fencing of quantum technologies. Law Technol Hum 7(1):68–83
Nousiainen K, Keski-Rahkonen J (2024) Future is quantum. Int J Law Ethics Technol 29
Palmer A (2023a) 'An Act of War': inside America's Silicon Blockade Against China. Available at: https://www.nytimes.com/2023/07/12/magazine/semiconductor-chips-us-china.html. Accessed 25 Aug 2025
Palmer A (2023b) The Silicon Blockade. N Y Times Mag:28–33
Parker E (2023) Promoting strong international collaboration in quantum technology research and development
Parker E (2024) The Chinese Industrial Base and Military Deployment of Quantum Technology: Addendum. Addendum to testimony before the U.S.-China Economic and Security Review Commission on February 1, 2024
Porsdam Mann S et al (2026) Quantum computing and ethical exceptionalism: lessons from classical computing. In: Aboy M, Corrales Compagnucci M, Minssen T (eds) Quantum technology governance: law, policy & ethics in the quantum era. Springer, Cham
Rasser M (2020) Rethinking export controls: unintended consequences and the new technological landscape. Center for a New American Security
Sarma SD et al (2005) Spin quantum computation in silicon nanostructures. Solid State Commun 133(11):737–746
Seskir ZC et al (2023) Democratization of quantum technologies. Quantum Sci Technol 8(2):024005
Shivakumar S, et al (2025) The limits of chip export controls in meeting the China challenge. Available at: https://www.csis.org/analysis/limits-chip-export-controls-meeting-china-challenge. Accessed 25 Aug 2025
Smith HL et al (2026) Quantum governance in the making: why standards matter. In: Aboy M, Corrales Compagnucci M, Minssen T (eds) Quantum technology governance: law, policy & ethics in the quantum era. Springer, Cham
Sparkes M (2024) The mysterious quantum export deal. New Sci 263(3499):18–18
Sparkes M (2025) No solace for quantum (earlier title: 'why quantum computers are being held back by geopolitical tussles'). New Sci 265(3530):12–12

Steinberg F, Wolff G (2024) Dealing with Europe's economic (in-)security. Global Pol 15(1):183–192

Stewart I (2024) Navigating uncharted waters: the unilateral shift in quantum computing export controls. Available at: https://strategictrade.substack.com/p/navigating-uncharted-waters-the-unilateral. Accessed 25 Aug 2025

Swayne M (2025) China sets 2030 metrology goals in push for chip, quantum and rare earth precision. Available at: https://thequantuminsider.com/2025/06/02/china-sets-2030-metrology-goals-in-push-for-chip-quantum-and-rare-earth-precision/. Accessed 25 Aug 2025

Taddeo M et al (2024) Consider the ethical impacts of quantum technologies in defence—before it's too late. Nature 634(8035):779–781

U.S. Government Accountability Office (2021) Quantum computing and communications: status and prospects, GAO-22-104422. Available at: https://www.gao.gov/products/gao-22-104422. Accessed 25 Aug 2025

Vigmostad TE, Meldahl HS (2024) Expanded Norwegian export controls for critical goods and technologies and updates to the EU Dual-Use List. Available at: https://www.wr.no/en/news/expanded-norwegian-export-controls-for-critical-goods-and-technologies-and-updates-to-the-eu-dual-use-list. Accessed 25 Aug 2025

Villasenor J (2025) DeepSeek shows the limits of US export controls on AI chips. Available at: https://www.brookings.edu/articles/deepseek-shows-the-limits-of-us-export-controls-on-ai-chips/. Accessed 25 Aug 2025

von der Dunk F (2009) A European "Equivalent" to United States Export Controls: European Law on the Control of International Trade in Dual-Use Space Technologies. Astropolitics 7(2):101–134

Wassenaar Arrangement Secretariat (2015) Wassenaar arrangement on export controls for conventional arms and dual-use goods and technologies - basic documents. Available at: https://www.wassenaar.org/app/uploads/2015/07/WA-DOC-15-SEC-001-Basic-Documents-2015-January.pdf. Accessed 25 Aug 2025

Watts R et al (2024) A systematic approach for identifying companies with economic moats. S&P Global

Yarkoni S et al (2022) Quantum annealing for industry applications: introduction and review. Rep Prog Phys 85(10):104001

Zhang C (2024) US puts export controls on quantum computers. Available at: https://www.aip.org/fyi/us-puts-export-controls-on-quantum-computers?mcid=e17e526d3b. Accessed 25 Aug 2025

Quantum Information Technologies and Public International Law: Strategic, Legal, and Geopolitical Dimensions

Elija Perrier and Mateo Aboy

Abstract The use of computational technologies by States for both offensive and defensive purposes has become a central feature of contemporary international relations. Quantum information technologies (QIT) are expected to influence these dynamics by transforming State capabilities in cybersecurity, encryption, and information analysis. This chapter examines how the strategic use of QIT by States intersects with the principles and rules of public international law. The analysis situates QIT within the jurisprudence of sovereignty, jurisdiction, and the use of force, drawing on the Tallinn Manual and related sources of international law. It also explores how game theory may illuminate patterns of quantum cooperation and competition among States in both peacetime and conflict.

Keywords Geopolitics · International law · Entanglement · Sovereignty · Tallinn manual

1 Introduction

Research and development in quantum information technologies (QIT)—including quantum computing, quantum communication, and quantum sensing—are increasingly driven by their potential strategic value to States. These technologies are not merely scientific innovations but prospective tools of influence and competition in international affairs. As quantum capabilities develop and mature, their potential implications for public international law, particularly in relation to the governance of cyber operations, sovereignty, and the use of force, warrant analysis.

E. Perrier (✉)
Centre for Quantum Software and Information, University of Technology,
Sydney, NSW, Australia

M. Aboy
Centre for Law, Medicine and Life Sciences (LML) & Centre for Intellectual Property & Information Law (CIPIL), University of Cambridge, Cambridge, UK
e-mail: eper2139@uni.sydney.edu.au; ma608@cam.ac.uk

M. Aboy et al. (eds.), *Quantum Technology Governance I*, Perspectives in Law, Business and Innovation, https://doi.org/10.1007/978-981-95-8371-3_7

Over recent decades, international legal scholarship and State practice have expanded to address the regulation of cyberspace activities. Central questions have included how existing legal norms govern State conduct in cyber operations, what constitutes an unlawful intervention or use of force, and how responsibility is to be attributed in complex technological environments. The emergence of QIT presents a new dimension to these discussions. The issue addressed in this chapter is therefore not whether QIT should be regulated under international law, but rather how existing doctrines apply when the underlying technologies are quantum in nature.

The inquiry is timely. State sovereignty increasingly depends on informational and digital infrastructure that supports governance, defense, and economic activity. The same infrastructures also represent potential vulnerabilities, as adversarial States may target or exploit them for strategic advantage. Developments in artificial intelligence and cyber systems already challenge existing legal categories. The advent of QIT adds further complexity: its non-classical characteristics, such as superposition and entanglement, could enable new modes of action that are operationally or conceptually distinct from those enabled by classical computing. These features may alter how States acquire, protect, and contest information, and thus raise questions of jurisdiction, attribution, and control under international law.

This chapter examines to what extent these technological developments require new legal instruments or can be accommodated within existing frameworks. It proceeds from the premise that international law already applies to State activities involving QIT, much as it does to other forms of cyber operation. However, the translation of familiar principles—such as due diligence, sovereignty, and the prohibition on the use of force—into the quantum domain demands interpretive care. Integrating quantum and legal reasoning requires attention to how quantum-specific phenomena translate into distinct capacities for State action, such as advanced decryption, simulation, or sensing capabilities that may afford informational asymmetries among States.

2 Geopolitical Impact of Quantum Technologies

2.1 Overview

The growing capabilities of QIT, especially advancements towards fault-tolerant quantum computational devices potentially capable of facilitating decryption of classically encrypted information have motivated increased consideration of the impact of QIT on national security, national infrastructure, economic competitive advantage and information ecosystems within and among States.[1] In this section, we survey the primary impact of QIT as they pertain to key characteristics of public international law and the law of conflict. As we discuss throughout, national

[1] Krelina (2021); Neumann et al. (2020).

security is an integral hallmark of the jurisprudential principle of State sovereignty at the heart of public international law. To study the geopolitical impacts of QIT, we map State behavior to its classification in terms of quantum computing, quantum communication and quantum sensing. Later in this article, we consider three strategic scenarios involving States and its effect on strategic behavior.

2.2 *Quantum Computing Strategic Impacts*

Quantum computing[2] has extensive potential application in strategic contexts. Impacts of quantum computing capabilities derive from the unique aspects of quantum computing itself, such as simulation of physical systems, including chemical and biological systems, materials synthesis and more efficient composite materials, in ways not technically possible on classical computers for certain classes of problems. But perhaps the primary application of quantum computers in State adversarial contexts lies in their ability to solve complex simulation, optimization problems and decryption. The potential use of quantum algorithms to solve optimization, search and decryption problems rapidly in ways that are infeasible on classical computers is central to their strategic impact. Of particular note is the ability to, in principle, solve certain classes of intractable problems (requiring exponential computational resources to solve) outside the reach of classical computing. We explore a few of these below.

2.2.1 Cryptography

Quantum algorithmic techniques (such as those based on quantum Fourier transforms and Shor's algorithm) for decrypting existing public-key cryptographic systems, such as RSA, Diffie-Hellman, and Elliptic Curve Cryptography represent what is generally considered the primary application of quantum computing in adversarial strategic scenarios among States, both in peacetime and during conflicts. Quantum cryptographic capabilities are (if realized) also anticipated to be critical for State intelligence agencies, enabling both decryption of intercepted communications from adversaries and the ability to test the resilience of a State's own (or its allies') cryptographic encryption regimes to adversarial attack. Because encryption is central to the functioning of modern States, the strategic benefits from even moderate capacities for such decryption are considered strategically significant. Defensively, post-quantum cryptographic protocols which aim to secure information and communications systems from quantum adversarial attack is already a major focus of research efforts among States.

---

[2] Nielsen and Chuang (2011).

2.2.2 Simulations

Quantum systems may be used in principle to more efficiently simulate certain classical systems faster than classical computers (and to incorporate more fine-grained information), relevant to, for example, scenario modelling, central to military planning. Quantum computers are also in principle able to more efficiently simulate other quantum systems themselves, a process essential for understanding complex materials and chemistry. Such simulations may in the future enable simulation and design better armor, explosives, and energy systems or model the use of for example biological agents by a State (or non-State) actor, enabling better preparedness against bioterrorism or chemical warfare. For example, the simulation of molecular interactions could help design antidotes or protective materials against chemical weapons.

2.2.3 Optimization and Machine Learning

Quantum algorithms offer potential for solving certain complex optimization problems,[3] such as logistics and resource allocation, supply chain management and mission planning (preconflict, and during conflict scenarios, for command and control systems), which are critical in military operations. Other more general applications include better or quicker decision-making, predictive analytics or verification procedures, though the extent to which quantum systems provide a practical advantage is yet unknown in general. An extension of such methods is the use of quantum algorithms (often in concert in most cases with classical algorithms) for quantum machine learning. Example prospective applications being researched include quantum-enhanced (hybrid) algorithms for rapid classification of data, such as for example satellite imagery, or processing large-scale datasets more quickly.

As we note below, quantum computing systems are necessarily embedded within classical computational architecture. Practically speaking, this means that State quantum computing infrastructure is likely to be cloud-based and distributed across quantum communication networks where fixed quantum computer edifices are interfaced via classical communication channels. Furthermore, as noted in our discussion of international law governing the application of QIT, strategic cyber operations and QIT-related activities among States will, as with their classical counterparts, occur in both peacetime and conflict scenarios.

[3] Farhi et al. (2014).

2.3 *Quantum Communication, Quantum Networks and Quantum Cryptography Strategic Impacts*

Quantum communication, quantum networks and quantum cryptography (which we examine in a communication context here specifically) have significant strategic implications for States. From a strategic perspective, quantum communication provides both opportunities and challenges for State actors. Nations with advanced quantum communication capabilities can secure critical infrastructure, military communications, and financial systems against quantum and classical cyber threats. At the same time, quantum communication intensifies geopolitical rivalries as States compete to develop superior quantum technologies, including quantum cryptoanalysis to decrypt adversaries' communications. Quantum communication combines QKD, entanglement-based protocols, quantum networks, and QRNGs to offer security and functionality. It is a cornerstone of the emerging quantum internet and has transformative implications for secure communication, distributed computing, and international strategic dynamics. That said, its implementation poses significant technological and geopolitical challenges.

2.3.1 Post-quantum Cryptography

Post-quantum cryptography has been a major focus of research efforts by States seeking to secure their networks against potential adversarial interference, interception and espionage. This is manifest in the long-term PQC program of NIST in the United States leading to a PQC standardization regime.[4] PQC is a major priority for quantum-capable nation states because of the information security affordances it potentially offers against an adversary using QIT, such as for espionage or during conflict.

2.3.2 Quantum Networks

One of the attractive potentials of quantum network technology is in overcoming limitations of (including attenuation) and risks of intervention in terrestrial fiber optics via the use of satellite-based quantum communication methods.[5] Examples include China's quantum experimental science satellite, Micius,[6] enabling satellite-based QKD and entanglement distribution.

[4] Alagic et al. (2022); Alagic et al. (2024).

[5] Liao et al. (2018).

[6] Lu et al. (2022).

2.3.3 Quantum Key Distribution (QKD)

QKD is a prospectively secure communication protocol that enables two parties to generate and share a secret cryptographic key with the assurance that any eavesdropping attempt will be detected. QKD offers the prospect of ultra-secure communication by leveraging quantum mechanics to detect eavesdropping. States may be able to use QKD for critical communication infrastructure, such as diplomatic, military, and intelligence channels of States, ensuring confidentiality and integrity in sensitive operations.

2.3.4 Quantum Internet and Strategic Infrastructure

Quantum communication networks, including quantum communication satellite-based systems, represent a prospective important form of peacetime and conflict QIT use. Such networks have particular dual use capabilities, especially in connecting national defense systems and critical industries securely and prospectively in conflict scenarios.

2.4 *Quantum Sensing*

A number of prospective use-cases of quantum sensing have potential strategic impact.

2.4.1 Submarine Detection

Submarine detection could have significant consequences for strategic relationships among nuclear States due to the consequences for a State's second-strike capability in the event of nuclear armed conflict. Existing methods of submarine detection rely upon magnetic anomaly detection, which measures disturbances in the Earth's magnetic field caused by a metallic substances within a submarine's hull. The prospective application of quantum sensors lies in their potential to improve sensitivity to these disturbances, enabling detection at greater distances. With the current state-of-the-art there are, however, significant technical challenges hindering the use of quantum sensors for submarine detection.[7] These include ocean noise (where magnetic disturbances from sources like ocean currents and mineral deposits, interfere with a submarine's magnetic signature), proximity requirements (all sensors, including, quantum sensors perform better closer to submarines), limited range (quantum magnetometers such as those utilizing nitrogen-vacancy center

[7] Rand (2023).

magnetometers have limited operational range), target variability (where submarines may vary their signatures via methods such as degaussing) and the movement of submarines themselves. Empirical analysis of current quantum sensing technology (and nascent technologies such as quantum gravimetry and synthetic aperture radar) suggest that near-term submarine tracking is unlikely.

2.4.2 Missile Tracking

Quantum sensors also have potential application missile tracking via improving the accuracy of inertial navigation systems used in ballistic missiles. Inertial navigation relies on accelerometers and gyroscopes to track an object's motion without external references. Quantum sensors could increase the precision of such instruments and thus enable finer-grained targeting. The technology could also provide an in principle advantage by reducing initial alignment errors, mitigating gyroscopic drift due to other noise sources (such as heat or kinetic energy), albeit doing so requires overcoming specific technical challenges to ensure they remain robust.

2.4.3 Quantum Sensor Networks

Quantum sensor networks may also be networked in order to create highly-sensitive quantum communication architectures. Quantum sensor and communication networks leverage the physical characteristics of quantum sensor technology and quantum communication protocols to create distributed networks of quantum sensors across wider geospatial distances while retaining the benefits of quantum communication security features. Quantum systems being used as quantum sensors are entangled with other quantum systems in long-range networks. An example candidate protocol theoretically explored is integrating quantum sensing and communication via entanglement.

A number of protocols exploring quantum sensor networks have emerged recently, including the QISAC protocol[8] leveraging Bell states for simultaneous quantum sensing and communication. In this case, Alice prepares and transmits entangled photon pairs to Bob via a quantum channel. Both parties perform randomized measurements on subsets of particles to confirm channel security with the remaining particles being encoded with information and used in sensing operations by Alice (such as for parameter estimation). Bob measures the received states, decodes the messages and retrieves the measurements statistics in question. Other proposals include cavity-based multipartite entanglement,[9] distributed quantum sensing systems using spin-squeezed atomic states leveraging non-local

[8] Liu et al. (2024).

[9] Brady et al. (2022).

entanglement for improved scaling effects.[10] Challenges include technical design and engineering issues especially at the NISQ stage,[11] but also more broadly the fact that quantum entanglement diminishes after each use (or measurement) of the quantum network itself. In quantum information science parlance, quantum entanglement is a resource[12] (meaning it is both a necessary resource for certain types of computation or information not otherwise possible and that it diminishes once used).

3 Technical Factors Affecting Strategic QIT

3.1 Classical and Quantum Strategic Taxonomy

In this section, we briefly examine a number of technical factors regarding strategic QIT use. As with the comparison between quantum and classical information processing itself (as is common in information sciences when describing classical and quantum channels[13]), strategic behavior of States related to QIT can be taxonomically classified in terms of quantum and classical relations:

3.1.1 Classical-to-Classical

Covering the use of classical information processing with respect to classical information technology (e.g. conventional cyberattacks).

3.1.2 Classical-to-Quantum

Covering the use of classical information processing to act in relation to QIT.

3.1.3 Quantum-to-Classical

Covering the use of quantum resources and QIT to act upon classical information (or information processing systems), as exemplified by for example quantum algorithms for decrypting classically encrypted information.

---

[10] Malia et al. (2022).

[11] Preskill (2021).

[12] Wootters (1998).

[13] Watrous (2018).

3.1.4 Quantum-to-Quantum

Involving the direct use of quantum-specific processes on quantum resources.

This taxonomy is a useful way to situate the interrelationships between quantum and classical technology in the context strategic behavior. There is also the added complexity of hybrid systems that leverage both classical and quantum (QIT will always be integrated within classical information systems infrastructure). We note both this and summarize this taxonomy in Table 1 below. We utilize this taxonomy in scenario modelling of strategic State behavior and our analysis of the implications under public international law below.

3.2 Quantum Systems are Classically Embedded

An important fact of QIT from a governance and strategic perspective is that all QIT is necessarily embedded within classical information processing architecture. The ontologically quantum characteristics of quantum information systems[14] (e.g., quantum states in superposition or entangled quantum states) cannot be directly

Table 1 Comparison of adversarial State classical, hybrid, and quantum information processing actions applied to classical, hybrid and quantum infrastructure. Classical to-classical attacks represent classical adversarial action against classical infrastructure

Information Processing	Infrastructure		
	Classical Infrastructure	Hybrid Infrastructure	Quantum Infrastructure
Classical Processing	State-sponsored cyberattacks targeting classical systems (e.g., hacking government databases, disrupting power grids).	Use of classical methods to infiltrate hybrid systems (e.g., exploiting weaknesses in hybrid cryptographic schemes).	Espionage on quantum research facilities using classical surveillance and analysis techniques.
Hybrid Processing	Quantum-informed attacks on classical systems (e.g., using quantum-inspired optimization to identify vulnerabilities in infrastructure).	State-backed operations combining classical and quantum methods to breach hybrid networks (e.g., intercepting classical-quantum communication).	Manipulation of quantum components in hybrid systems to disrupt or disable functionality.
Quantum Processing	Quantum cryptographic attacks on classical communication channels (e.g., breaking classical encryption using quantum computing).	Quantum-based interference in hybrid systems (e.g., using quantum simulations to disrupt hybrid networks).	State adversaries directly attacking quantum networks or systems (e.g., disrupting quantum entanglement or intercepting quantum communication).

[14] Bartlett et al. (2007).

observed. Rather, their representation is reconstructed via the results of classical measurement statistics arising from repeated measurements upon identically-prepared copies of the quantum system in question. These measurement statistics are in turn used to reconstruct, for example, quantum states via state or process tomography.[15] The inherently non-classical nature of quantum systems is represented classically by way of non-deterministic paradigms such as probability. In the language of quantum information, measurement is a quantum-to-classical channel. The manner in which quantum systems are controlled is also classically based: quantum control, such as the control required to have a quantum computer undertake a quantum computation, ultimately relies upon translating instructions and information from classical systems (the controlling system or human input channel) to quantum systems.

This is an important point to bear in mind. In cyber-attacks, such as penetration of an adversary State's cyber infrastructure, the actual computational processes underpinning that penetration within an adversary's classical network will be classical. It is not the case that for example a quantum algorithm could be deployed onto an adversary's classical network (to afford quantum advantage offered by such algorithms for example). For a State adversary with a quantum computer, in principle it may be possible to, for example, hack the classical infrastructure surrounding the quantum device to embed a copy of a particular algorithm by way of for example interfering with the classical description of quantum compilation[16] protocols, but this potential in turn relies upon mediating information between classical and quantum systems.

3.3 Direct Quantum-to-Quantum Offence is Difficult but Possible

In principle it is of course possible for two quantum systems to interact in ways that are 'directly quantum' in that the proximity of those systems causes them to be coupled in a quantum-specific way, such as via entanglement. However, engineered pure 'quantum-to-quantum' cyber operations would be at current technology levels incredibly challenging, if not impossible, to effect. This is because the direct interaction between two States' quantum systems without classical mediation requires networking of those quantum computers which physically means coupling of all or part of those systems to each other. While quantum computers—as with classical computers—are always coupled to their environment to some degree, the technical challenges to such coupling in an adversarial context are formidable. Thus the prospect of mobile QIT devices being utilized by State adversaries for espionage activities within a rival State are remote if not

[15] Greenbaum (2015); Mohseni et al. (2008).

[16] Khatri et al. (2019).

impossible due to the fundamental conditions required for quantum systems to remain robust, controllable and stable.

The exception to this scenario, which we explore further below, is where two States' quantum systems are entangled. It may seem fanciful that two State actors would willingly entangle their QIT resources despite being adversaries, but plenty of instances of adversaries sharing resources during competitive and even conflict scenarios abound throughout history. In the quantum case, a primary example would be the sharing of QIT by way of quantum networks. As discussed above, the networking of quantum computing can significantly affect the computational power and capabilities. The whole of a quantum internet is literally greater than the sum of its parts. This can be seen in elementary fashion by the fact that the number of computational states (and dimension of the Hilbert space) of an n qubit system is 2^n. Thus as the number of qubits n increases, the dimensionality of the Hilbert space increases exponentially. In peacetime, States would thus be motivated to network their quantum devices in order to leverage the computational gains from such cooperative coordination of shared resources. States may subsequently become adversaries—but may also decide to share resources during conflict.

The prospect of shared QIT resources, such as entangled quantum systems, is not completely implausible. In this scenario, in principle we have something resembling 'direct' quantum means of each State affecting the other via quantum actions which affect the mutually entangled quantum system. It should be noted that actually controlling such an attack (e.g. where one State decides to interact with a quantum network in order to disrupt it) would itself in most cases require classical inputs (i.e. classical inputs into the control regimes). Such quantum-to-quantum interference could take the form, in principle, of interfering with both quantum data and QIT processes themselves, such as how computation unfolds or how quantum communication over the network occurs.

3.4 *Classical-to-Quantum Cyberattacks can Interfere with QIT and Quantum Infrastructure*

While the prospect of a State actor interfering with another State adversary by way of direct quantum-to-quantum interaction may seem remote, classical-to-quantum adversarial behavior by States is possible. Such behavior is constituted by the use of classical information processing, such as conventional classical cyberattack strategies, directed towards a State adversary's quantum infrastructure. Because any QIT infrastructure is necessarily embedded within classical information systems—those which transmit information from the quantum system (e.g. via recording and storing the results of measurement) and into the system (via classical control signals, or classically-described protocols for state distillation or preparation)—those classical channels can be leveraged for adversarial activity.

3.5 *Most Adversarial Quantum Activity will be Locally Constrained*

The consequences of the foregoing are that, at least based on current and near-term forecasts, any use of QIT for State adversarial action is likely to be limited to mostly immobile QIT devices, or QIT devices whose mobility is constrained (such as those integrated into other mobile platforms). The most plausible *offensive* use cases are to do with quantum cryptography and quantum sensing where for example immobile networks of quantum computers are used to decrypt intercepted classical communications, or stationary quantum sensor networks are used to detect a State adversary's activities.

The exception, once more, is where adversarial action involves entangled quantum systems which are geographically remote, but which can be acted upon non-locally by one State's interaction with its own entangled quantum system. Such a scenario certainly would involve non-locality as a principle, but the actual action of a State (say which might seek to interfere with a joint quantum network in that way) would still require that they act locally upon their own local quantum system. This is because the physical substrate, such as the qubits of an entangled system, are for most intents and purposes local themselves. While they exhibit a degree of non-locality, the concentration of probability (measure) is in almost all realistic cases going to be within very narrow spatial bounds (in part because such systems need to be localized to be instantiated and controlled in the first place). The element of control remains, in this sense, local. Table 2 sets out some speculative examples of how classical information processing and cyber activities by one State could adversarially target and act against another State's quantum infrastructure.

3.6 *QIT Can Enhance Cyberattack Strategies*

As noted above, one of the major motivations for the use of quantum computing is the existence of certain algorithms which enable, in principle, the decryption of classically encrypted communications and data. The most celebrated of such algorithms is *Shor's algorithm*, a quantum algorithm based upon the class of quantum Fourier transforms which in principle provides a means of classically (within at most polynomial time) decrypting information encoded using classical encryption protocols such as RSA. While the practicalities of decryption using a quantum computer executing such an algorithm are complex and subject to constraints,[17] it is this potential impact which is of considerable, indeed major, focus of States, motivating much of the funding envelope driving research into quantum computing and QIT. Information confidentiality and encryption has a rich provenance throughout

[17] Hoofnagle and Garfinkel (2021).

Table 2 Taxonomy of classical-to-quantum adversarial actions by States including examples of how classical information processing can be used to disrupt or interfere with another State's quantum infrastructure

Type of Adversarial Activity	Examples
Disruption of Classical Control Systems	Interfering with the classical hardware or software responsible for controlling quantum systems, such as modifying pulse sequences or disrupting signal generators used in quantum gate implementation.
Hacking Classical Infrastructure Supporting Quantum Systems	Targeting classical systems that support quantum computers, such as data centers, control servers, or networks that transmit classical instructions to quantum systems.
Manipulation of Classical Instructions	Altering classical instructions used to initialize or operate quantum systems, such as tampering with qubit initialization parameters or gate sequences in quantum programs.
Classical Interference with Quantum Algorithms	Embedding malicious classical descriptions of quantum algorithms or Hamiltonians into the quantum system prior to quantum compilation, causing the quantum system to behave incorrectly.
Cyberattacks on Quantum Network Nodes	Launching classical cyberattacks on quantum network nodes to disrupt entanglement generation or transmission of quantum states.
Intercepting Classical Communications in Quantum Protocols	Intercepting or tampering with classical communication channels used in quantum key distribution or error correction protocols.
Physical Disruption of Quantum Systems	Using classical tools to physically disrupt the environment of a quantum system, such as inducing electromagnetic interference or modifying temperature controls.
Classical Malware in Quantum Systems	Embedding classical malware into the classical-quantum interface, such as corrupting firmware updates for quantum devices or injecting malicious code into classical simulators of quantum systems.
Disrupting Quantum Compilation Processes	Targeting classical compilers that translate high-level quantum algorithms into executable instructions for specific quantum hardware, causing errors in the generated quantum circuits.
Classical Attacks on Quantum Sensor Networks	Using classical computational or signal-jamming methods to disrupt the operation of quantum sensors, such as quantum radar or magnetometers, by interfering with their classical data processing layers.

State conflict and interactions.[18] The celebrated example of Turing's involvement in the decryption of the Third Reich's *Enigma* encryption device[19] is a practical case in point. All modern national security apparatuses rely upon modern encryption protocols for their communication and data integrity. Information security is also critical to fundamental strategic imperatives such as nuclear stances and doctrines that shape and define modern State geopolitics. In analogy with nuclear and other dual

[18] Bauer (2021).

[19] Turing (1939).

use technology, the fact dual use of such technology shapes governance approaches to it.

In practice, the use of QIT, such as quantum computing devices to execute variants of Shor's algorithm to break classical code represents a hybrid approach that would leverage both classical-to-classical eavesdropping and espionage techniques in order to gather data (we set aside the use of quantum sensing for this objective) and then quantum information processing techniques to decrypt and return the decrypted information to a classical register.

3.7 *Quantum Decryption Does Not Afford Omniscience*

We consider in more detail the technical aspects of the likely use of quantum information systems for decryption in sections below. However, it is important to note the practical constraints upon QIT used in cyberattacks, for example in cryptoanalysis, data gathering (eavesdropping) of deception attacks. QIT is not some sort of omniscient oracle. Thus even the application of Shor's algorithm to gathered and stored data will take considerable time across each possibility. Classical controls and constraints will continue to apply. Nevertheless, the use and combination of QIT in cyber offensive activities related to decryption is a significant consequence of the technologies that is shaping governmental and institutional responses to quantum technology.

3.8 *Quantum Decryption and Classical Infrastructure*

Offensive use of QIT can also be classified in ways that borrow from classical cybersecurity literature. Quantum-based offensive cyberattacks against classical information systems exploit weaknesses of those systems to enable and amplify their impact. They must also engage with classical systems and infrastructure. Examples include:

3.8.1 Data Gathering

Where classical data is stored in advance until quantum cryptoanalysis is possible.

3.8.2 Data Processing

Where information gathered in side-channel attacks can be more efficiently searched (e.g. using Grover-style algorithms noted above), or where the search for trajectories through complex networks may be optimized on a quantum computer.

3.8.3 Quantum Simulation

Where data is gathered in ways which may enable, for example, scenario modelling by States to plot effective cyber attack strategies.

3.8.4 Entanglement

Where entanglement might enable untraceable coordination among cooperating adversaries.

Such cryptoanalysis based attacks relying upon analysing data gathered or stored in registers include a classical component. Quantum-based methods, such as the application of Shor's algorithm and related decryption quantum protocols involve classical activities as well. Thus *store-now, decrypt-later* (SNDL) attacks may involve classical interception of classically-encoded communications for later decryption. Cryptoanalysis can also interfere with classical key distribution, such as Diffie-Hellman exchange protocols, allowing interception or impersonation.

3.9 Quantum Sensing

Quantum sensing also has application in adversarial and defensive cyber activities. We set out a few examples below:

3.9.1 Enhanced Side-Channel Attack

The sensitivity of quantum sensors to electromagnetic spectra and acoustic emission disturbances may allow collection of fine-grained or higher-resolution data as part of a broader cyber attack strategy.

3.9.2 Attack detection

Quantum sensing devices may be able to detect the use of interception devices themselves, (e.g., where low-power signals or perturbances indicative of interception technology or the equivalent of wire-taps are being used by an adversary). Other proposals of a more speculative variety include augmented quantum sensing used in radar systems.[20]

---

[20] Krelina (2021).

4 QIT Effects On Strategic Behavior

4.1 Dilemmas and Equilibria

The unique features of quantum information technology have implications for how States utilizing such technologies strategically behave in response to each other in ways that in principle differ from classical strategic behavior. We can assess this via studying scenarios involving quantum resources (such as quantum communication resources) while considering how States may act in cooperative or non-cooperative ways during peacetime or conflict. The strategic impact of quantum technology is modelled theoretically by quantum game theory[21] representing a subset of research into quantum strategies which considers differential effects of decision-making involving quantum information processing.[22] Because multi-agent games and behavior, including those of States, can be viewed in terms of distributed systems (and even modelled in part using distributed algorithms), quantum game theory has specific relation to circuit architecture and distributed quantum systems frameworks.[23] Implications of and results of quantum game theory include the following.

4.1.1 Different Equilibria

Quantum variations of classical games enable players to share entangled quantum states giving rise to equilibrium strategies where both players may achieve higher payoffs than in the classical Nash equilibrium context, such as in quantum versions of the Prisoner's dilemma which enable cooperative outcomes. These strategic outcomes are not feasible classically.

4.1.2 Strict Dilemmas

So-called 'strict dilemmas' where incentives and rational agency of players can lead to suboptimal and non-Pareto outcomes can in certain cases be supplanted where quantum resources are available (again the Prisoner's dilemma is the canonical case).

Intuitively, quantum resource availability alters classical cooperation and defection strategies. Classically, cooperation usually relies upon (i) external enforcement mechanisms such as treaties, third-party oversight or reputational considerations to motivate State behavior or (ii) repeated interactions among States to build trust or (iii) mutually shared resources or interests which are at risk if cooperation is not undertaken. The availability of quantum resources provides an effective

---

[21] Gutoski and Watrous (2007); Bostanci and Watrous (2022); Eisert et al. (1999).

[22] Guo et al. (2008); Meyer (1999).

[23] Bostanci and Watrous (2022); Chiribella et al. (2009).

self-enforcing mechanism. This is for two reasons. First, shared entanglement motivates honest behavior to reduce the chances of a State secretly changing its strategy or deceiving in communications due to the no-cloning theorem and measurement constraints.

Thus State communication may be encoded using entanglement methods or encrypted in ways that can detect changes in strategy and decision making (e.g. the decision to defect or not), motivating States to act honestly by the fact that their decisions are detectable or verifiable (the idea being that requiring State communication through quantum channels—because only communications via that channel were valid—say in prisoner dilemma contexts would give rise to such dynamics that are distinct from the classical case). Secondly, quantum protocols can verify randomness and therefore strategic behavior dependent upon randomness, such as where distribution of outcomes depends on an agreed procedure involving random sampling, providing a means of enforcing agreed upon outcomes via cryptographic protocols.

4.2 *Assumptions Behind Entanglement*

Entanglement-based protocols require, however, some degree of cooperation and are conditional on a number of assumptions including:

4.2.1 Cooperation on Quantum Resource Use

States must at some stage have agreed to share quantum resources (inadvertent entanglement is unlikely) e.g. such as via quantum communication networks (albeit States may later become adversarial) in order that entangled quantum states may be accessible by both.

4.2.2 Technical Capabilities

States must have the resources and technical expertise to utilize quantum resources (we touch upon this below in the context of strategic computational umbrellas where certain nation states have access to computational—AI or quantum—resources and others to not, affecting their strategic choices).

4.2.3 Rationality

States are assumed to be rational or mostly rational in order to recognize the benefits of cooperation over defection.

4.2.4 Economic Behavior

Another more speculative source of content for State economic strategic behavior is that of quantum economic behavior among States. This includes quantum analogues of classical economic behavior,[24] such as contracting, principal-agency theory, exchange of commodities and market design, along with information asymmetry principles.[25] States engaging in peacetime cooperative and competitive behavior often do so through economic channels and the availability of quantum resources via which to conduct economic activity thus gives rise to novel forms of strategic behavior. We consider the strategic behavioral activity of States with respect to QIT in more detail below.

5 Geopolitical Scenarios

5.1 Overview

The technical analysis of QIT gives rise to questions about the practical and applied scenarios in which QIT would give rise to strategic State behavior. Is the use of QIT give rise to unique geopolitical effects distinct from other computational and informational technologies? And what consequences might these effects have for international law? To consider how the technical prospects for use of QIT have consequences within the framework of international law discussed in the previous section, we consider strategic behaviors along different dimensions. Firstly, whether States are in *peacetime* (defined as the absence of State armed conflict) or in *conflict* (defined as the presence of State conflict, which may be binary between States or between alliances). For each such scenario, we consider whether States act *cooperatively* (such as trade partners in peacetime or allies in conflicts) or *adversarially* (such as economic competitors in peacetime or adversaries in war). Using this taxonomy, scenario modelling can then consider how different classes of QIT use may apply.

To provide illustrations for the types of activities, we set out some prospective examples in Table 3. These include: (i) *optimization problems*, such as logistical activities or strategic planning; (ii) *quantum simulations*, for materials discovery or strategic simulation; (iii) *cryptoanalysis*, including post-quantum cryptography cooperation or adversarial decryption; (iv) *machine learning and AI* enhanced using QIT; (v) *searching* and data mining using QIT (e.g. Grover-based algorithms); (vi) *quantum cloud computing* to enable wider interface among States to distributed QIT; (vii) *post-quantum cryptography* to strengthen State information security. We

[24] Ikeda and Aoki (2021).

[25] Ikeda (2021); Ikeda (2023); Ikeda and Aoki (2021).

Table 3 Strategic uses of QIT, highlighting the use of quantum technologies in peacetime and conflict, divided into cooperative and adversarial contexts

	Quantum Technology in International Relations			
	Peacetime		Conflict	
Category	Cooperative	Adversarial	Cooperative	Adversarial
Optimization Problems	Collaboration on logistics optimization for disaster relief or development of mutual infrastructure.	Monitoring adversarial advancements in logistics optimization or competitive trade strategy.	Joint optimization of logistics and planning for allied military operations.	Disrupting adversarial military planning or interfering with supply chains or predicting strategic behavior of adversaries.
Quantum Simulations	Joint research on quantum chemistry products, pharmaceuticals.	Simulating competitive markets or negotiations.	Development of advanced materials and defense strategies.	Weaponizing simulations to gain battlefield advantage.
Cryptoanalysis	Collaborative development of post-quantum cryptography.	Intercepting adversarial encrypted communications for market intelligence.	Testing secure communication systems among allies.	Decrypting adversarial communication networks during conflict.
Machine Learning and AI	Quantum enhanced shared civilian AI infrastructure for public benefit (e.g., smart cities).	Monitoring adversarial AI activities for potential military applications.	Using quantum computing with AI for battlefield intelligence and decision-making.	Using QIT with AI for autonomous military systems and cyber warfare.
Searching	Quantum data mining for global humanitarian purposes.	Data mining of market competitor communications.	Quantum sensing to track and search enemy troop movements using.	System search routing using to assist in cyberattacks on adversaries.
Quantum Cloud Computing	Shared quantum cloud for collaborative global research.	Quantum sensor networks for detection.	Secure quantum networks for inter-allied military coordination.	Enabling distributed use of QIT during conflict.
Post-Quantum Cryptography	Global collaboration to establish resilient cryptographic standards.	Developing countermeasures against adversarial cryptographic advancements.	Implementing quantum resistant communications among allies.	Exploiting vulnerabilities in adversarial cryptographic systems.

draw upon this taxonomy in the next section to develop scenarios used in our analysis of public international law implications of strategic QIT use further on.

5.2 Strategic Scenario Modeling

To study the implications of State strategic the use QIT (and its implications under international law) we consider simple scenarios of State strategic behavior related to QIT. The scenarios we use are designed to deliberately highlight the application of public international law principles to cyber activities primarily set out in the *Tallinn manual 2.0 on the International Law applicable to Cyber Operations* (the Manual).[26] Each scenario is constructed to focus upon the unique or *sui generis* aspects of QIT as they relate to State behavior, concentrating on the unique affordances that QIT enables which classical cannot. Our focus of this work is primarily upon adversarial behavior during peacetime and conflict, but we note the raft of international regulatory frameworks that would also apply to cooperative behavior in peacetime and during conflicts. For each scenario, we consider adversarial State behavior: in peacetime, we consider adversarial behavior as *competitive*; while in conflict situations, we consider such behavior as *offensive*. These can be itemized as follows:

5.2.1 Peacetime/Cooperative

Where each State seeks to coordinate their use of quantum resources to act cooperatively in order to achieve an objective, which may be the construction, or expansion, of distributed quantum infrastructure, global research initiatives and so on.

5.2.2 Peacetime/Adversarial

Where one or more States seeks to use quantum resources act adversarially to obtain an advantage over other States, such as by way of economic competitive advantage, or cyber espionage.

5.2.3 Conflict/Cooperative

Covering where States may enter into alliances or coalitions during conflicts affecting how they may use their quantum resources.

---

[26] Schmitt (2017).

5.2.4 Conflict/Adversarial

Where States use their quantum resources to seek to obtain a military advantage.

We also discuss briefly the consequences of asymmetric possession of QIT capabilities as asymmetries in technology can motivate State behavior, such as striking or acting (e.g. in anticipatory self-defense) to obtain an advantage before a technology gap becomes too great. In an elementary sense in which possession of QIT affords a comparative advantage with respect to a strategic decision, such as in conflict or negotiation, each scenario above represents a simple game whose structure, such as potential Nash equilibria, may be studied to inform toy models of strategic behavior. A game-theoretical approach to modelling impact e.g. the strength of inclination to take a particular action being reflection of a the weight or importance a State places on that action (such as a response to a cyber attack, or the use of QIT adversarially) is of independent research interest and able to draw upon the developing body of work on quantum games noted above. However, our focus is instead on using these scenarios to draw out their international legal implications. To this end, two main scenarios and variations on them.

5.3 *Scenario 1: Asymmetric Quantum Infrastructure*

In Scenario 1 (Table 4 below), State A has access to QIT while State B does not. We then consider two examples where State A utilizes its QIT adversarially: in peacetime to conduct industrial espionage and in conflict situations to decrypt military communications. We consider how this QIT asymmetry affects their strategic behavior and study consequences under international law in the next section.

Table 4 Scenario 1—Asymmetric Quantum Infrastructure

Item	Description
States	State A (with QIT) and State B (no QIT).
Technology	State A has access to an idealized quantum computer and quantum sensor network (comprising quantum sensors located within and outside its territory) connected by a quantum internet (within its territory)
Peacetime	State A conducts espionage via an SNDL decryption attack against State B, intercepting or conducting espionage to obtain data about State B's industrial production, storing it and decrypting it using its quantum computer. The interception occurs both within and outside its territory. The decrypted information is used to obtain economic competitive advantages.
Conflict	State A decrypts strategically sensitive military communications and uses its quantum sensor network to eavesdrop on State B and decrypt its communications. State A utilizes its ability to decrypt classical communications in order to determine classical private keys and protocols use by State B to encrypt its network. It uses that information to launch a cyber operation that disables State B's military surveillance network and to obtain strategic military advantage.

5.4 Scenario 2: Entangled Quantum Networks

In Scenario 2 (Table 5 below), we add more complexity and variation. State A and State B both share access to a single quantum resource, quantum internet e.g. distributed quantum network where both their quantum resources (e.g. qubit resources) are entangled.

6 International Law and Quantum Information Technologies

6.1 Overview

Having surveyed the QIT technology landscape, we now examine the sources of international law governing such strategic uses of quantum information technologies by States. As a set of information technologies, we consider how the use of quantum information technologies is situated within broader international law governing classical information systems, what are often denoted by the term 'cyber technologies'. We examine the main conventions, customs and other sources of international jurisprudence on information systems usage by States generally. There are no treaties at international law specifically designed to regulate the use of information technology or cyber activities by States. We rely upon key principles of international law and cyber activities of States as set out in the Tallinn Manual. We then provide scenario analysis of State adversarial interaction using QIT described

Table 5 Scenario 2—Entangled Quantum Networks

Item	Description
States	State A (with QIT) and State B (with QIT).
Technology	State A and State B share entangled quantum resources in the form of entangled qubit-based quantum computers and an entanglement-based quantum internet. State A and B initially entangled their quantum resources and participated in the establishment of a quantum internet across their jurisdictions. The quantum internet is used within each State and by each State internationally.
Peacetime	State A exploits the shared entangled resources to solve complex problems such as factoring large integers for cryptanalysis or simulating intricate molecular structures—tasks enhanced by quantum correlations. While both States use the quantum internet for secure scientific exchanges, State A covertly measures certain entangled qubits, subtly extracting sensitive patterns from State B's quantum data without triggering obvious alarms.
Conflict	State A intercepts or manipulates entangled qubits carrying State B's classified directives, thus undermining secure quantum key distribution and real-time strategic coordination. By exploiting its QIT, State A disrupts State B's critical communications and decision-making processes. The quantum network—once a cooperative computational platform—now amplifies State A's offensive capabilities, granting it intelligence and control over State B's most sensitive military operations.

above in order to identify any unique consequences or dilemmas arising under international jurisprudence from the use of such QIT.

The conceptual framing we adopt is that of typical international law analysis. Specifically (and as we discuss below), this ranks normative and legal imperatives according to the canonical principle of State sovereignty as set out in treaties, customary law and jurisprudence. State sovereignty sets out the justification for rights, obligations and interests of States under international law, including definitions of territorial and other sovereignty, actions which infringe upon sovereignty and actions by States justified in terms of preservation of State sovereignty. In practical terms, this situates QIT in instrumental terms, be it as infrastructure, a tool of State maintenance, or as an offensive or defensive technology.

The Manual is generally regarded as a leading, if not the leading, international law resource dealing with the application of international law to cybertechnology and computational technology for State-based conflicts. The Manual analyses how international law applies to cyber operations and cyber warfare. It was developed in connection with NATO Cooperative Cyber Defence Centre of Excellence by an international group of experts and analyses how existing international law (e.g., UN Charter, the laws of armed conflict, and State sovereignty) apply to cyber operations. The Manual examines international law doctrine as applicable cyber activities occurring both during peacetime and conflict scenarios. Given its influential status within jurisprudential scholarship on international cyber activities, we focus on the content Manual as a means of analysing the consequences of State use of QIT.

In later sections, we consider the extent to which international cyber jurisprudence may benefit from supplementary concepts to handle any unique consequences of QIT together with consideration of the types of international legal instruments that may be contemplated as a means of regulating (actively and pre-emptively) State strategic use of QIT.

Quantum computation used for decryption only (rather than say interception using quantum devices) will rely in most cases on classically gathering or intercepting information, inputting that information into a quantum computer executing a quantum algorithm to decrypt such information whose outputs will be rendered classically. Any action consequent upon this will be classical in nature. One way to frame this is by comparison with classical artificial intelligence technologies. The impact of AI can be framed as (i) epistemic, enabling more accurate prediction or greater information asymmetries whose actions are merely communication and messaging (e.g. responses to queries, outputs of computational processes) and (ii) agentic, where AI systems, such as AI-based agents (be they traditional or language model agents) may interact with the environment and world via acting, causally effecting some change. Quantum information systems may utilize quantum algorithms or forms of quantum advantage—to obtain advantages epistemically, but the specifically quantum actions which may be performed are limited (e.g. to where for example some uniquely quantum effect, such as entanglement, causes some change in environmental state). Simplifying, classical computation (e.g. classical AI) thinks and acts classically, while quantum computation thinks quantumly but (in the scenarios with which we are concerned) acts classically. To refine our analysis further, we continue with the classical-quantum strategic taxonomy set out above.

Before setting out a more fulsome analysis of key concepts from the Manual in relation to QIT, we include below discussion of a few recurring conceptual themes that arise when considering the effect and application of QIT. As we note above, QIT is anchored in the phenomena and laws of quantum mechanics. The unique features of quantum information processing systems as distinct from classical give rise to specific ontological and epistemic differences which have consequences for a number of ordinary, but relatively fundamental, concepts underpinning public international law jurisprudence. We list out a number below in advance of considering select sections of the Manual in detail. The primary phenomena we concentrate on are those of quantum superposition and quantum entanglement.

6.2 Quantum System Uncertainty

While great care goes into theoretical and applied means of governing quantum evolution via Hamiltonian specification, the outcomes of measurements of the evolved quantum states are stochastic. Jurisprudence on cyber activities in international relations as set out in the Manual distinguishes between physical, logical and social layers of cyberspace. This is premised upon a classical conception of the underlying physical substrate of information systems behaving classically, whose properties are in principle known or measurable and consistent and where uncertainty is in effect epistemic. As noted in earlier chapters, however, in general the outcome of measurements of quantum systems is inherently uncertain such as, for example, uncertainty with regard to position and momentum.

When a quantum state $|\psi\rangle$ is measured, the measurement postulate provides that it collapses into a relevant eigenstate. The superposition of a quantum state is thus not directly observable in the way that we can directly observe its representation. It is represented as an artefact of measurement statistics. In practice what this means is that many identical copies of the quantum system are prepared via state preparation procedures and measured. This jars somewhat with governance and law which is used to classical fundamental principles of persistence, continuity, identifiability and unity so that the object the subject of governance is ascertainable and definite. Understandably these classical assumptions permeate international law, including the treatment of cyber objects and activities in the Manual below. When considering the implications of quantum technologies it is important to recognize the differences between quantum and classical ontology (such as the fact that there is not one single continuous quantum system that remains in superposition as it is measured over and over, rather one must re-initialize quantum states or have multiple identically prepared instances available). However, the inherent ontological uncertainty of quantum systems does not mean that quantum systems are somehow magical, unknowable, uncontrollable and so on. Rather, as we argue below, the law is in the main equipped to adapt in ways that reckon with such quantum phenomena.

6.3 Jurisdiction

The inherent ontological uncertainty of quantum states gives rise to in principle uncertainty in their position descriptions. Quantum state positions, such as the state of for example an electron, are described by reference to probabilities (measures) over a range of positions. For example the position of an electron is described by a probability mass or density function such that repeated measurements allow that distribution to be estimate (subject to noise and so on).

This is exemplified by simple but illuminating 'particle-in-a-box' paradigms[27] which show how the distribution of an electron's position is not classical, but actually extends vastly just with asymptotically zero probability of being found outside the box. In practice, while uncertainty in quantum properties is a central feature, this sort of uncertainty doesn't particularly impact jurisdictional issues such as the territorial location of a single or multi-qubit system.

That said, our view is that since almost all of its probability measure is concentrated within very narrow intervals such that in practice the tails of the distribution can be essentially ignored from a jurisdictional perspective. In the case of entanglement, the question is more subtle because the combination of the ontological status of superposition and entanglement give rise, at least by many arguments in quantum mechanics and quantum foundations, to the fact that the physical position of the say entangled is construed as non-local. However, as we note below, proxy concepts such as the locus of control provide a means to conform to ideas in the jurisprudence of State jurisdiction.

6.4 Control

Classical jurisprudence for technology governance and cyber security is premised upon classical notions of control. Implicit, for example, in discussion of State responsibility to control its own use of cyber technology, or those of actors within its jurisdiction, is an idea of controllability of the cyber system itself: that it can be directed to evolve, function and perform in a particular way. Obligations of due diligence or obligations to take precautionary measures when utilizing cyber operations in armed conflict, for example, emphasize control to greater or lesser degrees. The law does countenance uncertainty and a lack of control over cyber systems—such as (discussed below) when a cyber attack otherwise lawful becomes unlawful because a failure to control it has led to unjustifiable collateral damage. There is also recognition that cyber systems are highly complex, such that it is often difficult to exert full control over them. Yet QIT is to a certain technical degree incongruous with these assumptions. Quantum state measurement outcomes are not controlled. At best the level of control over measurement statistics is managed via reliable

[27] Townsend (2000).

engineering such that the measurement statistics may be predicted with sufficient confidence.

6.4.1 Control in an Entanglement Scenario Is Complicated

When two States share entangled resources, which can be said to control that entangled system? And what does it mean to control such a system? In practice States sharing such resources would share an enormous number of identically prepared and entangled quantum states. By sharing this means that each physical qubit (which in aggregate would constitute a set of logical qubits) is physically located within the jurisdiction of a State (or otherwise controlled by it) such that the State can control how it interacts with its qubit. By measuring (or some other equivalent interaction), the State causes its own qubit and that of the other State to collapse into the measurement state with a given probability. Each State cannot control per se the outcome of the quantum measurement (and thus cyber operations e.g. subsequent computations contingent upon them).

Application of force in a conventional sense occurs by way of a State interacting with its own entangled qubits and this in essence causes, by virtue of entanglement, the measurement statistics of the other State to be correlated. Stochasticity aside, to the extent to which one State's measurements can be said to cause measurement statistics of the other State to be so correlated, then in effect the measuring State has exerted what the law would regard as some degree of control over the qubits of the other State.

6.4.2 Knowledge and Error Correction

Many State obligations relating to cyber activity are conditional to a greater or lesser degree on the knowledge of a State about that cyber activity. This includes customary laws regarding State due diligence, precautionary assessments by States about the impact of cyber operations and standards regarding reasonable foreseeability of consequences. International law does countenance uncertainty in a State's knowledge or epistemic state. Quantum information is derived via measurement statistics which are used to tomographically reconstruct the quantum state or process (Hamiltonian). This is usually (given current technology) infeasible for anything other than small multi-qubit systems. So what is and even can be known of the quantum system is subject to a heightened-degree of practical uncertainty viz-à-viz classical systems along with the fundamental differences that quantum systems are not in definitive states.

In general, international law already has mechanisms for dealing with technological or consequential uncertainty, but it is a noteworthy distinction to make to the extent that technical specificity may be a requirement under various rules or customs. Moreover, all quantum information processing requires error correction due to the sensitivity of quantum substrates upon which QIT is engineered.

The requirement for error correction means the types of control regimes applicable to them are distinct and made more complex. Error correction has important implications for the control of quantum systems because control regimes must account for the layering and encoding of, for example, error correction codes. They must also be directed in such a way that they do not undermine or interfere with the requirement for fault-tolerant error correction.[28] Error correction further limits the extent to which a quantum system may be diagnosed or surveilled.

6.4.3 Force

As we detail at some length below, the concept of force is central to the law of armed conflict and also cyber activities by States during peacetime. The Manual acknowledges that force for the purposes of cyber operations encompasses more than kinetic force, or even other physical catalysts, noting the central role that concepts of causality play in public international cyber law. Thus the application of force is framed usually in causal terms, where a cyber event has certain consequences. The application of force in a quantum setting is described by complex mathematical formalism and paradigms. Quantum paradigms of force differ in ways described by quantum causality.[29] Mostly this is not going to be directly relevant for State activities using QIT. However, in the case of entanglement, it is worth noting how the application of 'force' occurs: one State interacts—measures—its own qubits and, owing the ontological entanglement those qubits with the qubits of another State, this is deemed to cause wave functional collapse in that other State's qubits.

Force is not, however, propagated through intermediate space in the usual way of say a wave propagating through the electromagnetic field. Nevertheless, the framing of force in terms of causality does provide a means by which the usual jurisprudence may apply, noting however that the stochastic nature of quantum outcomes means that a State may not necessarily control the measurement outcome, so the classical description of causality remains distinct. In this sense quantum causality is conditioned by way of a certain probability of an effect rather than a certainty of outcome.

One of the other challenges in the case of quantum information technology and jurisprudence is the fact that tests for causality in the law tend to be counterfactual in nature. This means that the law seeks to examine what would likely have happened but for the intervention in question as a way of ascertaining its causal impact. However in the case of quantum mechanical systems, one can at best assert a different outcome with a certain or estimated probability. While uncertainty regarding counterfactual analysis is quite common in the law in the quantum case this uncertainty is irreducible. Even with all the information in the world, the type of

---

[28] Preskill (2018); Preskill (2021); Gottesman (1998); Gottesman (2010).

[29] Brukner (2014); Donoghue and Menezes (2020).

counterfactual analysis that the law engages in is problematised by the fact that quantum measurements are inherently random meaning their measurement outcomes are inherently uncertain.

6.5 Applicability of Tallinn Manual Information System Definitions to QIT

The Manual is divided into four Parts, each containing jurisprudential analysis and normative claims regarding the application of international law to cyberspace, computational and information technology in offensive and defensive contexts and communications protocols. Each Part is further decomposed into Sections comprising rules (conventional and customary) of public international law relevant to cyberspace activities and operations. The scope of the Manual is broad and has been subject to considerable scholarship since its publication.[30] Its focus is upon two fundamental principles of international laws of conflict. The first is that of *jus ad bellum*, the principle governing when and whether a State is permitted to use force. The second is the principle of *jus in bello* governing the use of force and the conduct of military operations by a State during conflict, including constraints designed to protect specific persons, objects, and activities.

The Manual also sets out extensive analysis on the public international law governing cyber operations during peacetime. Below we examine how the principles of international law set out in the Manual that are applicable to cyberspace carry over to quantum cyberspace which we define broadly as quantum information technologies canvassed above (with a comparison table set out in Table 6 in the Appendix).

In many cases, usual principles of cyberspace law are equally applicable and inherited in the case of quantum cyberspace scenarios by virtue of them being generically classifiable as cyber activities, cyber assets and so on. But in other cases, especially where the unusual properties of quantum mechanics are essential to the functioning, use or distribution of QIT, there are, we argue, specific differences (especially with regard to entanglement).

6.5.1 Cyberspace and QIT

Before examining a number of key provisions of the Manual and the implications of QIT for the jurisprudential analysis therein, we consider threshold issues of the extent to which QIT fits within established definitions of information processing and the subject matter of the Manual at all. We consider relevant definitions in the Glossary which relate to QIT. The term *cyber* is defined to connote a relationship

[30] Efrony and Shany (2018); Caso (2014); Fleck (2013); von Heinegg (2013); Kessler and Werner (2013).

with information technology which clearly countenances QIT detailed in earlier sections.

Cyber infrastructure (also synonymous with 'hardware') is defined as the communications, storage, and computing devices upon which information systems are built and operate. Cyber infrastructure would thus naturally encompass QIT infrastructure, both quantum-specific infrastructure and the classical infrastructure within which QIT is necessarily embedded.

Cyberspace is defined to include the environment formed by physical and non-physical components to store, modify, and exchange data using computer networks. A *cyber activity* is defined as any activity that involves the use of cyber infrastructure or employs cyber means to affect the operation of such infrastructure. Such activities include, but are not limited to, cyber operations. This latter term, *cyber operations* is defined to include the employment of cyber capabilities to achieve objectives in or through cyberspace. It is used in a predominantly operational context. Other relevant terms include *cyber reconnaissance*, including the use of cyber capabilities to obtain information about activities, information resources, or system capabilities. Clearly each of these terms covers within its meaning quantum information technology equivalence.

Cyber system is defined in terms of *computer system*. The definition of 'computer' itself is not included but would assume its ordinary meaning. *Computer system* is defined to include one or more interconnected computers with associated software and peripheral devices, including sensors and/or (programmable logic) controllers, connected over a computer network. Computer systems can be general purpose (e.g. a laptop) or specialized (e.g. the 'blue force tracking system'). Computer system thus includes single QIT devices, including quantum sensing and each node of a quantum. Although the foregoing definition incorporates connected (and thus distributed) computation in the classical distributed networks sense, the Manual also contains a definition of *computer network*, being a form of infrastructure of interconnected devices or nodes that enables the exchange of data. The data exchange medium may be wired (e.g., Ethernet over twisted pair, fiber-optic, etc.), wireless (e.g., Wi-Fi, Bluetooth), or a combination of the two. Computer networks would thus include networked quantum computers and, arguably, quantum communication network devices e.g. relying upon entanglement as a wireless technology. Similarly the definition of *internet*, being a global system of interconnected computer networks that use the Internet Protocol suite and a clearly defined routing policy, would cover in the main proposals for quantum internets and distributed quantum networks in general (albeit with some subtle, but immaterial, differences regarding what constitutes, for example, routing on a quantum network).

6.5.2 Quantum Data Terms

Other key definitions would also be likely to encompass QIT and quantum analogues of classical information processing concepts. For example, *data* is defined to mean the basic element that can be processed or produced by a computer to convey information with the fundamental digital data measurement identified as a byte. Although the qubits are usually distinguished from bits, qubits (and by extension quantum bytes) can be seen as a classical form of information subject to a quantum ontology: qubits, for example, remain representable (and usually are represented) in terms of bits assuming values of 0 or 1 (e.g. $|\psi\rangle = a \mid 0\rangle + b \mid 1\rangle$) albeit in probabilistic fashion.

Quantum data infrastructure (such as quantum memory and even simply the encoded data within a quantum system) would similarly fall within the concept of *data centers*, being defined as a physical facility used for the storage and processing of large volumes of data. A *database* is defined to include a collection of interrelated data stored together in one or more computerized files which would include storage of quantum data. The slight wrinkle here from a quantum perspective relate to superposition states and entanglement. Where data is in a superposition state, the concept of being stored together or stored is technically somewhat distinct from a quantum information perspective.

Recalling, unlike classical computers, most quantum computing is premised upon the ability to initialize identical states, measure a sufficiently large number of them to enable measurement statistics to be obtained (the whole process being denoted an experiment in some contexts). Thus, a state initialized in superposition contains probabilistic data and each experiment, once measured, collapses the relevant superposition (we use a simplistic non-multistate example here). One cannot simply access the data stored, that is, encoded, in a quantum system (such as a qubit) directly in the way that is possible with classical data, where measurement of the system does not interfere with it. Data in the quantum sense more closely refers to an abstraction which is effectively reconstructed via repeated experiments and interactions, rather than being identical to classical conceptions of storage.

Similarly, where data is encoded within entangled quantum systems (which by construction must be in a superposition state) that are distributed across the physical jurisdictional bounds of States (see below), the data within a quantum system controlled by a State can be affected by the measurement actions of another State on the entangled system. Thus again the classical conception of data has slightly different features to that of quantum data because as soon as one State measures the system, the data encoded within it changes due to the ontological collapse of superposition (and any decohering interactions). However, in practice identical preparation and measurement requirements could and would likely just be seen as a procedural element such that superposition state and entangled state quantum systems would meet definitions of data and other related terms, thus falling within classical definitions for the purpose of the Manual. The definition of data includes the use of data centers in distributed networks, stipulating that a data center can be used solely by users belonging to a single enterprise or shared among multiple enterprises, as in 'cloud computing' (see above) data centers. A data center can be stationary or mobile (e.g., housed in a cargo container transported via ship, truck, or aircraft). Once again, each of these definitions categorically encompasses QIT equivalents.

6.5.3 Cyberspace Definitions

There are a host of other technical terms defined in the Manual which the quantum analogues of which would likely fall within without much controversy. One particularly relevant definition given the offensive and defensive motivations for QIT use is that of *electronic warfare* being the use of electromagnetic (EM) or directed energy to exploit the electromagnetic spectrum. Electronic warfare covers the interception or identification of EM emissions (relevant to store-now decrypt-later quantum offensive strategies) and broadly put the employment of EM energy, prevention of hostile use of the EM spectrum by an adversary, and actions to ensure efficient employment of that spectrum by the user State. As discussed above, the use of QIT is not equivalent in action to that of classical information systems. Although all QIT systems rely upon the electromagnetic spectrum in some form or another, the 'action' of a quantum system is not, for example, a causal electromagnetic wave propagated locally through electromagnetic fields in the same way that say an electromagnetic pulse or even simple communication or signaling is in a classical context. The intended meaning of electronic warfare under this definition differs in a material sense. The use of QIT for offensive actions is still captured by other definitions, such as cyber activities, but quantum systems do not act in the same way as classical ones. For example, even in the case of State adversaries sharing entangled resources, the classical notion of one State acting on another by way of measuring an entangled set of qubits is not one of local (classical) action. Rather it is sometimes described as 'spooky' action at a distance.

The terms *cyber attack* and *cyber espionage* are defined by way of reference to Rules 92 and 32 respectively. Rule 92 defines a cyber attack as a cyber operation, whether offensive or defensive, that is reasonably expected to cause injury or death to persons or damage or destruction to objects. As the Manual notes, non-violent operations, such as psychological cyber operations and cyber espionage, do not qualify as attacks under the definition (which draws upon Article 49(1) of Additional Protocol I in its consequentialist requirement for the application of force or violence or other forms of causal interaction with similar effect). As with other jurisprudential conceptions of causality, proximity and effective causality is an issue when it comes to indirect actions that can be said to cause effects such as harm.

6.5.4 Ontological Cyberspace Stack

The Manual adopts a stacked or layer-wise hierarchical framing of cyberspace, defining it in terms of three layers (Rule 1.4, p12): (i) the *physical layer*, comprising the physical network components (hardware), (ii) the *logical layer*, corresponding of the connections that exist between network components, comprising higher-level abstractions such as applications, data and protocols for exchange of data across the physical layer and (iii) the *social layer*, comprising the stakeholders (individuals and groups) engaged in cyber activities. This hierarchy is important because certain rights, duties and obligations arising under the jurisprudential analysis of the Manual are cast in terms of distinct layers, akin to a governance stack.[31] Thus (as we note in more detail below) foundational principles of State sovereignty are construed according to all three layers of cyberspace. And further, as we analyze below, this has implications for the application of such principles. Thus while all QIT is physically embedded and relatively locally, the logical space exhibits different properties.

Thus for example, the application of principles of jurisdiction, sovereignty and control to entangled qubits arguably minimally must reckon with their non-locality in position space because, for example, the probability measure over such physical space that specifies the location of say an electron used as a qubit is almost entirely concentrated in what the law would regard as the physical site of the qubit. Yet when that physical qubit is entangled and/or forms part of a logical qubit via entanglement across jurisdictions, the logical layer of the logical qubit (and entangled system as a whole) is less easily specified in terms of simple geometric coordinates.

7 General International Law and Cyberspace

Part I *General International Law and Cyberspace* of the Manual sets out foundational principles of international law applicable cyberspace, noting that public international law already applies to States with respect to cyberspace activities. This principle that the law as it is, *lex lata*, already applies to cyberspace carries over to QIT in most respects. We examine the specifics of existing international law cyber principles, tracking the structure of the Manual and canvassing how and whether the application of the same to QIT-based cyber classifications varies in any material way.

[31] Perrier (2022).

7.1 Sovereignty

7.1.1 Sovereign Jurisdiction

Section 1 (*Sovereignty*) covers the canonical application of principles of State sovereignty (Rule 1), stipulating how this principle grants States exclusive authority over their cyber infrastructure. Despite abstractions of cyberspace as virtual, the situatedness and jurisdictional locality of cyberspace, that it is constituted by objects and involves activities conducted by persons and entities over which State sovereignty and jurisdiction applies (with no State sovereign over global cyberspace due to its partial location within other States). Cyberspace activities internally within a State's territory (Rule 2) are deemed subject to State sovereignty straightforward applications of sovereignty. This principle applies to both public (State) and private cyber assets for example, the determinative fact being whether a State may exercise sovereignty over the same rather than domestic configurations of ownership.

Such internal sovereignty is related to a State's *domaine reservé* (Rule 66), those areas of activity that are considered to fall exclusively within the domestic jurisdiction of a sovereign State, meaning they are not subject to interference or regulation by international law or external entities (where unlawful intervention is regarded as a breach of sovereignty). The physical layer of cyberspace is considered to be self-evidently subject to State sovereignty. The Manual suggests that sovereignty extends to a principle of control over aspects of the logical layer of cyberspace within a State's territory, giving the example of State legislation mandating interoperability protocols. This question of the relationship of *control* and sovereignty is something we examine below in the context of entanglement-based quantum communication networks shared among States where the actions of each State measuring its own entangled qubits has both a physical and logical effect on the quantum network and consequences for its use.

Rule 3 discusses the principle of *external sovereignty*, enabling conduct of cyber activities in international relations subject to constraints imposed by international law. The principle is considered to derive from the sovereign equality of States (as noted in, for example, article 2(1) of the UN Charter). That is, there is no supreme singular sovereignty of one State over another. States are thus free to enter into arrangements e.g. cyber treaties or issue *opinio juris* on customary law and practice relating to cyber operations.

In Scenario 1, the sovereignty of each State extends to its classical and cyber infrastructure within its jurisdiction, with both the classical and quantum cyber infrastructure of each State constituting an instrumental extension of its sovereignty. In Scenario 2, the sovereignty of each State over the entangled quantum system is more complex than in Scenario 1. The entangled quantum system exhibits non-local characteristics that do not directly fit into territorial or extra-territorial jurisdiction. Each State's sovereignty extends to control over the qubits physically located within its jurisdiction. However, this fact renders each State's exclusive control over its qubits is problematic (as noted above). The highly correlated nature of the entangled resource could possibly constitute a *de jure* and *de facto* object which is (to the extent of entanglement) subject to the joint sovereignty of each State.

7.1.2 Joint Sovereignty

Although not addressed in the Manual, the international law principle of condominium (or coimperium) may provide a source according to which jointly shared sovereignty, such as over entangled resources, may be analyzed. In international law, a condominium occurs when two or more States share and exercise governing authority over a particular territory without any single State enjoying exclusive sovereignty.[32] This concept has its roots in Roman and civil law traditions, where shared ownership and joint sovereignty were recognized legal constructs.

Historically, such arrangements involved the joint exercise of sovereign powers, as seen in European border territories or colonial holdings, while more recent examples often reflect limited forms of administration or regulatory oversight rather than full sovereignty. In a condominium, the States involved must manage and control their joint authority through carefully negotiated treaties or agreements, which set out principles that preserve the sovereignty of the other, such as those of non-discrimination, the free movement of persons and goods, the limits on military deployments, and the mechanisms for decision-making and dispute resolution. These arrangements are guided by principles of international law but have largely been supplanted by modern institutional regimes such as treaties and international bilateral and multilateral organizations.

7.1.3 Violations of Sovereignty

Rule 4 sets out the cyber equivalent principle that States are not permitted to conduct cyber operations that violate the sovereignty of another State, subject to exceptions recognized at international law (such as authorized by the UN Security Council) (see Rule 76) or pursuant to a State's right of self-defense. The obligation is owed only among States, not by States towards non-State actors. Thus while States have avenues to respond to non-State actor cyber attacks for example, the right to respond is not considered to subsist under the auspices of responses to violations of sovereignty (albeit a State may contravene their due diligence obligations by recklessly permitting such activity). The extension of the principle of sovereignty to private cyber infrastructure would similarly apply to QIT as a subset. Violations conducted against an adversary State within that adversary's own jurisdiction would constitute a violation of sovereignty regardless. The Manual notes that unlawful cyber operations against State cyber infrastructure may constitute

[32] Morrison (2012); Bantz (1998); Schneider (1987).

violation of State sovereignty (Rule 4) while setting out principles of sovereign immunity and inviolability (Rule 5).

Rule 4 sets out a number of criteria. The mere interception of a target State's signals from outside that State's territory does not violate State sovereignty because the cyber operation does not manifest within the target State's cyber infrastructure (subject to some qualifications regarding privacy). The three levels of violation include (i) physical damage, (ii) loss of functionality and (iii) infringement upon territorial integrity. Thus in Scenario 1, State A's interception of classical signals outside the territory of State B, and their decryption, would not constitute a violation of State B's sovereignty per se. Cyber espionage has no legal significance with respect to violations of sovereignty per se. In the Scenario 1 conflict case, State A's interference via disabling of State B's military surveillance network would constitute a loss of functionality amounting to a violation of sovereignty (but see below for whether unlawful or not). This may also constitute interference with the governmental functions of State B.

In Scenario 2, the complicating factor is the entangled nature of the shared quantum resources. Merely utilizing entanglement resources is not of itself a form of damage per se is proscribed as even cooperative activities may do so. But in a technical sense it may constitute a loss of functionality because of as noted before quantum entanglement is a resource. Whether the opportunity cost would equate to a loss of functionality (such as where States had previously agreed otherwise) is an unclear issue, but it does speak to the somewhat unusual legal implications that arise from entangled shared resources. Nevertheless, the use of such entangled resources in a way that both constitutes espionage and undermines functionality may constitute a violation if something like purpose or intent is factored into the cyber operation.

7.2 Due Diligence

Section 2 (*Due Diligence*) covers the general principle of due diligence, the obligation of States to exert due diligence in order to control activities (primarily of private actors) within their territory regarding objects over which it exercises sovereignty from harming other States (Rule 6) (the *Corfu Rule*[33]). The duty is not considered *lex lata* and even as a custom is not considered to be a positive obligation to prevent the use of cyber infrastructure (so not in the form of a guarantee to ensure this not occur, or even to take action such that it would be unlikely to occur), but rather is one addressed to not knowingly allowing such activities, something akin to a best endeavors obligation.

The question of knowledge of a State is further dealt with below. The jurisprudence considers whether transit (intermediate) States through which adversarial cyber activities were conducted bear responsibility. Rule 7 sets out considerations

[33] Corfu Channel Case (United Kingdom v. Albania), (1949) ICJ Rep 244.

regarding State burdens and duties for compliance with the due diligence principle. As noted therein, there is in general no strict liability obligation upon States to prevent cyber activities within their jurisdiction that would contravene international law. However, to the extent the general duty applies, it is considered to extend naturally to cyber operations and activities within a State's borders, which would encompass QIT as a subset thereof. A State's responsibility to act or mitigate such activities is qualified by their degree of actual or constructive knowledge. Scenarios 1 and 2 above only involve State actors, thus we eschew consideration of them in this context. However, we consider a few jurisprudential issues arising in the context of QIT use.

7.2.1 Knowledge

Obligations of due diligence rely upon jurisprudential standards of knowledge of States. As noted above and as is often the case with classical cyber operations, it can be difficult to identify specific activities or cyber operations per se, or challenging to establish causality. Such operations are often identified via their effects rather than, for example, surveillance of information processing itself. Similar challenges apply in the QIT case where, for example, monitoring a quantum computer that may be used to decrypt another State's classically encrypted information cannot be undertaken directly by observing quantum processes unfolding (albeit there may be alternative means of identifying the intent to, for example, implement Shor's algorithm).

7.2.2 Adverse Consequences

What constitutes "serious adverse consequences" for the purposes of Rule 2 is a matter of degree. Certainly in principle decryption strategies compromise another State's information security or significant espionage (such as, for example, cyber espionage enabling a weapon of mass destruction to be built) could arguably meet this threshold. To the extent that qualitatively such decryption would only be possible via using QIT (as part of a SNDL attack) would then, in principle, constitute the type of use of QIT that would form a causal factor in serious adverse consequences. However, the jurisprudential logic as encapsulated in the Manual on this first due diligence point is at a level of abstraction that the fact QIT was used for such purposes would not, arguably, materially change the legal analysis.

7.2.3 Control and Jurisdiction

A somewhat more interesting, albeit remote edge case, is the second consideration in the principle of State obligations regarding due diligence, namely that States must exercise due diligence over its instrumental (government) cyber infrastructure that it *controls*. Returning to our ongoing scenario where two States share entangled resources, it is conceivable that the principle ought to extent to control decisions by one State when interacting with its own entangled qubits, for example, with direct impact on the other State (such as acting on the entangled system in a way that adversely impacts the other State's ability to use the quantum system in some way). Again this toy model seems remote, but as we have noted above, it is entirely conceivable that States may share resources in competitive and even conflict scenarios. The jurisprudential distinction drawn between *jurisdiction* and *control* is germane. Although the discussion in respect of due diligence distinguishes between control exercised by a State versus non-State actors, the distinction is useful in the case of non-local quantum resources such as entangled QIT. It might be said, echoing our point above that the control of quantum resources is ultimately a local operation (even if it allows non-local action to occur), that when it comes to non-locality, control is 9/10ths of jurisdiction.

Section 3 (Jurisdiction) sets out general jurisprudential principles regarding the State exercising jurisdiction (derived from is sovereign status). Jurisdiction refers, jurisprudentially, to the competence of a State to regulate persons, objects and conducts under that State's municipal law, within international law limits, territorially (within its territory) or extraterritorially. Jurisdictional competence is parsed into three forms (Rule 8) (i) prescriptive (legislative); (ii) enforcement, covering State authority to enforce laws via executive and administrative action; and (iii) judicial (adjudicatory), having to do with the competence of a State's judicial bodies (courts) to regulate disputes over which they have jurisdiction. Rule 8 provides that subject to limitations, States may exercise territorial and extra territorial jurisdiction over cyber activities.

In this latter case, the use of classical and quantum information infrastructure for extra-territorial cyber activities such as cyber attacks or cyber espionage will often—as it is currently—be targeted extra-territorially. It should be noted that extra-territorial enforcement jurisdiction is more limited that the prescriptive jurisdiction, i.e. States may pass laws within the bounds of their prescriptive jurisdiction (e.g. with respect to activities outside their territory), yet the enforcement of them is limited primarily to within the State's territory. Rule 9 specifies that territorial jurisdiction applies to cyber infrastructure, cyber activities and so on with such a territorial nexus. In particular, Rule 9 (c) covers cyber activities having a substantial effect in a State's territory, while extra-territorial enforcement of jurisdiction is covered by Rules 10–12. As is the case with cyber activities, QIT-related activities (such as those integrated into classical cyber infrastructure) can in principle emanate from multiple States, across multiple States leading to contested jurisdiction over particular cyber activities.

In Scenario 2, multiple States sharing distributed quantum network infrastructure face novel and interesting jurisdictional challenges which we discuss above. In principle a State could legislate how quantum resources are to be used by virtue of its jurisdictional prerogatives. If State B were to utilize those entangle resources in a way consistent with State B's jurisdictional remit, then in dilemmas would obviously arise. The key point is again one of joint jurisdiction of correlated non-local resources distinct from the classical case.

7.3 Law of International Responsibility

Section 4 (Law of international responsibility) details primarily customary international law set out in the *International Law Commission's Articles on State Responsibility*[34] regarding State responsibility. State responsibility law sets out the legal criteria for attributing a cyber operation to a State (the responsible State) and the circumstances in which that act constitutes the use of force by the responsible State against another State (the injured State). It covers rules of evidence and how responsibility is attributed. As with classical cyber attacks, a State the recipient of cyber activities may have little time within which to respond under (ex ante) uncertainty.

In such cases States are under a duty to act and respond reasonably. Factors going to reasonableness include the nature scope and extent of a response, the reliability of information and the severity of the action. More severe responses generally impose a greater evidentiary burden. This can be problematic in the case of QIT: does decryption of military secrets, which may tip the balance in a conflict, constitute a highly severe use of QIT that would occasion more immediate reaction? And how would a State know? Moreover what counts as evidence subject of any disclosure obligation is problematic in the case of QIT e.g. is it measurement statistics, or algorithm specifications etc.? Rule 14 sets out that States bear responsibility for cyber activities attributable to them which constitute a breach of international legal obligations. The principle of responsibility is well established such that responsibility of a State is for internationally wrongful acts (including violation of its international law obligations). Those obligations differ in peacetime and during conflict and are not limited to adversarial rules, they can include a raft of other governing instruments. The definition is not sourced in international law itself and involves an intent to cause harm. The internationally wrongful character of a cyber attack does not depend upon its geographic source per se. Our scenarios above assume State responsibility for the use of QIT, but it may be that attribution of responsibility is unclear when shared or dual-use QIT resources are being used.

7.4 Cyber Operations Not Regulated Per Se

Section 5 (Cyber operations not regulated per se by international law) covers cyber activities by States which, while not the subject of specific regulation or *lex specialis*, may be subject to international law indirectly. The example given in Rule 32 (Peacetime cyber espionage) is of cyber attacks and espionage conducted outside State armed conflict. Cyber espionage is defined by the Manual to mean "any act

[34] Draft Articles on Prevention of Transboundary Harm from Hazardous Activities, with Commentaries, International Law Commission, Report to the General Assembly, 53 UN GAOR Supp. (No. 10), at 370–436, UN Doc. A/56/10 (2001).

undertaken clandestinely or under false pretenses that uses cyber capabilities to gather, or attempt to gather, information" (Rule 32) and may include cyber activities of surveillance, monitoring, capture, exfiltration of data or other information. Cyber espionage can be directed at all three layers of the cyberspace stack (physical, logical and social). Physically this may include embedding code during a manufacturing process which can be later activated or utilized. Logically this may include quantum algorithmic malware for example.

The view espoused in the Manual is that customary international law does not per se proscribe espionage due to the lack of State practice and *opinio juris*, but it may be conducted in a way or have effects that are unlawful under international law, such as where it constituted some other class of proscribed activity such as an unlawful cyber attack. In Scenario 1, the utilization of a quantum sensor network for espionage and eavesdropping can give rise to questions about the lawfulness of such activities. Thus, while cyber espionage is not itself proscribed by law, the purposive or causal-style analysis preferred in the literature would provide that if the effects of such activities prejudiced another State's rights, e.g. putting them at military risk, then such activities may fall foul of other provisions.

8 Use of QIT During Peacetime

Consistent with our partitioning of State activity between peacetime and conflict situations framed by cooperative or adversarial behavior, we consider specific consequences of QIT during peacetime. Part III (*International peace and security and cyber activities*) of the Manual covers the adversarial use of cyber technology during peacetime, focusing on a gradation of cyber activities which, while adversarial, fall short of the threshold for conflict scenarios. Rules 65 to 80 cover a variety of jurisprudential principles applicable to our scenarios above. We focus on a few of them related primarily to cyber espionage and, in particular, our second scenario and entangled resources. As with other parts of the Manual, the jurisprudential discussion concentrates upon generally applicable laws and principles.

8.1 Prohibition of Intervention

Sub-Part 13 (Peaceful settlement) deals with cyber activities during peacetime. Rule 65 covers the principles that States ought to engage in realistic attempts to settle their disputes involving cyber activities peacefully so as not to endanger peace and international security. Rule 66 of the Manual covers the principle of non-intervention (derived from the fundamental principle of sovereignty) that a State may not intervene, including using cyber activities, in the internal or external affairs of another State. The rule is considered a customary law of international law, often set out in

State dicta and *opinio juris*.[35] Internal affairs are related to the *domaine reservé* of a State, this includes political, economic and social configurations of a State.[36]

Coercion through cyber activities is not sufficient on its own to constitute a breach of the prohibition of intervention: the rule is purposive, that is, the coercion must be directed to target State's rights, duties or obligations (including its positions or actions), albeit there is debate as to whether depriving a State of control or resources may constitute a form of intervention. Cyber espionage is not considered using force because of the lack of a coercive element (Rule 32). Scenarios 1 and 2 above bears upon the question of intervention, in the former case, hacking into an adversary's critical cyber infrastructure; in the latter, the intervening act arises because of the entangled nature of the shared quantum resource among States in those scenarios.

In Scenario 2, because the measurement by one State (or other such interaction) of its own qubits has a physical (and logical) effect on the qubits of the other States, then those acts by the first State would reasonably be considered causally influencing the State in question. Using computational stateful paradigms, the state of the qubits is changed causally and thus the question would be whether such change of state constitutes breaches the prohibition. This causal influence on its face may satisfy a breach of the prohibition.

Clearly there is a need to distinguish between cooperative and competitive (adversarial) behavior in peacetime scenarios. Cooperative behavior by extension is that consented to by each State in question by virtue of its sovereign rights, which would and could encompass another State's use of entangled resources in a way that affects the first-mentioned State. In competitive scenarios, the situation is somewhat more complex. There is a jurisprudential question about the extent to which a State can be said to have consented to changes in the states of its entangled resources where such state changes lead to a competitive disadvantage.

8.2 The Use of Force and QIT

Part 14 (The use of force) of the Manual covers international law and jurisprudence regarding the use of force, focusing on the general prohibition on the use of force and exceptions such as Security Council authorized force (see Rule 76 below) and customary laws of State self-defense (Article 51 of the UN Charter, see Rule 71 below). The circumstances in which the use of force is constituted by cyber activities and, if so, is justified (*jus ad bellum*) remains an evolving area of international jurisprudence. Rule 68 encapsulates the prohibition in a cyberspace context, asserting that a cyber operation which constitutes a threat or use of force against the territorial integrity or political independence of any State (or is otherwise inconsistent

---

35 Corfu Channel Case (United Kingdom v. Albania) (1949) ICJ Rep 244.

36 Military and Paramilitary Activities in and against Nicaragua (Nicar. v. US) (1986) ICJ 14.

with the purposes of the United Nations) is unlawful under international law. The principle derives from both customary international law (such as Article 2(4) of the UN Charter[37]).

The thresholds that must be met by QIT are that (i) it is causally connected to the use of force, (ii) that it is a threat or use of force and that (iii) as a threat of use of force it undermines the territorial integrity or political independence (we leave questions of inconsistency with the purposes of the UN to one side). The application of the principle is purposive, not instrumental. It is not the use of cyber infrastructure, by one State, or even that it is the cyber infrastructure of another State which is per se affected, but rather the effects of such cyber activity. As to whether a cyber activity is attributable to a State, see the discussion on attribution earlier.

In the case of the use of QIT, there are a number of questions including as to the nature of the use and whether that may constitute the application of force which we discuss above. The use of QIT as an informational measure is addressed by considering its causal implications rather than any kinetic or physical application of force. This is somewhat complicated, as we note above, in the case of entangled resources because the use by a State of entangled resources may constitute in effect the application of force upon the entangled resources of another State.

Thus, in Scenario 2, in principle either State could interact with their own qubits in a way to affect the qubits of the other, thus constituting a physical (rather than simply indirect causal) connection between State action and effect. But as we note above whether this interaction would have led to a different outcome is precisely what makes quantum systems different: the same act by the same State on the same entangled qubit or qubit itself can give rise to different outcomes, such that any sense of determinism between a State's actions and the outcomes is different to the classical case.

8.3 *Prohibition on the Use of Force*

Rule 69 (*Prohibition of threat or use of force*) sets out a definition of when cyber operations constitute a use of force, namely when its *scale* and *effects* are comparable to non-cyber operations rising to the level of a use of force. The principle is drawn from jurisprudence, especially the *Nicaragua* judgment of the ICJ.[38] The threshold of the use of force is considered lower than that of "armed attack", the latter being a necessary condition to lawfully response in self-defense. The use of force with more serious consequences is considered a use that is "most grave".[39] There is debate on this point with the United States arguing any unlawful use of

[37] Charter of the United Nations (26 June 1945, 1 UNTS XVI).

[38] Military and Paramilitary Activities in and against Nicaragua (Nicar. v. US) (1986) ICJ 14.

[39] Military and Paramilitary Activities in and against Nicaragua (Nicar. v. US) (1986) ICJ 14.

force constitutes an armed attack. The Manual sets out a taxonomy for considering whether a cyber operation constitutes a use of force.

8.3.1 Severity

Severity of the cyber operation indicated by scope, duration and the intensity of consequences is the most significant factor, the more severe, the more likely it meets the use of force threshold. Thus physical harm or damage would constitute the use of force (such as hacking into an information infrastructure in order to cause physical harm).

8.3.2 Immediacy

The immediacy of the cyber operation is a second factor to consider. The more immediate, rapid, cyber operations affording less chance to respond peacefully also contribute. The more immediate, the more the operation may constitute the use of force.

8.3.3 Directness (proximate cause)

A closer causal proximity between the initial cyber operation and its effects is also important. The closer in temporal proximity, the more the operation may have the character of the use of force.

8.3.4 Invasiveness

The degree to which the cyber operation intrudes into another State's information infrastructure, with penetration of more critical infrastructure more likely to contribute to meeting the use of force threshold.

In general, as is usually the case in law, the more ascertainable the effects of a cyber operation are, the greater the evidence that can be adduced to justify the designation of a cyber operation as a use of force. Other factors include: (i) whether the operation has a military character (such as caused by military institutions of a State, or targeting those of another); and (ii) State involvement, whether States and their governmental instrumentalities execute the cyber operation, or whether other actors are involved. The threat of force (Rule 70) is similarly defined in terms of the threat of a cyber operation constituting an unlawful use of force.

The use of QIT could in principle meet the type of cyber operation (albeit in concert with classical infrastructure) that met severity, immediacy, directness or invasiveness constraints. For example, in the event that quantum sensing technology could effectively decloak nuclear-armed submarines (noting the current unlikeliness of this occurring, see section V D (Quantum Sensing) above), then the severity of this cyber operation would be considerable, potentially altering geopolitical balances of power. Other informational impacts, such as decryption of a State's critical communications infrastructure during peacetime (or conflict) could similarly meet such thresholds (Scenario 1). In the case of Scenario 2, interference with entangled quantum resources may be immediate, direct and potentially invasive and severe depending on how reliant the target State may be upon such resources into the future.

9 Use of QIT During Conflict

Once the use of force by way of a cyber operation constitutes an armed attack, two States can said to be in a conflict scenario. In this case, the classification of a cyber operation as an armed attack then triggers the availability of rights of self-defense against an armed attack under both Article 51 of the UN Charter and international customary law. Scenarios 1 and 2 above both envisage the use of QIT where conflict has arisen.

9.1 Self-Defense

Rule 71 (Self-defense against armed attack) both Article 51 and customary international law recognize the inherent right of individual and collective self-defense. Armed attacks must have trans-border characteristics (affecting the territorial or extra-territorial interests of a State). As noted in the Manual, the medium of attack is immaterial to whether the operation constitutes an armed attack,[40] thus in principle causal use of QIT can constitute an armed attack under this rule. The exact threshold at which cyber operation would constitute an armed attack is acknowledged as uncertain. An example discussed both in the literature and the Manual is the 2010 Stuxnet cyber operation[41] that caused damage to Iranian nuclear infrastructure (centrifuges). The Stuxnet attack was considered to constitute a use of force but views diverge on whether it satisfied an armed attack.

Moreover, there are also questions about whether a sequential and/or cumulative series of cyber operations may in aggregate constitute an armed attack, and whether less than physical damage may still notwithstanding constitute an armed attack for the purposes of international doctrine. Similar doctrines regarding reasonable foreseeability (and the recklessness or intentionality) of impacts also are considered in the Manual to be effects taken into account when assessing a cyber operation's

[40] Legality of the Threat or Use of Nuclear Weapons Advisory Opinion 1996 ICJ 226.

[41] Farwell and Rohozinski (2011).

classification as an armed attack or not (noting that intention is considered to not matter per se).

As a result, in Scenario 1, it may be plausible that the conflict use-case of QIT for decryption of strategic military information to afford a military advantage could be justified as a use of force in self-defense for example. In Scenario 2, the disruption of critical communications infrastructure in response to an imminent attack (see below) may also constitute lawful use of force by way of a quantum cyber operation.

9.2 *Necessity and Proportionality*

The use of force as a means of self-defense must accord with criteria of necessity and proportionality (Rule 72), twin principles that have long been recognized.[42] *Necessity* requires that non-forceful responses be insufficient to respond to the armed attack, not that there be no other option, albeit the existence of alternatives (e.g. firewalls or reasonably implementable countermeasures) would be factors in considering the legitimacy of the use of force in self-defense. *Proportionality* concerns the degree of necessary force, acting as a limit upon the extent and severity of a State's response (but noting that it is not a requirement to respond in kind). It is unclear about the extent to which, for example, decryption en masse of an adversary State's communications by way of QIT use may be disproportionate, but in principle the extent and severity of the consequences of such widespread decryption could factor into the analysis as to the proportionality of QIT use.

9.3 *Imminence, Immediacy and Anticipatory Self-defense*

Rule 73 (*Imminence and immediacy*) sets out that the right to use force in self-defense against a cyber armed attack arises if the attack is imminent and immediate. States need not wait idly by for attacks to eventuate before responding under the doctrine. Anticipatory self-defense is thus limited to cases where the attack is imminent. The concept of anticipatory self-defense refers to the use of force by a State to defend itself against an imminent armed attack that has not yet occurred but is about to happen.

This concept is rooted in customary international law and is often associated with the *Caroline Case (1837)*,[43] which established criteria for lawful self-defense in situations where the necessity is instant, overwhelming, and leaving no choice of

---

[42] Military and Paramilitary Activities in and against Nicaragua (Nicar. v. US) (1986) ICJ 14; Legality of the Threat or Use of Nuclear Weapons Advisory Opinion 1996 ICJ 226; Oil Platforms (Iran v. US) 2003 ICJ 161.

[43] Jennings (1938).

means, and no moment for deliberation.[44] The principle is sometimes expressed as the 'last feasible window of opportunity' meaning the last opportunity for a State to effectively defend itself, albeit distinctions between preparatory stages lacking the quality of imminence and the stage at which an adversary can be said to be capable of such an attack are germane to this issue. Moreover, strategic considerations, such as the need to act in an anticipatory fashion without signaling to an adversary about that action.

The signaling of intention and taking of preparatory actions by an adversary is generally considered a necessary (but not sufficient) condition for anticipatory preventative strikes against an adversary State, the standard being something like whether the potential target State can reasonably conclude that the adversary has formed the intention and has the capability to so attack. Being unable to form this conclusion limits the target State to responses that do not include the use of force.

The Manual also provides discussion for when collective self-defense is valid under international law. This would be particularly relevant in any case of quantum networks where one or more allied States seek to use the network against an adversary. This poses further interesting strategic and legal questions but we do not address this scenario directly here. One interesting question is the extent to which State B may have rights to anticipatory self-defense if it anticipates an imminent use of QIT that would have severe or catastrophic decryption effects. The extreme example of this is touched upon above where, for example, a State regards decryption that undermined its nuclear second-strike capabilities as severe enough to warrant the use of its own nuclear arsenal or other significant response.

10 QIT and Cyber Armed Conflict

Part IV (*The law of cyber armed conflict*) of the Manual sets out a detailed exposition of the application of the laws of armed conflict to cyber operations. Rule 80 notes that cyber operations fall within the subject matter of the law of armed conflict. The term "armed conflict" derives formally from the 1949 Geneva Conventions I-IV[45] (Article 2) and is considered jurisprudentially synonymous with "war". The Manual defines armed conflict to refer to a situation of hostilities (in our case, among States) including those using cyber means, with different threshold criteria

[44] Judgment of the International Military Tribunal Sitting at Nuremberg, Germany (30 September 1946), in 22 The Trial of German Major War Criminals: Proceedings of the International Military Tribunal Sitting at Nuremberg, Germany (1950).

[45] Convention (I) for the Amelioration of the Condition of the Wounded and Sick in Armed Forces in the Field (12 August 1949, 75 UNTS 31); Convention (II) for the Amelioration of the Condition of Wounded, Sick and Shipwrecked Members of Armed Forces at Sea (12 August 1949, 75 UNTS 85); Convention (III) Relative to the Treatment of Prisoners of War (12 August 1949, 75 UNTS 135); Convention (IV) Relative to the Protection of Civilian Persons in Time of War (12 August 1949, 75 UNTS 287).

in the case of international (Rule 82) and non-international (Rule 83) conflict. Cyber operations can become governed by the law of armed conflict even if they do not in themselves constitute an armed attack. The extent of the nexus is contextual, but relates in general to cyber operations in furtherance of hostilities.

10.1 Geographical Factors

As noted in the Manual (Rule 81), geographic considerations are relevant to characterization of the lawfulness of cyber operations. Cyber operations during conflict may be conducted in and upon the territory of State belligerents (with distinctions between international and non-international conflicts). Rule 82 sets out that an *international* armed conflict exists whenever there exist hostilities among multiple States (which may include cyber operations) (Article 2 of the 1949 Geneva Conventions) with contingencies for when States act by proxies or non-State actors. We focus only on such conflicts (not non-international) for our purposes. As with other principles governing adversarial behavior of States, there is debate about the threshold that must be met for an act by a State to constitute an international armed conflict, with some views that any armed conflict suffices, in contrast to other views that assert some greater *de minimis* level of conflict (such as with respect to intermittent border disputes, for example).

This is particularly relevant to cyber operations which are often gradated in scope and where cyber espionage plays an important preparatory and gradated role towards any hostilities that do emerge. In both Scenario 1 and Scenario 2, in principle once hostilities have commenced then the types of actions envisaged for State A ought to meet geographic criteria.

10.2 Cyber Attacks

Rule 92 sets out the definition of "cyber attack", being as noted above a cyber operation (offensive or defensive) that is reasonably expected to cause injury or death to persons or damage or destruction to objects. "Attack" is a jurisprudential term of art from which consequences flow such as regarding targeting (targeting civilians and civilian infrastructure is proscribed). The term connotes meanings of offensive or defensive violence against an adversary.[46] As noted in the Manual, acts of violence are not restricted to kinetic or vernacular definitions. Rather, the connotation is one of causality, hence the consequences caused by an action, such as a cyber operation, are the basis for classifying it as a cyber attack. In this regard, violence refers to the

---

[46] Protocol Additional to the Geneva Conventions of 12 August 1949, and Relating to the Protection of Victims of International Armed Conflicts (8 June 1977, 1125 UNTS 3).

consequences of an action, not necessarily the action itself. The idea of consequential harm is manifest in concepts of loss, danger, injury and other terms in various international law sources. The concept of causality encompasses reasonably foreseeable consequences including damage, destruction, injury or death. Thus using cyber operations to effect massive destruction or harm in some way would likely qualify that use as a cyber attack.

From a computational perspective, cyber operations against data and other 'non-physical entities' or entities that are more abstractly defined can be subject to an attack. So too may cyber operation-based interference with the functionality of an object, being equated to damage to the functionality of an object. This may include corruption of software control systems in ways that occasion harm. Other views hold that simply the interference with cyber infrastructure could constitute an attack rather than requiring further consequential harm. An important point of discussion in the Manual are cumulative effects on for example social functionality (such as mass email disruption), however this is viewed by some literature as too remote from the law of armed conflict itself. So too do cyber operations that are mere inconveniences, or even espionage, fail to meet the threshold of a cyber attack.

Moreover, the consequentialist approach to classification of attacks also encompasses attempted, but unsuccessful, attacks or those cyber operations whose intent is to cause harm but which may not have been executed, such as the backdooring of malware or viruses. A similar analysis in the QIT case would apply as in the classical case in this respect. Whether, for example, interference with shared entangled resources in Scenario 2 was sufficient to constitute an attack would, as with the classical case, be a question of context.

10.3 Other Armed Conflict Principles

Other armed conflict principles of relevance to considerations of QIT use include the two cardinal principles of customary international law of armed conflict recognized by the ICJ.[47] These are the principle of distinction (Rule 93), that the only legitimate object is the military forces of the enemy, and the prohibition of unnecessary suffering (Rule 104). These two rules essentially focus on minimizing targeting of non-combatants (civilians etc) and seek to impose precautionary obligations on States to avoid their harm. These concepts are manifest in the distinction between civilian objects and military objectives. A military objective (as a jurisprudential term of art) is defined in Rule 100 to include those objects which by their nature, location, purpose or use make an effective contribution to military action and whose total or partial destruction, capture or neutralization, in the circumstances ruling at the time, offers a definite military advantage. While the question of whether data as a category constitutes a military objective per se is debated, given the centrality of

[47] Legality of the Threat or Use of Nuclear Weapons Advisory Opinion (1996) ICJ 226.

data to modern State security and armed conflict operations, it is reasonable to assume that data can be a military objective (witness the importance of intelligence data throughout history) and one which would be the target of QIT-based uses of force as set out in Scenario 1 and Scenario 2.

The use of civilian objects for military purposes can render it a military objective. To this end, of particular interest to information technologies are dual use protocols discussed above. Rule 101 provides that cyber infrastructure used for dual civilian and military purposes is considered to be a military objective provided that its destruction offers military advantage. This draws upon the distinction (Rule 100) between civilian objects and military objects, drawing upon Article 52(1) of the Additional Protocol I.[48] Military objectives are thus those which make an effective contribution to military action such that attacking or harming them will provide a military advantage for the aggressor. This advantage must be definite.[49] Dual use considerations can give rise to precautionary obligations upon States to ensure that (consistent with the principles of distinction and prohibition of unnecessary suffering) civilian harm or harm to civilian infrastructure is mitigated.

As noted in the Manual, cyber activities present difficulties due to their dual use being often geographically or infrastructurally indistinguishable, such as in the case of networks used for dual civilian and military purposes. The extent to which attacks can be localized against distributed targets, such as internets, is thus important and is also relevant to considerations around proportional response. Rule 102 inheres a precautionary principle for careful deliberation before such dual use infrastructure is targeted. These considerations of dual use are important as QIT, along with other computational technologies, is likely to have a considerable dual use functionality. This is in part due to the considerable infrastructure required to support QIT: quantum computers are not envisaged as being as mobile as classical computational devices. They are in effect immobile in the main and would likely be utilized for a combination of State and civilian purposes given how challenging they are to construct.

10.4 Methods of Warfare

The Manual sets out consideration of the means and methods of cyber warfare, noting the general laws regarding legality of weapons and methods will also apply in the cyber case. Rule 103 defines means of cyber warfare in terms of cyber weapons and their associated cyber systems. Methods of warfare is defined to include cyber tactics, techniques and procedures by which hostilities are conducted. Both are terms of art within international jurisprudence. The Manual defines cyber weapons

[48] Protocol Additional to the Geneva Conventions of 12 August 1949, and Relating to the Protection of Victims of International Armed Conflicts (8 June 1977, 1125 UNTS 3).

[49] Pilloud et al. (1987).

in terms of cyber means that are used, designed or intended to cause damage or destruction, essentially the same criteria for rendering cyber operations a cyber attack (under Rule 92—see above). The term includes both cyber weapons and weapon systems, the former being an aspect of a system used to cause damage, destruction or injury. Cyber means is broadly considered to include devices, materiel, instruments, mechanism or software for cyber attacks.

The Manual distinguishes between computational systems which may be means of warfare, as distinct from cyber infrastructure (e.g. the internet) that is not considered to be a means of warfare, albeit due to a purported lack of control. In the case of a quantum internet, this may be different in that the internet in that case is limited and influenced by a limited number of States. Methods of warfare concerns strategies used, e.g. denial of service strategies rather than the instruments. Clearly the use of QIT would fall within these conceptual categories with similar rules applying. Thus in Scenario 2, State A ought to consider the effect of interfering with State B's quantum resources or quantum internet even if it only does so by interaction with its own entangled qubits.

The Manual also examines a range of applicable principles such as prohibitions on cyber warfare means or methods. These include: methods and means that cause superfluous injury or unnecessary suffering (Rule 104); prohibitions on indiscriminate use (Rule 105) including snowballing or viral-style effects that propagate and cyber booby traps, those cyber devices who may operate unexpectedly (and so be indiscriminate) (Rule 106). Rule 110 sets out consequential principles that mandate States using cyber means of warfare ensure they do so within the rules of law of armed conflict and that, additionally, where they are parties to Additional Protocol I, they undertake sufficient precautionary due diligence regarding the development, acquisition or adoption of new means to ensure compliance with said international obligations.

In the case of QIT, this arguably would involve something along the lines of considering how the application of QIT in various contexts has differential impacts by comparison with classical information technologies. This in turn relates to concepts flagged earlier on in our discussion about the imperative for detailed technological governance architecture for emerging QIT systems. These types of due diligence-style obligations on States provide motivation for how and why technology specific governance instruments are justified, even possibly required, from an international law perspective.

10.5 Conduct of Cyber Attacks

A number of rules in the Manual cover the actual execution and conduct of cyber attacks. Rule 111 reiterates that the conduct of attacks which is indiscriminate (e.g. striking targets that are not lawful targets, or fail to distinguish between civilian and non-civilian objects) are prohibited. This is drawn from Article 51(4)(a) to (c) of the Additional Protocol I and forms part of customary international law. The rule is distinguished from Rule 105 above in that it concerns cases where a system that may have the capacity for discriminate targeting in particular cases fails to meet such discriminatory criteria i.e. a discriminate means employed indiscriminately. Discriminability is thus considered a central tenet of the conduct of cyber warfare operations and in turn connects with obligations upon States to undertake reasonable precautionary analysis of the effects of their offensive cyber activities. Rule 112 covers the case where a cyber attack targeting cyber military objectives may in effect cause unlawful disproportionate impacts on protected classes of object (e.g. civilians or infrastructure). Thus even where a cyber attack itself on a dual use system may be proportionate it may fall foul of this requirement, though whether it does is clearly contextual depending on facts at the time.

Proportionality considerations relating to cyber attacks are considered in Rule 113, where a cyber attack is considered not meeting standards of proportionality (based upon the Additional Protocol I) in cases where damage to civilians, civilian objects or other protected classes is excessive in relation to the concrete and direct military advantage that may be afforded by doing so. The rule is a customary one of the international law of armed conflict. Its focus is on incidental harm and collateral damage which do not render a cyber attack unlawful per se, but does require a calculus between collateral harm and military advantage to be undertaken or demonstrated by an aggressor State.

Similar concepts as discussed above in terms of thresholds of cyber activities constituting armed attacks apply when determining whether a cyber operation may give rise to collateral harm sufficient to meet the proscription. Collateral harm is sometimes parsed into (i) immediate first-order effects and (ii) those which are delayed or intermediated by other events of actions. The Manual notes difficulties in assessing what constitutes excessive and what constitutes a sufficient military advantage, though notes a number of sources that discuss a preference for quantifiably concrete and direct impact in assessing military advantage. The principle inheres a precautionary element obliging States to act reasonably in conducting preliminary assessments of such trade-offs, as is required for conventional attacks (being an objective reasonableness test[50]).

However, certainty of outcome is not itself required especially given the difficulty of estimating collateral harm in advance. This touches to some degree on the inherent uncertainty of QIT use. Such precautionary principles are consistent with other principles espoused by the Manual of international law of conflict, such as the duty of State belligerents to take constant care during hostilities to avoid harming protected classes of object (Rule 114), requirements to verify targets as much as feasible to avoid harming protected classes of object (Rule 115) along with further rules obliging selection of means and methods of cyber attacks that respect similar principles and proportionality (Rule 117).

---

[50] Prosecutor v. Stanislav Galíc, Case No. IT-98-29-T, Trial Chamber judgment (Int'l Crim. Trib. for the Former Yugoslavia 5 December 2003).

Rule 118 sets out a rule where, in the event there exists an equivalence class of cyber attacks to obtain similar military advantage, States ought to select the cause of action (cyber attack) which minimizes harm and danger to protected classes of objects. Rule 121 further reiterates such precautionary principles, requiring States to take necessary protective precautions to avoid harm or danger to protected classes from cyber attacks (drawing upon Article 58(c) of the Additional Protocol I and protection against the dangers of military operations). The advanced capabilities of QIT do not create exceptions to this rule. Belligerents, such as State A in our Scenarios above, must still conduct a proportionality assessment to determine whether the collateral damage is justifiable. The speed, stealth, or complexity of QIT-enhanced attacks do not exempt States from this balancing test.

10.6 *Perfidy and Deception*

A number of rules deal with proscriptions against perfidy, where it is prohibited to kill or injure an adversary by resort to perfidy (Rule 122) e.g. harming surrendered or surrendering combatants after accepting their surrender. The underlying concept draws upon the notion of treachery set out in Article 37(1) of the Additional Protocol I. The rule of perfidy has four elements (i) inviting the confidence of an adversary, (ii) an intent to betray that confidence, (iii) a specific protection provided for in international law and (iv) death or injury of the adversary.

The Manual considers different views as to whether the Rule may encompass cyber systems, such as where States agree to a computational monitoring system and one State defects, or deceptive authentication mechanisms are used by one State. Perfidy is distinguished from cyber ruses, which are lawful and it does not apply to destruction of property. But it does relate (Rule 124) to the improper use of enemy indicators. While we do not focus on it in this paper, there are interesting game-theoretic considerations here that arise with respect to our Scenario 2 where States share entangled resources and can signal their decision to commit to certain strategies.

11 Comparison with Telecommunication Law

11.1 *International Telecommunication Union*

One final area of interest from the Manual we mention is that between quantum communication and international telecommunications law. Most States are party to international law instruments governing the regulation of international telecommunications, the primary example of which is the treaty regime set out in the International Telecommunications Union (a UN agency that regulates international telecommunication). As a subdivision of international law, international telecommunication law covers both the provision of telecommunication services and infrastructure and so plays a central role in classically facilitating cyber operations by States globally.

The regime is relevant both as a point of comparison with quantum communication and quantum internet proposals and as a model for how, in the event a quantum internet or similar is established among States, such quantum network infrastructure may be regulated. It is also instructive to analyze the extent to which the ITU regime may already encompass QIT systems. The ITU has already commenced a series of standards' development initiatives relating to QKD protocols,[51] covering functional requirements,[52] functional architecture,[53] key management[54] and control,[55] with additional research in the post-quantum cryptography domain also canvassed.

11.2 Sources of Law and Obligations of States

The primary sources of jurisprudential principle are set out in the ITU Constitution[56] and a series of International Telecommunication Regulations.[57] *Telecommunication* is defined as any transmission, emission or reception of signs, signals, writing, images, and sounds or intelligence of any nature by wire, radio, optical or other electromagnetic systems. The definition is regarded as technology neutral, thus can reasonably be considered to encompass quantum communication and non-classical methods of communicating within its scope. *International communications* as per the Manual concerns the transmission of data across State borders and through extra-territorial regions while an *international telecommunication service* is the provision of telecommunication capability among States.

The ITU Constitution sets out a number of principles, including the presumption as to the secrecy of communication of international correspondence (Article 37(1)). Rule 61 of the Manual, based on Article 38 of the ITU Constitution, sets out the principle that States must take measures to safeguard the establishment of

[51] Recommendation ITU-T Y.3800, (2019)/Cor.1 (2020). Overview on networks supporting quantum key distribution.

[52] Recommendation ITU-T Y.3801, (2020). Functional requirements for quantum key distribution networks.

[53] Recommendation ITU-T Y.3802, (2020). Quantum key distribution networks—Functional architecture.

[54] Recommendation ITU-T Y.3803, (2020). Quantum key distribution networks—Key management.

[55] Recommendation ITU-T Y.3804, (2020). Quantum Key Distribution Networks—Control and Management.

[56] Constitution of the International Telecommunication Union. (22 December 1992, 1825 UNTS 331).

[57] International Telecommunication Regulations. (WATTC-88, Melbourne, 9 December 1988); International Telecommunication Regulations. (WCIT-2012, Dubai, 14 December 2012).

international telecommunication infrastructure required for rapid and uninterrupted telecommunications. This includes maintaining any cyber infrastructure of a State established for this purpose. States are considered under an obligation of conduct equivalent to a 'best efforts' obligation, thus subject to reasonableness and feasibility. This includes a duty to maintain operational safeguards and ensure data can be reliably and efficiently transmitted.

11.3 Sovereignty and Telecommunication

The paramount nature of State sovereignty is recognized in the ITU constitution (Articles 35 and 34(2)). States retain a sovereign prerogative to suspend international cyber communication within their territory (and must give notice to other States of this) and may also stop transmission of private cyber communications contrary to municipal law (Rule 2). The ITU Constitution and Rule 63 set out principles whereby States ought not interfere with protected electromagnetic (radio) frequencies. State obligations are modified during armed conflict (a form of *lex specialis*) where for example jamming or other interference may be considered lawful in certain circumstances. Under Rule 64, States retain complete freedom regarding their military radio installations. While specific to the electromagnetic spectrum, the rules provide a basis for the development of jurisprudence for quantum communications. Moreover, the ITU framework serves as an example of the type of multilateral instruments which may be readily adapted for the governance of QIT use by States.

12 Discussion

Our analysis presented in this chapter suggests that the integration of quantum information technologies (QIT) into public international law represents an important, but not destabilizing, extension of existing cyber jurisprudence. While QIT introduces technical and conceptual differences from classical information systems, many of the foundational principles of international law—particularly those reflected in the Manual—remain adaptable to these emerging contexts. The discussion therefore points toward an incremental evolution of legal interpretation rather than a need for wholesale doctrinal reconstruction.

A key analytical contribution of this chapter is the development of a *classical-quantum strategic taxonomy* distinguishing interactions between classical and quantum systems—classical-to-classical, classical-to-quantum, quantum-to-classical, and quantum-to-quantum. This framework provides a structured way to describe State activity across hybrid infrastructures and clarifies that most foreseeable quantum operations will, at least in the near term, remain embedded within classical systems. It thus enables the application of established legal reasoning concerning cyber operations to quantum contexts, while still allowing for cases where the distinct properties of quantum systems—such as entanglement or decoherence—require refined interpretation.

In this chapter, we have also examined how QIT challenges certain assumptions implicit in international law about control, causation, and knowledge. Quantum systems are inherently probabilistic and non-deterministic, which raises questions about how legal doctrines premised on foreseeability or intent might apply. As we note above, however, these issues do not render existing doctrines inapplicable. Instead, they invite modest reinterpretations of control and responsibility. For example, in an entanglement-based network, jurisdiction may be better understood through the concept of *locus of control*—that is, a State's practical capacity to influence the behavior of quantum systems—rather than strictly territorial notions of sovereignty.

Our approach remains consistent with the general principles of State responsibility and due diligence, albeit applied to a more complex technical substrate. The use of quantum game theory to illustrate strategic interaction adds a further dimension to analysis of the strategic consequences of QIT. Quantum decision frameworks show that shared quantum resources may alter incentives for cooperation or defection, leading in some cases to more stable or transparent equilibria between States. These models are illustrative rather than predictive, but they demonstrate that established concepts of rational behavior and mutual deterrence can be adapted to quantum contexts without abandoning existing strategic theory or legal principle.

Our analysis also finds that quantum information capabilities are likely to enhance, rather than overturn, the structure of international law governing the use of force, espionage, and sovereignty. Quantum computing may provide new means of decryption or simulation, and quantum communication may strengthen the security of State networks, but these activities remain subject to familiar distinctions between lawful espionage, prohibited intervention, and the use of force. Similarly, while quantum technologies can amplify information asymmetries among States, they do not introduce forms of power that fall outside the conceptual reach of existing norms. International law's focus on effects—rather than on specific technologies—makes it capable of accommodating such developments.

From a governance perspective, QIT shares many of the characteristics of earlier dual-use technologies. Accordingly, existing mechanisms for technology control and transparency—such as those developed for nuclear and advanced cyber capabilities—offer templates for managing quantum risks. As evident via the comparison with international telecommunications law, existing institutional structures could, with adaptation, serve to coordinate emerging quantum communication networks and standards.

Overall, while QIT brings new technical possibilities and challenges, the existing body of international law provides a sufficiently flexible framework to address them. The distinctive features of quantum systems—stochasticity, superposition, and entanglement—complicate the application of established principles such as sovereignty and due diligence, but do not undermine them. International law's generality, its reliance on functional definitions, and its emphasis on effects rather than mechanisms all favor continuity. The likely trajectory of the law's response is therefore one of interpretive refinement rather than doctrinal rupture, as States and scholars progressively clarify how quantum technologies fit within the enduring structure of public international law.

13 Conclusion

Quantum technology is emerging as both a strategic capability and a domain that raises distinctive governance and interpretive questions for international law. Its unique characteristics create new modalities of information control and communication that may influence the conduct of States in both peacetime and conflict. Yet, as the preceding analysis suggests, these developments do not fundamentally displace the legal architecture already applicable to information technologies. Rather, QIT extends the scope of existing frameworks, inviting nuanced interpretation of principles such as sovereignty, jurisdiction, due diligence, and the use of force.

Our discussion has shown that international law likely possesses sufficient conceptual elasticity to accommodate the challenges posed by QIT. Most foreseeable applications of quantum computing, communication, and sensing will remain embedded within classical infrastructures, meaning that the majority of State activities involving QIT can still be assessed through the established doctrines of cyber law. Where refinements are needed—such as in attributing responsibility for actions within entangled systems or defining control in probabilistic environments—these can be achieved through incremental interpretation rather than through doctrinal overhaul. The adaptability of international law lies in its focus on the *effects* of State conduct rather than the *mechanisms* by which those effects are produced, making it resilient to technological evolution.

At the same time, QIT's technical affordances create novel patterns of strategic interaction. Quantum computing may, in principle, enable the decryption of classically secure information; quantum communication may render certain networks effectively tamper-proof; and quantum sensing could reshape the informational balance of power between States. These capabilities illustrate how informational asymmetry rather than kinetic capacity may increasingly define strategic advantage. They also reinforce the need to consider how existing principles governing espionage, intervention, and proportionality apply in contexts where causation and knowledge are probabilistic rather than deterministic.

While QIT remains in a developmental stage, its dual-use potential already engages existing export control and non-proliferation regimes. These mechanisms provide an immediate legal interface between quantum research and international governance, constraining technology transfer and shaping global distribution of capability. As the technology matures, similar instruments may offer a basis for more coordinated international oversight. Future governance models could include multilateral agreements establishing standards for QIT export controls, limiting quantum-enhanced offensive cyber operations, or promoting transparency in quantum sensing applications. Regional or global regulatory bodies might supervise the deployment of entanglement-based communication networks, drawing lessons from the institutional precedents of international telecommunications law. Verification regimes tailored to QIT—such as those auditing quantum key distribution networks or large-scale computation facilities—could further reinforce confidence and accountability among States.

In sum, QIT introduces new technical means through which familiar strategic behaviors are conducted, but it does not yet appear to necessitate a separate branch of international law. The central task is interpretive: to ensure that existing principles evolve in step with technological capability. In this sense, the governance of quantum technologies exemplifies the continuing capacity of public international law to adapt to scientific and technological change without losing its coherence or normative force.

Appendix

Table 6 Comparison of Definitions from the Tallinn Manual Glossary in Classical and Quantum Contexts. This table highlights differences and parallels between classical and quantum information concepts

Definition	Classical	Quantum
Cyber infrastructure	Includes classical hardware such as servers, storage devices, and communication networks.	Encompasses quantum-specific hardware like quantum processors, quantum communication devices, and the classical infrastructure supporting them.
Cyberspace	The environment formed by physical and non-physical components enabling data storage, modification, and exchange using classical computer networks.	Extends to include quantum networks and environments enabling entanglement based communication and quantum data processing.
Cyber activity	Any activity using classical infrastructure or means to affect its operation, such as hacking or data breaches.	Activities involving the use of quantum systems, such as quantum-enhanced encryption or quantum-based attacks on classical systems.
Cyber operations	Employment of classical cyber capabilities to achieve objectives in or through cyberspace, often involving offensive or defensive operations.	Utilizes quantum capabilities for objectives like secure quantum communication or quantum algorithm-based attacks on classical encryption.
Cyber reconnaissance	Use of classical tools to gather information about systems, networks, or capabilities, such as scanning or data mining.	Employs quantum techniques, like quantum-enhanced sensing, to detect adversaries or analyze systems with greater precision.

(continued)

Table 6 (continued)

Definition	Classical	Quantum
Computer system	Interconnected classical devices, including general-purpose and specialized systems, connected via classical networks.	Includes quantum computers, quantum sensing systems, and nodes of quantum networks integrated with classical systems.
Computer network	Infrastructure of interconnected classical devices enabling data exchange over wired or wireless media.	Extends to quantum communication networks, leveraging entanglement and quantum teleportation for secure data exchange.
Internet	A global system of interconnected classical networks using standardized protocols for communication and routing.	Incorporates quantum internet concepts, enabling secure communication using quantum protocols alongside classical routing systems.
Data	Basic digital elements processed or produced by classical computers, typically represented in bytes.	Quantum data represented by qubits, stored in superposition or entangled states, requiring repeated measurements for extraction.
Data center	Physical facilities housing classical infrastructure for data storage and processing, including cloud services.	Includes quantum data centers for storing and processing quantum information alongside classical data infrastructure.
Electronic war-fare	Use of electromagnetic energy to exploit or disrupt classical communication and sensing systems.	Could involve quantum sensing to detect electromagnetic emissions or quantum attacks targeting classical systems.
Cyber attack	Offensive or defensive operations causing injury, destruction, or damage using classical cyber means.	Quantum-based disruptions targeting classical or quantum systems, such as decoherence induction or interception of quantum communication.
Cyber espionage	Classical methods of covertly obtaining information, such as hacking or intercepting communications.	Quantum-enhanced espionage using quantum sensing or exploiting weaknesses in quantum communication protocols.

Acknowledgments This work was made possible through the generous support of the Novo Nordisk Foundation (NNF) via a grant for the scientifically independent Collaborative Research Program in Bioscience Innovation Law (Inter-CeBIL Program—Grant No. NNF23SA0087056).

References

Alagic G et al (2022) Status report on the third round of the NIST post-quantum cryptography standardization process. National Institute of Standards and Technology

Alagic G et al (2024) Status report on the first round of the additional digital signature schemes for the NIST post-quantum cryptography standardization process. National Institute of Standards and Technology

Bantz VP (1998) International legal status of condominia. Fla J Int Law 12:77

Bartlett SD et al (2007) Reference frames, superselection rules, and quantum information. Rev Mod Phys 79(2):555–609
Bauer C (2021) Secret history: the story of cryptology. Chapman and Hall/CRC
Bostanci J, Watrous J (2022) Quantum game theory and the complexity of approximating quantum Nash equilibria. Quantum 6:882
Brady AJ et al (2022) Entangled sensor-networks for dark-matter searches. PRX Quantum 3(3):030333
Brukner Č (2014) Quantum causality. Nat Phys 10(4):259–263
Caso JS (2014) The rules of engagement for cyber-warfare and the Tallinn Manual: A case study. In: The 4th annual IEEE international conference on cyber technology in automation, control and intelligent systems. IEEE
Chiribella G et al (2009) Theoretical framework for quantum networks. Phys Rev A Atom Mol Optic Phys 80(2):022339
Donoghue JF, Menezes G (2020) Quantum causality and the arrows of time and thermodynamics. Prog Part Nucl Phys 115:103812
Efrony D, Shany Y (2018) A rule book on the shelf? Tallinn manual 2.0 on cyberoperations and subsequent state practice. Am J Int Law 112(4):583–657
Eisert J et al (1999) Quantum games and quantum strategies. Phys Rev Lett 83(15):3077
Farhi E et al (2014) A quantum approximate optimization algorithm. arXiv:14114028 [quant-ph]
Farwell JP, Rohozinski R (2011) Stuxnet and the future of cyber war. Survival 53(1):23–40
Fleck D (2013) Searching for international rules applicable to cyber warfare—a critical first assessment of the New Tallinn manual. J Conflict Secur Law 18(2):331–351
Gottesman D (1998) Theory of fault-tolerant quantum computation. Phys Rev A 57(1):127–137
Gottesman D (2010) An introduction to quantum error correction and fault-tolerant quantum computation. In: Quantum information science and its contributions to mathematics, Proceedings of symposia in applied mathematics, vol 63, pp 13–58
Greenbaum D (2015) Introduction to quantum gate set tomography. arXiv:1509.02921
Guo H et al (2008) A survey of quantum games. Decis Support Syst 46(1):318–332
Gutoski G, Watrous J (2007) Toward a general theory of quantum games. In: Proceedings of the thirty-ninth annual ACM symposium on theory of computing (STOC '07). ACM
Hoofnagle CJ, Garfinkel S (2021) Law and policy for the quantum age. Cambridge University Press, Cambridge
Ikeda K (2021) Quantum contracts between Schrödinger and a cat. Quantum Inf Process 20(9):313
Ikeda K (2023) Quantum extensive-form games. Quantum Inf Process 22:66
Ikeda K, Aoki S (2021) Theory of quantum games and quantum economic behavior. Quantum Inf Process 21:27
Jennings RY (1938) The Caroline and McLeod Cases. Am J Int Law 32(1):82–99
Kessler O, Werner W (2013) Expertise, uncertainty, and international law: a study of the Tallinn Manual on Cyberwarfare. Leiden J Int Law 26(4):793–810
Khatri S et al (2019) Quantum-assisted quantum compiling. Quantum 3:140
Krelina M (2021) Quantum technology for military applications. EPJ Quantum Technol 8(1):24
Liao SK et al (2018) Satellite-relayed intercontinental quantum network. Phys Rev Lett 120(3):030501
Liu YC et al (2024) Quantum integrated sensing and communication via entanglement. Phys Rev Appl 22(3):034051
Lu CY et al (2022) Micius quantum experiments in space. Rev Mod Phys 94(3):035001
Malia BK et al (2022) Distributed quantum sensing with a mode-entangled network of spin-squeezed atomic states. arXiv:2205.06382
Meyer DA (1999) Quantum strategies. Phys Rev Lett 82(5):1052
Mohseni M et al (2008) Quantum-process tomography: Resource analysis of different strategies. Phys Rev A Atom Mol Optic Phys 77(3):032322
Morrison FL (2012) Condominium and coimperium. In: Wolfrum R (ed) Max Planck encyclopedia of public international law. Oxford University Press, Oxford
Neumann NMP et al (2020) Quantum communication for military applications. arXiv:2011.04989

Nielsen MA, Chuang IL (2011) Quantum computation and quantum information: 10th anniversary edition. Cambridge University Press, New York
Perrier E (2022) The quantum governance stack: models of governance for quantum information technologies. Digit Soc 1(3):22
Pilloud C et al (1987) Commentary on the additional protocols: of 8 June 1977 to the Geneva Conventions of 12 August 1949. Martinus Nijhoff Publishers, Geneva
Preskill J (2018) Quantum computing in the NISQ era and beyond. Quantum 2:79
Preskill J (2021) Quantum computing 40 years later. arXiv:2106.10522
Rand LE (2023) Schrodinger's technology is here and not: a socio-technical evaluation of quantum sensing implications for nuclear deterrence. University of Maryland
Schmitt MN (ed) (2017) Tallinn manual 2.0 on the International Law applicable to Cyber Operations. Cambridge University Press, New York
Schneider P (1987) Condominium. In: Bindschedler RL et al (eds) Encyclopedia of disputes installment 10. Elsevier
Townsend JS (2000) A modern approach to quantum mechanics. University Science Books
Turing AM (1939) Turing's treatise on Enigma. Unpublished Manuscript
von Heinegg WH (2013) The Tallinn manual and international cyber security law. In: Gill TD (ed) Yearbook of international humanitarian law, vol 15. T.M.C. Asser Press, The Hague
Watrous J (2018) The theory of quantum information. Cambridge University Press, Cambridge
Wootters WK (1998) Quantum entanglement as a quantifiable resource. Philos Trans R Soc London, Ser A Math Phys Eng Sci 356(1743):1717–1731

Index

M. Aboy et al. (eds.), *Quantum Technology Governance I*, Perspectives in Law, Business and Innovation, https://doi.org/10.1007/978-981-95-8371-3

FSC
www.fsc.org
MIX
Papier | Fördert gute Waldnutzung
FSC® C083411

Kolibri 360 GmbH
Ferdinand-Jühlke-Straße 7
99095 Erfurt, Deutschland
produktsicherheit@kolibri360.de